MIDDLE EAST 101

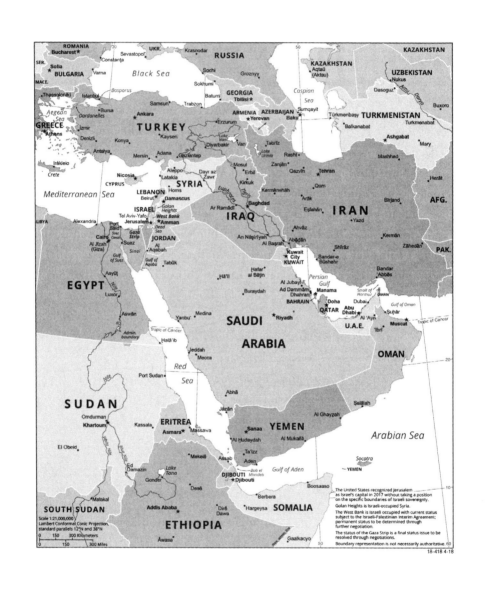

The United States recognized Jerusalem as Israel's capital in 2017 without taking a position on the specific boundaries of Israeli sovereignty.

Golan Heights is Israeli-occupied Syria.

The West Bank is Israeli occupied with current status subject to the Israeli-Palestinian Interim Agreement; permanent status to be determined through further negotiation.

The status of the Gaza Strip is a final status issue to be resolved through negotiations.

Boundary representation is not necessarily authoritative.

18-418 4-18

MIDDLE EAST 101

A BEGINNER'S GUIDE FOR DEPLOYERS, TRAVELERS, AND CONCERNED CITIZENS

Youssef H. Aboul-Enein and Joseph T. Stanik

Foreword by Gen. Stanley A. McChrystal, USA (Ret.)

Naval Institute Press
Annapolis, Maryland

Naval Institute Press
291 Wood Road
Annapolis, MD 21402

Library of Congress Cataloging-in-Publication Data

Names: Aboul-Enein, Youssef H., author. | Stanik, Joseph T., author.
Title: Middle East 101 : a beginner's guide for deployers, travelers, and
    concerned citizens / Youssef H. Aboul-Enein and Joseph T. Stanik ;
    foreword by General Stanley A. McChrystal, USA (ret.).
Other titles: Middle East one hundred one
Description: Annapolis, Maryland : Naval Institute Press, 2019. | Includes
    bibliographical references and index.
Identifiers: LCCN 2018054263 (print) | LCCN 2018055781 (ebook) | ISBN
    9781682474648 (ePDF) | ISBN 9781682474648 (epub) | ISBN 9781682474273 |
    ISBN 9781682474273(hardcover :alk. paper) | ISBN 9781682474648(ebook)
Subjects: LCSH: Middle East—History. | Islam.
Classification: LCC DS44 (ebook) | LCC DS44 .A25 2019 (print) | DDC 956—
dc23 LC record available at https://lccn.loc.gov/2018054263
♾ Print editions meet the requirements of ANSI/NISO z39.48-1992
    (Permanence of Paper).
Printed in the United States of America.

27 26 25 24 23 22 21 20 19   9 8 7 6 5 4 3 2 1
First printing

The authors dedicate this work to the members of the U.S. Armed Forces who have served, are serving, or will serve our country in the Middle East.

Contents

Foreword

Having had the honor and privilege of leading men and women in combat, I know firsthand that the most valuable resource a warrior brings to the theater of operations and ultimately the field of battle is his or her intellect. Cultivating one's mind takes commitment, discipline, and intellectual curiosity. In my 2013 memoir, *My Share of the Task*, I emphasize that leaders can step forward from any age and rank and that on some occasions I was led by soldiers who were junior to me and I benefitted from that experience. Also critical is the ability to yield to the experience and expertise of another soldier whose grasp of a tactical situation is superior to your own. Doing so communicates profound respect for the men and women with whom you serve, but it requires self-confidence and the ability to suppress your ego. These qualities are critically important as we seek warfighters with linguistic skills, cultural awareness, social media savvy, and technical prowess who can operate effectively in the complex tactical environments we confront today. This guide will help you launch your intellectual journey through the Middle East and aid your understanding of critical topics, such as the history, politics, and society of the region; nuances within the Islamic faith; the turbulent outcome of the Arab Spring; and battle against militant Islamists. The answers to the 101 questions posed will provide you with essential background on the Middle East, whether you have previously served there, are now serving there, or will be called on to serve there. I sincerely hope that this guide will encourage you to investigate more thoroughly this indispensably important part of the world.

To research and author this work, the Naval Institute Press paired two U.S. naval officers: one currently serving and grappling with developments in the Middle East and the other having served our nation in waters near Libya in the 1980s and in the Persian Gulf during Operation Desert Storm. Commander Youssef H. Aboul-Enein, MSC, USN, and Lieutenant Commander Joseph T. Stanik, USN (Ret.), bring to this undertaking a depth of knowledge and understanding of the region and the perspectives of two eras of naval service. Youssef, a Medical Service Corps officer, is a longtime adviser on the Middle East in the Department of Defense. He is well known for his tireless efforts to orient deploying units and for producing the widely read *Militant Islamist Ideology* (2010) and a series of Pentagon DVDs on a variety of subjects related to the region. Joe, a retired surface warfare officer, authored *Operation Eldorado Canyon: Reagan's Undeclared War with Qaddafi* (2003), the definitive work on U.S. military operations against Libya in the 1980s. In it, he reminds us that our national commitment to defeat international terrorism predated the tragic events of 11 September 2001. Youssef teaches at the National Intelligence University in Washington, DC, and previously served on the faculty at the National Defense University. Joe is a former history instructor at the U.S. Naval Academy and, after leaving active duty, served more than two decades as a high school history teacher in Baltimore City Public Schools. He is a frequent traveler to the Middle East and teaches Middle Eastern history at Anne Arundel Community College in Maryland. These gentlemen are warriors, scholars, and teachers whose writings and instruction will inform us for years to come.

Once I shared with my staff Gillo Pontecorvo's acclaimed film *The Battle of Algiers* (1966). Afterward I expressed my concern that we do not adequately understand what is happening "outside the wire." To overcome this deficit, we must ensure that our men and women receive in-depth instruction on the "human terrain" in their operating areas, and this process must begin not when hostilities erupt or when the deployment order is received, but months and even years in advance. As I write this, our country has troops engaged in combat in Afghanistan, Iraq, and Syria and has observed the seventeenth anniversary of the 9/11 terrorist attacks. As a twenty-first century warrior, you must dedicate yourself to maintaining a qualitative advantage over the enemy regarding the human and tactical dimensions of the battlespace. Having planned strategy for the conflicts in Iraq and Afghanistan and spent hundreds of hours evaluating intelligence before ordering the mission that killed Abu Mus'ab al-Zarqawi, the founder of al-Qa'ida in Iraq, I realize that both responsibilities tapped my knowledge and understanding of the culture, history, and politics of the Southwest Asian and Afghan theaters.

I hope you will view this work as the starting point in a lifelong study of the Middle East, avail yourselves of the authors' recommended readings and viewings, and join the professional policy discussion online with the U.S. Naval Institute (usni.org) and other sites, such as *Small Wars Journal* (smallwarsjournal.com) and *FDD's Long War Journal* (https://longwarjournal.org).

General Stanley A. McChrystal, USA (Ret.)

Former commander of the International Security Assistance Force and U.S. Forces Afghanistan and former commander of the Joint Special Operations Command

Preface

This guide to the Middle East was the idea of Tom Cutler of the Naval Institute Press. He brought us together to develop a resource that would provide essential background information to U.S. servicemen and women and federal employees deploying to the Middle East. We initiated this project by proposing 101 questions related to the geography, history, politics, and culture of the region. While volumes have been written on a variety of subjects involving the area, such as the emergence of Islam and Muslim conquest, Islamic law, the Crusades, the Ottoman Empire, the creation of Israel, the Iranian Revolution, and the Arab Spring, we will discuss these and many others in a few pages or less. Whether you are headed to the Middle East for the first time or are a veteran of multiple tours, our objective is twofold: first, to give you an informational edge in your area of deployment and, second, to encourage you to embark on your own journey to acquire more in-depth knowledge and greater understanding of an area of the world that has witnessed competition, invasion, and conflict since biblical times. You can pick up this book and start with Question 1 and read on to Question 101, or you can focus on a specific topic or historical era, or you can just open the book at any point and start reading. Browsing is a practical and relaxing way to acquire valuable information. If we leave you eager for more information about the region, then we have succeeded. We encourage you to browse the list of important books and DVDs in the selected bibliography. We also urge you to engage in online discussions on the Middle East with your brothers and sisters in the U.S. armed forces and civilian colleagues in federal service.

When it comes to recounting the rich history of the Middle East, we support the widely held belief that for many of the region's inhabitants, past events—such as the Crusades and the establishment of Israel—are as fresh and significant today as they were when they occurred. Since the origins of many modern conflicts can be traced back several centuries, there is intrinsic value in appreciating the process of establishing and expanding a Muslim state during and after the life of the Prophet Muhammad. For example, the seeds of the bitter feud between the Syrian and Iraqi branches of the Ba'th Party in the twentieth century were planted thirteen centuries earlier, when deep enmity emerged between the earliest adherents of Islam and later converts. After an opening chapter on the geography of the Middle East, we present the region's history chronologically, starting with the ancient Middle East and progressing to the post-9/11 world. Within this broad historical narrative, we have included questions about such critical topics as the fundamentals of Islam, the sources of Islamic law, Muslim philosophy and science, reform in the Middle East, the rise of nationalism, and the emergence of political Islam.

Now, get ready for your intellectual journey through the Middle East. You can travel light. Leave your preconceived notions at home. All you need to pack is an open and inquisitive mind.

Commander Youssef H. Aboul-Enein, MSC, USN
Gaithersburg, MD

Lieutenant Commander Joseph T. Stanik, USN (Ret.)
Arnold, MD

Acknowledgments

This volume on the Middle East would not have been possible without the necessary involvement of Tom Cutler and Jim Dolbow of the Naval Institute Press. Tom had the idea for a guidebook and was confident that we possessed the combined requisite academic background and operational experience to undertake this project. He challenged us to address 101 questions on the Middle East that would be assembled into a primer. In the summer of 2015, we met with Tom at the U.S. Naval Institute and, over donuts and coffee, fleshed out our vision of the manuscript. Jim carried the project forward as our acquisitions editor and brought the book to publication. We are very grateful to General Stanley A. McChrystal, USA (Ret.), for his interest in and support for this project and generous offer to write the foreword.

Youssef thanks the staffs of the United Service Organization (USO) at the Walter Reed National Military Medical Center in Bethesda, Maryland, and at several U.S. airports—most notably Reagan National—which provided him with a friendly and comfortable setting where he could ponder the 101 questions and write. The airport USOs proved invaluable, as he spent considerable time waiting for flights to and from his training assignments with deploying military units. A swimmer, he drew great inspiration while exercising with wounded warriors in the pool at the Walter Reed gym. These brave men and women, who glided through the water with the aid of their spouses, parents, sisters, brothers, girlfriends, or boyfriends, epitomize the true strength of America. The authors are humbled by your selfless service, your courage and perseverance, and the love and support of your families and friends.

Joe is grateful to Dr. Tyrone Powers, the director of the Homeland Security and Criminal Justice Institute at Anne Arundel Community College in Arnold, Maryland, who gave him the opportunity to develop and teach a course on Middle Eastern history. He is thankful for the steadfast support and encouragement of his colleagues and friends at the Department of History, U.S. Naval Academy, Annapolis, Maryland; New Era Academy, Baltimore, Maryland; the National Council on U.S.-Arab Relations, Washington, DC; and the Middle East Outreach Council (MEOC). One MEOC colleague suggested that he and Youssef answer 1,001 questions, not a mere 101. Of course, she was right, but that would produce a work too large for publication. Joe is enriched by the many friends he has made during his travels throughout the Middle East and prays for their good health and safety. Last, he acknowledges his many students over the past three decades. Their energy, curiosity, spontaneity, and goodness always kept him eager to begin the next school day.

Finally, we owe an incalculable debt to our wonderful wives, children, and—in Joe's case—grandchildren, who have supported our military careers over the years, held down the "home fronts" during our overseas deployments, and stood behind us as we undertook this important and worthwhile project.

The Physical and Human Geography of the Middle East

In this first chapter of our guide, we begin by discussing the importance of the region to Americans in the early twenty-first century. The remainder of the chapter is devoted to the region's physical and human geography. We examine the origin and use of the term "Middle East," identify major cities of and discuss urbanization in the region, identify the countries that make up the core states of the Middle East, locate important physical features, and describe major ethnic and religious groups.

1. What religious, historical, political, economic, and strategic factors have made the Middle East so important to the people of the United States?

The Middle East is the birthplace of the three Abrahamic, monotheistic religions: Judaism, Christianity, and Islam. The United States has a Christian majority, a sizable Jewish population, and a rapidly growing Muslim community. Americans, through their diverse faiths, can connect with the lands and peoples of the Middle East.

There is an overabundance of history in the Middle East. The region is the cradle of civilization, with two of the world's oldest settled communities, in Mesopotamia and Egypt, and it is home to cultures that have made major contributions to world civilization. Agriculture, organized religion, government, stone architecture, pottery, metal tools, writing, books, mathematics, and astronomy originated in the ancient Middle East.

Geopolitically, the Middle East lies at the juncture of Europe, Africa, and Asia, and it contains a number of vital waterways. The region was long contested by competing imperial powers—Great Britain, France, Austria, and Russia—and by rival blocs led by the United States and the Soviet Union during the Cold War.

Regarding the region's role in the global economy, the Middle East contains massive oil and gas reserves. Of the estimated 1.646 trillion barrels of proven oil reserves worldwide (2017), approximately 803 billion barrels are found in the Middle East, with some 266 billion barrels in Saudi Arabia alone. Additionally, Iran, Qatar, and Saudi Arabia rank among the world's ten largest gas producers.[1]

Finally, the region is strategically important to the United States. Israel is the oldest democracy in the region, and the United States and Israel enjoy a very close relationship. In a 2009 speech at Cairo University, President Barack Obama (2009–17) affirmed the special ties between the American and Israeli people: "America's strong bonds with Israel are well known. This bond is unbreakable. It is based upon cultural and historical ties, and the recognition that the aspiration for a Jewish homeland is rooted in a tragic history that cannot be denied."[2] The United States has maintained a long-term military presence in Afghanistan, fighting insurgents and supporting the national government, and plans to keep troops there beyond 2019. In 2011 it ended Operation Iraqi Freedom and Operation New Dawn and withdrew all troops from Iraq, but in 2014 it began deploying thousands of military advisers and special forces troops to Iraq and Syria to fight the Islamic State of Iraq and Syria (ISIS). In 2011 the United States participated in military operations in Libya that led to the removal of the dictator Mu'ammar al-Qaddafi. The U.S.-led war on terrorism is focused on the Middle East, where U.S. forces conduct special operations and air and drone strikes against ISIS in Iraq and Syria, al-Qa'ida affiliates in Yemen and Africa, and al-Shabab in Somalia. The United States has supported the Yemeni government and Saudis in their battle against Iranian-backed Shi'a Houthi rebels in Yemen. Turkey, a Muslim country, is a democracy—

albeit flawed—and a North Atlantic Treaty Organization (NATO) ally that appears to be moving closer to Russia's orbit as its relations with the United States grow increasingly strained. The United States has strategic relationships with authoritarian states, such as Egypt and Saudi Arabia and other Arab countries of the Persian Gulf, and emerging democracies, such as Iraq, Jordan, Kuwait, and Oman. For decades a fundamental U.S. policy in the Middle East has aimed at containing the power and influence of the Islamic Republic of Iran. In 2015 Russian president Vladimir Putin (2000–2008, 2012–present) deployed Russian combat forces to Syria to support the brutal regime of President Bashar al-Asad, an indication that strategic competition among great powers continues over the Middle East.

2. What is the origin of the term "Middle East"?

For centuries Arabs have referred to the region running eastward from Cyrenaica in eastern Libya across to Syria and Iraq, to Iran, as al-Mashriq (the Lands of the Rising Sun), which led the French to call the area the Levant ("rising"). They call the remainder of North Africa, spanning from Tripolitania in western Libya to Morocco, al-Maghrib (the Lands of the Setting Sun). Finally, they refer to Arabia as al-Jazeera (the Peninsula) because it is bound on three sides by water—the Red Sea, Arabian Sea, and Persian Gulf.

For well over a century, the area east of Europe (and the broader Western world) and west of China (and the rest of East Asia) has been considered the Middle East. Europe naturally served as the geographical fulcrum in the nineteenth century, owing to its power and influence over much of the world. Great Britain had the most extensive empire, and Greenwich, England, through which passes the prime meridian (zero degrees longitude), was a significant global reference point. In short, the term "Middle East" was created and advanced by outsiders and is a legacy of imperialism. It was likely coined in the 1850s by the India Office of the British government. In 1902 the American naval strategist Admiral Alfred Thayer Mahan (1840–1914) popularized the term, using it to describe the region between Arabia and India and centered on the Persian Gulf. Ironically, the term has attained conventional usage; the people of the Middle East also refer to the region by that name.

3. Which countries make up the core Middle East?

In addition to the inherent controversy over the term "Middle East," there are also different views on which countries comprise the region. It is difficult to achieve uniformity of opinion because academics, government agencies, and private organizations have different definitions and, in some instances, use a different term altogether. Furthermore, the Middle East is often redefined when prevailing political circumstances change. Before the terrorist attacks of 11 September 2001, maps of the region routinely included Egypt, Turkey, the Fertile Crescent (Iraq, Syria, Lebanon, Israel, the Palestinian territories, and Jordan), the Arabian Peninsula (Saudi Arabia, Kuwait, Bahrain, Qatar, the United Arab Emirates, Oman, and Yemen), and Iran. Many maps today reflect the United States' long war in Afghanistan, shifting the region to the northeast. Hence, parts of Egypt and Turkey are often lopped off, and Afghanistan and Central Asian states are more prominently displayed.

The British government had used the term "Near East" in the past, which also included the Balkan Peninsula in southeastern Europe. Scholars often use the term "Near East" to describe the region before the advent of Islam and the term "Middle East" to mark the period that coincides with the Islamic era. The U.S. Department of State also uses the term "Near East" in the title of the bureau that handles Middle Eastern and North African affairs. The American scholar Marshall Hodgson used the term "Nile to Oxus Region" to avoid any trace of Eurocentrism.[3] The U.S. military referred to the area as Southwest Asia during Operation Desert Storm, but that description excludes Turkey and Egypt. In some instances, the word "central" has replaced the word "middle" altogether. The former Central Treaty Organization (CENTO) and the current U.S. Central Command (CENTCOM) are good examples.[4]

The area of responsibility of CENTCOM "covers the 'central' area of the globe," stretching from Egypt to Central Asia.[5] It does not include Turkey, the countries of the Caucasus Mountains (Georgia, Armenia, and Azerbaijan), Israel, the Horn of Africa (Sudan, South Sudan, Eritrea, Ethiopia, Djibouti, Kenya, and Somalia), and most of North Africa. Furthermore, responsibility for the Horn of Africa was transferred to U.S. African Command in 2008. Israel is part of the U.S. European Command's

AOR because EUCOM has permanent assets that could come to its aid in a time of extraordinary crisis. The U.S. Department of State's Bureau of Near Eastern Affairs defines the region as consisting of the Arab world (including the Western Sahara, but excluding Mauritania, and the Horn of Africa), Israel, and Iran. The bureau does not handle relations with Turkey, Pakistan, and Central Asia.[6] The Central Intelligence Agency's definition of the Middle East includes the countries of the Arabian Peninsula, the Fertile Crescent (including Israel), Turkey, the Caucasus, and Iran, but it excludes Egypt.[7] Interestingly, the agency's maps of the region often include Egypt.

The Middle East Institute, a nonprofit organization located in Washington, DC, has supported "various disciplines relating to the Middle East and North Africa, as well as Afghanistan and Pakistan, since 1945."[8] The Middle East Studies Association, also a nonprofit organization, based at the University of Arizona, defines the Middle East as "the area encompassing Iran, Turkey, Afghanistan, Israel, Pakistan, and the countries of the Arab World from the seventh century to modern times."[9] As one can see, the definitions of the region are numerous and varied.

What definition should we use for our guide? Considering the significant degree of overlap among these definitions, we will define the core Middle East as Egypt, Turkey, Iran, the countries of the Fertile Crescent, the states of the Arabian Peninsula, Cyprus, and Afghanistan. Nevertheless, our definition will stretch temporarily to cover other countries and territories as we study the region's history.

4. What are the differences among the terms "Middle East," "Arab world," and "Muslim world"?

We cannot base our definition of the Middle East on the Arab world because the Arab world does not include the non-Arab countries of the region—Israel, Turkey, Iran, Cyprus, and Afghanistan. Similarly, we cannot base our definition on the Muslim world because the Muslim world includes countries that are outside the region, such as Indonesia, Malaysia, Pakistan, Bangladesh, and Nigeria.

The term "Arab world" connotes the Arabs' culture, ethnicity, and language, yet it generates disagreement among the Arabs themselves. The controversy can be traced to the argument over 'Uruba (Arabness). In the strictest definition of the word, an Arab is a person from the Arabian Peninsula. Arabs from the peninsula often argue that their Arabness is purer, because they are desert nomads or Badawi (Bedouin), not farmers or city dwellers, and because they come from central Arabia, not the Red Sea or Persian Gulf coasts, which have been influenced by global trade and are more cosmopolitan.

A more liberal definition of what it means to be Arab emerged with the rise of modern nationalism. This version defines an Arab, irrespective of faith, as a person who speaks the Arabic language and adheres to Arab traditions, culture, and heritage. The Cairo-based League of Arab States uses this more inclusive definition, which explains why the African nations of Somalia, Djibouti, Comoros, and Mauritania are members of the league. It is important to recognize that 'Uruba predates Islam but does not predate tribalism, meaning there are Arab Christians, Arab Jews, and of course, Arab Muslims. Unfortunately, the pressures of tribal loyalty, sectarianism, and regional politics have eroded the idea of a unified and inclusive Arab world. For example, at the time of writing, the al-Asad regime in Syria had abandoned its advocacy of Arab nationalism—actually ridiculing the 'Urban ("pure" Arabs or Bedouin)—and replaced that ideology with militant, absolute "Syrianism."[10]

The term "Muslim world" casts a vast net that includes areas of the globe where Islam is the predominant expression of faith. It refers to the community of 1.6 billion Muslims who share a common *aqida* (creed) yet have many *manahij* (paths or interpretations) and ethnicities. Of the world's Muslims, only an estimated 300 million are Arabs. The Organization of Islamic Cooperation, founded in 1969, comprises fifty-seven nations, including Arab countries and several large non-Arab nations, such as Indonesia (the world's most populous Muslim state) and Nigeria (the largest Muslim country in Africa).[11]

5. What are the major urban centers of the Middle East, and how has rapid urbanization affected the region?

The Middle East and North Africa, despite their widespread desert terrain, have large urban populations and the highest rates of urbanization in the world. The population has exploded throughout this expansive region since the mid-twentieth century. Approximately 105 million people lived there in 1960; more than four times as many lived there in 2016.[12] Cairo had a population of 2 million in 1950 and 16 million in 2000; its population in 2017 was 18.8 million. Similarly, Istanbul had 2 million people in 1950 and 12 million in 2000. The city had 14.2 million inhabitants in 2017. Cairo and Istanbul are the two largest cities in the Middle East. Tehran, with 8.4 million people, Baghdad, with 6.6 million, and Riyadh, with 6.2 million, round out the top five.[13]

One should examine the issue of urbanization through the lens of ancient, medieval, and modern urban centers. Jericho, on the Palestinian West Bank, is one of the world's oldest inhabited cities, dating back 11,000 years. Ancient cities that still thrive include Alexandria, Damascus, Tripoli (Lebanon), Antioch (present-day Antakya, Turkey), and Jerusalem. These cities contain multiple layers of human history, extending to the modern era. Cairo, a medieval city, started out as al-Fustat, a military camp for Arab warriors during the great conquest of the seventh century, and grew into the capital of the Shi'a Fatimid caliphate in the late tenth century. The oil boom of the 1970s transformed small, remote settlements—such as Riyadh and Jiddah in Saudi Arabia, Dubai and Abu Dhabi in the United Arab Emirates, Doha in Qatar, Manama in Bahrain, and Kuwait City—into modern, prosperous, cosmopolitan cities.

Rapid urbanization has generated an insatiable demand for public services and scarce resources, exerting great pressure on national economies and central governments to provide adequate access to food, housing, education, and medical care. Furthermore, as the oil-producing states have achieved a higher standard of living, a growing share of their energy reserves is being consumed domestically, making less available for export.

Urbanization directly affects national security and domestic stability. Growing populations along the Tigris and Euphrates Rivers have led to threats and near-conflict among Iraq, Syria, and Turkey over access to water. A conflict between Egypt and Ethiopia could erupt if Ethiopia dams the Blue Nile tributaries without Egypt's consent. For decades, people have migrated from the countryside to the cities, searching for meaningful employment and a better life. Tens of thousands of refugees, fleeing civil war and the violence of radical Islamist groups, have recently swelled the population of cities, strained critical services and resources, and led to the creation of new urban centers, such as the large Syrian refugee camp at Zaatari, now one of Jordan's largest cities.[14]

The Middle East has a very youthful demographic profile. Approximately 50 percent of the population is eighteen years of age or younger, and about two-thirds of the population is under thirty. These developments have put even greater pressure on governments because young people are demanding quality education, decent jobs, and a political voice—some of the very causes of the Arab Spring protests of 2011. Many young men—and women—have become so discouraged by their current circumstances that they have turned to radical Islam.

6. What are important physical features of the Middle East, including mountain ranges and plateaus, rivers and valleys, deserts and arid areas, and waterways?

Picture for a moment the landscape of the Middle East. Which physical feature is foremost in your mind? Most likely, you conjured up deserts—hot, vast, and empty. Deserts and arid regions are indeed abundant throughout the region, but other significant topographical features also deserve attention.

First, there are several important mountain ranges and high plateaus. In Turkey the Taurus Mountains run along the Mediterranean Sea coast, and the Pontic Mountains line the Black Sea coast. Between the two ranges, the Anatolian Plateau dominates the Turkish interior. In Iran the Elburz Mountains stretch along the southern coast of the Caspian Sea, and the Zagros Mountains run roughly parallel to the coastline of the Persian Gulf. Like Turkey's interior, Iran's is dominated by a large plateau, the Iranian. The Turkish and Iranian highlands are noted for heavy seismic activity and are home to isolated communities of Kurds, Azeris, and Armenians.

Hillside agriculture and pastoral nomadism are practiced in the mountainous terrain of Turkey and Iran. The foothills do not require irrigation since the rainy season supports the growth of grasses and shrubs. Mountain nomads roam in a seasonal migration cycle. In the winter and spring, they live at low elevations where grass is plentiful; in the summer, they move to higher pasture lands. On the other hand, sedentary farmers are dependent on an organized irrigation system during the dry season. The mountain ranges of Turkey and Iran have a Mediterranean climate: semiarid in the interior and cooler and wetter along the coast.

Other mountain ranges of note include the Lebanon and Anti-Lebanon Mountains; the Western and Eastern Hajar Mountains in Oman; the Hijaz, Asir, and Yemen Mountains along the Red Sea coast of the Arabian Peninsula; and the Hindu Kush of Afghanistan.

Second, several important rivers and alluvial valleys are found in the Middle East. Rivers support the region's largest population centers and areas of highest agricultural development. The most well-known river systems in the Middle East are the Tigris and Euphrates and the Nile, anchors of some of the world's oldest civilizations. The Tigris and Euphrates begin in Turkey and flow through Syria and Iraq to the Persian Gulf. The area between the Tigris and Euphrates is called Mesopotamia, a Greek word meaning "land between the rivers." It is part of the Fertile Crescent, which arcs across Iraq and Syria and stretches south along the Mediterranean coast to the Sinai Peninsula. The Nile, whose source can be traced to lakes in the central African highlands, flows through South Sudan, Sudan, and Egypt to the Mediterranean.

Third, the Middle East boasts the largest continuous arid region in the world. It has both high deserts, in Iran and Afghanistan, and low deserts, in Saudi Arabia (al-Nafud, al-Dahna, and Rub al-Khali). The Rub al-Khali is the epitome of the Arab desert. It is exceedingly hot, dry, and desolate. Other desert systems include the Judean in Israel and Palestine, the Negev in Israel, the Syrian, and the Saharan in North Africa.

Because most of the region receives little annual rainfall, many ingenious irrigation systems have developed out of necessity. These systems include *qanats* (underground channels) in Iran and Oman, desalinization plants in the Persian Gulf states, and drip irrigation in Israel. On the other hand, the seaward side of the highlands of Asir, Yemen, Hadhramaut, and Dhofar, all on the Arabian Peninsula, are lush because they benefit from the monsoon rains of Indian Ocean.

The deserts are expanding at an alarming rate, and reforestation has been undertaken to stem desertification, but Israel's efforts in this regard went too far. The trees were depleting the country's groundwater, and many had to be removed.

Water is in short supply throughout the region, and the struggle for this essential resource has the potential to lead to conflict. Three examples illustrate this concern. First, Jordan and Israel have had a long dispute over water from the Jordan River and its tributaries. Second, Israel limits Palestinian water usage in the occupied territories. Third, Syria has objected to Turkey's construction of the huge Tabqa Dam and Keban Dam on the Euphrates. Turkey was implementing the Greater Anatolian Project, which sought to harness the power of the river for the economic benefit of its Kurdish population. The two countries traded threats, but the issue was resolved peacefully. Regional talks on water resources have been held since the Madrid Conference of 1991.

Bedouin are called "people of the camel" because they depend on the animal for transportation and make use of its milk, meat, hair, hide, and even bone. They are proud of their lifestyle and regard themselves as the best representatives of Arab culture and virtues. In years past, city dwellers, townspeople, and farmers considered them violent and uncivilized; conversely, the Bedouin considered themselves superior to the settled population because of the freedom they enjoyed. The number of Bedouin is declining, however, as more and more of them are being forced into settlements by their governments.

Finally, the Middle East is home to several strategic waterways and chokepoints. The Turkish Straits (the Bosporus, Sea of Marmara, and Dardanelles) connect the Black and Aegean Seas and separate Europe from Asia. In some places, the straits are about as wide as the Potomac River. The great city of Istanbul, formerly Constantinople, is located on the Bosporus, not far from the Black Sea. The straits are important to Russia and Ukraine, whose warm-water merchant and naval shipping passes through them.

The Suez Canal, Red Sea, and Bab al-Mandab connect the Mediterranean Sea to the Indian Ocean. The French built the canal, which opened in 1869; the British gained control of it in the 1880s; and the Egyptians nationalized it in 1956. Since 1975 it has been enlarged and upgraded to accommodate most supertankers.

The Strait of Hormuz, which connects the Persian Gulf to the Indian Ocean, is only twenty-one miles wide at its narrowest point; its shipping channel is only two miles wide. A huge quantity of the world's oil is carried through the strait: 17 million barrels per day, which is about 30 percent of seaborne-traded oil or 18 percent of all traded oil in 2015. By 2016 the estimated daily volume of oil shipped through the strait stood at 18.5 million barrels.[15]

7. What are the major ethnolinguistic groups of the Middle East?

Ethnic groupings are primarily based on language. In addressing this question, we will examine the following Middle Eastern ethnolinguistic groups: the Arabs, Hebrew speakers, Persians, Turks, Kurds, and Armenians.

Arabs

The Arabs are the largest ethnic group in the region. Broadly and simply, an Arab is someone who speaks Arabic as his or her first language. Arabic is a member of the Semitic group of languages. In Arabic, the traditional definition of "Arab" is nomad or Bedouin. As discussed earlier, there is plenty of disagreement over what constitutes being an Arab. There are Arabs of the Arabian Peninsula and Fertile Crescent, and there are many Arabs who live outside these areas. The latter group includes populations that were Arabized starting in the seventh century. Moreover, some see a division within the Arab world between the eastern Arab world (al-Mashriq) and the western Arab world (al-Maghrib). The dividing line is drawn through the middle of Libya.

While language, culture, and history unite the Arabs, the paradox of Arabic is that it is both a unifying and centrifugal factor in the Arab world. In effect, there are two forms of Arabic in use simultaneously: spoken (dialectic or vernacular) Arabic and standard (common) Arabic. Spoken Arabic involves several regional dialects, some of which are dissimilar, and these differences contribute to the region's diversity and complexity. Standard Arabic, which is derived from classical Arabic, is learned in school. Classical Arabic is the language of the Qur'an, the Muslim book of sacred scripture. Standard Arabic is used in written works, such as books, magazines, and newspapers, TV and radio broadcasts, class lectures, and mixed groups of Arabs. Spoken Arabic, which differs by region, is the popular language used in plays, personal letters, and movies. It is the language of the street and *suq* (marketplace). The Egyptian dialect is widely understood among Arabs because thousands of TV shows and movies have been produced in Egypt and distributed throughout the Arab world.

Hebrew Speakers

Hebrew is also a Semitic language, and Hebrew and Arabic are very similar. For example, in Hebrew, the New Year is called Rosh Ha-shannah, and the word for house is *beth*. New Year and house in Arabic are Ras as-sana and *bayt*, respectively. The Jewish Diaspora ("diaspora" means dispersal or scattering) produced two languages related to Hebrew: Yiddish, which is a combination of Hebrew and medieval German, and Ladino, which is a mix of Hebrew and Spanish. Hebrew was revived as a living language in the late nineteenth and early twentieth centuries by Eliezer Ben-Yehuda, who is acknowledged as the "Father of Modern Hebrew." His son, Ben-Zion, was the first person to speak Modern Hebrew as his mother language.

Persians

Persian is an Iranian-group language within the Indo-European linguistic family, which originated in southern Russia and Central Asia. The Iranian group includes the following Middle Eastern languages: Persian, Tadjik, Pushtun, Kurdish, Baluch, Bakhtiari, and Armenian. Persian is the official language of Iran, while approximately 25 percent of the population of Iran is Turkish speaking and 10 percent is Arabic speaking.

Turks

Turkish is a Turkic-group language within the Altaic family of languages, which arose near the Alti Mountains of Central Asia. Turkish is related to Japanese, Korean, and Mongol. The Turks, who originated in Central Asia, swept into Iran, Anatolia, Russia, and Syria. The Turkic group includes the following Middle Eastern languages: Azeri, Qashqai, Qajar, Turcoman, Turkmen, Uzbek, Khirgiz, and Kazakh.

Kurds

Kurdish is an Iranian-group language that consists of several dialects. The Kurds live in an area that sweeps across Iran, Iraq, Syria, Turkey, Azerbaijan, and Armenia. A unified, independent Kurdish state will be difficult to establish because no country wants to give up territory to create it. The Kurds came closest to creating their own state under Salah al-Din over eight hundred years ago. Following World War I, the victorious Allies considered the Kurdish case for an autonomous nation but decided instead to make the territory around Mosul, with its huge oil reserves, part of the postwar British mandate in Iraq. Today, the Kurds of northern Iraq enjoy a virtually independent status under the autonomous Kurdistan Regional Government. In a 2017 plebiscite, the Kurds of northern Iraq voted overwhelmingly for independence, a move rejected by the central government in Baghdad.

Armenians

Armenian is another member of the Iranian group of languages. Armenians live in Armenia, Turkey, Iran, Syria, Cairo, Beirut, and the Armenian Quarter of the Old City of Jerusalem. Their historic homeland is in eastern Turkey and the Caucasus Mountains.

8. What are the major religious denominations of the Middle East?

Earlier we emphasized that the Middle East is the source of the three Abrahamic, monotheistic religions: Judaism, Christianity, and Islam. More than 90 percent of the population of the Middle East is Muslim.[16] Several countries in the core region have measurable Christian minorities, and Israel has a majority Jewish population.

Islam

Sunni Muslims make up 87 to 90 percent of the Muslim faithful worldwide.[17] The name "Sunni" derives from the *sunna*, the customs, manners, sayings, and actions of the Prophet Muhammad. Sunnis acknowledge the legitimacy of the first four caliphs, who led the *umma* (community of Muslims) after the Prophet's death in 632, and adhere to the *sunna*.

Shi'a Muslims make up about 10 to 13 percent of the Muslim world. The term "Shi'a" stems from Shi'at 'Ali (Partisans of 'Ali). 'Ali was Muhammad's cousin and son-in-law, and his supporters believed that he deserved to be the first caliph. Importantly, he is revered by Shi'a as their first leader (imam) and the spiritual authority of their faith. In the Middle East, Shi'a constitute a Muslim majority in Iran (90–95 percent), Iraq (65–70 percent), and Bahrain (65–75 percent). They are also a majority in Azerbaijan (65–75 percent), which lies outside the core Middle East, and are a significant minority in Lebanon (25–30 percent), Kuwait (20–25 percent), and Saudi Arabia (10–15 percent).[18] Several important Shi'a shrines are located in Iraq. Iraqi dictator Saddam Hussein, a Sunni, long repressed his country's majority Shi'a population.

There are two important offshoots of Shi'ism: the Druze and 'Alawis. The Druze, also known as al-Muwahhidun (the Unitarians), are strict believers in absolute monotheism. They follow a secret rite advanced by Shaykh al-Darazi in the early tenth century. He preached that the Fatimid caliph al-Hakim bi-Amr Allah was a manifestation of God. Druze teachings are contained in the six-volume *Al-Hikma al-Sharifa* (The Noble Knowledge). Many beliefs and practices set the Druze apart from other Muslims. They live principally in Syria (3 percent of the overall population), Lebanon (5–6 percent), and Israel (1–2 percent).[19] The Jumblatt family of Lebanon is Druze.

The 'Alawis (followers of 'Ali) have an eclectic set of doctrines more secretive than those of the Druze. Their holy book is *Kitab al-Majmu* (Book of the Collections). They have adopted some Christian festivals and rituals, including a Mass-like ceremony. About 12 percent of the population of Syria is 'Alawi.[20] Small 'Alawi communities also exist in Turkey and Iraq. The al-Asads of Syria are well-known 'Alawis. Some Muslims regard the Druze and 'Alawis as heretics, but most accept them.

The Kharijites (Seceders) are the third-largest group of Muslims, after the Sunnis and Shi'a, but they make up a tiny percentage of the global Muslim community. They continued to profess Islam but established a breakaway Muslim community a few decades after the death of Muhammad. They denounced 'Ali's decision to participate in the arbitration of a dispute over the caliphate. The only remaining Kharijite sect today is the Ibadhis, who live in present-day Oman and Algeria.

Christianity

Owing to war, persecution, and discrimination, the Christian population of the Middle East has rapidly declined. In the early twentieth century, Christians made up approximately 14 percent of the population of the Middle East; by 2010 they were only 4 percent.[21] The population of Lebanon is between 34 and 41 percent Christian; Egypt, 9 percent; Syria, 5 to 9 percent; Israel, 3 percent; and Iraq, 1 percent.[22]

Many Christians in the region follow the Roman Catholic or Orthodox branches of the faith, but indigenous Christian sects that existed before the advent of Islam have persisted. Nestorians believe that Christ has separate and distinct divine and human natures within his being. Condemned as heretics at the Council of Ephesus in 431, they took refuge in Persia and founded the Church of the East. The Nestorian Christians of Iraq, Iran, and Syria are known as Assyrians. Many Assyrians speak Aramaic, a Semitic language. Tariq 'Aziz (1936–2015), who served as Iraqi foreign minister and deputy prime minister, was Assyrian.

The Copts are the oldest Christian sect in Egypt. Old Egypt (or Coptic Cairo) is the center of the Coptic community in Egypt's capital; Asyut, in central Egypt, also has a large Coptic population. Butros Butros Ghali (1922–2016), a former Egyptian foreign minister and UN secretary-general, was a Copt. The Copts are Monophysite Christians who believe that Christ has a single, divine nature. They were branded as heretics in 451 by the Council of Chalcedon, which established the doctrine that Christ has two natures—fully human and fully divine—perfectly combined in one person. The Nestorians and Monophysites were persecuted because of their beliefs under the Byzantine Empire, which defended orthodox Christianity. The Jacobites are Syrian Monophysites.

Judaism

Large communities of Jews lived in Arab countries and Iran long before the creation of the State of Israel in 1948. Before the seventh century, there were significant Jewish communities in present-day Iraq, Iran, Yemen, Egypt, and Saudi Arabia. These Eastern Jews spoke Arabic or Persian.

Sephardic Jews (or Sephardim) were forced out of Spain by the Christian Reconquista (Reconquest) of the fifteenth century. Because "convert, leave, or die" were the Jews' only options, they settled in North Africa and the lands of the Ottoman Empire. Many were brought into the empire through the personal intervention of the Ottoman sultan Bayezit II. Thriving Jewish communities developed in Thrace and the Balkans; they speak Ladino. Today Eastern and Sephardic Jews are collectively known as Mizrachim or Mizrahi Jews. The term Mizrachim is derived from the Hebrew word *mizrach* ("east").

Ashkenazic Jews (or Ashkenazim) settled in Europe and Russia. They speak Yiddish. In Israel today, political tension exists between the Ashkenazim and Mizrachim communities. The former were the original settlers and founders of modern Israel and continue to dominate national politics, while the latter, who are politically conservative, complain of not having a public voice commensurate with their majority status. The Mizrachim also tend to be socially conservative because they historically lived in large Muslim communities and never dealt with the notion of a separation between religion and politics.

Yazidism

Approximately a half million Yazidis live in northern Iraq. Primarily ethnic Kurds, they have preserved their religious identity despite centuries of oppression, violent attacks, and threats of genocide. It is believed that a Sufi (Muslim mystic) founded Yazidism in the twelfth century. The faith is distinctly non-Abrahamic but contains elements of Islam and pre-Islamic beliefs, namely, Zoroastrianism, Christianity, and ancient Mesopotamian religions. Its tenets include baptism, from Christianity; circumcision and a prohibition on eating pork, from Judaism and Islam; and reverence of fire as a manifestation of God, from Zoroastrianism. The Yazidis' alienation and subsequent persecution derive from their worship of the fallen angel Melek Taus, the Peacock Angel. Unlike Satan from the Judeo-Christian tradition, Melek Taus was forgiven by God and restored to heaven. Nevertheless, owing to the central importance of the fallen angel, the Yazidis acquired a mistaken reputation as devil worshippers. That false representation during the current age of Islamic extremism has proved deadly. Targeted for extermination by ISIS, the Yazidis took refuge in the rugged mountains of Iraqi Kurdistan.[23]

Zoroastrianism

We will discuss the tenets of Zoroastrianism, the ancient Persian religion still practiced by small communities in Iran, India, Pakistan, and Central Asia, in the answer to Question 11.

It is essential to recognize that many inhabitants of the Middle East who have religious beliefs that predate Islam are leaving the region to escape persecution and threats to their existence from Muslim extremists. By providing safe havens, the Western democracies of the twenty-first century are helping to preserve some of the world's oldest expressions of worship.

9. What are the differences between the Sunni and Shi'a branches of Islam?

The Prophet Muhammad died in 632 without explicitly designating a caliph (temporal successor). A number of his followers argued that his successor should come from a member of his family—specifically his son-in-law and cousin 'Ali Ibn Abu Talib. Other Muslims believed that Muhammad's successor should be selected through the custom of tribal consensus. Both groups cited statements from the Prophet to support their views. In the end, the first four caliphs—Abu Bakr, 'Umar, 'Uthman, and finally 'Ali—were chosen through consensus by tribal leaders, and they led the *umma* from 632 to 661.

From 656 to 680, the Muslim community was racked by a series of civil conflicts known as the Fitna Wars. "Fitna" means temptation in Arabic. 'Ali during his caliphate (656–61) fought a number of challengers who refused to acknowledge his selection as caliph. During the early Fitna period, one find references to the Shi'at 'Ali (Partisans of 'Ali) and Shi'at Mu'awiya (Partisans of Mu'awiya). Mu'awiya latter was the governor of Damascus and 'Ali's most formidable opponent. After the assassination of 'Ali in 661 and the death of Mu'awiya, who served as caliph until 680, the struggle for leadership of the *umma* resumed, with Husayn, 'Ali's son and the Prophet Muhammad's grandson, challenging Mu'awiya's son Yazid. The slaughter in 680 of Husayn and his tiny band of rebels at the hands

of Yazid at Karbala, in present-day Iraq, is a key event in the development
of Shi'ism. Shi'a commemorate the martyrdom of Husayn each year on
'Ashura, the tenth day of the Muslim month of Muharram, as a day of
mourning and atonement. All Shi'a Imams are descendants of Muhammad through 'Ali and Husayn. After Karbala, Shi'a no longer sought the
caliphate.

An important difference between Sunnis and Shi'a is the latter's reverence for the Imams, who they believe are *ma'soum* (possessing a divinely
infallible character that is free from sin) and serve as intercessors between
humanity and God. Sunnis, on the other hand, contend that this reverence
for the descendants of 'Ali detracts from the worship of God and veers into
idolatry.

2

The Ancient Middle East

This chapter begins with an investigation of the pre-Islamic Middle East. We highlight the contributions of several ancient city-states, nations, and empires to world civilization, discuss characteristics of the Roman (Byzantine) and Persian (Sassanid) Empires and the rivalry between them at the advent of Islam, and examine Arab society in the early seventh century.

10. What are some essential legacies of the ancient civilizations of the Middle East?

Many enduring innovations of civilization originated in the Middle East during the three millennia before Islam. "To understand the development of Islam and Islamic civilization, we must recognize that the Middle East region into which Islam expanded was a rich repository of centuries of accumulated intellectual exchanges, religious experiences, and administrative practices," wrote historians William L. Cleveland and Martin Bunton. "Islamic society built upon these existing foundations and was shaped by them."[1] As we address this question, we will consider the contributions of ancient Middle Eastern societies, the origins of the Arabs, the concept of a pre-Islamic age of ignorance (as viewed in Islamic history), the geopolitical situation in the region at the advent of Islam, and essential characteristics of pre-Islamic Arab society.

By 5000 BC, a settled community had emerged at Jericho, in ancient Palestine, but a more developed civilization had begun in Sumer, in southern Mesopotamia. City-states existed at Ur, Lagash, and Uruk by 3500 BC, and the following twelve hundred years marked the development of Sumer's culture and economy. Ample irrigation and good weather facilitated the development of agriculture, which in turn led to the proliferation of cities. With the countryside supporting the city-states, urban inhabitants could devote more of their attention to language, art, government, religious ritual, and commerce. Sumerian merchants traded throughout the Persian Gulf and as far away as the Caspian Sea and Indus Valley regions. Each city-state developed unique religious and political traditions. Typically, it had a king and its own protective god. The king would appeal to the god on behalf of his people.

In 2340 BC Sargon of Akkad (r. ca. 2340–2284) conquered the Sumerian city-states and established an expansive empire. The Akkadians, a nomadic, Semitic people from central Mesopotamia, then adopted the Sumerians' culture. Conquest and assimilation are recurring themes in Middle Eastern history. Nevertheless, Sargon's empire was difficult to govern because diverse peoples are natural obstacles to unity and authority. They have allegiances to different gods and resist being governed by an outsider, but Sargon minimized opposition and enhanced his legitimacy by adopting and preserving Sumerian culture.

The Hebrews were the first people to practice Abrahamic monotheism. The name of their god, Yahweh, cannot be uttered out of reverence and means "He who brings forth." Another early name for god is Elohim, which means "gods." The Aramaic Elah and the Arabic Allah derive from this name. Yahweh, the Hebrew tribal god during the time of Abraham and the Patriarchs, became a universal god, in Jewish belief, supplanting all others. Jewish doctrines concerning monotheism and law were developed between 1300 and 1000 BC, the time from Moses to King David. From the late eleventh century to 900 BC, Saul, David, and Solomon unified the Hebrew tribes and established a kingdom. Solomon built a magnificent temple in Jerusalem to centralize worship. The kingdom eventually split into the northern Kingdom of Israel and the southern Kingdom of Judah, and civil war ensued. In 722 BC, the

Assyrians defeated Israel, and in 586 BC, the Chaldeans destroyed the temple and took the Judeans as captives to Babylon. Yahweh traveled with them, strengthening the concept of monotheism; here was one god, not residing in a remote temple, but living with his people. The Persian Achaemenid ruler Cyrus (ca. 600–530 BC) defeated the Chaldeans and, in 538 BC, permitted the Jews to return to Jerusalem and rebuild their temple. God lived in the temple, but he also existed beyond it. In AD 70, the Romans destroyed the second temple, and the Jews were sent into exile. Monotheism, the great contribution of the Hebrews to civilization, had a profound influence on their concept of political legitimacy. The Jews were united in one faith and equal before God. Their rulers attempted to dispense justice with this reality in mind.

In 522 BC, Darius I (ca. 550–486 BC) assumed the throne of the Persian Empire. He fought off his chief rival, Gaumata, after a prayer to the god Ahura Mazda—further evidence of the power of monotheism. In this case, the religion was Zoroastrianism. The role of Ahura Mazda is evident in this passage from *The Behistan Inscription of King Darius* (ca. 520 BC), in which Darius I thanked his god for his victory:

> Says Darius the king: . . . Gaumata the Magian took . . . both Persia and Media and the other provinces; he seized (the power) and . . . became king. . . . There was not a man neither a Persian nor a Median nor any one of our family who could make Gaumata . . . deprived of the kingdom; the people feared his tyranny; . . . afterward, I asked Ahura Mazda for help; Ahura Mazda bore me aid; . . . I smote him; I took the kingdom from him; by the grace of Ahura Mazda I became king; Ahura Mazda gave me the kingdom.[2]

After the Achaemenid dynasty (550–330 BC), Persia was ruled by Alexander the Great as part of his Macedonian Empire. Subsequently it was ruled by the Seleucid dynasty (330–247 BC), the Parthians (247 BC–AD 224), and the Sassanids, who succumbed in the Arab conquest of 651.

The Roman consul Marcus Crassus (112–53 BC), who ruled the Roman republic as a member of the Triumvirate with Julius Caesar and Gnaeus Pompey, led a force of 50,000 to fight the Parthians and achieve military glory. In 53 BC, the Parthians crushed Crassus and his army at the Battle of Carrhae, in southern Turkey near the border with Syria. To mock Crassus' personal wealth and the splendor of Rome, his Persian foes were said to have poured molten gold down his throat.[3] As you read of these military campaigns, think of the many armies from antiquity to the present day that have swept through and battled in the Middle East.

Alexander's empire diffused classical Greek language and culture throughout the ancient Middle East, a process known as Hellenization. The Roman Empire, established by Caesar Augustus (r. 27 BC–AD 14), then spread Hellenistic civilization throughout its vast domain. In AD 295, the Roman Empire split into western and eastern halves. The western branch collapsed in 476, but during the sixth century, the eastern Roman emperor Justinian (r. 527–65) restored much of the empire's lost territory. Persia and Rome became great competitors in the Middle East. This rivalry influenced the spread of Islam in the seventh century.

Muslims refer to the period before Islam as the Jahiliyya (age of ignorance). From the Muslims' perspective, the civilizations, artifacts, and unjust practices of the ancient Middle East were elements of the Jahiliyya as a time devoid of reason and light and rife with ruthless tribalism. A notorious example from the Jahiliyya, referenced in the Qur'an, was the pre-Islamic practice of female infanticide. The revelation of the Qur'an through the Prophet Muhammad (ca. 570–632) began a new age—an age of enlightenment—for the Arabs. They now had a holy scripture, just as the Jews and Christians had their own Abrahamic sacred books. Modern Arab and Muslim views of the ancient Middle East depend on the individual and the way he or she interprets God's commandment against the worship of graven images. Modern intellectuals, politicians, and businesses have used ancient artifacts as symbols of nationalism. *Al Ahram*, the Egyptian newspaper, displays the Great Pyramids on its masthead, the logo for EgyptAir is the Eye of Horus, and Iraqi president Saddam Hussein rebuilt parts of Babylon and Nineveh to re-create the glory of the Babylonian Empire. A Muslim fundamentalist today might argue that it does not make sense to use or glorify artifacts from the Jahiliyya. Other Muslims argue that these artifacts must be preserved to inform about the past and are not objects of idolatry to be destroyed. Tragically, the Taliban and ISIS have taken the extreme step of destroying ancient monuments in the Middle East, some of them United Nations Education, Scientific, and Cultural Organization (UNESCO) World Heritage sites. Furthermore, these violent groups have engaged in the illegal sale of antiquities to generate revenue.

11. What were the characteristics, strengths, and weaknesses of the two major powers in the Middle East at the advent of Islam: the Byzantine Empire and the Sassanid Empire?

In the early seventh century, two powers dominated the Middle East: the Roman Byzantine Empire and the Persian Sassanid Empire. The western half of the Roman Empire fell in AD 476, but the eastern branch—later called the Byzantine Empire, with its capital at Constantinople—lasted until 1453. In AD 224, the Sassanids took Persia and Mesopotamia from the Parthians. They built their capital at Ctesiphon, near present-day Baghdad, and established themselves as the political successors to the Parthians and as the preservers of the nomadic warrior tradition. Their dynasty survived until 651.

The Byzantines dominated the eastern Mediterranean littoral, the Balkans, Anatolia, and Egypt, which supplied the empire with grain. They were renowned for their high Greek culture, monumental architecture, military prowess, and leading role in the formation of Orthodox Christian doctrine. The Sassanids also ruled vast territory, stretching from modern-day Iraq eastward across Iran to Turkmenistan, Afghanistan, and Pakistan. They built a sophisticated empire based on trade, diplomacy, cultural exchanges, and military strength. Both empires practiced universal, monotheistic religions, but Zoroastrianism evolved into a dualistic faith with one supreme being representing good and the other representing evil. The Byzantines did not tolerate religious dissent and fought Christian heresies and non-Christian beliefs within the empire. The Sassanids were generally tolerant of other faiths, but they also persecuted a major heresy, Mazdakism, within their domain. Moreover, they treated non-Persian subjects as uncivilized, thus mirroring the Romans, who used the term "barbarian" to describe anyone who was not Roman. Both the Byzantines and Sassanids viewed Arabia as an unruly backwater, and each employed a confederation of Christian Arab tribes in the northern part of the country as a buffer against tribes in the south. The Ghassanid confederation was allied with Byzantium; the Lakhmid tribes were allied with Persia.

The Byzantines were duophysite Christians, believing Christ had two natures: human and divine. In 313 the Roman emperor Constantine (r. 306–337) recognized Christianity as a legitimate religion in the Roman Empire, and in 380 Emperor Theodosius (r. 379–395) made it the official religion of the state. By the mid-fifth century, only duophysite Christianity was tolerated in the empire. Between 325 and 451, church councils condemned other views of the nature of Christ. Orthodoxy enhanced unity and universalism within the empire but led to the persecution of non-duophysite heresies, particularly in Syria and Egypt, which produced a significant number of Christian dissenters.

The Sassanid Persians advanced Zoroastrianism as the state religion. Zoroastrianism was founded by a Persian prophet, Zoroaster, in the seventh century BC. He preached that Ahura Mazda, the sun god, was equal to goodness and truth and was in eternal conflict with Ahriman, the devil, who was equivalent to evil and falsehood. The faith of Zoroaster was universal and open to all people, requiring no tribal or social pedigree for acceptance into the Zoroastrian community. It started as a monotheistic religion but became a dualistic theology through the teachings of Mazdak, a Magian priest, in the late fifth and early sixth centuries AD. He preached a doctrine of dualism that became known as Mazdakism, in which Ahura Mazda was equal to Ahriman, light was equal to darkness, good was equal to evil, and truth was equal to falsehood. This duality helped Zoroastrianism gain many adherents. Sassanid rulers and Zoroastrian priests fought Mazdakism, which they regarded as a heresy. Mazdak was killed, and thousands of his followers were either put to death or forced to flee. The state-sanctioned version of Zoroastrianism became known as Mazdaism—named for Ahura Mazda. Aside from the repression of the Mazdakis, Sassanid society could be described as generally tolerant. Jundishapur University, in what is today southwest Iran, became a leading center of Hellenistic culture and scholarship. Nestorian Christian, Jewish, and Buddhist scholars moved there and thrived.

The Sassanids bequeathed two great legacies to Muslim civilization, one in agriculture, the other kingship. The Sassanids advanced agriculture with the concept of a hydraulic state. Because agricultural prosperity depended on reliable irrigation, the governing authority had the responsibility to maintain and manage the water supply. The Sassanids also refined kingship with the Circle of Justice, illustrated in the figure below. God blesses and glorifies the king, imbuing him with charisma. The king supports the priests who administer justice, ensuring the people are not oppressed. The people produce food and support the soldiers. The soldiers protect the people and defend the king. The king protects the kingdom from outside threats by supporting the soldiers. Society remains stable so long as the components of the circle are kept in balance; justice equals balance. The Circle of Justice was carried into the Islamic era: god was Allah, the king was the caliph or sultan, and the concept of balance corresponded to justice (*'adl*). The opposite of *'adl* is *fitna*, a term introduced in Question 9.

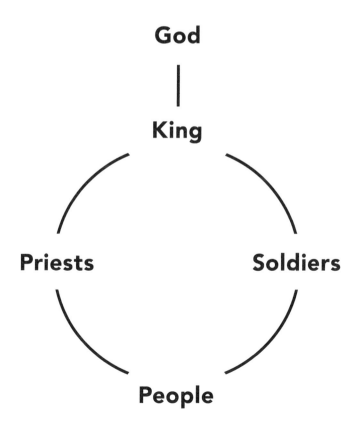

The Byzantines and Sassanids became bitter rivals. For nearly ninety years, beginning in the mid-sixth century, they fought over territory in the heart of the Middle East. They also battled heresies in their empires. After decades of conflict, they were militarily exhausted, financially spent, and left with heavily damaged cities and farmland. By the early 600s, a power vacuum existed in the Middle East. Islam would fill that void.

12. What were the social institutions and practices of pre-Islamic Arabia?

Originating in the Arabian Peninsula, early Arabs were divided into two branches: "pure" Arabs and Arabicized Arabs. The pure Arabs are descended from Yarub Ibn Yashjub Ibn Qahtan. They are also known as Qahtanites, South Arabians, or Yemenis. The Arabicized Arabs migrated to the north and are descended from Adnan, a descendant of Isma'il, the son of the patriarch Abraham and his Egyptian concubine, Hagar. They are also known as Adnanites, North Arabians, or Qays. The distinction between the pure and Arabicized Arabs would influence politics in the *umma* after the death of the Prophet Muhammad. According to the Arab and Muslim traditions, all Arabs are descendants of Isma'il, and the Bible and the Qur'an state that the Arabs are descendants of Sam (or Shem), the oldest son of Noah. The terms "Semite" and "Semitic," derived from the name Shem, were coined by the German historian August Ludwig von Schlozer (1735–1809) in the late 1700s.

Throughout the Arabian Peninsula, ancient Arabs were organized into clans, clans into tribes, and tribes into tribal federations, which centered around the major urban areas of Mecca, Taif, and Yathrib (later Medina). Mecca's was the largest and most prosperous of the tribal federations. Muhammad's tribe, the Quraysh, sat at the apex of the tribal oligarchy. The rulers of Mecca were the Banu (Sons of) 'Abd ash-Shams clan, part of the Quraysh tribe and parent clan to the Banu Umayya, which would govern the Muslim Empire from 661 to 750. The Prophet Muhammad belonged to the less influential Banu Hashim. The rivalry between clans continued after Muhammad's death and profoundly influenced early Muslim politics.

In our discussion of pre-Islamic Arab society, we focus on the caravan trade, tribalism, poetry, and religion. The caravan trade was the primary source of wealth in the area around Mecca in the Hijaz region of western Arabia. Mecca was an entrepôt for goods shipped between Ethiopia and Yemen in the south and Syria in the north and from India to the Mediterranean world. The city was also important because it had a well; was the site of the Ka'ba, which contained hundreds of tribal idols; was the site of the annual pilgrimage to honor the gods; and was the venue of the annual poetry fair, held near the Ka'ba.

Ancient Arab tribes were extended families that migrated together and held property in common. Tribes protected their members against other nomads and settled people. The Arabs were belligerent and zealous in defending their honor, on which their freedom depended. Raids and feuds were important components of tribal culture and frequently turned into wars between tribes. The tribe was led by a shaykh who was selected by a council of tribal elders representing different clans and leading families. Traditionally, the newly chosen leader was well respected and noted for his generosity and bravery. He governed the tribe through a consultative council, in Arabic *majlis ash-shura*, and by consensus. His principal responsibilities were protecting the tribe, upholding tribal honor, and administering justice. By providing security and material support for the clans, he garnered their loyalty. All members of the tribe could approach and petition the shaykh.

Poets were held in high esteem in Arab society. They served as tribal historians, chronicling acts of bravery and honor and recounting the practice of pre-Islamic Arab virtues (*muruwwa*). Those virtues included bravery in battle; chivalry in conducting raids; perseverance in misfortune; determination in revenge; defiance toward the powerful; safeguarding the weak; charity to women, children, and the poor; hospitality and protection to guests; allegiance to the tribe; and commitment to keeping promises. The Suq O Kadh was a four-month truce observed during the annual poetry fair. The best poems were hung in the Ka'ba and bore the title "Mu'allaqat" ("Suspended Odes"; in modern Arabic, this term means "commentaries"). As increasing numbers of Arabs moved to the cities, they became more and more interested in individual success and monetary gain and cared less about traditional values and tribal concerns. Many Arabs, including Muhammad, were deeply concerned about the decline of *muruwwa*. By the time Muhammad began preaching, Arab chivalry had declined to such a degree that exploitation of the weak and dispossessed was commonplace. Many concerned Arabs viewed Muhammad's message of social justice as an effort to restore *muruwwa*.

Religion in pre-Islamic Arabia was mostly animistic and polytheistic. There were hundreds of tribal gods, and 360 totems were housed in the Ka'ba. Over the years, there was a gradual movement toward the notion of Allah (God). Al-Lat was one of three chief goddesses prominently revered in Mecca; the others were al-Uzza and Manat. The term "al-Lat" was also used to describe the Mesopotamian goddess of the underworld, and Arabs seemed to have ascribed the term "al-Uzza" to the Greek goddess Aphrodite. According to Muslim tradition, the Ka'ba was built by Abraham and Isma'il after God spared Isma'il's life. (In the Old Testament God spares the life of Abraham's son Isaac.) They erected it in the Holy Precinct, which had been staked out by Adam, as directed by God, to remind him of the paradise he had lost. The structure served as a house of worship dedicated to the one God. Abraham placed a black stone, a meteorite, in the Ka'ba. Small pieces of the Black Stone, a gift from heaven, are all that remain of the original Ka'ba.

Mecca benefitted greatly from the presence of the Ka'ba. It was considered *haram* (sacred) and was the place where idols were kept and winning poems from the poets' festival were displayed. All disputes, even a blood feud between two tribes, had to be set aside in the vicinity of the Ka'ba. A blood feud was a seemingly intractable conflict that could last for decades. Indeed, in the area around the Ka'ba, disputes could be discussed and hopefully resolved. The Ka'ba was a profitable attraction in Mecca. It was the centerpiece of Meccan society and became the temporal heart of Islam.

Although polytheism was prevalent, other religious practices existed in pre-Islamic Arabia. Jewish communities had dwelt in the peninsula for several centuries, and non-duophysite Christians fled to Arabia to escape persecution by Byzantine authorities, who had assumed the role of the true defenders of Christian orthodoxy. Tension existed between Arabs who followed the monotheism of Judaism and Christianity and those who worshiped tribal gods, followed Roman and Greek cults, or even venerated Egyptian deities. Aggravating this tension was the intolerance of monotheists toward any hint of polytheism. Arguably, the most vivid account of the unbridled power of monotheism during the Roman era was provided by Hypatia (370–415), the Alexandrian mathematician, astronomer, and philosopher. She witnessed the destruction of the library of Alexandria and suppression of neo-Platonic philosophy by zealous Christians and was herself murdered by a mob.

3

The Prophet Muhammad
and the Emergence of Islam

This chapter covers the life and career of the Prophet Muhammad, focusing on his efforts to establish a viable Islamic social and political order. We also provide an overview of the fundamentals of Islam, including a discussion of the meanings of jihad, an introduction to the Qur'an, and the reading of sample passages from the holy book.

13. Why are the life, career, and character of the Prophet Muhammad so crucial to understanding the rise and spread of Islam?

The life, career, and personal attributes of the Prophet Muhammad are central to the story of Islam.

We discussed in chapter 2 the protracted conflict between Rome and Persia for hegemony in the Middle East. In the century of Muhammad's birth, the Arabian Peninsula also witnessed great tumult. In 525 the Christian Kingdom of Axum, located in northern Ethiopia, invaded southern Arabia and defeated the Himyarite Kingdom, a Jewish state that had flourished in Yemen since the late second century BC. In 570, the year of Muhammad's birth, an Ethiopian military force, with war elephants in the vanguard, moved on Mecca. The attack failed. The role of God in saving the city is recounted in Sura 105:1–5 ("The Elephant") of the Qur'an:

See you not how your Lord dealt with the Companions of the Elephant.

Did He not make their treacherous plan go astray?

And He sent against them Flights of Birds,

Striking them with stones of baked clay.

Then did He make them like an empty field of stalks and straw, (of
   which the corn) has been eaten up.[1]

An alternative theory for the Ethiopian defeat is that its army was the victim of disease, either smallpox or bubonic plague, the latter of which might be traced to the Plague of Justinian, which ravaged the Mediterranean world and Middle East in the mid-sixth century.

Muhammad was born in Mecca into the Quraysh tribe and the Banu Hashim, a prominent clan whose members served as custodians of the Ka'ba. Muhammad's father, 'Abdullah, died before he was born; his mother, Amina, died when he was six years old. He was raised by his grandfather 'Abd al-Muttalib for two years. He was then cared for by a Bedouin clan, affording him the opportunity to perfect spoken Arabic and master Arab values. Finally, he was taken in by his uncle Abu Talib, a wealthy merchant who served as his protector and sponsor.

Muhammad became a merchant and caravanner and quickly acquired a reputation for being honest and forthright. Had he died at the age of forty and never become a prophet, he would have been known locally as al-Amin (the trustworthy one). Unable to achieve wealth within his clan, he went to work for Khadijah Bint Khuwaylid, a wealthy widow who operated a caravan network. She was impressed with his integrity, noting that he operated her caravans with an accurate accounting, and proposed marriage; she was fifteen years his senior. Muhammad's marriage to Khadijah assured financial security and afforded him the opportunity to meditate on several important issues, such as monotheism, the decline of Arab virtues, and social justice. Khadijah bore several sons and daughters, but only daughter Fatima outlived Muhammad.

Muhammad often meditated in al-Hira, a cave on what is now known as Jabal an-Nur (Mountain of Light) near Mecca. During his life, he had encountered the adherents of other monotheistic religions. He knew Christian tribes in the Najran region of Arabia and had many conversations with the Nestorian monk Bahira. Three Jewish tribes lived in the city of Yathrib, north of Mecca. He shared in the longing of many Arabs, worthy descendants of Abraham, to have their own scriptures.

Muhammad received his first revelation at the age of forty on the twenty-seventh of the Muslim month of Ramadan—a date revered by Muslims as the Night of Power. The revelations were delivered to Muhammad by the angel Gabriel, who commanded him to "recite" (*iqra* in Arabic): "recite in the name of your Lord who created, created man from clots of blood! Recite! Your Lord is the most bountiful one, who by the pen taught man what he did not know" (Qur'an 96:1–5). Khadijah encouraged Muhammad to listen to the revelations. She became his first convert. Other early converts were his cousin 'Ali Ibn Abu Talib and his friend Abu Bakr.

Muhammad continued to receive regular revelations and began preaching publicly in 610. He and his followers encountered resistance from the Quraysh, who attempted to stop him and his message. They perceived him as a threat to the socioeconomic order of Mecca. He preached about a new social order and a monotheism that threatened the Meccan economy, which benefitted greatly from the revenue derived from pilgrimages. According to Muhammad, adherence to Islam outweighed tribal loyalty, and all Muslims were equal and brothers in the eyes of God. He defended the rights of the poor and oppressed and asserted that the rich and powerful had an obligation to provide for the disadvantaged members of society. In effect, Muhammad was creating a new tribe based not on blood ties, but on the idea of monotheism, which attracted the poor and those without tribal protection. Muhammad attracted large numbers of the Arab underclass and became the leader of a community that would outnumber the tribes of pre-Islamic Arabia and supplant the ruling Meccan aristocracy.

The Quraysh stepped up their persecution through boycott and verbal abuse. In 615 some converts went to Christian Ethiopia for protection. This event is regarded as the first *hijra* (migration). Muhammad did not travel to Ethiopia because it was too distant for carrying out his work.

The years 619 to 622 were a period of crisis and introspection for Muhammad and his followers. He began to question his calling. In 619 both Khadijah and Abu Talib died. With the death of Abu Talib, Muhammad lost his protection. He was stoned by children in Taif when he sought refuge there. He was forced to live in the desert, away from Mecca. The year 619 was probably the worst year of his life.

That same year, Muhammad performed the Isra' (Night Journey), during which Gabriel led him from Mecca to the site of al-Masjid al-Aqsa (al-Aqsa Mosque) in Jerusalem. He then ascended through seven levels of heaven on a winged, Pegasus-like creature called Buraq, an event that Muslims call al-Mi'raj (literally, "the ladder" and the origin of the English word "mirage"). He ascended from the rock that is now housed by the Dome of the Rock in Jerusalem. In heaven he observed the Creation in one night, received instruction on Islam from God, and met other prophets. It is still debated by theologians whether Muhammad's journey was physical or metaphysical.[2] Because of this remarkable experience, Jerusalem is the third-holiest site in Islam, after Mecca and Medina. Of note, the rock inside the strikingly beautiful Dome of the Rock shrine is also believed by followers of the three monotheistic faiths to mark the spot where Abraham nearly sacrificed Isaac, his son by Sarah in the Old Testament, or Isma'il, his son by Hagar, according to Islamic tradition.

Despite the many troubles involved, Muhammad continued to preach publicly. His Meccan revelations dealt with God and his attributes, especially the concept of monotheism, judgment day, rewards, and punishments.

During 620–622, the pressure on Muhammad and his followers from the Meccan hierarchy reached its height. In 621 Muhammad conferred with tribal representatives from Yathrib at al-Aqaba. According to the Pledge of Aqaba, they offered a home to him and his followers in exchange for his services as a permanent mediator. Two of the three pagan Arab tribes in Yathrib were feuding, which weakened their solidarity against the three Jewish tribes. Meanwhile, a plot against Muhammad's life in Mecca was uncovered. The migration of Muhammad's followers to Yathrib began on 16 July 622 (the first day of the Muslim month of Muharram), which marks the beginning of the Islamic calendar. The migration took two months to complete. After all of Muhammad's followers had departed Mecca, Muhammad left the city with Abu Bakr and arrived in Yathrib in September. This group of Muslims, known as the Muhajirun (Emigrants), would play a critical role in Islam's political development.

Yathrib soon became known as Medina, short for al-Madina an-Nabawi-yya (City of the Prophet). In Medina the Muslims built the first mosque, and Muhammad served as chief executive, judge, legislator, commander of the army, *and* prophet. His successors, the caliphs, had only temporal authority. His Medinan revelations consisted of laws concerning prayer, almsgiving, fasting, and performing the pilgrimage; social and political ordinances governing marriage, divorce, inheritance, and legitimate authority; and rules regulating business practices.

The Pledge of Aqaba evolved into the Constitution of Medina, best described as a compact, which served as the basis for a commonwealth or Islamic state. Muhammad created a tribal federation, consisting of the Muhajirun, the Ansar (helpers, or Medinan converts), and the tribes of Yathrib. The federation marked the beginning of a distinct Muslim community bound to other tribes through the compact. *Umma*, a term difficult to define, connotes a religious and political union, deemphasizes individual tribes, and prescribes a means of interacting with non-Muslims. Muhammad, who had been selected to serve as the Grand Arbiter of Yathrib, became the de facto ruler of the Yathrib Tribal Confederation. At this early stage, Muhammad governed more non-Muslims than Muslims, and the former were more interested in his arbitration skills than in his prophecy. The constitution trumped tribal law and tribal loyalties and created a sense of unity among different groups. Jews and Christians could live and practice their religion within the Muslim state so long as they were peaceful, restricted proselytization, and paid taxes. They were respected as Ahl al-Kitab (People of the Book). The word "book," in this case, refers to a written scripture. Tolerance of other religions was an important attribute of the *umma* and a major reason why Islam spread so rapidly at the time.

In 623 Muhammad married 'A'isha, daughter of Abu Bakr. That same year, he began a campaign to capture Mecca. The Muslims opened the conflict by raiding lucrative Meccan caravans. Although the raiding started out as an act of tribal revenge and a source of income, it then assumed a religious purpose: fighting nonbelievers, principally the Meccans who threatened the *umma*. *Ghazwi* (raiding) evolved into jihad (holy war) and provided a powerful and dynamic vehicle for the spread of Islam. In effect, the Muslims were fighting against people who were fighting Islam. Peace would come through submission to Islam or acceptance of Muslim authority. Conversely, the Romans had fought ruthless wars against Germanic tribes, the Parthians, and others, expecting their submission to Roman rule. The Roman historian Tacitus (d. ca. AD 120) described the harsh reality of the Pax Romana: "They [the Romans] ravage, they slaughter, they seize by false pretenses, and all of this they hail as the construction of empire. And when in their wake nothing remains but a desert, they call that peace."[3]

In 624 'Ali Ibn Abu Talib married Fatima. By that year—two years after the *hijra* to Medina—two major factors were spurring the spread of Islam: the Constitution of Medina and raiding. The constitution offered a framework for social and political organization and accounted for the People of the Book. Muhammad had been invited to Yathrib to serve as a permanent mediator to resolve local disputes. This act marked the first time that a group of tribes had secured the services of a permanent mediator. Muhammad's decisions, which were final, enjoyed religious sanction.

The People of the Book—Christians, Jews, and Sabians (ancient south Arabian monotheists)—enjoyed legal status. They were treated with tolerance, were protected, and were not forced to convert so long as they accepted Muslim authority. The idea of a book or scripture is significant to Muslims as the word of God. Nevertheless, Muslims believe that the Jewish and Christian scriptures became corrupted when men attempted to write them down, introducing fabrications and errors. Muslims believe that the People of the Book seek truth and have not fallen away. Muslims recognize three sacred books in addition to the Qur'an: the Torah, Psalms, and Gospels.

Raiding became *jihad fi sabil Allah* (warfare in the cause of God). Caravan raiders, in effect, became religious warriors, and raiding became a leading cause of the rapid expansion of Islam. The practice was carefully regulated, however; Muslims would fight only those who resisted them, and only combatants could be attacked. Furthermore, during the expansion, the Muslims were often welcomed by local inhabitants who had been oppressed by their imperial masters.

The idea of a Dar al-Islam (Abode of Islam) and a Dar al-Harb (Abode of War) began with the Muslim community in Medina. A principal goal of the Muslims at this critical time was the expansion of the *umma*'s boundaries, or Dar al-Islam, the territory governed by Muslims. The Dar al-Harb is the territory outside the Dar al-Islam where the inhabitants have not accepted a truce (*'ahd*) offered by Muslim authorities; hence, the Dar al-Islam contains the Dar al-'Ahd (Abode of Truce). In the opinion of several political Islamists, the Middle East mandates governed by Britain and France after World War I and the State of Israel are examples of the Dar al-Harb being implanted into the Dar al-Islam. Would militant Islamists expand their political power indefinitely if they had the opportunity? Probably yes, but this is a challenging goal made more difficult by the emergence of the modern nation-state and the revulsion many Muslims have toward the imposition of Islam, particularly an extreme interpretation of the faith, through coercion and intimidation. Think of how the expansion of ISIS in Syria and Iraq has assaulted the sovereignty and territorial integrity of Muslim and non-Muslim countries alike. ISIS also conducted or inspired horrific terrorist attacks in Europe, the United States, Asia, and the Middle East, killing both Muslims and non-Muslims.

In 624 Muhammad came into conflict with the Jews of Medina. Initially, he and the Jews had enjoyed good relations. He fasted on their Day of Atonement, and Muslims prayed toward Jerusalem. The Jews, on the other hand, contended that his teachings conflicted with the Torah. Muhammad responded that the Hebrew scriptures were flawed, corrupt, and incomplete, and the Qur'an was correcting them. He subsequently developed new traditions that distinguished Muslim and Jewish religious practices. For example, he designated Ramadan as the month of fasting and introspection and changed the *qibla* (direction of prayer) to Mecca. He also accused the Jewish tribes of siding with the Meccans. Although he had developed a framework for dealing peacefully with the People of the Book, violence broke out between Muslims and Jews. The Jewish tribes were expelled from Medina, and many Jews were killed.

That same year, the Muslims began a series of battles against the Meccans. At the Battle of Badr, three hundred Muslims defeated a thousand Meccans. Before the action at Badr, information had reached Muhammad and his followers that the Meccans had seized Muslim property in Mecca and placed it on the caravan to Syria to be sold to the highest bidder. The following year, at the Battle of Uhud, seven hundred Muslims were defeated by three thousand Meccans and retreated to Medina. Fortunately for the Muslims, the Meccans did not follow up their victory. The last contest, the Battle of the Trench, took place in 627. A large Meccan force was sent to destroy the Muslims, but the Muslims dug a dry moat around Medina that thwarted the Meccan cavalry and forced the Meccans to lay siege to the city. The Muslims outlasted them.

In 628 Muhammad led a peaceful delegation of pilgrims to Mecca. As the Muslims approached the city, the Meccans offered a ten-year truce, the Hudaybiyya Pact, which permitted the Muslims to make the lesser pilgrimage the following year. The agreement made it clear that the Muslim community was not going to be eliminated. Around this time, two notable Arab warriors (and formidable foes of Muhammad) who would play important roles in the Muslim conquest joined the Muslim community: 'Amr Ibn al-'As and Khalid Ibn al-Walid, the latter of whom is known as the "Drawn Sword of Islam."

In 629 the Muslims performed a lesser pilgrimage, but the Meccans broke the truce by attacking a Muslim ally, the Banu Kuz'aa. A year later, Muhammad marched on Mecca with 10,000 faithful. They met little resistance and captured the city peacefully. Muhammad cleansed the Ka'ba of all idols, and many Meccans converted to Islam. With Mecca in its grasp, the Muslim community enjoyed a sense of completeness.

Also in 630, Muhammad launched a military expedition against the Byzantine Empire's Arab vassals, the Ghassanids. The following year became known as the Year of Delegations, during which tribal representatives from the Hijaz and Yemen visited Muhammad and pledged their loyalty. Most tribes converted sincerely to Islam, but some converted in name only to avoid further conflict with the Muslims and to share in the spoils of war. Muhammad demanded that all allies profess Islam or accept Muslim governance.

Four months after the pilgrimage of 631, the Ka'ba was declared *haram* (sacred) and forbidden to pagans and polytheists. Muhammad performed a farewell pilgrimage in early 632 and in his sermon on Mount Arafat he professed, "This day I have perfected your religion for you, completed My favor upon you, and have chosen for you Islam as your religion" (Qur'an 5:3). He then spoke of the unique bond of the faith: "Learn that every Muslim is a brother to every Muslim and that the Muslims constitute one brotherhood. . . . All those who listen to me shall pass on my words to others and those to others again; and may the last ones understand my words better than those who listen to me directly."[4]

Muhammad died in his house in Medina in June 632. At the time of his death, almost all the tribes of the Arabian Peninsula were under the banner of Islam. Some tribes embraced the faith, others joined for material gain, and still others allied themselves with the ascendant power in Arabia. The tribes were given the choice of professing Islam or signing a compact and joining Muhammad's tribal confederation. Unlike Jesus, who had relatively few followers at the time of his death, Muhammad had established a thriving state and had laid the foundation for a vast empire by the time he passed away. The expansion of territory under Muslim control, in turn, spurred the growth of Islam, which spread by example, persuasion, intermarriage, and (to a degree) compulsion. The religious and political domains were combined in the Muslim state, and Muslims argued that Muhammad was chosen and inspired by God and that his state cannot be re-created because his successors were not chosen by God. The basis for law was to be the Qur'an and hadith, the reported sayings and actions of Muhammad.

Muhammad is one the most significant figures in history, and his life is worth studying for several reasons. First, according to Muslims, he served as the human conduit through which the true word of God was revealed to humanity. The revelation of the Qur'an is considered by many believers as his only miracle. Second, to Muslims, he is the last (or the seal) of the Abrahamic prophets; that is until the return of Jesus, who will come as son of the Maryam and prophet of Islam, not as the son of God, as according to Christian belief. Third, he was the founder of an Islamic community that became a state and expanded into a vast empire after his death. Fourth, unlike Jesus but much like Moses, he engaged in warfare to defend the community, yet he made provisions for the care of widows and orphans and the treatment of prisoners. It had been tribal custom for a shaykh to keep a fourth of the spoils, but Muhammad took only a fifth and gave much of that away. Fifth, his life provides the best example of Muslim behavior. Believers study the Qur'an's verses and hadith to determine in a particular circumstance "What would Muhammad do?" His emphasis on social justice and devotion to monotheism won many converts.

Knowing and understanding the life and teachings of Muhammad are of singular importance. This understanding can help non-Muslims get to the core of the faith, root out misconceptions, and appreciate the diverse perspectives of the 1.6 billion adherents of the faith.

14. What are the fundamental tenets of Islam?

"Islam" means submission, surrender, or obedience to the will of God. It is related to the Arabic word for peace, *salaam*. "Islam" and *salaam* have the same three-letter root (s-l-m). A Muslim will greet another Muslim by saying, "As-salaamu alaykum" (Peace be with you). The response is "Wa alaykum as-salaam" (And with you, peace). A Muslim is someone who has submitted to and obeys the will of God. Do not confuse the terms "Islam" and "Muslim." One is the religion; the other is a person who practices the religion.

The Nature of God

The word for God in Arabic is "Allah." In Islam, Allah is the eternal, all-powerful, and omnipresent being. In Christian belief, God has human form. Think of the white-haired, bearded God creating Adam in Michelangelo's paintings on the ceiling of the Sistine Chapel. Allah, however, does not have human characteristics, but instead has ninety-nine attributes, among them being the Merciful, Compassionate, Creator, Almighty, Provider, Compeller, and Preserver. Muslims create personal names for their sons by attaching the term *'abd* (servant) before one of the attributes, as in 'Abd ar-Rahman (servant of the Merciful) or 'Abd al-Jabar (servant of the Compeller). Muslims use the invocation "Bismillah ar-Rahman ar-Rahim" (known as the Bismillah)—"In the name of God, the Merciful, the Compassionate"—before they begin a task, such as a news broadcast, a journey, a speech, a letter, an entry in a notebook, or an exam. The invocation contains two attributes of Allah: the Merciful and the Compassionate.

The Fundamentals of Islam

The three fundamentals of Islam are faith (*iman*), practice (*ibada*), and morality (*ihsan*).

Faith

Regarding the first fundamental—faith—Muslims believe absolutely and uncompromisingly in one God; angels; *jinn*, from which the English word genie derives; revealed books; messengers and prophets; the Day of Resurrection; and the Day of Judgment. The Muslim cosmology, which is similar to that of Christianity, consists of God, angels, humans, *jinn*, and Shaytan or Iblis (Satan or the Devil). A channel of communication exists between angels and humans. When God wants to communicate with a man or woman, he sends an angel. *Jinn* coexist on earth with humans; they are made of fire, not flesh. Rebellious *jinn* have become devils. "Shaytan" literally means "adversary." Shaytan was the leader of a group of angels who refused to pay homage to Adam and were expelled from heaven. Both Muslim and Christian theologians debate whether such beings as Satan and *jinn* are physical beings or representations of base human desire and behavior.

The Christian and Muslim concepts of the Day of Resurrection and Day of Judgment are similar, but the Muslim descriptions are more tangible than the Christian ones. On the Day of Resurrection for Muslims, corporeal resurrection takes place. Then, on the Day of Judgment, every person answers for his or her lifetime of words and deeds; rewards or punishments are meted out in either heaven or hell. Martyrs bypass judgment and go directly to heaven. The following passage from the Qur'an vividly illustrates the end of time, the horrors of hell, and the paradise of heaven:

> The Day that the Trumpet shall be sounded, and you shall come
>   forth in crowds;
> And the heavens shall be opened as if there were doors,
> And the mountains shall vanish, as if they were a mirage.
> Truly Hell is as a place of ambush,
> For the transgressors a place of destination:
> They will dwell therein for ages.

Nothing cool shall they taste therein, nor any drink,

Save a boiling fluid and a fluid, dark, murky, intensely cold,

A fitting recompense (for them).

For that they used not to fear any account (for their deeds),

But they (impudently) treated Our Signs as false.

And all things have We preserved on record.

"So taste you (the fruits of your deeds); for no increase shall We grant
   you, except in Punishment."

Verily for the Righteous there will be a fulfillment of (the heart's)
   desires;

Gardens enclosed, and grapevines;

Companions of equal age;

And a cup full (to the brim).

No vanity shall they hear therein, nor Untruth:

Recompense from your Lord, a gift, (amply) sufficient,

(From) the Lord of the heavens and the earth, and all between, (Allah)
   Most Gracious: None shall have power to argue with Him.

The Day that the Spirit and the angels will stand forth in ranks, none
   shall speak except any who is permitted by (Allah) Most Gracious,
   and He will say what is right.

That Day will be the sure Reality: Therefore, whoso will, let him take
   a (straight) return to his Lord!

Verily, We have warned you of a Penalty near, the Day when man will
   see (the deeds) which his hands have sent forth, and the Unbeliever
   will say, "Woe unto me! Would that I were (mere) dust!" (78:18–40)

The graphic descriptions of heaven and hell contained in the Qur'an
and in Byzantine and Persian literature and beliefs influenced medieval
European writers, notably the Florentine poet Dante Alighieri (d.
1321), who used them in his fourteenth-century masterpiece, the *Divine
Comedy*.

During judgment, no one stands between an individual Muslim and
God. The mosque, the Muslim place of prayer, emphasizes this point. The
word "mosque" derives from the Arabic word *masjid* (place of prostration),
and in a mosque, no one stands between God and a Muslim during prayer.

Everyone prays together, and all are considered equal before God. There are no pews, chairs, or private boxes. Most Muslims pray and confess directly to God, while Shi'a pray to God through intercessors who are descended from the Prophet Muhammad. Sunnis argue that this practice detracts from the worship of God.

In Sunni tradition, there is no formal clergy, but several occupations take on the trappings of a clergy: *'alim* (a religious scholar; pl. *'ulama*), *qadi* (a judge), mufti (a legal expert capable of delivering a fatwa or legal opinion), and imam (a prayer leader). Concerning the last term, any devout Muslim chosen from a group can serve as an imam. *'Ulama* frequently lead prayers and deliver the Friday sermon. The word "imam" with a small *i* differs from the word "Imam" with a capital *I*. The latter is a Shi'a spiritual and temporal leader. In contrast to Sunni Islam, Shi'ism has clerical ranks, such as *marja al-taqlid* (a source of emulation, a grand ayatollah), ayatollah (a sign of God), *hujjat al-Islam* (an authority on Islam), mullah (a teacher), and *ta'lib* (seminarian). Rank is earned through extensive study, demonstrated knowledge and expertise, and recognition by one's peers. Unlike Christian clergy, Shi'a clergy do not have responsibility for a geographical area, such as a diocese or district. In general, Shi'a clergy are apolitical and chiefly influenced by followers. Ayatollah Ruhollah Khomeini, who led a successful revolutionary movement in the 1970s, represented the exception, not the rule, regarding overt Shi'a political involvement.

A consensus of Muslim scholars believes that humanity has free will within the constraints of God's law and is not subject to predestination. In the Qur'an, the angels ask God why he did not create humans like them—that is, without free will: "Behold, your Lord said to the angels: 'I will create a vicegerent on earth.' They said: 'Will You place therein one who will make mischief therein and shed blood?—while we do celebrate Your praises and glorify Your holy (name)?' He said: 'I know what you know not.'" (2:30). An opposing idea in early Islam was that God is all-powerful; therefore, humans had no choice but to obey his laws. It took time for the idea of free will, a subject of great debate among Muslim scholars, to dominate this discourse.

Practice—The Five Pillars

Practice, the second fundamental of Islam, consists of the Five Pillars, which are the profession of faith (*shahada*), prayer (*salat*), fasting (*sawm*), almsgiving (*zakat*), and pilgrimage (hajj).

The most basic pillar is the profession of faith: "There is no god but God, and Muhammad is the Prophet of God."[5] The profession of faith is repeated at every prayer and is recited over a newborn baby. Conversion to Islam is straightforward: With a sincere heart, the convert recites the *shahada* before two witnesses.

Prayer is performed five times per day. The times are *fajr* (dawn), *zuhr* (noon), *'asr* (mid-afternoon), *maghrib* (sunset), and *'isha* (nightfall). Muslims face Mecca during prayer. In a mosque, the *qibla*, or direction toward Mecca, is marked by a niche in the wall called a *mihrab*. Muslim prayer is characterized by worship and adoration rather than supplication (*du'a*), which is separate from *salat*. The Qur'an does not specify a set ritual for prayer, but according to hadith, prayer consists of a specific number of prostrations (*raka'at*) and recitations. Muslims perform ritual washing (*wudu*) before praying. Prayer is a powerful democratizing force in Muslim society. Individuals pray side by side. The call to prayer is recited by a *muezzin* from a minaret. Prayer can be done anywhere; it does not have to be at a mosque. The exception is the noon prayer on Friday, Yawm al-Juma' (Day of Gathering), which must be performed in a congregational mosque to hear the sermon (*khutba*). The sermon covers a spiritual or moral topic based on that day's Qur'an reading. Since sermons often mention the name of the ruler, they can be very political and thus objectionable to many Muslims. Friday is not a day of rest akin to the Jewish Sabbath or Sunday for Christians. On the contrary, in many Muslim countries, it is a major market day in addition to a day of communal worship. Influenced by the West, most Muslim countries now observe a two-day weekend. Turkey adopted Saturday and Sunday as its weekend; the Persian Gulf states, Thursday and Friday; and Egypt, Jordan, and Palestine, Friday and Saturday. Throughout the Muslim world, Friday has indeed become a day of rest.

Fasting is performed during the month of Ramadan, the ninth month of the Muslim calendar. During daylight hours, Muslims abstain from eating, drinking, smoking, sex, vulgar language, and angry thoughts. Children under the age of puberty and the aged are exempt from fasting. Soldiers in battle, the infirm, travelers, and pregnant, menstruating, or nursing women may postpone the fast. Fasting reminds Muslims of the less fortunate, and it reinforces one's unselfish concerns. It also serves as a penitential rite, giving Muslims an opportunity to reflect on their lives and practice controlling their desires. One-thirtieth of the Qur'an is read each night of Ramadan. The night of the twenty-seventh day of Ramadan—the Night of Power—is observed as the night when God began sending revelations to Muhammad. Non-Muslims living in or visiting Muslim countries should be mindful of Ramadan and show respect by not eating, drinking, or smoking in public. 'Id al-Fitr (Feast of the Breaking of the Fast), a three-day celebration, marks the end of the monthlong fast.

To meet the obligation of almsgiving, Muslims donate 2.5 percent of their net worth (property and income) above a specified minimum in a given year. In several countries, alms are collected by a government agency. In Turkey, submitting the *zakat* is voluntary; in Saudi Arabia, Muslims are encouraged to donate to official agencies to ensure the money is used for worthy causes. In Pakistan, the former dictator General Muhammad Zia-ul-Haq (1924–88) approved legislation for *zakat* to be withheld from one's pay, an unpopular act that was later rescinded. The Qur'an argues that one should not be compelled to perform acts of faith. The funds from *zakat* are used to support mosques, hospitals, schools, the poor, orphanages, and homeless shelters and to cover the costs of collecting the alms and administering the charities.

Most of the activities of the annual pilgrimage to Mecca commemorate events in the life of Abraham. The pilgrimage is performed during Dhu al-Hijja, the twelfth month. Hajj reinforces the sense of community and equality in Islam. Muslims are required to perform the hajj once in their lifetime, so long as personal conditions—particularly health and finances—permit. Male pilgrims wear two white, seamless cloths. Women are unveiled and wear a simple white gown. No jewelry is permitted. Pilgrims abstain from anything that would distract them from the meaning of the pilgrimage.

Pilgrims perform many rituals and participate in several activities from the seventh through the tenth of the month. They enter the courtyard of the Great Mosque in Mecca, kiss or face the Black Stone, perform seven circumambulations of the Ka'ba (*tawaf*), and pray at the place where Abraham stood near the Ka'ba. These activities emphasize Muslim unity and God's presence at the center of the universe. Pilgrims then run seven times (*sa'y*) between the nearby hills of Safa and Marwa, reenacting the desperate search by Hagar for a caravan to rescue her and Isma'il before both died of thirst in the desert. At nearby Muzdalifa, the pilgrims gather forty-nine pebbles to be thrown at three stone pillars, representing devils who tempted Abraham. The devils, also mentioned in the Old Testament book of Genesis, were another test of his faith. On the ninth of the month, pilgrims gather on the Plain of Arafat, where they perform *wuquf* (standing) under the mountain where Muhammad delivered his farewell sermon. Prayers are recited there from noon to sunset, the Prophet's last sermon is read aloud, and pilgrims stand humbly before God, examining their conscience and seeking forgiveness for themselves and all Muslims. They regard *wuquf* as a brief, earthly rehearsal for the Day of Judgment.

The tenth of Dhu al-Hijja marks 'Id al-Adha (Feast of the Sacrifice). Muslims commemorate Abraham's near sacrifice of his son Isma'il by sacrificing camels, sheep, and goats. Abraham sacrificed a ram in place of Isma'il. (Some Muslims argue that the ritual sacrifice is done in remembrance of Isaac, Abraham's son by Sarah.) The feast demonstrates a willingness to part with precious items and is an act of charity. During the 'id, it is customary for pilgrims to eat only a small portion of the sacrificial meat and give the rest to the poor. Afterward, some pilgrims go to Medina to visit Muhammad's tomb, but this visit is not an official part of the hajj.

Morality

Morality, the third fundamental of Islam, demands righteousness in one's private and public life. One's actions and relations with others are generally classified into five categories or levels: *mandatory* (*fard* or *wajib*), which includes circumcision and performing the Five Pillars; *recommended* (*mustahab*), which includes praying more than five times per day and keeping a beard, following Muhammad's example; *permitted* (*mubah*, *mandub*; neutral, *halal*), which includes having more than one wife, but only if the man can treat all of them equally, taking medicine that contains alcohol, and smoking, although some Muslims argue that smoking is a sin; *reprehensible* (*makruh*), which includes divorce and cremation, although some Muslims argue that cremation is forbidden because it interferes with the necessity of a whole body on the Day of Resurrection (actions that are reprehensible, while technically not sins, should be avoided because they could lead a person to sin); and *forbidden* (*haram*), which includes gambling, abusing drugs, drinking alcohol, eating pork, committing adultery, committing theft, committing murder, and lying. *Shirk*, belief in other gods or associating any of God's creations with God, is the only unforgivable sin, which has its origins in the first commandment's injunction against putting any other god before God.

15. What are the different meanings of jihad?

Can jihad be considered a sixth pillar? There are two categories of jihad: greater (inner) and lesser (outer). Greater jihad is the striving or struggling to lead an ideal Islamic life. Lesser jihad involves performing one's worldly obligations, such as providing for one's family. Lesser jihad also includes holy war. A holy war can only be declared by a caliph, but there has not been a caliph since 1924. The Qur'an requires that Muslims fight against people who wage war on them, but it specifically forbids Muslims from continuing to fight when there is a chance of concluding peace: "Fight in the way of God, with those who fight with you, but aggress not, for God loves not the aggressors" (2:190). It also states, "Let there be no hostility except to those who practice oppression" (2:193). Many in the West mistakenly think that jihad only refers to holy war; similarly, Muslim extremists have narrowed the definition to mean war against those they perceive as enemies of Islam. Muhammad is said to have affirmed that greater jihad encompasses the effort to lead a moral, upstanding life while lesser jihad includes warfare.

16. How is the Qur'an organized, what are some of its essential teachings, and how does it compare to the Old and New Testaments?

"Al-Qur'an" literally means "the recitation." It is the literal word of God as revealed to Muhammad by the angel Gabriel—the same heavenly messenger that appears in the New Testament—and then passed by Muhammad to humanity. It contains the basic and central beliefs of Islam. The idea of *logos* ("word" in Greek) differs between Christianity and Islam. In Christianity, Christ is the word of God. "The word became flesh and lived among us" (John 1:14). In Islam, the Qur'an is the actual word of God as uttered to humankind.

The Qur'an is revealed and recorded in Arabic, which has particular significance to Muslims. While knowing Arabic is beneficial, it is not a requirement for being a Muslim, and most Muslims in fact are non-Arabic speakers. Unquestionably, knowledge of Arabic permits Muslims to gain deeper insight into their faith. Since the Qur'an was revealed in Arabic, it cannot be faithfully translated into another language; therefore, a translation is only the translator's rendering of the divinely revealed Arabic text. Children study the Qur'an to learn Arabic, and it forms the basis for Arabic oratory and grammar. Furthermore, according to Islamic teaching, the original Qur'an—Umm al-Kitab (Mother of All Books)—is kept in heaven. The following passage addresses the significance of Arabic and refers to the Umm al-Kitab: "We have revealed the Qur'an in the Arabic tongue that you may understand its meaning. It is a transcript of the eternal book in Our keeping, sublime, and full of wisdom" (43:3–4). Although this point has been the subject of debate among Muslim scholars, it is believed that the Qur'an is an eternal, uncreated object. Muslims accept three other revealed books: the Torah, Psalms, and Gospels. They claim, however, that these three holy books are flawed; that is, they were corrupted by humans. The Qur'an, as revealed through Muhammad—the last of the prophets— corrected the errors in the other Abrahamic sacred books. Muslims have a special tolerance for Jews and Christians, despite their imperfect scriptures. This point is made clear in the following passage from the Qur'an:

If the People of the Book accept the true faith and keep from evil, We will pardon them their sins and admit them to the gardens of delight. If they observe the Torah and the Gospel and what is revealed to them from their Lord, they shall enjoy abundance from above and from beneath.

There are some among them who are righteous men; but there are many among them who do nothing but evil. . . .

Say: "People of the Book, you will attain nothing until you observe the Torah and the Gospel and that which is revealed to you from your Lord."

That which is revealed to you from your Lord will surely increase the wickedness and unbelief of many of them. But do not grieve for the unbelievers.

Believers, Jews, Sabians, and Christians—whoever believes in God and the Last Day and does what is right—shall have nothing to fear or regret. (5:65–69)

The People of the Book are tolerated by but not equal to Muslims. It is important to remember that each of the Abrahamic faiths advances the preeminence of its version of monotheism. Nevertheless, it must be emphasized that the intolerance of non-Muslims as practiced by extreme Islamists who selectively read and interpret the Qur'an to advance their radical ideology is not in accordance with general Islamic teachings and traditions.

The Qur'an contains 114 chapters. The chapters are called *suwar* (sing. *sura*) and are arranged in descending order of length after Sura 1, "Al-Fatiha" (The Opening). A verse is called an *aya* (sign; pl. *ayat*). There are 6,236 *ayat* in the Qur'an. The Qur'an is not a narrative per se; the longest narrative is the story of Joseph, son of Jacob. The book is exhortative, inspirational, and legalistic. The ninety Meccan *suwar* are short and direct. They speak of God, warn unbelievers, and describe the Day of Judgment. The twenty-four Medinan *suwar* are lengthy and legalistic, delineating rules and procedures for marriage, divorce, inheritance, warfare, and commerce. Many regulations reflect the political reality Muhammad faced after settling in Medina.

The Qur'an is meant to be read aloud, and Muslims regard it as a means through which they can commune with God. Furthermore, as the following *aya* states, the Qur'an cannot be duplicated, "Say: 'If men and *jinn* combined to write the like of this Qur'an, they would surely fail to compose the like, though they helped one another as best they could'" (17:88).

The Qur'an serves as the foundation of Islamic law (Shari'a). As a source, it is indisputable, but it does not provide answers for every circumstance, and there are frequent disagreements over the interpretation of particular Qur'anic verses. Hadith and other sources provide guidance where the Qur'an does not. An example of law contained in the Qur'an is the rule on the number of wives a man can take. The Qur'an permits a man to have up to four wives, but if he cannot be fair to all of them, he must marry only one. Thus, the Qur'an provides justification for those Muslims who argue that polygamy is permitted and for those who advocate monogamy.

The Qur'an mentions several prophets and saintly figures. There are Arabs, such as Salih, Hud, Shuayb (Jethro, father-in-law of Moses) as well as Muhammad (only Shuayb is also mentioned in the Bible); New Testament figures, such as Jesus, John the Baptist, Mary (the mother of Jesus), and Zechariah (the father of John the Baptist); and several Old Testament prophets, such as Adam, Noah, Abraham, Lot, Isaac, Isma'il, Jacob, Joseph, Job, Moses, Aaron, David, Solomon, Jonah, and Elijah. Some prophets are mentioned by nicknames in the Qur'an. For example, Abraham is "Friend," and Moses is "the Word of God."

The Qur'an contains violent verses, but its tone compares to the imagery in the Old Testament books of Deuteronomy, Numbers, and Samuel. Especially troubling today is the habit of militant Islamists to select specific verses of the Qur'an to advance their worldview and even negate Meccan passages, which they believe were superseded by the Medinan verses. This reductionism is a hallmark practice of many militant religious movements that seek simple answers to complex questions and are not inclined to approach scripture holistically—a practice that requires balancing contradictory verses in a book. Theologically, this pattern is alarming. If a Muslim believes the Qur'an is the word of God yet advocates wholesale *naskh* (abrogation), then one is tacitly admitting God can make mistakes.

Sample Passages from the Qur'an

Read the following six excerpts from the Qur'an, especially if you have never read the Muslim holy book before either in its entirety or in part. As you read, consider the following questions: How does the tone of the verses strike you? How does the text of the Qur'an compare with other scriptures that you may have read? What are some of the recurring themes contained in the passages? Can you tell which passages were revealed in Mecca and which were revealed in Medina? What rules and regulations governing food and worship are contained in the passages? Are Muslims required to follow rules and regulations without exception? Why does the Qur'an emphasize reward and punishment? How does it depict them? What do the passages say about the fidelity of the People of the Book, the veracity of their scriptures, and their relationship to the Muslim community? Does knowledge of the teachings of Judaism or Christianity facilitate your understanding of Islam? In the last passage ("The Light"), what metaphors convey the universality of Islam?

Furthermore, as you read these sample passages or others from the Qur'an, appreciate how militant Islamists might spin the meaning of a fragment of scripture to support their extreme modernist ideology. A fragment of scripture—any scripture—can be used to justify or defend just about any action or point of view, and the Qur'an is no exception.

From "The Opening" (1:1–7):
In the name of Allah, Most Gracious, Most Merciful.
Praise be to Allah, the Cherisher and Sustainer of the worlds;
Most Gracious, Most Merciful;
Master of the Day of Judgment.
You do we worship, and Your aid we seek.
Show us the straight way,
The way of those on whom You have bestowed Your Grace, those
     whose (portion) is not wrath, and who go not astray.

From "The Heifer" (2:173–74):
He has only forbidden you dead meat, and blood, and the flesh of swine, and that on which any other name has been invoked besides that of Allah. But if one is forced by necessity, without willful disobedience, nor transgressing due limits, then is he guiltless. For Allah is Oft-forgiving, Most Merciful.

Those who conceal Allah's revelations in the Book, and purchase for them a miserable profit, they swallow into themselves nothing but Fire; Allah will not address them on the Day of Resurrection. Nor purify them: Grievous will be their penalty.

From "The Family of Imran" (3:67–71):

Abraham was not a Jew nor yet a Christian; but he was true in Faith, and bowed his will to Allah's (Which is Islam), and he joined not gods with Allah.

Without doubt, among men, the nearest of kin to Abraham, are those who follow him, as are also this Messenger and those who believe: And Allah is the Protector of those who have faith.

It is the wish of a section of the People of the Book to lead you astray. But they shall lead astray (Not you), but themselves, and they do not perceive!

You People of the Book! Why reject you the Signs of Allah, of which you are (Yourselves) witnesses?

You People of the Book! Why do you clothe Truth with falsehood, and conceal the Truth, while you have knowledge?

From "The Women" (4:163–69):

We have sent you inspiration, as We sent it to Noah and the Messengers after him: we sent inspiration to Abraham, Isma'il, Isaac, Jacob and the Tribes, to Jesus, Job, Jonah, Aaron, and Solomon, and to David We gave the Psalms.

Of some apostles We have already told you the story; of others We have not; and to Moses Allah spoke direct;

Messengers who gave good news as well as warning, that mankind, after (the coming) of the apostles, should have no plea against Allah. For Allah is Exalted in Power, Wise.

But Allah bears witness that what He has sent unto you He has sent from His (own) knowledge, and the angels bear witness: But enough is Allah for a witness.

Those who reject Faith and keep off (men) from the way of Allah, have verily strayed far, far away from the Path.

Those who reject Faith and do wrong,—Allah will not forgive them nor guide them to any way—Except the way of Hell, to dwell therein forever. And this to Allah is easy.

From "The Repast" (5:1–2, 5–6):

O you who believe! fulfill (all) obligations. Lawful unto you (for food) are all four-footed animals, with the exceptions named: But animals of the chase are forbidden while you are in the sacred precincts or in pilgrim garb: for Allah does command according to His will and plan.

O you who believe! Violate not the sanctity of the symbols of Allah, nor of the sacred month, nor of the animals brought for sacrifice, nor the garlands that mark out such animals, nor the people resorting to the sacred house, seeking of the bounty and good pleasure of their Lord. But when you are clear of the sacred precincts and of pilgrim garb, you may hunt and let not the hatred of some people in (once) shutting you out of the Sacred Mosque lead you to transgression (and hostility on your part). Help you one another in righteousness and piety, but help you not one another in sin and rancor: fear Allah for Allah is strict in punishment. . . .

This day are (all) things good and pure made lawful unto you. The food of the People of the Book is lawful unto you and yours is lawful unto them. (Lawful unto you in marriage) are (not only) chaste women who are believers, but chaste women among the People of the Book, revealed before your time, when you give them their due dowers, and desire chastity, not lewdness, nor secret intrigues if anyone rejects faith, fruitless is his work, and in the Hereafter he will be in the ranks of those who have lost (all spiritual good).

O you who believe! when you prepare for prayer, wash your faces, and your hands (and arms) to the elbows; Rub your heads (with water); and (wash) your feet to the ankles. If you are in a state of ceremonial impurity, bathe your whole body. But if you are ill, or on a journey, or one of you comes from offices of nature, or you have been in contact with women, and you find no water, then take for yourselves clean sand or earth, and rub therewith your faces and hands, Allah does not wish to place you in a difficulty, but to make you clean, and to complete his favor to you, that you may be grateful.

From "The Light" (24:35–40):

Allah is the Light of the heavens and the earth. The Parable of His Light is as if there were a Niche and within it a Lamp: the Lamp enclosed in Glass: the glass as it were a brilliant star: Lit from a blessed Tree, an Olive, neither of the east nor of the west, whose oil is well-nigh luminous, though fire scarce touched it: Light upon Light! Allah does guide whom He will to His Light: Allah does set forth Parables for men: and Allah does know all things.

(Lit is such a Light) in houses, which Allah has permitted to be raised to honor; for the celebration, in them, of His name: In them is He glorified in the mornings and in the evenings, (again and again), by men whom neither traffic nor merchandise can divert from the Remembrance of Allah, nor from regular Prayer, nor from the practice of regular Charity: Their (only) fear is for the Day when hearts and eyes will be transformed (in a world wholly new),

That Allah may reward them according to the best of their deeds, and add even more for them out of His Grace: for Allah does provide for those whom He will, without measure.

But the Unbelievers, their deeds are like a mirage in sandy deserts, which the man parched with thirst mistakes for water; until when he comes up to it, he finds it to be nothing: But he finds Allah (ever) with him, and Allah will pay him his account: and Allah is swift in taking account.

Or (the Unbelievers' state) is like the depths of darkness in a vast deep ocean, overwhelmed with billow topped by billow, topped by (dark) clouds: depths of darkness, one above another: if a man stretches out his hands, he can hardly see it! for any to whom Allah gives not light, there is no light!

4

The High Caliphate

In this chapter, we examine the era of the High Caliphate, the period from the late seventh century to the mid-tenth century when the Islamic community, or *umma*, was largely united and governed by a caliph—the successor to the Prophet Muhammad. The apparent unity, however, was not without division and factionalism, as branches emerged within Islam and non-Arab Muslims asserted themselves within the empire. We investigate the institutions, achievements, weaknesses, and demise of the Rashidun, Umayyad, and 'Abbasid caliphates and the emergence of powerful Shi'a, Persian, and Turkish dynasties that challenged the authority of the caliph and the Sunni-Arab elite.

17. How were the first caliphs—the temporal successors to the Prophet Muhammad—chosen?

The term "caliph" means successor. In the context of Muslim history, the term derives from *khalifat rasul Allah* (successor to the Prophet of God). Therefore, the caliphs followed Muhammad as the leaders of the Muslim community. The Qur'an uses the word "caliph" when it refers to King David: "O David! We did indeed make you a caliph (vice-regent) on earth, so judge you between men in truth and justice" (38:26). Another reference to political authority in the Qur'an is the injunction to "obey God, obey the Messenger, and those charged with authority among you" (4:59).

As Muhammad lay dying, he issued no instructions to his followers concerning the selection of his successor. He had been the Prophet, political leader, arbiter, lawgiver, chief judge, and military commander of the *umma*. His death in 632 created a crisis for the fledgling state, which needed a leader to direct its affairs. The central question became, Who should rule in place of the Prophet?

A dispute immediately arose between three groups within the *umma*, which complicated the selection process. The first group, the Muhajirun, comprised Meccan converts who had immigrated to Medina to escape the persecution of the Meccan oligarchs. They fell under the dominance of the Quraysh tribal elite, namely, the Umayyad clan (or Banu Umayya), and were regarded as the "insiders," synonymous with the Arab Muslim elite. The second group, the Ansar, comprised Medinan converts. They were associated with lesser Quraysh clans and were regarded as "outsiders" (or later "second-class Muslims") by the Muhajirun. Their ranks were dominated by the Mawali (clients; sing. Mawla), or non-Arab Muslims, who were converting to Islam in rapidly increasing numbers. Making the succession crisis even thornier were the motives of the third group, the Arab tribes. Some tribes had readily accepted Muhammad's revelations, others had converted for material gain, and a few had agreed to a compact with Muhammad that allowed them to retain their tribal gods and not make the declaration of faith. Following the death of Muhammad, Abu Bakr and 'Umar Ibn al-Khattab feared that many tribes would renounce their ties to the *umma*, causing Muhammad's federation to scatter as if driven by harsh Arabian winds.

After Muhammad's death, the companions (early followers of the Prophet) secured the election of Abu Bakr. He was nominated by 'Umar and elected by a council of Quraysh elders. He was chosen because he was a member of the Quraysh, was a devout and modest man, was one of the first converts, was Muhammad's closest friend and father-in-law, and enjoyed a good rapport with the tribes. A large group of Ansar, however, favored the election of 'Ali and claimed that Muhammad had designated him as his successor. The controversy over what Muhammad might have said or intended about succession lies at the center of the schism between Sunni and Shi'a Muslims. The latter embrace a hadith attributed to

Muhammad in which he instructed his followers, while pointing to 'Ali, "If you follow me, follow 'Ali."[1] Sunnis, on the other hand, cite a hadith in which Muhammad, while on his deathbed, responded to a companion who had asked who his successor would be. He answered, "My community does not gather in consensus and make an error."[2] Muhammad died without affirming 'Ali, who was considered by many as too young to lead a huge tribal federation and who was not officially presented as a candidate to the Quraysh elders. The dispute between companions and supporters soon split the community, a schism that divides Islam to this day. For example, the long-running rivalry between the Syrian and Iraqi branches of the Ba'th Party arguably can be traced to the contest between Muhajirun and Ansar over where the capital of the caliphate should be: Kufa, in present-day Iraq, Damascus, or Medina.

18. What factors contributed to the success of the Arab conquest in the seventh and eighth centuries?

By the time of the Prophet Muhammad's death, he had unified most of Arabia under the banner of Islam. His first successor, Abu Bakr (r. 632–634), used persuasion, political manipulation, and force to bring back to the *umma* the tribes that had fallen away after the Prophet's death. Under the second caliph, 'Umar (r. 634–644), the incredible Muslim expansion began. The first conquests outside Arabia were carried out by three armies. An army of Muhajirun fought the Byzantines to the north. This army won the Battle of Ajnadayn in Palestine (634), captured Damascus (635), triumphed at the Battle of Yarmuk, in present-day Jordan (636), and took Jerusalem (638). A second army made up of Ansar struck eastward and clashed with the Persian Sassanids. In 636 the Ansar army was victorious at the Battle of Qadisiyya on the Euphrates River, and a year later it captured Ctesiphon, the Sassanid capital, and all of Iraq. A mixed Muhajirun-Ansar force swept into Africa. It captured Babylon-on-the-Nile, near present-day Cairo (641), took Alexandria (642), and secured Libya (644). By 711, only a century after Muhammad had received his first revelation, an army led by Tariq Ibn Ziyad crossed the narrow waterway at the Pillars of Hercules, renamed Jebel Tariq (Mountain of Tariq or Gibraltar), and landed in al-Andalus—the region of Andalucía in present-day Spain. (The Arabic term "al-Andalus" literally means "the Vandals"; in actuality, the Muslims encountered Visigothic tribes in the Iberian Peninsula.) Also in 711, an army led by Muhammad Ibn Qasim reached Sindh and established a coastal Muslim enclave in what is today Karachi, Pakistan.

Several factors account for the stunning success of the Muslims during the great wave of expansion. Politically, the Byzantine and Sassanid Empires had seen their resources severely depleted by decades of warfare between them. Moreover, they lost the support of their respective Christian Arab allies: the Ghassanid tribal confederation for the Byzantines and the Lakhmid Kingdom for the Persians. Militarily, the Arabs used tactics that took advantage of local topography and that included the use of long-range camel transport and quick strikes out of the desert on horseback. Furthermore, the Muslim armies comprised soldiers who had extraordinary warfighting skills. Practically every Arab male, before Islam, had been reared in tribal warfare and could ride a horse, wield a sword, string a bow, and launch a spear. The skills practiced in raiding rival tribes were readily applied to campaigns of expansion. Socially, many subject peoples saw the Muslims as saviors from oppressive empires that stifled religious freedom and imposed high taxes. For example, when the Muslim armies expanded into Christian lands, they presented the inhabitants with three options: convert to Islam; freely practice Christianity, while living in peace and paying the *jizya* (a head tax on non-Muslims); or resist and continue to suffer the consequences of war. Muslim leaders recognized that one of the main grievances among the Christians of the Byzantine Empire was high taxation; therefore, they set taxes well below what the Byzantines had imposed. Also economically, booty from conquest—the spoils of war—was a huge inducement for individual warriors to join the Muslim forces and fight to expand the empire.

Muslim armies, despite their spectacular success, experienced many close calls. For example, at the Battle of Yarmuk, the Muslims won a narrow victory over the Byzantine army thanks to a timely sandstorm, which they used to their advantage, and the actions of a group of courageous Muslim women, led by Hind Bint 'Utbah, the wife of Umayyad leader Abu Sufyan. They rallied Muslim soldiers, exhorting them to halt their withdrawal and regroup, which they did. Unfortunately, many of today's Islamic extremists are unaware of the diverse factors that accounted for the overwhelming success of the Muslim conquest. They tend to reduce the Prophet Muhammad to a one-dimensional being—a warlord—while ignoring his exemplary roles as a Muslim, political leader, husband, father, and friend.

19. How did the Rashidun caliphs govern the Muslim empire, what were their major accomplishments, and what were the causes of their downfall?

The era of the Rashidun, or Rightly Guided Caliphs (632–661), witnessed the greatest expansion in the history of the Islamic world. By 661 the empire stretched from Cyrenaica, in Libya, to the Oxus River, in Central Asia. The leadership of the Rashidun marked the last time one caliph governed all Muslims. The four caliphs (Abu Bakr, 'Umar Ibn al-Khattab, 'Uthman Ibn 'Affan, and 'Ali Ibn Abu Talib) had known Muhammad personally, and the community knew them.

Abu Bakr ruled for only two years (632–634), but he acted forcefully to preserve the *umma*. After Muhammad's passing, many tribes recanted their pledge to Islam. Many of them sought to avoid paying the *zakat*, and their apostasy was the first great challenge to the post-Muhammad community. Abu Bakr made it clear that once a person professes Islam, there is no turning back. How his pronouncement can be reconciled with the Qur'an, which states that "there be no compulsion in religion" (2:256), is still a matter of debate, as scholars formulate Islamic-based counterarguments to radical Islamist ideologies. To restore the unity of the *umma*, Abu Bakr waged what became known as the Ridda (Apostasy) Wars against restive tribes and false prophets who roamed the desert. By securing the Arabian Peninsula, he provided Islam with a solid base for the great expansion to come. He died peacefully—the only Rashidun to do so—and was immediately succeeded by 'Umar.

Caliph 'Umar (r. 634–644) was a stern leader but was well known for his simple habits and humble nature. He oversaw the first wave of expansion outside the Arabian Peninsula and the beginnings of an imperial system of government. He organized and expanded the army, creating an intelligence-gathering service and enlisting former rebellious tribes. Under his leadership, political competition between the Muhajirun and

Ansar began. Regarding political appointments, 'Umar slightly favored the emigrants.

In the conquered territories, Muslim administrators set up several governing institutions. First, the *jizya* was imposed on all adult male non-Muslims. Later, during the Umayyad caliphate, non-Arab Muslims were required to pay the poll tax, further widening the gap between Muhajirun and Ansar. Second, military commanders established *amsar* (garrison towns) at Basra and Kufa in present-day Iraq and at al-Fustat in Egypt as a means of keeping their armies and the local population separated. The garrison system made it easier for the soldiers to maintain their Islamic zeal, and it prevented conflict between soldiers and nearby inhabitants. The effectiveness of this separation is debatable: It was inevitable that social interaction and intermarriage would take place and influence both Muslims and non-Muslims because Islam was evolving from a desert-based to an urbanized religion. The conversion process was very gradual—achieved through the model behavior of bivouacked armies, commercial interaction, and some coercion. Third, a central treasury in Medina, the *diwan*, managed the distribution of war booty and supervised the collection of taxes. It allocated shares of the bounty according to *sabiqa*, the precedence determined by the date of a person's conversion to Islam. Since the Muhajirun in Syria had a higher precedence than the Ansar in Iraq, *sabiqa* reinforced the social division within the *umma*. While later converts resented *sabiqa*, it provided an impetus for further expansion. The only way a new convert could be assured of receiving a payout from the *diwan* was through the acquisition of more territory. Finally, 'Umar implemented a bureaucracy to regulate commerce and manage the welfare of orphans and widows. He appointed a woman to regulate the markets of Medina and installed judges (sing. *qadi*, pl. *qudah*) to settle disputes within the *umma*. The judges became the *'ulama*, the class of Muslim scholars and jurists. In 'Umar's day, a *qadi* was often assisted by a *mufti*, who, like a law clerk, helped him draft legal opinions (sing. fatwa, pl. *fatawa*).

Owing to the existence of the garrison camps and the religious tolerance shown by Muslim administrators to their non-Muslim subjects, the inhabitants of some places, for example Egypt and Iraq, noticed little change. They welcomed the retention of Byzantine and Persian

civil servants and engineers and the continued use of the bureaucratic
and administrative languages to which they were accustomed. In 644
'Umar was murdered by an aggrieved Persian slave and was succeeded by
'Uthman, a member of the Umayyad clan.

'Uthman (r. 644–656) was elected over 'Ali by a *shura* (council) of
Muhajirun that had been named by 'Umar on his deathbed. Often
characterized as a weak leader, 'Uthman had two great accomplishments:
He ordered the codification of a definitive version of the Qur'an and
completed the conquest of Persia. Whereas 'Umar had slightly favored the
Muhajirun in appointments, 'Uthman was solidly pro-Muhajirun and anti-
Ansar. For example, he revised the *sabiqa* system to benefit the Muhajirun
by demanding more tax revenue from the provinces to support the Quraysh
elite in Mecca. Furthermore, the Muhajirun governor of Iraq had alienated
the local population, so Kufans blocked his return from Medina and
named their own governor. 'Uthman's governor in Egypt infuriated the
local population, a number of whom traveled to Medina and protested
to the caliph. 'Uthman promised to appoint a new governor but secretly
conspired to murder the protesters. They caught wind of the plot, and
disgruntled Egyptian soldiers entered 'Uthman's home and assassinated
him and his wife while they were praying. The slaying is considered Islam's
first politically motivated murder.

A *shura* comprised of Muhajirun and Ansar members selected 'Ali as
the fourth caliph (r. 656–661). By the time of his accession, the dispute
between the two groups had reached a level of extreme hostility. Elected
under pressure from Egyptian rebels and supported by Iraqi Ansar, he
became identified with the Ansar and was soon regarded as an outsider,
despite his extremely close connections to Muhammad. The Quraysh elite
had opposed 'Ali's election and doubted that he would bring the killers of
'Uthman to justice. They fomented a rebellion in Mecca and confronted
'Ali at Basra, in Iraq. The uprising was led by A'isha, the daughter of
Abu Bakr and widow of Muhammad. She was resentful of 'Ali, who had
suggested to Muhammad that he consider divorcing her over accusations
of infidelity. The ensuing Battle of the Camel (656) was the first conflict
between Muslims. This period of civil strife is referred to as the Fitna
(Sedition) Wars. 'Ali defeated his opponents on the battlefield but entered

into a larger conflict with Mu'awiya, the governor of Syria and a prominent member of the Umayyad clan. He had been ordered by 'Ali to step down from his post but had refused. Furthermore, he would not recognize 'Ali as the caliph until 'Ali found and punished the murderers of 'Uthman. The armies of 'Ali and Mu'awiya met at Siffin in 657. At a crucial moment in the battle, Mu'awiya's army was losing, but it tricked 'Ali's forces by placing Qur'ans on the tips of their spears and pleading for arbitration to resolve their dispute. 'Ali acquiesced, and the arbitrators ruled that 'Ali should step down as caliph and a new election take place. Some of 'Ali's supporters, later known as Kharijites (Seceders), protested his decision to pursue arbitration, arguing that he had been unfaithful to the will of God, and deserted him. During the negotiations, Mu'awiya brought in reinforcements from Damascus. 'Ali recognized his mistake, refused to resign, and established a new capital in Kufa. In 660 Mu'awiya declared himself caliph but kept his capital in Damascus. The following year, a Kharijite assassinated 'Ali. Thereupon, his older son, Hasan, succeeded him as caliph, but Mu'awiya repudiated the selection. After a period of negotiation, Hasan relinquished the caliphate and retired to Medina. His decision strengthened Mu'awiya's grip on power. The year 661 marked the start of the Umayyad caliphate, but 'Ali's second son, Husayn, would continue to oppose Mu'awiya and his son and successor, Yazid, until 680.

20. How did the Umayyad caliphs govern the Muslim empire, what were their major accomplishments, and what were the causes of their downfall?

Mu'awiya stabilized the *umma* following the turmoil of 'Ali's caliphate. He consolidated and expanded his rule but still had problems with troublesome areas, like Iraq, which was an Ansar stronghold. By the time of his caliphate, there were two power blocs: the Medina-Iraq axis, dominated by the Ansar, and the Mecca-Damascus axis, dominated by the Muhajirun. To gain control over Iraq and other quarrelsome territories, he appointed stern governors. Making Damascus his capital had a profound effect on governing the empire. Experienced Byzantine bureaucrats were retained in their posts, and Syria offered a central location, far from the heart of Arabia, and a cosmopolitan atmosphere.

Mu'awiya felt politically secure enough to name his successor, establishing a tradition that ran counter to Arab tribal custom. He designated his son Yazid as his heir, and the latter assumed the caliphate in 680. That same year, the Ansar in Kufa encouraged Husayn to confront Yazid over the caliphate. He accepted a truce offered by Yazid at Kufa to resolve their differences, but he and his followers were ambushed at Karbala on AH 10 Muharram 61 (10 October 680). Husayn had an army of 72 warriors; Yazid had between 1,000 and 10,000, which shows the degree to which this event has been mythologized. Husayn and all his followers were killed and became Shi'a revered martyrs. Shi'a loathe Yazid as the murderer of Husayn and commemorate 'Ashura as a day of mourning and atonement. Karbala is a key event in the development of Shi'ism. Henceforth, all Shi'a imams would be descendants of 'Ali through Husayn, and Shi'a would no longer openly contend for the caliphate.

In 683 Yazid was assassinated and his teenage son Mu'awiya II became caliph, but the young ruler died a year later. Marwan, a relative of Mu'awiya II, reluctantly assumed the caliphate. His accession inaugurated a period of significant Umayyad accomplishments. Noteworthy caliphs, such as 'Abd al-Malik (r. 685–705), 'Umar II (r. 717–720), and Hisham (r. 724–743), effectively created an Arab empire by implementing several important institutional reforms.

'Abd al-Malik, a son of Marwan, made Arabic the administrative language, minted Arab coinage that replaced Byzantine and Persian coins, and standardized weights and measures. He carried out a major building program that included the Dome of the Rock in Jerusalem. To uphold the unity of the empire, he governed Ansar-dominated areas with draconian authority and crushed many rebellions. By the end of the seventh century, factionalism had been contained and territorial expansion resumed. When his son al-Walid (r. 705–715) succeeded him, no one complained; the hereditary system had been accepted and normalized.

The Umayyad caliphs would adopt many of the trappings and customs of Byzantine and Persian monarchs, and they gradually claimed spiritual authority in addition to their temporal powers. They would bestow on themselves such titles as the Shadow of God on Earth, which imitated the aura and mystery of Byzantine and Persian despots.

In 711 Muslim armies under the command of Tariq Ibn Ziyad crossed the Strait of Gibraltar and entered Spain. The Battle of Tours (732), in central France, marked the furthest point of Muslim expansion into Western Europe. At Tours a Christian army under the Frankish leader Charles Martel (d. 741) repelled a Muslim incursion. Meanwhile, Muslim armies reached Transoxiana (Bukhara and Samarqand), western China, Khwarizm (around the Aral Sea), and areas of modern-day Pakistan (Baluchistan, Sindh, and Punjab).

Caliph 'Umar II endeavored to infuse in the *umma* fairness and equality for all Muslims. In particular he eliminated the *jizya* for non-Arab Muslims and abolished many taxes that predated Islam. Conversely, non-Muslims fared poorly under 'Umar. He forced Jews and Christians to wear clothing that denoted their faith, prohibited them from riding camels and horses, and required them to obtain permission to build houses of worship.

Hisham's reign marked the high point of the Umayyad caliphate. He completed the reform of the tax system begun by 'Umar II. The new system included *zakat*, paid by Muslims; *kharaj*, a property tax paid by property owners; a land tax paid by peasants based on the amount of their produce; and *jizya*, paid by non-Muslims. He undertook major irrigation projects and completed the conquests of Spain and Transoxiana.

After Hisham's caliphate, factionalism and widespread political dissent increased dramatically, weakening Umayyad governance and hastening the demise of the dynasty. The groups opposing the Umayyads included the Mawali, who had assumed positions of notoriety within the empire but were still considered second-class members of the *umma*; older Ansar, who had helped build the Muslim state but had been shut out of the caliphate; Shi'a, who openly resisted the Umayyads and backed the 'Abbasids, a branch of the Hashimite clan; Kharijites, who opposed a hereditary caliphate; the mixed Persian-Arab population of Khurasan, in northeast Persia, which had become a major commercial center and a hotbed of anti-Umayyad protest; and pious Muslims, who viewed the Umayyads as corrupt and decadent. Opposition to the Umayyads coalesced under the leadership of the 'Abbasids, who descended from Muhammad's uncle al-'Abbas.

In 747 the 'Abbasid revolution broke out in Khurasan, led by Abu Muslim, a Persian. The rebellion sought to revive Islamic fundamentals in the caliphate. In 749 'Abbasid forces took Kufa. A year later, Abu Muslim defeated the Umayyad army; the last Umayyad caliph, Marwan II, was killed after he had fled to Egypt, and Abu al-'Abbas as-Saffah (r. 750–754) was proclaimed the first 'Abbasid caliph. In the aftermath of the 'Abbasid victory, a surviving Umayyad prince who had escaped the eradication of the caliphal household established a state in Córdoba, Spain, that would last until 1031.

The Umayyads transformed the Muslim state into a vast, prosperous empire, yet they were vigorously opposed for several reasons. They were corrupt, decadent, and worldly; they established a hereditary caliphate; and they discriminated against non-Arab Muslims, creating a caste system within the *umma*.

21. How did the 'Abbasid caliphs govern the Muslim empire, what were their major accomplishments, and what were the causes of their downfall?

The 'Abbasids ruled the *umma* from 749 to 1258, a period of more than five hundred years; in contrast, the Umayyads governed for roughly ninety years. The 'Abbasids descended from a branch of the Hashimite clan headed by al-'Abbas, an uncle of Muhammad. They and the Umayyads were both Quraysh, but a closer family connection to the Prophet increased the political legitimacy of the 'Abbasids.

Since most Muslim expansion had taken place by 750, the 'Abbasids inherited a great empire, and their long reign was characterized by the incorporation of large numbers of non-Arabs—especially Persians—into important positions in society and government. Islamic theology, law, and civilization reached their maturity under the 'Abbasids. The diversity and immensity of the empire and long-distance trade networks contributed to this maturing process. Trade carried Islam to Indonesia, Malaysia, the Philippines, and coastal China, and Muslims began to dominate the lucrative spice trade between Asia and Europe.

The years 750 to 945 marked the high point of Muslim civilization, which far surpassed that of early medieval Europe. The caliphate functioned independently until 945; thereafter, viziers (senior officials) and military commanders controlled the caliph, who ruled in name only. The caliph oversaw religious matters and embodied the unity of the *umma*; the vizier directed the affairs of government.

The 'Abbasids had mobilized dissidents and disaffected members of the *umma* to overthrow the Umayyads, but anti-'Abbasid revolts soon broke out owing to economic troubles and social discontent. Supporters, particularly the Ansar and pious Muslims, embraced the idea of a ruler descended from the family of Muhammad but were soon appalled by the opulence of the 'Abbasid court, the same complaint that had been leveled against the Umayyads. By the late eighth century, the Muslim Empire had cloaked itself in the trappings of Eastern despotism. Members of the court exhibited an extravagant lifestyle, boasted lavish palaces and clothing, and became increasingly dependent on a large foreign bureaucracy. Persian notables served the government and gradually Persianized the state.

Caliph al-Mansur (r. 754–75) built a new capital—Baghdad—on the Tigris River in 762. "Baghdad" is a Persian word meaning "Gift of God"; the city is also known in Arabic as Medinat as-Salaam (City of Peace). A planned city with round double walls, four gates, and the royal palace in the center, Baghdad became an exquisite imperial city and the center of gravity of the known world; its splendor and opulence were unparalleled.[3] Under al-Mansur, notable Persian families began serving as senior government officials, including court viziers. The Persians demonstrated their literary and scientific prowess over the Arabs, who felt demeaned and feared that the 'Abbasid revolution was being dominated by Persians.

The golden age of the caliphate was the ninth century. The Baghdad of Caliph Harun ar-Rashid (r. 786–809) provided the setting for the magical tales of *The 1001 Nights*. The zenith of the 'Abbasid caliphate occurred during the reign of al-Ma'mun (r. 813–833). He founded Bayt al-Hikma (House of Wisdom), a university and research center where scholars translated Greek, Roman, and Persian scientific, literary, and philosophical works into Arabic and preserved them for later transmission to Europe. The institute researched mathematics, physics, optics, geography, astronomy, chemistry, medicine, and neo-Platonic thought. Algebra, alchemy, and alcohol (the distilled medicinal) are legacies of the 'Abbasid quest for *'ilm* (knowledge). Interestingly, the word *'ilm* appears more frequently in the Qur'an than the word "jihad" does.

As the power of the 'Abbasid caliphate began to wane, conquests halted and cracks appeared in the imperial edifice. The state had become too large and heterogeneous for the central government to manage, and a primary concern for the caliph was maintaining popular support and the loyalty of his subjects. Minor states emerged and asserted their independence in the ninth century; most notable were the Buyids and Tulunids. The Shi'a Buyids ruled western Persia and Iraq from 932 to 1055. The Tulunid state in Egypt was founded by the 'Abbasid-appointed governor Ahmad Ibn Tulun, a Turk, who arrived in Egypt in 868. His independent dynasty would rule Egypt until 905.

Iqta', the grant of land to an individual in exchange for military or government service, was begun by the 'Abbasids. It was analogous to awarding a fief in medieval Europe. People with their own land became increasingly independent of the central authority. The rise of independent states and autonomous landholdings created a shortage of available military forces for the 'Abbasid state. A solution was to import Turkish *mamluks* (slaves) from Central Asia and train them for royal service. Al-Mu'tasim (r. 833–842) was the first caliph to employ Turkish soldiers, who were well disciplined and great horsemen. Over the years, they asserted their autonomy and developed their own power base. Al-Mu'tasim's action marks the beginning of Turkish influence in the Middle East.

By the mid-tenth century, the Mawali were providing all serving viziers and had established themselves as the genuine power in the empire. The first challenge to caliphal preeminence occurred in 945, when the Shi'a Buyids seized control of the government in Baghdad. They were fierce infantrymen who had served the caliph. After asserting their control over the caliph, they retained him as a figurehead ruler. Their prominent role in the 'Abbasid state created a split between the religious and political spheres. The caliph's name and the *shahada* were stamped on one side of coins, while the name of the Buyid amir (prince) appeared on the reverse along with the title shahanshah (King of Kings). The coins conveyed the image of Shi'a political power and Sunni religious authority. This concept is contrary to Islam, which recognizes no separation between religion and politics. The Buyids retained power until the Seljuk Turks occupied Baghdad in 1055. The Seljuks, who were Sunni Turks, replaced the Shi'a Persian Buyids as the dominant power in the 'Abbasid state.

The power of the 'Abbasid caliphate had shriveled considerably by the late twelfth century, when Caliph an-Nasir (r. 1180–1225) reasserted royal authority with the aid of *futuwwa* (youthfulness) organizations. *Futuwwa* societies were medieval youth groups that advocated a strict code of chivalry based on *muruwwa*. They provided valuable muscle to save the caliphate, which enjoyed a brief revival. In 1258 the Mongols invaded Iraq, annihilated the 'Abbasid family, and devastated Baghdad. The unity of the *umma* was shattered. Today, it is not uncommon for Muslims to blame the Mongols for the decline of Muslim civilization. The pressures from Mongols in the east and crusaders in the west would plant seeds of radicalization within Islam and spur the rise of militant ideologues.

22. What distinguishes the three main Shi'a sects: the Zaydis, Isma'ilis, and Twelve-Imam Shi'a?

Shi'a Muslims believe that 'Ali and his successors should have rightfully governed the *umma* following the death of Muhammad. After 'Ali's brief caliphate, no other Shi'a leader considered touched by God ruled the Muslim empire. The supreme Shi'a authority is the Imam, and 'Ali is regarded as the first. His older son, Hasan, succeeded him as caliph, but the Umayyad caliph Mu'awiya rejected his accession, and after lengthy negotiations, Hasan dropped his claim to the caliphate and retired to Medina. The third Imam, Husayn, Hasan's brother, continued the dispute with Mu'awiya and led a rebellion against Mu'awiya's son, the Caliph Yazid, but Husayn and his small rebel band were massacred by Yazid's huge army at the Battle of Karbala in 680. Today, Shi'a Muslims are divided into three major branches: the Zaydis (or Fivers), Isma'ilis (or Seveners), and Twelve-Imam Shi'a (or Twelvers, Ja'faris, or Imamis) and a number of sub-branches.

Zaydis are prevalent today in Yemen and the Horn of Africa. In 740 Zayd Ibn 'Ali (695–740), a son of the fourth Imam, 'Ali Zayn al-'Abidin, rebelled against the Umayyad caliph Hisham. His followers believed that he was the rightful fifth Imam, not his brother Muhammad al-Baqir. The Zaydis continued a line of Imams, which descended from 'Ali and Fatima and passed through Zayd. The Zaydi Imam, unlike Imams of the Isma'ili and Twelve-Imam Shi'a, must be a physical presence, not a concealed being. By the late 800s, Zaydis ruled independent states in Tabaristan, in northern Iran, and Yemen. The Zaydi Imams of Yemen ruled the country until 1962.

Over the years, the Zaydis have absorbed into their practice a great deal from the Hanafi school of Sunni jurisprudence. As a result of battlefield pressures, the militant Islamist group al-Qa'ida in the Arabian Peninsula (AQAP) has declared publicly that it is not at war with Zaydis in general, but with the Zaydi Houthi religious-political movement and its Iranian supporters. The rebel Houthis who took control of Sana'a, Yemen's capital, in 2015 aspire to restore the Zaydi imamate—an idea unpopular with many Yemenis. There is also concern that the Iranians will attempt to convert the Houthis from Zaydi (Five-Imam) to Twelve-Imam Shi'ism.

The Isma'ilis claim descent from 'Ali and Fatima through Isma'il Ibn Ja'far (ca. 721–755), the seventh Imam, believing that Isma'il was the true seventh Imam, not Musa al-Kazim, his brother. For Isma'il's followers, he is the last Imam, and many Isma'ilis believe he is not dead but lives on in a hidden state. After Isma'il passed from the scene in the mid-eighth century, anti-'Abbasid revolutions broke out and several branches of the movement sprang up: the Qarmatians in Syria, Palestine, Iraq, and Bahrain; Fatimids in Syria, Tunisia, and Egypt; Druze in Syria, Lebanon, and Israel; 'Alawis in Syria, Turkey, and Iraq; Nizaris, also known as the Assassins, in Syria and Iran; and Khojas in South Asia, East Africa, Britain, Canada, and Massachusetts. The Khojas, an offshoot of the Nizaris, are today a great philanthropic organization led by Prince Shah Karim al-Husayni, Agha Khan IV (b. 1936). His father, Prince Aly Khan (1911–60), was married briefly to the American actress Rita Hayworth (1918–87).

Hunted by 'Abbasid authorities, the Isma'ilis went underground in Syria and North Africa, where they formed a network of propagandists and developed an esoteric theology. (An overview of the Isma'ili Fatimid caliphate can be found in the response to Question 23.)

Twelve-Imam Shi'a—as their name implies—follow a line of a dozen Imams, running from 'Ali through Muhammad al-Baqir and Musa al-Kazim to Muhammad al-Muntazar; the Imams are believed to be *ma'soum* (infallible). The sixth Imam, Ja'far al-Sadiq (ca. 702–765), developed the leading school of Shi'a jurisprudence, which bears his name. The faithful also believe that it is through the intercession of the Imams—a practice known as *tawa'sul*—that they connect with God. The twelfth Imam, Muhammad al-Muntazar al-Mahdi (b. ca. 868), went into hiding or a state of occultation for nearly seventy years, starting in 874. After a period of brief contact with his followers, he resumed his hidden state, which continues to the present. It is imperative to note that according to Twelve-Imam Shi'a doctrine, he did not die; he disappeared. Consequently, he is known as the Hidden Imam. He is regarded as a messianic figure, who will return at the end of time to avenge the oppressed and establish a perfect society where peace and justice prevail, paving the way for the return of Jesus.

Within the Twelve-Imam Shi'a community, it is believed that the more devout and learned a person is the more capable that person is to determine the will of the Hidden Imam. *Mujtahids* are legal scholars capable of performing *ijtihad* (independent reasoning) to reach legal decisions. After the twelfth century, *ijtihad* was shunned by Sunni Muslims but was continued by Shi'a as a valid basis for legal reasoning. There are two ways that Shi'a can communicate with the Hidden Imam: through political dissent during times of difficulty or by personal contact as judged by one's peers. If a scholar demonstrates the ability to communicate with the Hidden Imam, that person will be highly regarded and respected. Therefore, having the ability to channel the Imam's spiritual power is paramount in Shi'a society. It serves as a great source of legitimacy for religious leaders. Throughout history, *mujtahids* have been independent of secular authority.

Ayatollahs, the highest-ranking Shi'a clerics, are *mujtahids*. Along with all Imams, they inherited from 'Ali an infallible understanding of the Qur'an and teachings of the Prophet Muhammad and the true interpretation of the law. Consequently, many Shi'a see temporal government as contrary to the will of the Hidden Imam.

While Sunnis and Shi'a appear similar in practice, there are notable differences between the two, mainly over the issues of leadership and jurisprudence. Moreover, Sunnis regard Shi'a veneration of the Imams as a form of idolatry. Nevertheless, they both believe that "right practice and intent" identifies one as a Muslim and that it is up to God to judge. By the late seventh century, political power in the *umma* was dominated by Sunnis, but the Shi'a were not irrelevant. While Shi'a are a minority in most countries of the Muslim world, Sunnis generally tolerate them and rarely refer to them as heretics. Inevitably, political developments occasionally exacerbate tensions between the two communities.

Knowing the principles of Islam, recognizing differences between Sunni and Shi'a, and appreciating divisions within Shi'ism will enhance your understanding of the human terrain as you travel through the Middle East.

23. How did non-Arab, non-Sunni groups—mainly the Shi'a, Persians, and Turks—achieve ascendancy in the *umma*?

During the last three centuries of the 'Abbasid caliphate, non-Arab, non-Sunni Muslims asserted their power and autonomy vis-à-vis the central authority in Baghdad. As 'Abbasid power waned, some ethnoreligious groups wrested political power from the caliph, reducing him to a figurehead; others established independent dynasties, ensuring a permanent political fragmentation of the *umma*. In response to this question, we will examine the rise of four groups: the Fatimids, a Shi'a Arab dynasty; the Buyids, a Shi'a Persian dynasty; and the Ghaznavids and Seljuks, Sunni-Turk dynasties.

The Isma'ili Fatimid movement was begun by Abu Muhammad 'Abdallah al-Mahdi Billah, who sought to abolish the 'Abbasid caliphate and restore the leadership of Islam to the house of 'Ali and Fatima. He failed to take control of Syria and fled to North Africa, where he overthrew the Aghlabid dynasty and established a political base in present-day Tunisia. He became the first caliph of the Fatimid dynasty (r. 909–934). In 969 Fatimid general Jawhar (d. 992) took advantage of political instability in Egypt, occupied al-Fustat, and claimed the whole country for the Isma'ilis. That same year, Fatimid caliph al-Mu'izz li-Din Allah (r. 953–975) moved from Tunisia to Egypt, where he founded the city of Cairo (Medinat al-Qahira), near al-Fustat. The Fatimid caliphate further weakened the authority of the 'Abbasids and undermined the unity of the *umma*.

The reign of Caliph al-Hakim bi-Amr Allah (r. 996–1021) was very controversial. He was a capricious ruler and often conducted himself like a madman. He claimed to be a divine manifestation, and this assertion was advanced by the Isma'ili propagandist Shaykh Muhammad ad-Darazi (d. 1018). Ad-Darazi's teachings would evolve into the Druze religion. Following the death of al-Hakim, ad-Darazi's disciples were persecuted and fled to Syria.

The Fatimids can claim several achievements. They founded al-Azhar Mosque and University in the late tenth century, built a profitable long-distance trade network, introduced an army of slave soldiers from Central Asia, and extended their authority to Libya, Syria, Palestine, and the Hijaz. They did not attempt to convert their Sunni subjects and honored the religious freedom of Jews and Christians. In 1171 the Fatimid vizier Salah al-Din (1137–93), a Sunni Kurd, proclaimed himself sultan upon the death of the caliph and established the independent Ayyubid sultanate.

The Buyids were Persian Shi'a who had been employed as mercenaries by the 'Abbasid caliph. By the mid-tenth century, they had seized the reins of government in Baghdad and soon dominated the caliph, whom they retained as the titular spiritual ruler, thus maintaining the fiction of a unified Muslim nation. Their control of the vizierate and ascendancy over the caliph drove a wedge between religion and politics in 'Abbasid society. The Buyids were ousted from power in 1055 by the Seljuk Turks, who became the new masters of the declining 'Abbasid caliphate.

Turkic peoples originated in Central Asia; they gradually converted to Islam. Warriors from Turkish tribes had fought for the Umayyads in Persia, and the 'Abbasids had employed them as *ghazis*, or border warriors. During the reign of Caliph al-Mu'tasim, the 'Abbasids began bringing boys from Central Asia into the empire to serve as slave soldiers.

The Sunni Turk Ghaznavids had served as *ghazis* for an independent Sunni Persian dynasty, the Samanids, in the tenth century. The seat of their empire was the town of Ghazna in present-day Afghanistan. The empire's founder, Sebuktegin (r. 977–997), had received an *iqta'* from the Samanids in return for his service as a military commander and local governor. Their empire, which reached its height in 1035, contained eastern Iran, all of Afghanistan and Pakistan, and parts of northern India. They introduced Islam into India but did so forcefully, creating a great backlash. The Ghaznavid state lasted until 1186.

The Sunni Seljuk Turks had served both the Samanids and Ghaznavids as *ghazis* in Transoxiana and were rewarded with landholdings. The Seljuk dynasty ruled large parts of the Middle East and Central Asia from 960 to 1302. They took Khurasan in 1040 from the Ghaznavids and entered Buyid-controlled Baghdad in 1055, having been invited by the 'Abbasid caliph, a fellow Sunni. Their goal was to restore caliphal authority. The Seljuk Empire, the leader of which bore the title Sultan of the East and the West, encompassed Azerbaijan, Armenia, Syria, Palestine, Iraq, Persia, and the Caucasus region. In 1071 Seljuk leader Alp Arslan (r. 1063–72) scored a major victory over the Byzantines at the Battle of Manzikert, adding most of Anatolia to the empire and opening the area to large-scale Turkish settlement. They established their capital at Konya, in southern Anatolia, but the empire crumbled following the death of Malikshah (r. 1072–92). The last remnant of the empire, the Sultanate of Rum, a vassal of the Mongols, dissolved in 1308.

The Seljuks spurred several significant developments in Middle Eastern history, including the Turkification of vast areas, the revival of Sunni authority in the heart of the Muslim world, the dissemination of Persian administration and culture, and waves of Turkish migration into the Byzantine heartland—Anatolia.

At this point in our discussion, we need to emphasize two broad historical trends that began during the late 'Abbasid period: the dominance of nomads and the slave-soldier system. Nomads emerged as a dominant social force in the Middle East in the thirteenth century; their power and influence would persist in some areas until the early twentieth century. They earned a status equal to city dwellers and large landowners owing to a substantial decline in agricultural production. What caused this decline? Successful agriculture depended on irrigation. The central government had to operate a well-managed irrigation network to deliver water to arid and semiarid zones. A poorly maintained system could lead to drought or increased salinity of the soil. After 945 the 'Abbasid state fragmented, and the central government's power declined. As a result, the empire's irrigation infrastructure deteriorated, and agricultural production suffered.

The years 945 to 1200 marked a period of increased marginal use of the land, especially in Iraq. Large tracts of farmland became grazing land. Consequently, farmers produced fewer crops, and fewer crops caused famine, rioting, a decline in national income, and rebellion against the central government.

Nomadism also influenced the nature of warfare, and a dichotomy in military technology emerged. Sedentary military technology, which was highly organized, well structured, and relied heavily on large armies and elaborate fortifications, lagged behind the mobile warfare of nomads, who employed horses, bows and arrows, swords, and lances. Nomad warriors, who could outflank and surround a conventional force, were brought to heel by the widespread use of gunpowder weapons beginning in the late fourteenth century.

Under the slave-soldier system, rulers would take boys, usually Turkish boys from Central Asia, for use as soldiers or civil servants. While technically slaves, many rose to serve in prominent positions in the military or government service. With nomads ascendant, whole tribes infiltrated into an area for military service, most notably during the eleventh, twelfth, and thirteenth centuries. Overpopulation in Central Asia forced one Turkish tribe after another into Iran, Azerbaijan, and Anatolia.

Ibn Khaldun (1332–1406), a North African Muslim historian, is renowned for his theory governing the rise and fall of civilizations. In his classic work, *Al-Muqaddima* (The Introduction), he espoused the concept of *'asabiyya* (group solidarity or tribalism) as the motivating force behind conquering nomad empires. *'Asabiyya* dissipates after the nomads settle down, their power declines, and they are engulfed by the next wave of nomads.

5

Islamic Law and
Medieval Muslim Civilization

This chapter provides an overview of Islamic law (Shari'a), including a discussion of the law's influence on the lives of men and women in traditional Muslim societies. It also covers major institutions of medieval Islam and the contributions of Muslim scholars, scientists, theologians, artists, and architects to human civilization.

24. What is the nature of the political-religious ("mosque-state") dichotomy in the Muslim world?

Because Shari'a is a veritable minefield of interpretations, it is a challenging topic to study. Nevertheless, we will embark on as concise and informative a tour as possible. The fundamental problem facing non-Muslims in the West as they strive to understand Shari'a is their ingrained acceptance of the concept of a divide between religion and politics. While the Western world worries about combining church and state, many Muslims worry about splitting them apart. For Muslims, this dichotomy was not a problem until the modern era, when the rise of such concepts as nationalism, social Darwinism, and Marxism challenged the religious foundation of all three Abrahamic faiths. Journalist and Middle East scholar Thomas W. Lippman, in *Understanding Islam*, writes, "Christ's injunction to 'render unto Caesar the things that are Caesar's and to God the things that are

God's' is alien to Islam—in fact, it's opposite. In the words of Bernard Lewis, 'Such pairs of words as Church and State, spiritual and temporal, ecclesiastical and lay had no real equivalent in Arabic until modern times, when they were created to translate modern ideas; for the dichotomy which they express was unknown in medieval Muslim society and unarticulated in the medieval Muslim mind.'"[1]

The debate over the role of Islam in the state is not new. During the 'Abbasid era, Islamic scholars debated whether the Prophet Muhammad had established a social order or a state in Medina. Since his mission was to serve as a messenger of God, some argued that all his actions were directed toward the revelation and spread of God's word. Following this reasoning, he was never commanded by God to govern a state but did create a social order to advance the divine message.

Scholars argued further that since Muhammad was chosen by God, his social order could not be replicated by his successors, who (except for 'Ali, the fourth caliph) would be untouched by divine guidance. Furthermore, the Qur'an does not dictate how Muslims are to govern themselves, but it does require that Muslims establish *'adl* (justice), engage in *shura* (consultation), and select a *wali al-'amr* (guardian or person in charge), generally understood as a male leader in the Abrahamic tradition. The Qur'an, however, does not specify the means of dispensing justice, holding consultation, or choosing a leader.

Scholars also debated the role of the state in enforcing morality. Some argued that if the state did not enforce religious morality, the strength and unity of the community would erode, and the survival of the faith would be threatened. Other scholars pointed out that if the state did work to ensure morality, it would be required to interpret the teachings of Islam and impose a particular version of the faith on both followers and nonfollowers. Whenever an Islamic state is established, the vital question becomes "Upon whose interpretation of Islam is it based?"

In the previous chapter, we discussed the "mosque-state" division that occurred when the Buyids seized control of Baghdad in 945. Their viziers, who governed the empire, took names that contained the word *dawla* (state), while the caliphs, who exercised religious authority, had names that contained either the word *din* (faith) or "Allah." This division was never legitimized by Shari'a but became a de facto political arrangement.

During the Ottoman period, the sultan, who was the supreme authority in the empire, governed with the advice and consent of the *'ulama*, who operated separately from the other ruling institutions. Another governing arrangement produced further division between the religious and political spheres: If a legal question could not be resolved by consulting the Qur'an or hadith, the sultan would address the issue.

There is no provision for secular law evolving from Islamic law. Two legal systems concurrently exist side by side in most of the Islamic world: a religious system and a secular system. Under the religious system, the Shari'a courts, supervised by religious judges, handle issues of personal status, such as marriage, divorce, and inheritance. The governing practice of *shura* also occurs within Islamic law. The Qur'an states, "Whatever you are given here is but a convenience of this life: but that which is with God is better and more lasting: it is for those who believe and put their trust in their Lord . . . establish regular Prayer; who conduct their affairs by mutual Consultation" (42:36–38).

In a secular system, grievance or civil courts, headed by civil officials appointed by a secular ruler, administer uncodified, unsanctioned secular law, usually dealing with criminal infractions, taxes, and commerce. In traditional settings, the ruler maintains an audience with his subjects (*mazalim*, a pre-Islamic process that continued under Islam) during which he administers *'urf*, or customary law. (*'Urf* means "that which is known.")

A fundamental legal issue facing the Muslim world is how to legitimize secular law—that is, how to give it religious sanction or base it on religious law. In post-Taliban Afghanistan and post–Saddam Hussein Iraq, the drafters of the new constitutions patched over this issue by stating that no law could violate or exist contrary to Islam, yet this arrangement opens the door to choosing an interpretation of Islam and imposing it on Muslims and non-Muslims alike. Arguably, it will take an era of Islamic reformation to produce a modern law code derived from elements of the Qur'an. The task will take great courage, astute thinking, and wisdom to develop a new legal framework. With 1.6 billion Muslims worldwide, there is a multitude of views on the relationship between Islam and the state and diverse views on how to apply Islamic law in one's day-to-day life. Opinions range from those who believe that Islam has a primary role in government to those who believe that the union of Islam and politics would generate more inflexible and restrictive religious practice. For the present, the union of Islam and politics threatens to persecute Muslims who disagree with the religious interpretations of the ruling class as well as non-Muslims who do not adhere to the faith. Some Muslims argue that institutions, such as the caliphate, are political traditions grounded in neither the Qur'an nor the Prophet Muhammad's sayings or actions.

25. What are the sources of Islamic law (Shari'a)?

Shari'a is Muslim holy law, although the word means "pathway." For the Bedouin of the desert, it took on the meaning of "a beaten path to a watering hole." Thus, Shari'a is a metaphor, representing the straight path to eternal salvation. Following the straight path demands righteousness in each person's private and public lives. *Fiqh* (jurisprudence) is the term that most closely conveys the practice of Islamic law.

There are two fundamental sources of Islamic law: the Qur'an and the sunna-hadith. The Qur'an is the only indisputable source of law; to Muslims, it is infallible and immutable. Sunna is the collected sayings and actions of the Prophet Muhammad governing correct Muslim belief and behavior. Therefore, after the Qur'an, it is the most important source of Muslim law. Hadith (pl. *ahadith*) is a statement, authenticated by a chain of reliable witnesses (*isnad*) that recounts a saying or act of Muhammad or an act of one of his companions of which he approved. Hence, it is an authoritative source of Shari'a. (The terms "sunna" and "hadith" can be used interchangeably, but they are different. The former is an action or saying of Muhammad; the latter is the report of that action or saying.)

The science of scrutinizing hadith began in the ninth century, less than three hundred years after Muhammad's death. The important task of researching hadith was performed by dedicated scholars. Different collections of hadith are recognized by different sects, and the Shi'a have their own collections, including the traditions of the Imams. Six books of Sunni hadith emerged from this effort. The leading works are by

Isma'il al-Bukhari (d. 870) and Muslim Ibn al-Hajjaj (d. 875). Islamic jurisprudence began with the search for valid hadith.

Hadith is used in addition to the Qur'an as a source of law because the Qur'an does not cover all situations. Hadith covers much more and amplifies particular verses in the Qur'an. If a legal ruling can be made using the Qur'an or hadith, then that resolves the issue under consideration. Many Muslims cling to fragments of Qur'anic verses and hadith to justify personal choices, unique customs, a particular worldview, or even militancy and terrorism. A believer from any faith can use fragments of scripture to justify almost anything.

If a ruling cannot be made using the two fundamental sources, scholars can employ three subsidiary sources to extend and elaborate on the Qur'an and hadith: *qiyas*, *ijma*, and *ijtihad*. *Qiyas* is analogical reasoning. Accordingly, if a certain action is allowed or prohibited by the Qur'an or hadith, a similar action is also allowed or prohibited. For example, wine is prohibited, because it is intoxicating; therefore, all alcoholic beverages are prohibited. Some scholars, however, accept the ban on wine only, not other intoxicating beverages, while others believe that alcohol is permitted so long as it is not drunk to excess. In another example, some scholars have equated the size of a bride's dowry and the loss of her virginity with the value of goods stolen by a thief and the amputation of his limb. Other scholars have argued that the dowry is the exclusive property of the bride and is a form of prepaid alimony. Others still, pressured by tribal custom, contend that the dowry belongs to the male guardians of the bride. These divergent opinions illustrate the diversity of interpretations governing Muslim morality. Inevitably, interpretations of scripture are influenced by tribal, cultural, historic, and political concerns.

Ijma is scholarly consensus regarding a legal question. In many cases, it includes accepted customs that do not conflict with the Qur'an and sunna-hadith. Muhammad once declared, "My community does not gather in consensus and make an error."[2]

Ijtihad, which we introduced in chapter 4, is independent reasoning, judgment, or speculation. Since the twelfth century, Sunnis have not widely accepted it as a legal procedure. The use of *ijtihad* returned in the nineteenth century, and it is increasingly used today. The Shi'a, on the other hand, have a long tradition of using *ijtihad*, which they consider a valid source of law. A *mujtahid* is a person who is qualified to practice *ijtihad*.

There are dangers involving the use of *ijtihad*. Using *ijtihad* could conflict with orthodoxy and could create tension and loopholes regarding personal behavior. There are also benefits, however, in using independent reasoning. It can deal with issues not dreamed of in Muhammad's time and is increasingly useful in an age of modern technology, globalization, and political ferment.

The human links between the body of Islamic law compiled by the *'ulama* and its application are trained judges (sing. *qadi*, pl. *quda)* and juris-consults (sing. mufti). A *qadi* considers a legal case and issues a decision; a mufti, that is, a legal specialist, can issue a fatwa, an opinion on a specific legal question. A *muhtasib* is a market inspector who works for a *qadi* and ensures that commerce is conducted honestly. There is no supreme court in Islam, except in Iran, where the modern Council of Guardians can review acts of parliament and strike down laws that are judged to violate Islam.

26. What are the differences among the schools of Sunni jurisprudence?

The four schools of Sunni jurisprudence (sing. *madhhab*) are Hanafi, Maliki, Shafi'i, and Hanbali. The schools are named for scholars who codified aspects of Islamic law and practice in the late eighth and early ninth centuries. As their teachings spread throughout the Middle East and North Africa, the schools adapted to or absorbed local customs. Before long, practice had become so diverse that adherents of the same school living in different parts of the Muslim world had differences of opinion. Today, many Muslims subscribe to more than one school, following teachings that fit their personal needs and attitudes.

Approximately 75 percent of Sunni Muslims follow the Hanafi *madhhab*. The school, which is noted for tolerance, is common in India, Pakistan, Afghanistan, and lands of the former Ottoman Empire. Hanafis use *qiyas* based on the Qur'an, not hadith; therefore, their analogies are strictly derived. They also use *ijma* and Greek logic to reach a decision.

The Maliki rite is flexible, owing to the influence of local, tribal, and pre-Islamic customs. It is prevalent throughout Africa. *Qiyas* can be based on hadith, but there is disagreement over the use of *ijma*. Most Maliki *'ulama* argue that rulings agreed to by a majority of scholars are both valid and necessary to deal with a rapidly changing world. Other scholars take a more restrictive view, believing that the only binding decisions reached through consensus are those of the companions of the Prophet Muhammad.

The Shafi'i *madhhab* is prevalent in Southeast Asia and the nations of the Indian Ocean littoral. It is a synthesis of the Hanafi and Maliki schools. Shafi'is put great emphasis on *qiyas*, allow the use of *ijma*, and permit the careful use of *ijtihad* based on the Qur'an, hadith, and *qiyas*.

The Hanbali school is rigid and inflexible. *Ijtihad* is not permitted, *qiyas* is rarely used, and only *ijma* from the companions can be used. The Hanbali rite is dominant in Saudi Arabia, where Wahhabi Muslims preach that the only sources of Shari'a are the Qur'an and hadith. The Taliban of Afghanistan and Pakistan combined aspects of the Hanbali and Hanafi schools with the pre-Islamic tribal code of Pashtunwali, producing an extreme interpretation of Islam. Violent Islamist groups that adhere to aspects of Hanbali jurisprudence and fragments of scripture that support their ideologies include al-Qa'ida, ISIS, Boko Haram of Nigeria, and al-Shabab of Somalia.

In medieval Islam, other schools existed—namely, the Mu'tazili and Ash'ariyya rites—that merged Greek philosophy and Islam. In the eighteenth century, the Sunni Ottomans reached an accommodation with the Shi'a Safavids of Persia, recognizing the Shi'a Ja'fari school as a fifth *madhhab*, which was tolerated in Mecca and Medina. The arrangement lasted until the early twentieth century, when Ottoman rule collapsed in the Hijaz.

Shari'a is traditionally taught in madrasas, or religious schools, which developed in the eleventh and twelfth centuries, following the compilation of the hadith. One or more *madhhabs* are taught in each madrasa. In medieval Cairo, large madrasas contained multiple vaulted halls facing a courtyard, each hosting a different *madhhab*. When evaluating today's madrasas, critics scrutinize their curricula to assess whether the schools are creating scholars capable of helping people navigate the complexities of society and faith or producing political Islamists or militant jihadists for the battlefield, as when ISIS-run schools cultivated child fighters to serve as the Cubs of the Caliphate.

When approaching the topic of Islamic law, have a curious and open mind, and endeavor to appreciate the complexities inherent in any faith tradition. By doing so, you will be better prepared to cope with the human challenges and diversity present in the Middle East and among the world's 1.6 billion Muslims.

27. How does Islam affect men and women in traditional Muslim society?

The Qur'an significantly improved the status of women in seventh-century Arabia. Although it is a great reforming document, it does not accord women equality with men; instead, it granted them "complementarity." In traditional Islamic society, a man and a woman are not equal, except in faith, but each complements, or completes, the other, and together they form a whole person. Each half of the union contributes unique abilities and skills for the well-being, security, and goodness of the family.

In pre-Islamic Arabia, women were sold to their husbands for a dowry, paid to their fathers or other male relatives. The Qur'an changed this practice by making the dowry payable to the bride, not her family, thus giving women the right to possess property. Furthermore, a woman cannot be forced to marry against her will. If the marriage ends in divorce, the wife is entitled to her dowry.

The Qur'an allows a man to have up to four wives, provided he can love and treat them equally, but there are passages that question this conclusion. For example, the Qur'an suggests that a man can be married to more than one wife but makes it clear that doing so is difficult to carry out: "Marry women of your choice, Two or three or four; but if you fear that you shall not be able to deal justly (with them), then only one" (4:3). Conversely, the Muslim holy book declares that men are unable to be fair with respect to women: "You are never able to be fair and just as between women, even if it is your ardent desire: But turn not away (from a woman) altogether, so as to leave her (as it were) hanging (in the air). If you come to a friendly understanding, and practice self-restraint, Allah is Oft-forgiving, Most Merciful" (4:129). The two verses lead to different interpretations. Many Muslims believe that the former permits more than one wife. While others argue that the latter instructs a man to take only one wife. Nevertheless, the Qur'anic prohibition against more than four wives was a significant reform because polygamy was unrestrained in pre-Islamic Arabia.

In Islam, divorce is permitted—but discouraged—for both men and women. In the case of women, this was a significant development in Arab society. Before Islam, divorce was an unregulated male prerogative, and women had no right to seek one. The manner of divorce is different for men and women. A man can still repudiate his wife without stating a cause. A woman's ability to initiate a divorce remains limited and involves a more complex legal process than that required for men. Her request for divorce must be presented to a *qadi*.

Islam guarantees women a share of an inheritance. This was a revolutionary social development because women had no right to inheritance in pre-Islamic Arab society. In general, females receive half the share that a male receives from a deceased person's estate, but a wife always inherits before her children do. Again, this is not equal treatment, but it was an improvement over the way that inheritance was practiced before Islam. Today, some Muslims argue that the inheritance rules were most faithfully observed when males—whether husbands, fathers, or brothers—provided the principal means of support, but the pressures of modern family life have eroded this convention; therefore, Muslim inheritance and family laws need reform.

The Qur'an requires for both men and women modesty, appropriate dress, and decorum toward the opposite sex. The following passage pertains to men: "Say to the believing men that they should lower their gaze and guard their modesty: that will make for greater purity for them: And Allah is well acquainted with all that they do" (24:30). The Qur'an calls for men to avoid lust and to dress acceptably. In the Arab world, short sleeves are not widely worn, and except in tourist venues, short pants are almost never seen. This verse provides guidance on modesty for women:

And say to the believing women that they should lower their gaze and guard their modesty; that they should not display their beauty and ornaments except what (must ordinarily) appear thereof; that they should draw their veils over their bosoms and not display their beauty except to their husbands, their fathers, their husband's fathers, their sons, their husbands' sons, their brothers or their brothers' sons, or their sisters' sons, or their women, or the slaves whom their right hands possess, or male servants free of physical needs, or small children who have no sense of the shame of sex; and that they should not strike their feet in order to draw attention to their hidden ornaments. And O you Believers! Turn you all together towards Allah, that you may attain Bliss. (24:31)

The Qur'an states that women must lower their gaze, not display their beauty, cover their bosoms, and dress modestly. Beauty is traditionally defined as the hair and figure, but it does not mean that they should cover their faces. Many Muslim women wear a *niqab* or *burqa'* that conceals their faces. Doing so reflects either a strict fundamentalist interpretation of the Qur'an or adherence to tribal custom. Today, veiling has become a form of political protest among many women, particularly when the state makes an issue of it. The question of whether a woman wears a *burqa'* goes back to the issue of practice versus interpretation. It indicates the strong influence of tribal custom, which prevails over Islam in many everyday situations. Of note, the veil was adopted by the Prophet Muhammad's wives in Medina as a status symbol, emulating the fashions of aristocratic women in Byzantium and Persia. On the other hand, Muhammad's first wife Khadijah did not wear a veil.

Islam improved the treatment and status of women, but it still upholds the preeminence of men in many instances. For example, a woman's testimony in a trial is worth half of a man's. Therefore, it would take four male witnesses to an act or eight female witnesses to prove a charge of adultery or fornication. The worst example of inequality is the abhorrent custom of honor killings, which is viewed by scholars as a blending of Islam and tribalism. According to this practice, a woman—often a wife or daughter—is murdered for committing an immoral act—whether actual or perceived—to restore the honor of a tribe, clan, or family. Since honor killings are still practiced in many parts of the Middle East, as a military man or woman serving in the region, you must be aware of this tribal-influenced practice, which some Muslims equate with their faith.

28. What are essential characteristics and institutions of medieval Muslim urban and rural societies?

In response to this question and the next, we will discuss the structure of medieval Muslim urban and rural life, the accomplishments of Muslim science and technology, and Muslim achievements in architecture and art.

Many Western historians are obsessed with the factors behind the rise of the West. They emphasize the influence of European cities, which functioned as autonomous, political-corporate entities, thriving on competition and economic enterprise. For example, medieval Venice had a republican form of government and substantial commercial interests. It also had guilds or trade organizations that set prices and wages, regulated production, and looked after the social welfare of its members.

By contrast, many Western historians have gone out of their way to convince others that the typical Middle Eastern city was poor, corrupt, disorganized, and ungovernable. They emphasize plagues, poverty, and ignorance. In reality, medieval Middle Eastern cities were well-functioning political units and highly developed cultural centers. We must avoid these unhelpful and inaccurate generalizations.

Most medieval cities in the Middle East followed a common layout. Let's use Jerusalem as an example. There were different quarters for each religious community (Muslim, Christian, Jewish, and Armenian), and each community had its own schools and courts. Mixed courts handled cases involving multiple religious groups. Markets were located both outside the city and on the border of each quarter. Within each market, whole streets were devoted to a particular craft, product, or service. The center of the market was reserved for the most valuable goods, such as jewelry, silks, spices, and perfumes. In the Muslim quarter, the *muhtasib* (market inspector) ensured that weights and measures were true, prices were fair, and shops were clean. The market provided a safe meeting place for people of diverse origins. Regarding urban dwellings, families typically owned a home that was walled off from the surrounding neighborhood, and its principal rooms faced a central courtyard.

Several important organizations and institutions defined the character of medieval Muslim cities. Those entities included guilds, trading companies, *futuwwa* organizations, Sufi orders, and *waqf*.

Guilds were organized according to trade and ethnic group. For example, lettuce grocers in Istanbul were typically Albanians, and gold and silver merchants were Armenians. Guilds regulated industries, controlled wages and prices, and dealt with the social concerns of their members.

Trading companies were similar to joint stock companies in the West. Members shared the costs, risks, and profits of a business venture, such as importing spices from Asia. In most cases, the companies were controlled by prominent merchant families who sent traders all over the world. They established commercial centers in locations as far-flung as Canton, China; Malacca, in Southeast Asia; and Zanzibar, on the east coast of Africa. To facilitate commercial transactions, the medieval Muslim world established a universal system of coinage and adopted a form of checking that allowed funds to be transferred safely between cities.

The Arabic word *futuwwa* means "youthfulness." A *futuwwa* group was a cross between a Muslim young men's association and an urban band of youths. The brotherhoods followed *muruwwa*—the code of Arab virtues—and operated clubs where the members participated in a variety of athletic activities. They also protected neighborhoods. One group helped restore the authority of 'Abbasid caliph an-Nasir in the late 1100s.

Sufism differs significantly from the Islam of the *'ulama* because it involves a profound mystical religious experience. (The Arabic word *sufi* means "woolen," which refers to the coarse wool cloaks worn by wandering holy men.) Sufis hope to achieve a level of spiritual consciousness that neither law nor formal ritual can provide. Specifically, they seek a personal union with God and attempt to reach this goal through meditation and esoteric practices.

In the twelfth century, Sufis organized into lodges (*zawiyyas*) under a master (or shaykh) who served as their spiritual guide. Sufism is roughly analogous to Christian monasticism. Sufi disciples, or full-time members, devote themselves to study, spiritual exercises, and upkeep of the lodge. Associate members keep jobs and raise families. Lodges are more comparable to Western social clubs, such as the Rotary, Kiwanis, and Lions, than to monasteries. Religious services consist of standard prayer and a unique activity, such as singing, chanting, or whirling.

Waqf is a difficult term to translate. It is similar to a nonprofit under-taking or endowed charitable pursuit. In practice, a benefactor designates a parcel of land as *waqf,* not for profit. The land will not be taxed, and all income beyond administrative costs will go to a designated charity. A *waqf* can be handed down from generation to generation; family members act as trustees. It is used to fund a variety of activities, such as hospitals, libraries, orphanages, soup kitchens, primary schools, law schools, Sufi lodges, and public fountains. There are examples of women, like members of the imperial Ottoman household, who became notable philanthropists and established *waqf* trusts. During the medieval caliphate, slave soldiers were forbidden to marry but eventually were permitted to maintain con-cubines and families. Because their property reverted to the ruler upon their deaths, many established endowments to keep the property in their families.

Think about how the feudal system operated in the West during the Middle Ages. A lord would grant a parcel of land (a fief) to a subordinate nobleman in return for the nobleman's loyalty and military service. In a time of conflict, the nobleman honored his pledge and provided his lord with a specified number of armed, mounted knights.

In the medieval Middle East, an *iqta'* was analogous to a fief in medieval Europe, and it formed the governing basis of rural society. Like a fief, it was a payment of land to a ruler's or lord's leading and most loyal soldiers. It began as a temporary system whereby the lord moved his landholders to new locations after a few years. This practice made it clear that the lord owned the land; it was not hereditary. The system later became hereditary, and beginning in the sixteenth century, *iqta'* holders stayed put. Landlords collected the *kharaj,* gouged the peasants for fees, and passed on the property to their heirs. They became powerful local leaders who in many instances challenged central authority.

29. What are significant works and accomplishments of medieval Muslim scholars, scientists, theologians, artists, and architects?

Medieval Muslim civilization played an essential role in the progress of human history for two reasons: it preserved and transmitted classical knowledge and was a major contributor to new knowledge. This great advance of learning was achieved by Muslim and non-Muslim scholars alike.

Preservation of Classical Knowledge

Many people in the West believe that the Muslim conquest of the Middle East stifled its artistic, literary, and scientific creativity. On the contrary, the Muslims collected, translated, and preserved classical texts from Greece, Rome, and other civilizations and then transmitted them to the West—an immeasurable gift that would help launch the European Renaissance.

The principal sources of classical knowledge were Byzantium, Persia, China, and India. The Byzantines preserved Roman civilization and Hellenistic philosophy and science. Alexandria and Edessa were major centers of Greco-Roman learning. The Sassanians were the custodians of Persian literature and science. They operated a major research center at Jundishapur and preserved knowledge of astronomy, medicine, pharmacology, and Zoroastrianism. The Chinese invented gunpowder and paper. When the Arabs moved into Central Asia in the mid-eighth century, they encountered a Chinese rocket corps. Paper reached Baghdad from China in the late 700s. The Indians were accomplished astronomers and mathematicians who developed a numbering system, including the zero, the decimal system, and nautical devices, such as the astrolabe.

Leading centers of Muslim scholarship and science were Baghdad, Córdoba in al-Andalus, and Cairo. In Baghdad's Bayt al-Hikma, scholars translated the works of several Greek philosophers and scientists, including Plato, Aristotle, Hippocrates, Galen, Euclid, and Ptolemy. They also translated the famous Persian folktale *Khalila wa Dimna*, a collection of fables in which the main characters are animals. Córdoba was a seat of mathematics and medicine, while Cairo's al-Azhar University was renowned for its legal scholarship.

Starting in the mid-tenth century, the central authority in Islam became weak and fragmented. This breakup of the Muslim world had a counterintuitive effect on science and learning. The rivalry between emerging empires actually stimulated science and technology. Each ruler wanted to have the best poets, philosophers, physicians, and scientists in his court.

A veritable bidding war emerged for itinerant scholars who could command high wages.

The two epicenters for transmitting Muslim culture to Europe were Sicily and Toledo, Spain. Sicily was taken back from the Arabs by the Normans in the eleventh century. It was a violent takeover, but Norman rulers, especially Roger II (r. 1130–54), became great patrons of Islamic literature, science, and philosophy. After the first Reconquista in 1085, Arabic-speaking Christians and Jews in Toledo translated many preserved classical works from Arabic into Latin.

Achievements of Muslim Scholars and Scientists

The Arab conquests brought Muslims into contact with the philosophical ideas of the Hellenistic world, and those ideas found their way to the Bayt al-Hikma in Baghdad, where the works of Aristotle and Plato were translated by Syrian Christians into Arabic. The translations inspired several Muslim philosophers and theologians, such as al-Kindi, al-Farabi, Ibn Sina, Ibn Rushd, al-Ash'ari, and al-Ghazali.

Al-Kindi (ca. 801–873), "the Philosopher of the Arabs," considered the search for truth the ultimate human endeavor, surpassed only by religious devotion. Al-Farabi (ca. 872–950) labored to reconcile Greek philosophy and Islamic teachings. Ibn Sina (ca. 980–1037), known as Avicenna in the West, was a physician and philosopher who commented extensively on Aristotle. Ibn Rushd (1126–98), known as Averroes in the West, wrote at length on the philosophy of Aristotle and the works of Muslim theologians. The Christian theologian Thomas Aquinas (ca. 1224–74), who wrote a monumental treatise on the synthesis of faith and reason, obtained his knowledge of Aristotle from the writings of Ibn Sina and Ibn Rushd. Al-Ash'ari (ca. 874–935), who was influenced by the writings of Ibn Hanbal (ca. 780–855), founder of the Hanbali *madhhab*, argued that God's revelation, not reason, was the best guide for human behavior. Accordingly, he emphasized that faith was absolute and that Qur'anic scripture should be accepted literally. Al-Ghazali (ca. 1058–1111) used Aristotelian logic to prove the basic tenets of Islam. In *The Restoration of Theology*, he sought to reconcile orthodoxy, mysticism, and rationalism.

Muslim historians were the first scholars to attempt to structure history by looking for patterns in the rise and fall of dynasties, peoples, and civilizations. These efforts culminated in the fourteenth century with Ibn Khaldun's monumental *Al-Muqaddima*. In it, he linked the rise of states to their feelings of group solidarity and their decline to its erosion. He also investigated what today would be called the social contract between the ruler and the governed.

Muslim mathematicians made great advances in algebra, plane and spherical trigonometry, and the geometry of planes, spheres, cones, and cylinders. Our "arabic" numerals were actually transmitted by Arabs from India to Europe. Al-Khwarizmi (ca. 780–850) developed algebra. Thabit Ibn Qurrah (ca. 835–901) was an accomplished translator of Greek texts and an authority on exponential theory. 'Umar al-Khayyami (1048–1131), also known as Omar Khayyam, was an accomplished poet and mathematician who wrote a major treatise on solving algebraic equations.

In medical science, the Muslims built on the great work of the ancient Greeks. Ibn Sina wrote the *Canon of Medicine*, which was produced in Hebrew, Arabic, and Latin and remained in use in European medical schools until the seventeenth century. The surgeon al-Zahrawi (ca. 936–1016) wrote *Kitab al-Tasrif* (*The Book of Medical Methods*), a multivolume text on diseases, injuries, and medical practices, including surgery. Mansur Ibn Ilyas (ca. 1380–1422) mapped the circulatory and nervous systems in *Tashrihi Mansuri* (*Mansur's Anatomy*), an atlas of the human body. Ibn al-Haytham (ca. 965–1040) known as al-Hazen in the West, challenged Galen's explanation of vision as rays emitting from the eyes and presented a new theory based on the physics of refraction and reflection. He described the human ocular system in *Book of Optics*. Another leading ophthalmologist, Hunayn Ibn Ishaq (ca. 809–873), a Nestorian Christian, translated several Greek medical texts, mainly the works of Galen, into Arabic.

Muslims were skilled astronomers and astrologers. Knowledge of the movements of the stars and planets aided ocean and desert navigation. Early Muslims also believed that heavenly bodies affected the lives of individuals, cities, and empires. They were heavily influenced by Persian and Indian astrologers. Many Muslim rulers retained court astrologers. Indian and Persian scientists also shared their knowledge of astronomy with their

Muslim counterparts, who achieved new heights in the field, including the naming of hundreds of stars and questioning Ptolemy's geocentric model of the solar system. Al-Battani (ca. 858–929) measured the length of the solar year, and his work aided the research of the Polish astronomer Nicolaus Copernicus (ca. 1473–1543), who formed a heliocentric model of the heavens. Al-Buruni (ca. 973–1048) was an accomplished astronomer and geographer. He measured the diameter of Earth and wrote an encyclopedia of India. Al-Fazari (d. 777) was the first Muslim to design an astrolabe following the visit of an Indian mission to Baghdad. An astrolabe, which is the forerunner to a modern sextant, is a device for making precise measurements of latitude by determining the height of stars and planets above the horizon. Al-Zarqali (ca. 1029–87) improved al-Farazi's astrolabe.

Geography and cartography in the Muslim Middle East emerged from a blending of intellectual curiosity and long-distance trade. Al-Idrisi (ca. 1100–1165) drew an extraordinarily detailed map of the known world. It revealed the source of the Nile River to be lakes in central Africa; European explorers would not confirm this fact until the mid-nineteenth century. Muslim scientists knew the Earth was round and measured its circumference to within a few miles.

Muslim Art and Architecture

Muslim artists illustrated manuscripts with calligraphy, abstract designs, beautiful pictures of plants and animals, depictions of everyday life, and ceremonial activities of men and women. Calligraphy became the highest form of art. Other artistic creations included enameled glass; carved wood, stone, and ivory; engraved metal trays; jeweled rings, pendants, and daggers; embroidered silk; leather book bindings; carpets; and glazed pottery and tile. Early Muslim artisans produced a form of porcelain with a metallic glaze known as lusterware. By the eleventh century, they were making blue and white porcelain similar in quality to the exquisite wares imported from China. Later, Ottoman artists would make their own signature ceramics, known as fritware, which is fabricated from clay mixed with ground glass or quartz. Their brightly fired plates and tiles took their name from the town of Iznik, which became the center of the Turkish pottery industry.

Some of the best proportioned and most lavishly decorated buildings ever erected are the large congregational mosques of the Muslim world's leading cities. Muslim architects also built beautiful palaces, schools, hospitals, Sufi lodges, mausoleums, and caravanserais (caravan lodges) and designed gardens with reflecting pools and fountains. In addition to mastering a style of their own, Muslim architects frequently converted existing buildings for their religious use. For example, the Basilica of Saint John the Baptist in Damascus became the Umayyad Mosque, and the domed Basilica of Hagia Sophia in Constantinople became a mosque following the Ottoman conquest of the city. The domed mosque became the signature feature of Ottoman architecture. The exquisite Dome of the Rock in Jerusalem is the first great work of Muslim architecture. Erected by the Umayyads in the late seventh century, the shrine marks the spot where the Prophet Muhammad ascended to heaven during his Night Journey. The Fatimids and Mamluks of Egypt built huge mosques, schools, and palaces in Cairo. Many of the structures served multiple purposes. A notable example is the massive Sultan Hasan Mosque and Madrasa, built in the mid-fourteenth century during the Mamluk era. Its madrasa contains a large courtyard with four open, vaulted halls, or *iwans*. Each *iwan* serves as the place of instruction for one of the four Sunni *madhhabs*. Mamluk architecture is one of the most spectacular of the medieval era. It is marked by large, multipurpose buildings; huge facades; tall portals; layers of red and white stone called *ablaq*; stalactite-like carvings, known as *muqarnas*, above portals and windows and in corners beneath domes; intricately carved domes over tombs; and tall multilevel minarets.

In years long past, schoolchildren in the West were taught that the victory of the Frankish leader Charles Martel over Muslim forces at the Battle of Tours in 732 saved European—and by extension, Western—civilization. (One of the authors of this guide remembers such a lesson in elementary school.) We must remind ourselves that Charles was part of the European Dark Ages. His standard of living was very basic, and the quality of life for his subjects was exceedingly primitive and precarious. On the other hand, the world of Islam was in full flower at the time, as evidenced by its power, wealth, scholarship, art, and architecture. How different do you think European history—and world history, for that matter—would have been if the outcome at Tours had been the opposite?

It is also important to note that Islamist extremists regard Muslims who would take great pride in the achievements described above to be Hellenized and thus apostates. ISIS prohibited the study of science in Mosul and al-Raqqa, creating a society that was unrecognizable to any of the great caliphates of the golden age.

6

Invaders, Conquerors, and Warriors

T he questions in this chapter span the years from the late eleventh to the early sixteenth century. We start by investigating the origins of the Christian Crusades to the Middle East, examine their outcomes, and evaluate their impact on Europe and the Muslim world. We also consider the Mongols, nomadic warriors from Central Asia who gained control over most of the Middle East; the Mamluks, slave soldiers who governed Egypt and established a prosperous regional empire; and Tamerlane, the nomad conqueror-ruler who, like the Mongols conquered vast territory in the Middle East and Central and South Asia.

30. What were the political, economic, social, and religious factors that contributed to the First Crusade?

One of the most controversial historical events of the past millennium was the Christian military effort to liberate the Holy Land from Muslim control. Known collectively as the Crusades, these efforts left an indelible mark on the peoples of the Middle East and Europe that still resides in their collective memory. The term "crusade" is derived from the Latin word for cross: *crux*. The crusaders wore crosses on their uniforms, emphasizing that theirs was a Christian military movement.

A good starting point for a discussion of the Crusades is the eleventh century. The Seljuk Turks were moving into the Middle East from Central Asia in large numbers. They brought their families and tribal structure with them and served as hired warriors for several Muslim petty dynasties. By 1055 they had taken Baghdad from the Shi'a Buyids, reaffirmed the primacy of Sunni Islam, and propped up the 'Abbasid caliph. In 1071 they defeated Byzantine forces at the Battle of Manzikert, in eastern Anatolia, and their victory opened the area to Turkish settlement. Seljuk migration put tremendous pressure on the Christian population of Anatolia and alarmed the Byzantine emperor, who appealed for help from the West. In the early 1090s, the Seljuk Empire reached its height under Malikshah (r. 1072–92), stretching from Central Asia to Anatolia and the Levant and from the Caucasus to the Persian Gulf. The Mongol invasion weakened and fragmented the Seljuk state. The Rum Seljuks, who represented the last vestige of the once vast empire, survived until 1302.

A combination of political, economic, feudal, and religious factors led to the start of the Crusades. Regarding politics, in Western Europe, relations between the pope and the continent's monarchs, especially the Holy Roman emperor, were strained. The papacy had been weakened by the Investiture Controversy, (the dispute over whether the pope or the emperor had the authority to appoint bishops), but had rebounded by the mid-eleventh century, when the emperor ceded some authority to the pope on the selection of clergy. A crusade could expand the pope's influence and strengthen his power vis-à-vis the monarchs.

Economics was another critical factor. The High Middle Ages witnessed a European commercial revival. Merchants knew that lucrative trade opportunities existed in the Middle East. A crusade could enable merchants to establish trading posts in the region.

The third factor involved the feudal system. The eleventh century marked the height of the feudal era, yet the medieval system of inheritance could compel an ambitious young man to join a crusade. Younger sons of the nobility wanted to own land, but the practice of primogeniture prevented them from inheriting it from their fathers. They might obtain it in the Holy Land. Furthermore, there was great insecurity in Europe. Young knights or warriors were always itching for a fight to boost their reputation and increase their material wealth. A crusade might channel their energies and promote stability in Europe. One way to unite a disparate group of people is to promote the existence of an external enemy—in this case, the Turks who were threatening the Christians of the Middle East.

Finally, there were significant religious factors. As we discussed above, relations between the pope and the monarchs of Western Europe were frigid. Worse yet, there was no relationship to speak of between the Roman and Eastern churches. The pope and the Orthodox patriarch had excommunicated each other in 1054. An attempt at reconciliation had failed, and a permanent schism resulted. The pope saw a crusade as a compelling opportunity for the Roman church to regain its sway over Eastern Christianity. Also of religious significance was the pope's promise that service in a sacred campaign to free the Holy Land would earn a Christian warrior the absolution of all sins and eternal salvation. For Christians of the Middle Ages, attaining a place in heaven was their paramount concern.

31. What factors account for the crusader victory at Jerusalem in 1099?

In the mid-1090s, Byzantine emperor Alexius I Comnenus (r. 1081–1118) appealed to the leaders of Western Europe for help against the Turkish invaders and for the protection of pilgrims traveling to the Holy Land. Pope Urban II (r. 1088–99) took up the emperor's request and issued a papal bull in 1095, calling for all Christians to join in a war against the Turks to recover the holy sites. The First Crusade began in 1096.

At the end of the eleventh century, the geopolitical situation in the Middle East favored a European invasion. The 'Abbasid caliphate was weak; Malikshah's Seljuk Empire had fragmented into feuding mini-states in Aleppo, Mosul, and Damascus; and a rival Shi'a caliphate, the Fatimids, ruled from Egypt.

The People's Crusade, also known as the Peasants' or Popular Crusade, which comprised tens of thousands of untrained fighters and several women and children, served as a prelude to the First Crusade. Led by the charismatic cleric Peter the Hermit (ca. 1050–1115), the irregular force marched across Europe to Anatolia. In the Rhineland, it slaughtered several thousand

Jews. The crusaders reached Constantinople and crossed the Bosporus into Anatolia, but a force under the Rum Seljuk sultan Kilij Arslan (r. 1092–1107) routed the Christians on the outskirts of Nicea, killing most of them.

The First Crusade was led by the generals Raymond of Toulouse (d. 1105), Godfrey of Bouillon (d. 1100), Hugh of Vermandois (d. 1101), and Bohemond the Norman (d. 1111). Other generals included Baldwin (d. 1118), brother of Godfrey, and Tancred (d. 1112), nephew of Bohemond. Four separate crusader armies arrived at Constantinople in late 1096 and early 1097, making their encampments outside the walls of the Byzantine capital a tangible threat to the emperor's hold on power. Alexius successfully transported the crusaders across the Bosporus and away from Constantinople, but the crusaders refused to submit to his leadership and had no intention of honoring their pledge not to seize and hold Byzantine territory.

Before the crusaders could take the city of Nicea, which had been left undefended by Kilij Arslan, Alexius rescued Kilij Arlan's family, reunited them with the sultan, and claimed the city for himself. The crusaders were furious about the emperor's preemptive act. In 1098 Baldwin moved east and took Edessa, while most of the crusaders continued south to Antioch and placed the city under siege. The city held out for nine months, but the Muslim population was ultimately betrayed by an Armenian armorer and guard named Firuz, who had converted to Islam. He permitted a small group of crusaders to scale one of the towers of the city, after which the raiders threw open a city gate to the Franj army. ("Franj" is the term Arab Muslims used for Europeans and derives from Franks.) Bohemond soon had complete control of the historic city.

The struggle for Antioch marked the first unified Muslim effort to halt the Christian invaders. Karbuqa (d. 1102), the Seljuk *atabeg* of Mosul, organized a relief expedition, but at the city walls, the attack failed owing to rivalries among Seljuk leaders. (*Atabeg* is a Turkish word that means "prince-father." The *atabegs* started out as guardians for the princes of the Seljuk clan but—as so often happens in Middle Eastern history—they eventually became de facto rulers.) Damascus and Aleppo were ruled by two other Seljuk *atabegs* who were also brothers: Duqaq (d. 1104) in Damascus and Ridwan (d. 1113) in Aleppo. Duqaq undermined Karbuqa by stating that the Mosul *atabeg* was only fighting for himself. As a result, Karbuqa's warriors lost their ardor for combat.

As the crusaders continued their march toward Jerusalem, the Muslims went to great lengths to portray them as inhuman, accusing them of committing the unthinkable act of cannibalism during the siege of Ma'arra, in Syria. Following this incident, the crusaders moved down the coast with impunity; the Arab population was terrified.

The Fatimids, who had wrested control of Jerusalem from the Seljuks in 1098, did not have enough men and resources to defend the city adequately. Nevertheless, after their offer of a truce was spurned by the crusaders, they braced for a devastating siege. As the scorching summer of 1099 dragged on, the encamped crusaders were increasingly desperate to reduce the city's defenses. They were also in dire need of wood for the construction of siege engines and ladders. The Fatimids had cleared the area around Jerusalem of trees, forcing the crusaders to search for wood as far away as Samaria. They found enough to build two siege towers, a battering ram, and a few catapults—not enough to take a city the size of Jerusalem. The crusaders then resorted to dismantling the ships of the Genovese fleet for their wood and rope. In the end, the breaching action of only one siege tower led to the fall of Jerusalem on 15 July. The city was taken in six weeks without a significant battle having been fought.

The crusader victory at Jerusalem contrasted with the Arab conquest of the city in the seventh century. The Muslims had been magnanimous and respectful of the local population. The crusaders, on the other hand, carried out wanton destruction, looting, and murder. Thousands of inhabitants, including Jews and indigenous Christians, were slaughtered.

The conquest of Jerusalem in 1099 marked the end of the military phase of the First Crusade. The crusaders next established states in Jerusalem, Antioch, Edessa, and Tripoli. The Latin Kingdom of Jerusalem assumed hegemony over the other states: the County of Tripoli, Principality of Antioch, and County of Edessa. The states were set up as feudal establishments where Muslim peasants and laborers were forced into serfdom.

To a significant degree, the First Crusade succeeded because the Muslim world was not united in its resistance to the invaders. Some Muslims sided with the crusaders to undermine their Muslim rivals, the Fatimids of Cairo defied the 'Abbasid caliphate, and the Seljuk Empire had splintered. Similarly, it is important to note that from 1099 to 1187, the crusader kingdoms challenged one another for power and influence. Two crusader factions soon emerged: The first group sought to coexist peacefully with Muslims as a means of weakening their Christian foes, and the second maintained a hostile attitude the toward Muslims.

32. How did the Muslim world react to the Crusades and ultimately drive the crusaders from the region?

Muslims who survived the fall of Jerusalem became refugees, flooding into Islam's major cities. From the tops of minarets, the faithful received the bitter news of the loss of Jerusalem. Despite the initial shock, the Christian victory in the First Crusade had little impact on the Muslim world. Many Muslim leaders were unperturbed because, except for Jerusalem, the crusaders had not captured any city of great significance, such as Aleppo, Baghdad, Cairo, Damascus, or Mosul.

After 1100 the Muslims became more unified and effective as a fighting force. In 1104 a Muslim force halted a crusader advance at Harran, in southeastern Anatolia. Fifteen years later, Ilghazi (d. 1122), the ruler of Aleppo, defeated Roger of Antioch (r. 1112–19). Yet just as their momentum was building, the Muslims suffered a series of setbacks. Persistent jealousies and assassinations disrupted military and political efforts.

A branch of Isma'ili Shi'ism, the Nizaris—known as the Assassins—was founded by Hasan as-Sabbah (d. 1124), a Persian Shi'a. He sought to reestablish orthodox Shi'ism with a movement that was stridently opposed to the Seljuks, whom he viewed as an invading force and detested for their defense of Sunni Islam. He served as the agent for an Isma'ili Imam who was purported to be the son of Nizar (ca. 1047–97), the eldest son of Fatimid caliph al-Mustansir Billah (r. 1036–94). The Imam was never seen. Nizar claimed that his father had designated him as his successor, and during a conflict with his younger brother, al-Musta'li (1074–1101), he fled Cairo and was later murdered. Hasan had supported Nizar in his claim to the caliphate and consequently became a foe of the Fatimids as well. After the death of Nizar, his followers took refuge in a mountain fortress at Alamut, in the Elburz Mountains of northern Persia. Hasan began a targeted assassination campaign against his enemies, knowing that fighting pitched battles would not be realistic. According to legend, his assassins would partake in ritual hashish before embarking on a mission. He created a Nizari state in Syria and Iran that was composed, not of territory, but of scattered fortresses. By 1140 assassinations had reached their zenith, and then Zangi, the *atabeg* of Mosul (r. 1127–46), put an end to the Nizari campaign of murder. Alamut acquired an undeniable reputation for terror, but it was also a great intellectual center. It hosted scholars and had a great research library.

Muslim-organized resistance to the crusaders had begun in earnest under Zangi, who established his own kingdom at Mosul in 1127 and took Aleppo the following year. He rallied Muslim forces and defeated the crusaders at Edessa in 1144. In reaction to Zangi's victory, Pope Eugene III (r. 1145–53) preached the Second Crusade (1147–49), which was led by Emperor Conrad III of the Holy Roman Empire (r. 1138–52) and King Louis VII of France (r. 1137–80).[1]

After Zangi's assassination by the hand of a slave in 1146, his territory was divided between his sons: Sayf al-Din (d. 1149), who controlled Mosul, and Nur al-Din (1118–74), who governed Aleppo. (This division of Zangi's territory hardened the rivalry between Syria and Iraq that has persisted to the modern era.) Instead of striking at Aleppo, which was closer to Edessa, the crusaders attacked Damascus with a large force. The *atabeg* of Damascus, Mu'in al-Din Unar (d. 1149), sought help from Nur al-Din and Sayf al-Din to ward off the crusaders. When Nur al-Din's army arrived at Damascus, the crusaders retired to Jerusalem. The Crusade failed owing to a poorly conceived strategy. Many historians believe that the decision to attack Damascus instead of Aleppo was a great mistake; the crusaders never recaptured Edessa.

Years earlier, Ayyub, a Kurdish soldier and political leader from Iraq, had transported Zangi and his army to safety across the Tigris River after they had suffered defeat in battle. Zangi rewarded Ayyub with a governorship in Lebanon, and after Zangi's death, Ayyub's brother Shirkuh (d. 1169) and Ayyub's son Salah al-Din (1137–93) distinguished themselves as military officers in service of Nur al-Din. Shirkuh, who emerged as Nur al-Din's most capable general, was dispatched to Cairo to safeguard the wealth of Egypt, which was essential in support of military operations against the crusaders. In 1169 Salah al-Din became grand vizier under the Fatimid caliph following the death of Shirkuh, who had held the post. In 1171 he proclaimed himself the sultan, after he had defended Egypt from a crusader advance and removed the caliph, who was near death. Salah al-Din's Ayyubid dynasty would rule Egypt until 1250, when they were succeeded by the Mamluks.

Salah al-Din employed a careful strategy against the crusaders. He sought to regain Muslim territory peacefully if possible, by force if necessary. By seeming unpretentious, he hoped that other Muslim leaders would not regard him as a threat to their power and positions after the crusaders had departed from the region. He was a savvy diplomat, not a military genius. Although he failed to wrest Acre and Tyre from the crusaders, he nearly succeeded in uniting the Muslim world under his leadership.

Taking charge of Egypt set Salah al-Din on a collision course with Nur al-Din, but he remained safe by avoiding open conflict with his overlord. When Nur al-Din died in 1174, Salah al-Din gained control of Damascus; in 1181 he seized Aleppo. In 1183 he combined Syria and Egypt into an enlarged Ayyubid Empire.

In 1182 Reynauld of Chatillon (d. 1187), former prince of Antioch, who had been imprisoned by Nur al-Din for fifteen years, attempted to raid Mecca, which naturally earned him the enmity of Muslims. In 1185 Raymond, the count of Tripoli and regent for the king of Jerusalem, signed a four-year truce with Salah al-Din. A year later, Reynauld violated the truce by raiding a Muslim caravan bound for Mecca. In 1187 Salah al-Din retaliated and defeated the crusaders at the Battle of Hattin, in the north of present-day Israel. Crusader resistance crumbled, and Salah al-Din's army soon captured Jerusalem.

The Third Crusade (1189–92), also known as the Kings' Crusade, was led by Richard the Lionheart of England (r. 1189–99), Philip Augustus of France (r. 1180–1223), and Frederick Barbarossa of the Holy Roman Empire (r. 1155–90). The crusaders took Acre after an extended, brutal siege but failed to capture Jerusalem. Salah al-Din dealt cautiously and effectively with the invaders. He countered the English king's religious arguments for a crusade by emphasizing the sacredness of Jerusalem to Muslims. He granted pilgrimage rights to Christians, ransomed captives, and did not condone violent tactics, although his men carried out a bloody attack at Jaffa without his approval. Meanwhile, Richard proposed to marry off his sister Joanna to al-'Adil, the brother of Salah al-Din, hoping to establish a Christian-Muslim kingdom, but Salah al-Din rebuffed the offer.

Salah al-Din held many advantages over Richard. First, time was on his side; he could wait the crusaders out. Second, he enjoyed "home field advantage." At the Battle of Hattin, he cut off the Christian army from its water supply. And third, he was able to mute the power of the crusaders without having to defeat them completely. By offering generous terms, he discouraged them from launching a new crusade, which was tantamount to a Muslim victory. From 1189 to 1191, Salah al-Din tried but was unable to take Acre. Two years later, he died in Damascus. The Ayyubids would resist the crusaders for several more decades with the help of the Mamluks, slave soldiers in their service.

The crusaders never reached the Holy Land during the Fourth Crusade (1202–4). Instead, the crusaders, mostly Venetians, occupied and sacked Constantinople and placed one of their own on the throne of the Byzantine Empire. The Crusade was, in essence, a European attack on Byzantium, and it drove an irretrievable wedge between Roman and Orthodox Christianity.

The Franj invaded Egypt, the wealthiest country in the Muslim world, during the Fifth Crusade (1218–21). Led by King Andrew II of Hungary (r. 1205–35), Duke Leopold VI of Austria (r. 1198–1230), and Count William I of Holland (r. 1203–22), the crusaders took Damietta in the delta and then marched on Cairo. Sultan al-Kamil (r. 1218–38), son and successor of al-'Adil I (r. 1200–18), halted their advance and expelled them from Egypt.

The Sixth Crusade (1229) involved little fighting, yet it achieved the temporary transfer of Jerusalem from Muslim to Christian control. Al-Kamil, who was busy campaigning against rebels in Syria, signed a truce with the Holy Roman emperor, Frederick II (r. 1220–50), which allowed the German ruler to hold the lease on Jerusalem and other cities in the

Holy Land for ten years. When the lease expired, Jerusalem reverted to Muslim control. The subsequent Barons' Crusade (1239–41) restored the Kingdom of Jerusalem, and the city remained in Christian hands until 1244, when Khwarizmian forces, allies of the Ayyubids, devastated the city and massacred its Christian population. Not until 1917, during World War I, did Christendom again govern Jerusalem. In December of that year, forces of the British Empire under General Edmund Allenby paraded into the holy city.[2]

The Seventh Crusade (1248–54) was led by King Louis IX of France (r. 1226–70), the future Saint Louis. For a second time, the crusaders invaded Egypt, hoping to secure a base for an advance on Jerusalem. They landed in the delta in 1249 and defeated an Egyptian army led by Sultan as-Salih Nagm al-Din Ayyub (r. 1240–49), who died later that year. His wife, Shajar al-Durr (d. 1257), succeeded him as ruler of Egypt. In 1250 a Mamluk army defeated Louis and took him prisoner. After his wife, Margaret, ransomed him, he traveled to the Levant, where he helped fortify coastal fortifications. He returned to France in 1254.

King Louis also led the Eighth Crusade (1270); the objective again was the capture of Egypt. This time the crusaders landed in Tunisia in the heart of North Africa and planned to march on Egypt from the west. Shortly after the crusaders had arrived in Tunisia, dysentery swept through their encampment. The disease killed Louis and ravaged the Christian ranks. The campaign was soon abandoned, and the surviving crusaders withdrew across the Mediterranean.

Over the next two decades, the Mamluks of Egypt expelled nearly all the remaining crusaders from the Middle East. Two years before the collapse of the Eighth Crusade, the Mamluk sultan Baybars (r. 1260–77) captured Antioch. Sultan Qalawun (r. 1279–90) captured Tripoli in 1289. Two years later, Sultan al-Ashraf (r. 1290–93) conquered Acre, the last major city under crusader control. By 1293 the remaining Christian outposts—Beirut, Sidon, and Tyre—were evacuated.

Begun in 1095, the era of the Crusades lasted almost exactly two centuries. Well before the conclusion of this violent period in Middle Eastern history, a highly charged and negative view of Arabs and Muslims had emerged among the people of the Christian West. Similarly, Muslims became increasingly intolerant of Christian Europe. They had regained their self-confidence by the time of their victory in Jerusalem in 1187, but their subsequent actions against the crusaders became extremely brutal and destructive. The chivalry of Salah al-Din did not outlive him.

33. What is the legacy of the Crusades from Christian and Muslim points of view?

In both Christendom and the Dar al-Islam, the Crusades elevated the concept of a holy war to extreme heights. To medieval Christians, a crusade entailed going on an armed pilgrimage to liberate the Holy Land from Muslim authority and earning from the church the guarantee of eternal salvation. In addition, armed religious orders—brotherhoods of warrior monks such as the Knights Templar and Knights Hospitaller—emerged during the Crusades. In the aftermath of the Crusades, the demonization of Islam and Muslims was firmly entrenched among Christian clergy and academics.

To Muslims, the crusader attack from the west and the Mongol invasion from the east in the mid-thirteenth century exerted extraordinary pressures on the Muslim world, pressures that spawned the growth of radical Islamic expression. For example, the Hanbali theologian Taqi al-Din Ibn Taymiyya (ca. 1263–1328) preached an extreme and intolerant form of Islam. He declared Christians and Jews to be infidels and Muslims who did not share his views to be apostates. Militant Islamist ideologues today study his treatises and embrace his ideas.

There were, however, positive aspects of the Crusades. The European world was introduced to the advanced technology and science of Islam's golden age. Furthermore, because of the Crusades, Europeans' diet was altered forever by the introduction of spices and citrus fruit. European trade increased, and the Italian city-states became very wealthy and influential. European leaders recognized that trading networks were more valuable than the acquisition of land. A vibrant middle class emerged, and feudalism declined. European merchants developed systems of banking and credit, which facilitated trade. After the thirteenth century, most Europeans were resigned to Muslim control over the holy places, so long as access was granted to pilgrims.

European civilization benefitted greatly from the Crusades, acquiring several new wares, innovations, and food items from the Middle East, including musical instruments; pigeons; a code of chivalry; heraldic devices; gunpowder; waterwheels; fashions; furniture, such as the sofa; linens; mirrors; the idea for the rosary; dyes; the compass; architectural innovations, such as the pointed arch; spices; incense; coffee; a variety of plants, such as the rose; vegetables, such as scallions; cereals, such as carob, millet, and rice; fruit, such as lemons, melons, and apricots; and sugar. In the mid-thirteenth century, Venetian and Genoese merchants abandoned roman numerals for arabic numbers to facilitate business accounting. On the other hand, the people of the Middle East acquired only a few goods and ideas from the European invaders, namely, chain mail, the use of pads under armor, the crossbow, and castle design.

Understanding the legacy of the Crusades is important for military personnel deploying to the Middle East because this legacy still influences the image that many Muslims and Christians have of one another. For example, Christian and Muslim terrorists, among them the Norwegian bomber-gunman Anders Breivik and al-Qa'ida founder Usama Bin Ladin, espoused similar views of the Crusades. Both sides argued that their faith was under siege, and extreme violence was required to save it, revealing a shallow and mythic understanding of this critical era in human history. Arguably, the most obvious legacy of the Crusades is a negative one: the furtherance of the language and practice of religious extremism.

34. How did the Mongols establish a vast empire, and what were their governing institutions and religious practices?

In response to this question and the next three, we will discuss the impact that Mongol invaders from Central Asia, the Mamluks of Egypt, and the great warrior-conqueror Tamerlane had on the society and culture of the Middle East.

In the late twelfth century, the Mongols under Jenghiz (Genghis) Khan (ca. 1162–1227) built a huge tribal confederation. While over 90 percent of the population under his control was Turkish, the Mongols constituted the leadership. He ruled as the Great Khan (lord or ruler) until 1227. By 1300 his descendants governed most of the Eurasian land mass.

The Mongols' main military asset was their extraordinary ability to move hundreds of thousands of mounted warriors rapidly over great distances. On the march, Mongol fighters typically depended on three or four mounts; when desperate for nourishment, they would drink a concoction of horse milk and blood. Mongol officers bore a title based on the number of troops they commanded. For example, an officer who led ten men was known as an *arban*; a commander of tens of thousands was a *tumen*.

The Mongols launched two major military invasions: east to China and west to the Middle East, which they reached in the early 1200s. A crisis in Central Asia triggered the latter invasion. Central Asian Turkish tribes allied with the Mongols were being oppressed by another Mongol federation, the Kara-Khitay. Jenghiz Khan quickly subdued and absorbed the Kara-Khitay Mongols. Years later the Khwarizmian Turks in Turkmenistan and Uzbekistan, led by Shah Muhammad II (r. 1200–1220), were harassing another Mongol ally. In 1221 the Mongols brutally defeated the Khwarizmian army, remnants of which fled to Anatolia and the Fertile Crescent. Two decades later, the Mongols defeated the Rum Seljuks of Anatolia and reduced them to vassals, but the conquerors permitted the Turkish tribes to establish dozens of principalities.

In 1258 Hulegu Khan (ca. 1218–65), a grandson of Jenghiz Khan, reached Baghdad. The caliph refused the Mongol's ultimatum to surrender and abdicate, which prompted Hulegu to attack the city. By the time he finished, the 'Abbasid caliph and hundreds of members of the royal family had been slaughtered, and the once-great city lay in ruins. In one sudden, violent stroke, the Mongols ended the 'Abbasid caliphate, which had survived for more than five centuries.

By the mid-thirteenth century, the Mongols were poised to conquer much of the known world, but after they seized Damascus in early 1260, a succession crisis in Mongolia forced Hulegu to depart the Middle East and return home. Because the Mongols did not use a hereditary method of succession, Hulegu and other descendants of the dead khan competed for the title. Qubilai (Kublai) (r. 1260–94), another grandson of Jenghiz Khan and a brother of Hulegu, won out and became the Great Khan.

Back in the Middle East, Hulegu's military commander, General Kitbuqa (d. 1260), advanced toward Egypt and the Hijaz. A Mongol victory could have spelled the end of Islam. In September 1260, Mamluks under Sultan Qutuz and General Baybars defeated the Mongols at the Battle of Ayn Jalut, in the Galilee region of Israel. The Mongols had been beaten by a military opponent who was just as fierce and skilled as they were.

Under Qubilai, the vast Mongol empire was divided into four *ulus* (states): the Yuan *ulu* in China and Mongolia, the Chaghatay in Central Asia, the Golden Horde in Russia, and the Il-Khanid in Persia, which had been established by Hulegu in 1256. It is essential to note that the Mongols in China adopted Chinese culture and that the Golden Horde, which ruled the vassal states of Kiev and Muscovy, contributed to the rise of a Russian national identity.

The Great Khan ruled his empire through a general assembly (Ikh Kuraldai). He appointed the prime minister, subordinate officials, judges, shamans, and military commanders. In each *ulu*, the Mongols readily adopted local customs and culture but followed their tribal law code, known as Ikh Zasig; Arabs referred to it as "Yasa," which is derived from the Mongol name. The Mongol code, which dealt with family issues, taxes, and criminal violations, paralleled Islamic law and was accepted by Muslims as a secular code, so long as it did not conflict with Shari'a. The Arabic word for politics, *siyasa*, is derived from *yasa*, which means "to manage, steer, tend or train animals, particularly horses."[3]

Parallel usage of Yasa and Shari'a harmonized Mongol government with Islam and made it easier for the Mongols to govern Muslim-populated areas. On the other hand, the Hanbali theologian Ibn Taymiyya preached that Mongols should be regarded as apostates until they gave up Yasa and followed Islamic law exclusively. Yasa was used until the sixteenth and seventeenth centuries in areas ruled by the Mongols.

The huge Mongol Empire remained united until Qubilai's death, in 1294. After his passing, the four *ulus* went their separate ways, and by the fifteenth century, all of them had collapsed. The Ming dynasty replaced the Yuan in 1368. The Chaghatay survived until the end of the fourteenth century, when it was taken over by Tamerlane. The Il-Khanid state lasted until 1353. Abu Said (r. ca. 1316–35), the last notable Il-Khanid khan, made peace with the Mamluks, but his empire fragmented into a number of mini-states, which in turn were absorbed by Tamerlane. The Golden Horde, which had converted to Islam, also split into petty states and drifted into a closer alliance with the Mamluks. In 1395 it also fell to Tamerlane.

Throughout the Mongols' history, they either followed or tolerated diverse religious beliefs. Their attitude toward religion was one of ambivalence; they were tolerant when necessary; brutal when appropriate. Originally, they were shamanists who believed in a host of natural and tribal gods. Tengri, the Eternal Blue Sky, was their chief deity. On the other hand, Hulegu's wife, Doquz Khatun, was a Nestorian Christian, and several Mongols embraced Buddhism.

By the end of the thirteenth century, the Mongols, most notably the Il-Khanids, were converting in large numbers to Islam. Mahmud Ghazan Khan (r. 1295–1304) adopted Sunni Islam as the state religion. Later Il-Khanids experimented with different Muslim sects. An Il-Khanid coin from the early 1300s contained the *shahada* and the Shi'a saying "'Ali Wali Allah" ("'Ali is the authority of God"), leading one to conclude that the Il-Khanid Mongols had adopted Shi'ism as the state religion. Another coin minted some twenty years later contained the names of the four Rashidun and had dropped the 'Ali text, indicating that the state had returned to Sunni Islam.

35. What is the legacy of the Mongols in the Middle East?

The Mongols have a mixed legacy in the Middle East. For many people today, their name denotes utter destruction. Some inhabitants of the region blame the decline of Muslim civilization on the devastation wrought by the Mongols. One of the authors of this work has met Arabs who firmly believe that since the Mongol conquest, Islamic civilization has never attained its former glory.

Despite the Mongols' record of violence, they neither destroyed Islam nor uprooted Muslim culture. In terms of destruction and violence, their legacy is arguably worse than the crusaders' but, then again, maybe not. The Mongols built an observatory at Maraghah in northwest Persia, which became their version of Bayt al-Hikma. Scholars wrote Persian poetry and history and collected Il-Khanid fables, and the famed astronomer Nasir ad-Din at-Tusi (1201–74) studied the heavens from Maraghah.

The Mongols introduced Chinese art, architecture, fashion, and agricultural know-how to the Middle East; established a postal system that could transport a letter from Persia to China in about a week; and pioneered the use of paper currency. Based on this record, one can see why the Mongols' legacy in the Middle East is still the subject of healthy academic debate.

36. Who were the Mamluks of Egypt, what were their accomplishments, and what factors led to their downfall?

The Arabic verb *malaka* means "to own." The word *mamluk* is a past participle that means "owned." Therefore, *mamluk* means "slave," "owned man," or (in a historical context) "slave soldier." In Egyptian history, there were two distinct periods of Mamluk slave-soldier government: 1250–1382 and 1382–1517.

The first Mamluks, from the Turkish Kipchak tribe, lived in an area north of the Caspian Sea. They were brought to Egypt to serve the Ayyubid sultanate. This line of Mamluks, which would produce twenty-four sultans, is called the Bahri Mamluks because they were garrisoned on the island of Rhoda in the Nile River. (*Bahr* means sea in Arabic.)

The years 1250 to 1279 witnessed the establishment of Mamluk rule in Egypt. The subsequent period, 1279 to 1382, was characterized by dynastic rule and relatively smooth succession. From 1250 to 1257, Egypt was jointly ruled by the first Mamluk sultan, Aybeg, and his wife, Sultana Shajar al-Durr, the widow of the last Ayyubid sultan, as-Salih Nagm al-Din Ayyub. In 1257 Aybeg and Shajar al-Durr were separately murdered, and two years later, Qutuz, a high-ranking Mamluk official, seized power in a military coup, deposing Aybeg's son, 'Ali. In 1260 Mamluks under Sultan Qutuz and General Baybars defeated the Mongols at the Battle of Ayn Jalut, stopping the Mongol advance on Egypt. Baybars then killed Qutuz and became the fourth Mamluk sultan.

Baybars (r. 1260–77) established firm Mamluk control of Egypt. He liberated Antioch from the crusaders; increased the size of the army and navy; sponsored major public works projects, such as the building of citadels, harbors, and canals; and expanded foreign trade. One successor, al-Mansur Qalawun, the seventh sultan (r. 1279–90), established dynastic rule; forged friendly relations with Mediterranean powers; built forts, hospitals, and mosques; and liberated Tripoli (in present-day Lebanon) from crusader control. Al-Ashraf Khalil, the eighth sultan (r. 1290–93), drove the crusaders from Acre, which left them with only the Lebanese enclaves of Beirut, Sidon, and Tyre, all of which would fall to Muslim forces by 1293.

During the second period of Mamluk rule, 1382–1517, succession to the sultanate was not hereditary. Circassian slaves from the Caucasus comprised this line of Mamluks, which produced twenty-three sultans, and were referred to as Burji Mamluks because they were quartered in the Citadel in Cairo. (*Burj* means tower in Arabic.) Whenever the sultanate became vacant, cohorts of slave soldiers backing various candidates for the office would engage in violent barracks warfare until a new sultan emerged.

As we discussed in the previous section, the system of taking foreign boys into slavery to serve in a standing army began with the 'Abbasid caliphate in the ninth century. Many families gave up their sons willingly, knowing that their children, though technically slaves, might rise to great positions of power and influence in an imperial city, such as Cairo. The boys spent years honing their skills in swordsmanship, archery, mounted warfare, and the use of such weapons as the mace and lance.

Under the Mamluks, patronage of the arts and architecture flourished. The U.S. Marine Corps officer's dress sword and the colossal multiuse structures in Cairo are tangible reminders of the era of Mamluk rule. Islamic radicals attacked Mamluk leadership as un-Islamic. Led by Ibn Taymiyya, they charged the Mamluks with usurping religious authority, although from 1261 to 1517 the Mamluks kept in their custody a shadow caliph who had survived the Mongol annihilation of the 'Abbasid family. The Mamluks limited the caliph's powers to the administration of *zakat* and *waqf* and the installation of a new sultan; meanwhile, they introduced non-Islamic statutes, namely, customary law and the equality of a woman's testimony in court. They observed various teachings from all the Sunni schools of jurisprudence instead of following only one. Consequently, the Mamluk law code was an eclectic amalgam of customs, rules, and laws.

New military technologies and the deterioration of the Egyptian economy proved to be the undoing of the Mamluks. They took great pride in their horsemanship but neglected infantry tactics and adopted neither muskets nor artillery. Their emphasis on commerce caused a decline in agricultural production, a famine ensued, and bloody riots broke out. In the late 1400s, during the early period of European exploration, the Mamluks lost their monopoly on the trade of luxury goods from the East Indies to Europe. Finally, the Black Plague devastated Egypt in the thirteenth century.

In 1516 the Ottomans crushed the Mamluks with modern gunpowder weapons at the Battle of Marj Dabiq (Meadow of Dabiq), in northern Syria.[4] The Ottomans took control of Egypt but retained the Mamluks as local rulers. In 1798 Napoleon Bonaparte invaded Egypt; his lopsided victory over the Mamluks at the Battle of the Pyramids severely weakened their power and influence. Mehmet 'Ali, the autonomous pasha of Egypt, massacred several hundred Mamluk leaders and their families in 1811, effectively eliminating them as a rival source of power.

37. What is the legacy of Tamerlane and his descendants in the Middle East?

Tamerlane (1336–1405)—also referred to as Timur-e-Lang or Timur the Lame—was born in the Chaghatay *ulu* in present-day Uzbekistan. He was an ethnic Turk who served as an officer in the Turco-Mongol branch of the Chaghatay army. He gained power and legitimacy through marriage and rapid conquests. He adopted the title *gurkan* (son-in-law) to describe his relationship to the khan of the Chaghatay state. He would become the epitome of the nomad conqueror-ruler; this is arguably his greatest legacy.

Tamerlane consolidated his power and carried out his major conquests during the period 1369–1405. He subdued the fragmented Il-Khanid state in 1393. This victory gave him control over Afghanistan, Iran, Kurdistan, and Iraq. He defeated the Golden Horde in 1395, which added Azerbaijan, Georgia, Armenia, and southern Russia to his realm. He captured northern India in 1399 and seized Aleppo and Damascus in 1401. A year later, he crushed Ottoman forces under Sultan Bayezit I at the Battle of Ankara and transported the vanquished Ottoman leader in an iron cage back to his capital at Samarkand. He then made the Ottomans in Anatolia his vassals. In 1405 he died peacefully as he made preparations to invade China.

In Central Asia, Tamerlane is celebrated as a great leader and warrior; in Baghdad, Damascus, and Delhi, however, he is regarded as a violent scourge who destroyed great cities and built pyramids of human skulls. The Muslim political philosopher Ibn Khaldun commended Tamerlane for unifying much of the Muslim world, and it is reported that while Ibn Khaldun was negotiating the surrender of Damascus with Tamerlane, the Turco-Mongol warrior questioned him at length on the history, politics, and societies of North Africa. Ibn Khaldun was so impressed by his intellectual curiosity that he wrote a character study of Tamerlane.

Tamerlane's conquests coincided with the rise of the nomad conqueror-ruler and the decline of the settled way of life for many inhabitants of the Middle East. He was the roaming warrior-leader par excellence. Nearly always on campaign, he spent about two weeks per year in Samarkand. His absence from the capital resulted in an insecure base of power, and because there was no permanent central authority, he had to be an unyielding ruler to hold the empire together.

A prevailing view of Tamerlane is that he, like the Mongols, inflicted excessive destruction, yet his constant campaigning had a positive effect on both the economy and culture of the region. Long-range commerce flourished and a far-ranging postal service succeeded owing to the extensive road system that was built to facilitate the movement of Tamerlane's army. Persian was established as the primary administrative and literary language of the Muslim world, prompting a renaissance of both Turkish and Persian letters. On the other hand, Tamerlane eradicated the Nestorian Christian community in the east, forcing them to take refuge in Iraq. During the Timurid era, Islamic orthodoxy declined, as rulers switched between the Sunni and Shi'a branches of Islam, owing to either their personal preferences or their political hopes of attracting a loyal following. Sufi and shaman influence became evident throughout the empire.

Tamerlane was succeeded by his son Shahrukh (r. 1405–47), but his empire began its decline immediately after the elder man's death. This development is illustrative of how a charismatic leader, like Tamerlane, has great difficulty establishing a stable, durable regime. After he had passed from the scene, the Mamluks regained control of Syria, and the

Ottomans asserted their authority over Anatolia. A power struggle between Shahrukh's sons hastened the demise of Tamerlane's state.

A remnant of Tamerlane's once vast empire would endure for another four centuries. Babur (ca. 1483–1530), his great-great-great-grandson, established the Mughal (or Mogul) dynasty in India. His successors governed the country as independent monarchs until 1747 and under the tutelage of the British East India Company until 1858.

7

The Rise of the Ottoman
and Safavid Dynasties

I n this chapter, we look at the rise and expansion of two great dynasties
of the early modern era in the Middle East: the Ottoman Turks, who
ruled a vast empire in the Middle East, southeastern Europe, and North
Africa for several centuries, and the Safavids of Persia, who restored the
position of shah, made Shi'ism their state religion, and governed territory
encompassing present-day Iran, part of Iraq, Pakistan, and Afghanistan. We
also investigate the decline and collapse of the Safavid state, signs of decline
in the Ottoman Empire, and cultural achievements of both dynasties.

38. What accounted for the rise and expansion of the
Ottoman Empire under the first ten sultans?

The Ottomans were members of the Kayi tribe, which in turn was part of
the Oghuz tribal federation. The Oghuz tribes had migrated into Persia
and Anatolia alongside the Seljuk Turks, and they formed the backbone
of the Seljuk cavalry. This is a superb example of a tribe moving into
an area and serving a larger tribe or more powerful dynasty. According
to Ottoman tradition, following an important victory over the Byzantine
army, the Seljuk sultan awarded the Kayi leader Ertogrul a fief at Sogut,
in northwestern Anatolia. As the Seljuks fragmented, several fiefs evolved
into petty states or principalities. The Ottomans began their ascent to

power as *ghazis* (Muslim frontier warriors). The *ghazis* were a dynamic fighting force that observed a strict moral and ethical code and was devoted to a particular spiritual guide, usually a Sufi master.

For the most part, the early Ottoman rulers were charismatic, effective leaders; the first ten sultans were unequaled in their character and leadership abilities. The dynasty began with Ertogrul's son Osman I (r. 1280–1326), who became the leader of the early Ottoman state around 1280. He took the title Ghazi (Supreme Warrior) and declared his independence from the Seljuk sultan in 1300. He expanded Ottoman territory in northwest Anatolia and battled the Byzantines at Bursa, Iznik, and Izmit. In 1326, while on his deathbed, his forces took Bursa, which became the first Ottoman capital. "Ottoman" is a European term derived from the Turkish name Osman; subjects under Osman's rule were called Osmanli. In Arabic Osman is 'Uthman.

Orhan I (r. 1326–60) was the first Ottoman to adopt the title of sultan. From 1330 to 1341, a succession crisis in Constantinople weakened Byzantine power in the Balkans. Stefan Dušan, king of Serbia (r. 1331–46), supported one candidate, a member of the Palaeologus family; the other candidate, John Kantakouzenus, gave his daughter Theodora in marriage to Orhan and enjoyed support from the Ottomans. Kantakouzenus emerged the winner and, as Emperor John VI Kantakouzenus (r. 1347–54), allowed the Ottomans to conduct forays across the Turkish Straits. The emperor's invitation to the Ottomans proved to be a fateful decision. On their third raid in 1354, the Ottomans took the fort at Tzympe on the Dardanelles and established a bridgehead on the European side of the Turkish Straits. Ottoman expansion in Europe rapidly followed. This portion of the empire became known as Rumelia; the Asian half was known as Anatolia. In 1354 Orhan took Ankara through suasion, not force, because his *ghazis* would not battle other Muslims. He introduced the practice of recruiting Christian boys from the Balkans for service in the Ottoman military and government, following their conversion to Islam and completion of training. This practice was institutionalized in the *devshirme* system, which is discussed below.

Murat I (r. 1360–89) outflanked the Byzantines at Constantinople and drove into Europe. He conquered Thrace in 1361, Macedonia and Bulgaria in 1371, and Serbia in 1389. In 1366 he established a new capital at Adrianople (Edirne) in Thrace. This act signaled a shift in the center of gravity of the empire toward Europe. The Ottoman victory over the Serbians at the Battle of Kosovo in 1389 opened the region south of the Danube to conquest. Although Murat lost his life, Kosovo marked the first great Ottoman victory over a Christian army. For the Serbians, the battle reinforced their national identity. The Serbian strongman Slobodan Milošević used the Battle of Kosovo to stoke sectarian hatred toward Muslims during the Bosnian War of the early 1990s.

Having conquered large tracts of European territory, the Ottomans faced the problem of governing a large Christian population. Their expansion into Europe mirrored the early Arab conquest in that the subjugated population was treated magnanimously. While Christians were required to pay tribute, they enjoyed political and religious autonomy. For sectarian and taxation reasons, many welcomed the Ottoman conquerors. For example, the Bogomil heresy was persecuted by Orthodox Christian authorities, but the movement mattered little to the Ottomans.[1] Moreover, Stefan Dušan of Serbia had imposed an excessive tax burden on his peasants, requiring them to work two days per week, but the Ottomans mandated only two days of labor per year. As a result, peasants pledged loyalty to the Ottomans in droves, facilitating their conquest.

Bayezit I (r. 1389–1402), known as Yilderim (Thunderbolt), carried out the first Ottoman siege of Constantinople, from 1394 to 1398, but the operation failed. He also pushed deep into Thrace and Bulgaria and defeated a large Christian force at Nicopolis in 1396. A year later, the Ottomans overwhelmed the Turkish state of Karaman, in Anatolia, as part of a campaign to subdue petty Turkish rulers in Anatolia. The offensive incurred the anger of Tamerlane because many of the local leaders were his allies or vassals. In 1402 the armies of Bayezit and Tamerlane met at Ankara, where the Timurids achieved a stunning victory. The sultan was captured and died while he was transported as a war prize back to Samarkand. Tamerlane's success put the brakes on Ottoman expansion, and he reduced the remnants of the Ottoman state in Anatolia to vassalage. Tamerlane died in 1405, and his empire declined.

After a ten-year interregnum, Mehmet I (r. 1413–21) bested his brothers in a power struggle and emerged as sultan. He campaigned in the Aegean,

Balkans, and Anatolia, restoring territories lost by Bayezit. Murat II (r. 1421–44, 1446–51), a Sufi, preferred a peaceful and contemplative way of life. He abdicated in favor of his young son Mehmet, but his retirement was short-lived. A large Christian military coalition, led by the rulers of Poland-Hungary, Wallachia, Albania, and Transylvania, invaded eastern Bulgaria to preempt an Ottoman invasion of Hungary. Murat took back the throne and repelled the Christians at the Battle of Varna in 1444. His victory opened Central and Eastern Europe to Ottoman expansion.

In addition to lighter taxes and religious tolerance, other factors also aided Ottoman expansion in Europe. First, the Ottomans took advantage of a growing power vacuum in the Christian and Muslim worlds. Through a practice called *devshirme*, which means "gathering" in Turkish but is frequently construed as "boy levy," the Ottomans recruited Christian boys in Rumelia and converted them to Islam. The brainiest boys prepared for government service, while the others were trained as highly skilled infantry soldiers, known as janissaries (new troops). The boys' primary loyalty was to the sultan, who provided for their personal needs, educated and trained them, and afforded a few of them access to the highest levels of Ottoman power. Ironically, it was not uncommon for Christian families to support *devshirme*. Service to the sultan was considered a way to achieve upward mobility because a family giving up its son might benefit from his future position within the imperial government.

Second, the Ottomans exploited new military technology, remaining on the cutting edge of advancements in weaponry and ordnance until the late sixteenth century. The Ottomans were the first power in the Middle East to use gunpowder weapons. The other great "Gunpowder Empires" of the early modern era in the Middle East were the Safavids of Persia and the Mughals of India. The term was coined by the scholar Marshall Hodgson in the third volume of his classic work, *The Venture of Islam: Conscience and History in a World Civilization.*[2]

Mehmet II (r. 1444–46, 1451–81), known as Fatih (the Conqueror), was a capable scholar, but his greatest achievement was the capture of Constantinople in May 1453. His attack force included more than 50,000 troops, about 125 ships, and several heavy artillery pieces. In a display of tactical ingenuity, he had his ships towed overland using greased logs, which permitted them to pass around a massive chain that blocked warships from one of the water approaches to Constantinople. Mehmet beseeched the inhabitants of Constantinople to stay and demonstrated great tolerance for Jews, Christians, Greeks, and Armenians. He organized non-Muslims into *millets* (confessional communities) that would manage their own judicial, ecclesiastical, and educational affairs. The city was the natural center of the empire and was renamed Istanbul, which was derived from the Greek phrase meaning "in the city." He brought most of the southern Balkans and Greece into the empire, gained control over the Black Sea and islands of the Aegean, secured most of Anatolia, and acquired Crimea. In 1480 his troops briefly occupied southern Italy.

Bayezit II (r. 1481–1512), a poet by avocation, achieved naval superiority in the Mediterranean, using naval warriors known as sea *ghazis*. He faced an uprising of Shi'a Turcoman tribes in Anatolia who had been emboldened by Shah Isma'il of Persia. Selim I (r. 1512–20), called Yavuz (the Stern or Implacable), forced his father to abdicate when the Shi'a rebellion reached Bursa. He crushed the rebellion and then defeated Isma'il at the Battle of Chalderan, in eastern Anatolia, in 1514. The Persian forces used spears and swords against Ottoman muskets and artillery. In 1516 Selim I defeated the Mamluks at the Battle of Marj Dabiq and wrested control of Syria. A year later, he seized Cairo and the Hijaz, on the Red Sea coast of Arabia. Again, the Ottoman foe lacked modern weapons. After conquering Egypt, a surviving member of the 'Abbasid family—the shadow caliph residing in Cairo—allegedly transferred the caliphate to Selim. During his relatively short reign, he tripled the size of the empire.

Suleyman I (r. 1520–66), hailed as Kanuni (the Lawgiver) throughout the empire and known as the Magnificent in the West, was a man of both the sword and the pen. He reformed the Ottoman legal code, streamlining statutes that improved both public administration and the regulation of inheritance, salaries, rank, ceremonies, commerce, taxes, and feudal matters. He championed education and elevated the status of Jews and Christians in the empire. He proved his military mettle by capturing Belgrade and Rhodes. He also undertook campaigns against Vienna in 1526 and 1529, but both efforts failed. After the Battle of Mohacs in 1526, Hungary was added to the empire. He drove the Portuguese fleet from the Red Sea and defeated the Persians twice, taking Baghdad, southern Iraq, and the Persian Gulf. Under the Treaty of Amasya (1555) with the Safavid Persians, the Ottomans retained Iraq, Armenia, Kurdistan, and Basra. The Ottoman fleet took all of North Africa, except Tunis and Morocco. Suleyman I's reign marked the zenith of the Ottoman Empire, as its power, institutions, and culture flourished.

Selim II (r. 1566–74), variously nicknamed the Drunkard, Sot, or Debauched, was not the most capable heir to the throne, but he *was* the son of Suleyman's favorite wife, Hurrem (Roxelana). By 1571 his forces had seized Tunis and Cyprus, but his navy suffered a major setback at the hands of a Christian coalition at the Battle of Lepanto that same year. The Spanish then captured Tunis, but the Ottomans reclaimed it in 1574. Does Selim II's reign mark the beginning of the end of the empire? He was certainly more concerned with affairs of the harem than matters of state, and as a result, the empire suffered. By his death, the empire had passed its peak. A long period of stagnation and decline followed, but the empire was far from finished.

39. What were the major institutions of the Ottoman government?

In the Ottoman state, the sultan was the supreme authority. He was commander in chief of the military, chief enforcer of Shari'a, and—after 1517—the caliph, yet he was not an absolute ruler. He governed with the advice of his imperial council, the clergy, the military establishment, and the women of the harem, particularly his usually headstrong and politically astute mother. While the Ottoman court had its share of intrigues and violence, a primitive form of checks and balances did exist. By ruling with the guidance of key individuals and institutions, the sultan remained faithful to the Qur'an's directive to practice *shura* (consultation) when making major decisions that affected the lives of many.

There were dichotomies in the Ottoman system, principally the inner-outer split, which indicated that an individual's importance derived from his or her proximity to the sultan because the power of the ruler radiated outward. In the early stages of the empire, the sultan was the undisputed head of the government, yet he could be overruled in religious matters. In later years, he became a mere figurehead. It is also important to recognize the two Ottoman social classes: the *askeri* and the *reaya*. The former was the Ottoman ruling class, while the latter encompassed all other people in the empire—the workers and producers.

The four branches of the Ottoman government—administrative, military, scribal, and cultural—were supervised by the sultan. The first three branches were staffed by slaves or members of the Ottoman family; slaves did not serve in the cultural branch.

The administrative branch consisted of the harem, inner service, and outer service. The harem was the private residence of the sultan and his family, including his concubines. The inner service comprised the powerful chief black eunuch, who oversaw the harem; chief white eunuch, who supervised the royal household staff; the sultan's spiritual adviser (a Sufi); the sultan's mother; and the sultan's family. Because the harem comprised—in large part—captured women, some concubines provided to rival states valuable intelligence on Ottoman trade, military preparations, and the state of relations between the sultan and his ministers and generals. The outer service consisted almost exclusively of the imperial council, or divan, which was the first layer of government outside the inner service.

The five core members of the divan were the grand vizier, chief scribe, janissary commander, and chief judges of Anatolia and Rumelia. The grand vizier was the chief administrator of the outer service, who had the power to oversee all government functions. The sultan appointed him and could overrule his decisions. The chief scribe oversaw foreign affairs and fiscal matters. The janissary chief commanded the infantry and answered only to the sultan. The chief judges, or *qadis*, administered justice in the European and Asian halves of the empire. The judiciary was further divided into religious and military courts. A *qadi* presided over the former, a military judge (*qadi asker*) over the latter.

The empire was divided into provinces (*vilayet*), each headed by a provincial governor (*beylerbey*), and each province was further divided into districts (sing. *sanjak*), led by a district representative (*mutasarrif*). Finally, each district was subdivided into fiefs. Under the Ottomans, a fief was known as a *timar*.

The military branch contained an assortment of combat and supporting elements. The janissaries, who were crack infantrymen trained in the latest firearms, formed the core of the army and included approximately

10,000 troops by the mid-sixteenth century. They were recruited through
the practice of *devshirme* (described in the response to Question 38), were
under the direct control of the sultan, and were completely dependent on
him. (An embroidered spoon was woven into their headdresses, symbol-
izing this relationship.) The janissaries observed a strict code of discipline,
and owing to their Christian origins, the sultan could use them to fight his
Muslim enemies.

Royal or regular *sipahis* were the sultan's cavalry. Royal pages and
janissaries filled their ranks. Feudal *sipahis* were free-born Muslim
cavalrymen commanded by a provincial governor. Nearly identical to the
iqta' system described in chapter 5, the award of a *timar* to an Ottoman
nobleman ensured a ready number of *sipahis*. Each property holder was
free to exploit the resources of his *timar*, so long as he reported for duty to
the sultan with the specified number of battle-ready horse soldiers. Both
types of *sipahis* had remarkable striking power. Their weaponry typically
included sword, lance, javelin, mace, and bow and arrow.

Initially, the sultan required his nobles to rotate from one *timar* to another,
to prevent the rise of rival centers of power. Later, they were permitted
to settle in one area, and the *timars* became hereditary. A system of tax
farming (*iltizam*) soon developed. The landholder–tax farmer (*multizim*)
would squeeze his peasants for tax money and then provide cash to the
sultan in place of *sipahis*. The practices of hereditary landholding and tax
farming contributed to the weakening of the empire. The *sipahis* declined
in power and influence relative to the janissaries, whose esprit de corps
was fortified by their devotion to the Bektashi Sufi order. Furthermore,
Suleyman favored the janissaries over the *sipahis* within the Ottoman
military establishment.

In the early 1500s, the Ottoman navy had a fleet of approximately
four hundred ships. It was commanded by a *kapudan pasha*. The technical
services included engineering, logistics, artillery, and ordnance branches.
Akinjis were irregular cavalry, while *'azabs* were irregular infantry. These
fighters served as frontline cannon fodder. They risked their lives for one
purpose: the acquisition of booty.

The scribal branch consisted of the executive office of the divan, chan-
cery, and treasury. Its skilled bureaucrats drafted government documents,

maintained records, collected taxes, paid government salaries, and met other monetary obligations.

Last, the cultural branch oversaw religious matters, education, and law. It was staffed by Muslims, not slaves. The shaykh al-Islam, who managed the branch, was nominated by the grand vizier, and the sultan either approved or rejected the nomination. He was the chief mufti and, as a one-man supreme court, ruled on the Islamic appropriateness of laws or decrees issued on behalf of the sultan. He had the power to revoke an order of the sultan but did so infrequently. He appointed all religious officials except the two chief judges. A rudimentary system of checks and balances existed between the cultural branch and the sultan.

40. What accounted for the rise and development of the Safavid state?

The Safavid dynasty, which ruled Persia from the start of the sixteenth century through the mid-eighteenth century, marked a crucial stage in the development of the Persian-Iranian state. The Il-Khanid *ulu* of the Mongols fragmented in the 1350s and was absorbed by Tamerlane, whose empire crumbled in the fifteenth century. In the fourteenth century, Persia had been about 80 percent Sunni; today, Iran is 95 percent Shi'a. In the medieval era, Persia witnessed a resurgence in Sufism. The Safavid brotherhood was a prominent Sufi order.

The Safavids were ethnic Turks. They spoke Turkish but advanced Persian culture. They adopted Persian as their everyday language, but from the fourteenth century until 1922, the court language in Persia was Turkish. The original Safavid leaders were Sufi shaykhs who followed a militant Sufi order in Azerbaijan led by Safi al-Din (d. 1334), a Sunni Muslim. He founded the Safavid order in the early 1300s. His descendants controlled the mosque at Ardabil, which served as the Safavid base.

Like the Ottomans, the Safavids were nominally Sunni in belief but Sufi in practice. After the demise of the Il-Khanid state in the late 1300s, the Safavids became Shi'a Muslims. Scholars are not sure why they became Shi'a. They may have done it to differentiate themselves from the Ottomans. Because western Persia was caught between Sunni and Shi'a orbits, it was relatively easy for its inhabitants to tilt to Shi'ism. The area making up western Persia and eastern Anatolia was a veritable cauldron of religious practices: Sunni, Shi'a, and Sufi.

Tamerlane conquered Persia in the late fourteenth century, but the Safavid order continued to grow. The decline of Tamerlane's empire following his death led to the emergence of several small dynastic states in Persia, most of them ruled by rival nomadic tribes, such as the Black Sheep and White Sheep Turcomans.

Under the leadership of Shaykh Junayd (d. 1460) and the protection of the Black Sheep Turcomans, who were Shi'a, the Safavids began converting large numbers of Turks in Azerbaijan and Anatolia to Shi'ism. When the Black Sheep Turcomans betrayed Shaykh Junayd and drove him from Ardabil, he formed political and marital alliances with the White Sheep Turcomans of eastern Anatolia, who were Sunnis.

Junayd's successor Shaykh Haydar (d. 1488) developed distinctive red headgear for his Turkish converts. Wearing these caps, the Safavid cavalry soldiers became known as *kizilbash* (Turkish for "redhead"). This development marked the emergence of the Safavids as a military and political force, in addition to being a Sufi order. The *kizilbash* earned a solid reputation as *ghazis* among the heterodox Turcoman tribes of western Persia and eastern Anatolia. They regained their base at Ardabil.

In the late fifteenth century, there were several competing powers in the region. The Ottomans were consolidating their empire in Anatolia and the Balkans. The Shi'a Black Sheep Turcomans competed with the Sunni White Sheep Turcomans in eastern Anatolia, taking turns as the protectors of the Safavids. At the end of the fifteenth century, the Safavids with their *kizilbash* troops challenged the White Sheep for leadership of the region. The latter resisted and went about capturing or killing members of the Safavid family. By 1494 the only prominent Safavid still standing was seven-year-old Isma'il, the grandson of Junayd. He went into hiding and eluded capture.

In 1500 Isma'il and his *kizilbash* followers fomented a rebellion against the White Sheep Turcomans in Anatolia. Turkish Shi'a tribal warriors supported Isma'il, and in early 1501, he decisively defeated the White Sheep. That same year, Isma'il was proclaimed shah (Persian for "king") by the *kizilbash*. A year later, he took Tabriz from the White Sheep and established the Safavid state. Within a decade, he controlled all of Persia.

Shah Isma'il (r. 1501–24) established Shi'ism as the state religion with a simple edict: "Convert or die." He and his followers, especially his soldiers, believed that he was divinely inspired and that he was receiving guidance from the Hidden Imam. His Sufi poetry espoused his divinity.

The principal source of Isma'il's power was the *kizilbash*, who provided him with military strength and revenue; in return, he rewarded them with fiefs. His rule posed a direct threat to the Ottomans because the janissaries belonged to the Bektashi Sufi order. They were Sunnis, but they revered Isma'il as a great Sufi leader. They studied his poetry and were fascinated by the mystery cult that surrounded him. What kept the janissaries in line was their loyalty to the Ottoman sultan. He had to deal with his Persian adversary; battle lines were drawn between Selim I and Isma'il.

At the Battle of Chalderan (1514), Ottoman musketry and artillery crushed Isma'il's army. The battle profoundly affected Isma'il's claim of divinity, which was now suspect. Henceforth, he downplayed it. He lost some of his luster and credibility, but his state did not collapse. A power struggle ensued between Isma'il and the *kizilbash*, who wanted to establish a ruling oligarchy drawn from their ranks, but the shah managed to stay ahead of them. He also embraced gunpowder technology.

Under Isma'il, orthodox Shi'ism was taken up and advanced, and the Safavids became its chief guardians. Orthodoxy provided unity and stability for the state, and Shi'ism served to differentiate Persia from the Ottoman Empire. Scholars were brought from Lebanon and Iraq to codify Shi'a practice and doctrine. By the late sixteenth century, Shi'ism in Persia was firmly established and well-articulated. Religious centers were set up, the chief of which was in Qom. Traditions, clerical hierarchy, and ritual practices, including public flagellation for atonement of sin, were developed by the end of the century.

Persian Shi'a initiated the Ta'ziya, the passion play commemorating the death of Imam Husayn, the Prophet Muhammad's grandson, at Karbala in 680. The Ta'ziya is an iconic feature of Shi'a culture because it re-creates an important event and is highly interactive. The audience cheers the actors playing Husayn and his followers and jeers the actors portraying Caliph Yazid and his troops. The play provides Shi'ism with a strong identity, but it is a public event, not a religious act. The reign of Isma'il was a defining period in modern Persian-Iranian history. He restored the institution of the shah, made Twelve-Imam Shi'ism the state religion, and oversaw the formulation of Shi'a doctrine and practice.

Shah Tahmasp (r. 1524–76) reasserted central control over the country by neutralizing the power of the *kizilbash*. He sparred with Sultan Suleyman for several years but in 1555 signed the Treaty of Amasya, which stabilized the frontier between the two empires.

'Abbas (r. 1588–1629) was the most accomplished shah of the Safavid era. He built the great capital at Isfahan and improved civil administration, seeking to establish a dynamic, centralized state that would function on par with the Ottomans. He formed a corps of slave soldiers—the *ghulams*—comprising Christian boys from the Caucasus. He hoped that a regular, professional army, like the janissaries, would enable him to rein in the power of the *kizilbash*, who had become a threat to the Safavid government.

Aside from creating a modern army, 'Abbas's program of reforms ultimately failed. First, agricultural production declined as cheap New World silver flooded into the country, debasing the national currency and driving down the cash value of crops. Consequently, nomads became more prominent in the countryside. Second, although he broke the power of the *kizilbash*, he could never check the strength of nomadic warriors, particularly their tribal cavalry. He never had enough *ghulams* to control the nomads. And third, he spent more time in his capital than on campaign, indicating that the era of the nomad conqueror-ruler was drawing to a close. Parts of Persia became increasingly autonomous, while central control was becoming more the exception than the rule. Despite these setbacks, the reign of 'Abbas marked the zenith of Safavid authority in Persia. His successors were generally incompetent and incorrigible.

41. What contributed to the decline and collapse of the Safavid state?

From 1629 to 1722, the power of the Safavid shahs along with the central authority of the state steadily wore away. The country suffered from famines, insurrections, the instability wrought by nomadic warlords, and—most significantly—weak, incompetent shahs who had been sheltered in the harem during their formative years. Shah Sultan Husayn (r. 1694–1722), who undertook matters of state with a demonstrably carefree demeanor, was the last independent Safavid ruler.

Resistance to the central government increased, especially in Afghanistan, which had long been targeted for forced conversion to Shi'ism. The Safavids carried out harsh measures against the Afghan population, including taking the daughters of Afghan officials for the pleasure of Safavid governors. In 1709 the Pashtun tribal leader Mirwais Khan Hotak (d. 1715) fomented an uprising against the Safavid governor, killed him, and declared the independence of southern Afghanistan. In 1718 Afghans invaded Persia and four years later took Isfahan and removed Sultan Husayn from power. The Afghan victory underscores how corrupt and ineffective the Safavid shahs had become.

The Ottomans now confronted a threatening Sunni force on their border, instead of a hostile Shi'a power. Nevertheless, the Ottomans were reluctant to fight the Afghans because they were fellow Sunnis. In 1724 the Russians responded to the Afghan threat and occupied the territory around the Caspian Sea. The Russian deployment prompted the Ottomans to act. They invaded Persia and thus became tacit allies of the Russians. Afghan military efforts collapsed in the face of the Russian incursion and Ottoman invasion. The Afghans sued for peace and ceded territory in western Persia. In 1724 the Russians and Ottomans signed a treaty in which they recognized each other's territorial acquisitions in Persia and pledged to support the Safavids in the ongoing struggle against the Afghans. The Safavids took refuge in Khurasan, where they established a rump state.

In 1726 Nadir Afshar, a Turcoman Afghan warlord, joined the court of Tahmasp II, serving as his army commander. He also served as the regent for puppet shahs until 1736. In 1729 he expelled the Afghans from Isfahan, and by 1735 he had recovered all lost Safavid territory. A year later, upon the death of the child shah 'Abbas III, he coerced tribal leaders to elevate him to the Persian throne; he took the name Nadir Shah (r. 1736–47). In 1739 he defeated Mughal armies near Delhi, and after he had emptied the Mughal treasury, he reinstated the Mughal ruler as his vassal.

Nadir Shah attempted to reconcile Sunnis and Shi'a by establishing a fifth *madhhab* of Islamic jurisprudence, the Shi'a-based Ja'fari school. In

1743 Ottoman and Persian clerics met at Najaf and papered over differences between the two branches of Islam. Ultimately, Nadir's initiative was a great failure. Many Sunnis balked at a number of Shi'a beliefs and practices, namely, veneration of the imamate and temporary marriage. It is worth noting that this event marks the beginning of an independent Shi'a clerical class in Persia. Clerics worked independently of the government and—by virtue of *waqf*—were not dependent on the ruler for support. They had a profound influence on Persian-Iranian society and the politics of the nineteenth and twentieth centuries, which culminated in the Constitutional Revolt of 1906 and Iranian Revolution of 1979. Nadir was murdered by his troops in 1747. He had become a cruel tyrant and exhibited signs of insanity.

The years 1747–94 were a time of political decline, foreign intervention, and domestic chaos in Persia. The Safavids were unable to gain complete control of the country. From 1750 to 1779, the Persian Zand dynasty governed southern Persia on behalf of a Safavid puppet shah. In the 1770s, the Qajars, a *kizilbash* tribe, asserted their independence in northern Persia. In 1794, under Agha Mohammed Khan (ca. 1742–97), they established a dynasty that would last until 1922.

The Safavid dynasty (1501–1794) made essential contributions to the formation of the modern Persian-Iranian state. It laid the groundwork for a central governing authority and established Shi'ism as the state religion. It must be emphasized that the history of the dynasty is relevant in light of current developments. Militant Islamist groups, such as al-Qa'ida and ISIS, refer to Shi'a as al-Safawiin (the Safavids). The label is meant to sow sectarian anger by reminding Sunnis of forced conversions to Shi'ism and the Shi'a's undermining of Ottoman expansion into the heart of Europe by presenting a hostile Shi'a force on the eastern frontier of the empire. The Safavids took advantage of an Ottoman army, on campaign in Europe, to seize Shi'a holy sites in Iraq.

42. What initiated the decline of the Ottoman Empire?

The demise of the Ottoman Empire was a significant development of the early twentieth century because it has influenced relationships between nations of the Middle East and Europe to this day. Determining when the empire began its decline is a complicated historical task because there are so many scholarly opinions, ranging from the advent of the European age of discovery to Napoleon Bonaparte's invasion of Egypt. Setting aside this debate, we can see that the seeds of decline were sown as early as the reign of Suleyman.

Several important factors explain the decline of the Ottoman state. First, following the death of Suleyman, the empire suffered from increasingly mediocre civilian and military leadership. Sultans became increasingly involved in the affairs of the harem and neglected the functions of government. Beginning in the early 1600s, Ottoman princes were "imprisoned" in the harem. They did not gain practical experience as either military commanders or provincial governors. The military establishment, including the janissaries, became civilianized, and many soldiers took up commerce and the trades. Bureaucrats bought their offices and sold subordinate posts to other office seekers, and everyone in the ruling establishment gouged peasants and laborers with exorbitant taxes and fees. Senior military posts and political offices were awarded on the basis of family ties, not merit. Finally, autonomous rulers emerged in the provinces, even establishing their own dynasties, most notably Mehmet 'Ali of Egypt in the early 1800s.

Second, the fighting edge of the Ottoman military declined significantly. A technology gap developed between the empire and Europe. The Ottomans had enjoyed military superiority for so long that they neglected to keep up with the West. The janissaries still used firearms, but their discipline and fighting skills had deteriorated. They browbeat the sultan into giving them more liberties and personal benefits. They married, started businesses, and resisted campaigning. By the seventeenth century, the *devshirme* system had ended. Janissaries were recruited from the general population, and the sons of janissaries joined the corps. By the 1680s, the Ottoman government acknowledged the military decline, but it was too late to reverse it completely. In 1699 the Ottomans ceded Hungary after they had lost a war to Austrians, who had employed superior arms and tactics. The effectiveness of the janissary corps continued to wane during the eighteenth century. Its members acted more like a Praetorian Guard or urban gang than a formidable combat force.

Third, the empire suffered from severe economic problems. The Ottoman currency was based on silver, but it had become devalued by the flood of cheap silver from America into Europe. The Ottoman economy never overcame the astronomically high inflation. Additionally, new trade patterns emerged to the Ottomans' extreme disadvantage. The Europeans bypassed the Middle East, particularly Ottoman-controlled territory, sailing around Africa to reach the riches of East Asia. By the sixteenth century, the Portuguese were well established in Africa, the Persian Gulf, India, and East Asia, and the Spanish had major territorial holdings in the Americas. Losing control over east-west overland trade was a severe blow to the Ottoman economy. The Ottomans were also locked out of European markets by the policy of mercantilism, a system of trade that was stacked against them. Owing to their country's deteriorating economy, the government could not afford military improvements. Overtaxed peasants flocked to the cities.

And fourth, Ottoman society suffered from scientific and cultural stagnation. By the seventeenth century, the Ottomans consistently exhibited a militantly negative attitude toward science. For example, in 1577 Sultan Murat III (r. 1574–95) built an observatory near Istanbul. A plague broke out, and the 'ulama blamed the epidemic on research being performed at the observatory; the janissaries destroyed it in 1578. Meanwhile, Europe was experiencing the full flowering of the scientific revolution and Enlightenment. Ottoman religious leaders saw Western culture and science as a threat to Muslim society. In 1730 the first Arabic-alphabet printing press was introduced. A fatwa was required because religious and political authorities were concerned about the corruption of the Qur'an and complaints from calligraphers who feared that they would be put out of work.

It is significant to note that the Ottomans took steps to check their decline. They knew that they must emulate Europe to reverse their fortunes and revive the era of Suleyman. From the mid-1600s through the early 1700s, the Koprulu family supplied a series of reforming viziers. Mehmet Koprulu (r. 1656–61) initiated a program to reform the empire at all levels. He fought corruption and graft, defeated the Venetians, and smashed revolts in Transylvania and Anatolia. His son Ahmet (r. 1661–76) restored *devshirme* and implemented measures to strengthen the Ottoman government. In 1669 the Ottomans seized Crete, and in 1676 they took Ukraine. In 1683 the Ottoman army, under Grand Vizier Kara Mustapha (r. 1676–83), marched to Vienna and placed the city under siege. King Jan Sobieski of Poland (r. 1674–96) arrived with a large army and saved the Hapsburg capital. Between 1683 and 1774, the empire experienced setbacks and victories. The Austrians rolled the Ottomans back to the Balkans, and in 1699 both powers signed the Treaty of Karlowitz, which confirmed the cession of Hungary to the Austrians. In 1703 the janissaries who opposed the treaty deposed Sultan Mustafa II. In 1718 the Austrians again defeated the Ottomans, and the latter forfeited Belgrade under the terms of the Treaty of Passarowitz.

The years 1718 to 1730 were known as the Tulip Era. As the price of tulips skyrocketed in Europe, owning bulbs became a symbol of wealth and conspicuous consumption. Paradoxically, in the Ottoman Empire, it was a time of artistic, architectural, and literary achievement as well as military and political stagnation. It marked the beginning of Istanbul's effort to learn more about and from the West. In 1721 the Ottomans sent an embassy to France, and that generated a mania for French culture, namely, food, fashion, furniture, and gardening. During the 1730s, the Comte de Bonneval (1675–1747), a French convert to Islam, operated a school of geometry and artillery for selected military units. Characteristically, the existence of the school was kept secret out of fear that the janissaries would destroy it.

In 1739 the Ottomans rebounded and retook Belgrade, which was sealed by the Treaty of Belgrade. The empire's rise and its long decline were marked by both peaks and valleys. A year later, the Ottomans signed a capitulation treaty with France, the first of many with European powers. Capitulations were concessions granted to the citizens of a foreign state. The 1740 treaty stipulated low duties for French imports; no arrest of a French citizen, except in the presence of a French diplomat; no trial of a French citizen, except in a French consular court; and the recognition of Roman Catholics in the empire as French citizens. Treaties with Great Britain, the Netherlands, and Russia would follow. The Ottomans signed these lopsided treaties because they were desperate for foreign trade; they needed Western goods and hard currency. The system of capitulations became corrupt with the sale of certificates of citizenship by European embassies and consulates to Christians and Jews of the empire. The practice generated great resentment among Ottoman Muslims.

The Ottomans had to deal with rebellions in Arabia and Egypt in the eighteenth century. In the Arabian Peninsula, the fundamentalist religious scholar Muhammad Ibn 'Abd al-Wahhab (ca. 1703–92) preached a strict interpretation of Islamic law and theology. In the 1740s, he joined forces with Muhammad Ibn Sa'ud (d. 1765), the leader of a tribal federation in central Arabia. Their religious-political partnership would ultimately lead to the founding of the Kingdom of Saudi Arabia in the twentieth century. The Wahhabis rejected Ottoman rule and from 1803 to 1818 controlled the holy cities of Mecca and Medina. Meanwhile, in Egypt the Mamluk governor Ali Bey al-Kabir (r. 1768–72), took advantage of the war between Russia and the Ottoman Empire to assert his independence from the sultan and dispatch his army to the Hijaz and Syria, which the army briefly held. He was deposed and murdered by his military commander, Abu al-Dahab (r. 1772–75), who signed his own commercial treaty with the British governor in Bengal. In the late eighteenth century, the Ottomans regained a tenuous hold on Egypt, but their achievement was short-lived. In 1798 Napoleon Bonaparte invaded and occupied the country; French forces held it until 1801. Following the eviction of the French, domestic troubles in Egypt lead to the rise of Mehmet 'Ali Pasha, who would create the modern Egyptian state and establish a dynasty that would rule the country until the Egyptian Revolution of 1952.

Starting in 1769, the Russians and Ottomans fought a five-year war that resulted in a significant Russian victory. The subsequent Treaty of Kuchuk Kaynarja was a watershed event in Ottoman history. The empire ceded considerable territory to a European power and extended to that power tremendous influence over a large sector of the population. The treaty recognized Russian sovereignty over Crimea and established a Russian protectorate over the Orthodox Christians of the empire, but it allowed the sultan to retain the role of caliph over the Muslims of Crimea.

43. What were significant cultural achievements of the Ottoman and Safavid states?

The rival Ottoman and Safavid dynasties attained extraordinary achievements in the fields of art and architecture. Throughout their far-flung empire, the Ottomans built exquisite mosques, palaces, madrasas, hospitals, mausoleums, baths, fortresses, and bridges. They were heavily influenced by Byzantine builders, especially in the use of great domes. The master of Ottoman architecture was Mimar Sinan (ca. 1489–1588), a former janissary and military engineer who became Suleyman's court architect and designed more than three hundred buildings over his long career. He solved the conundrum of how to fit a giant dome onto a square building by employing graceful arches and half domes. His signature creations are the Mosque of Suleyman in Istanbul and the Mosque of Selim in Edirne. Ottoman calligraphers advanced their refined skill to high art, producing exquisite government documents and designing for each sultan an emblematic signature, known as a *tughra*. Coinage served a practical purpose and achieved a level of sublime beauty. Mints in Cairo, Tunisia, Aden, and Istanbul produced coins of the same weight, facilitating trade by enabling a merchant from Cairo to use Egyptian coins in Yemen or Tunisia, and vice versa, with little need for exchange. The early centuries of the empire were renowned for scholarship in the fields of theology, philosophy, history, geography, mathematics, and astronomy. *Kitab-i Bahriye* (Book of Navigation, 1521), by the Ottoman admiral, geographer, and cartographer Piri Reis (ca. 1465–1553), contains detailed maps of the known world, including the eastern edge of the Americas. The Ottomans built an astronomical observatory in Istanbul in the late sixteenth century, but—as noted above—it was destroyed by the janissaries. The codification of administrative law, which supplemented Shari'a, was undertaken by the Ottomans. This effort was an early attempt to separate religious and secular law.

Shah 'Abbas the Great advanced commerce and manufacturing in the Persian Safavid Empire. He recruited skilled artisans from China to produce exquisite ceramics and glazed tiles, and the Chinese potters passed their know-how on to their Persian counterparts. Under 'Abbas the manufacture of carpets became a major industry, employing thousands of

weavers. Persian carpets were in high demand overseas. At the end of the
sixteenth century, 'Abbas moved his capital to Isfahan in central Persia and
began construction of one of the most extraordinarily beautiful cities in the
world. His architects revived the art of urban planning and designed a city
in which broad, straight avenues connected the palace and royal gardens in
the northern portion of the city to the residential area in the south. A large
rectangular park, with shopping arcades, a polo field, and the magnificent
Shah's Mosque occupied the city center. The mosque, one of the most treasured places of worship in the Muslim world, is covered with elaborately
decorated blue tiles. Any visitor to Isfahan will no doubt concur with the
Persian saying "Isfahan is half the world." The Blue Mosque in Mazar-i-
Sharif, Afghanistan, is another superb example of Safavid blue-tile architecture. The Safavids were also masters at painting astonishing murals and
exquisite miniatures, depicting paradise, battles, and the wonders of nature.

8

The Rise of Western Influence in the Middle East

I n this chapter, we examine the origins of European imperialism in the Middle East, specifically the strategic interests of the major European powers—Russia, Austria, Great Britain, France, and Germany—as they relate to the Ottoman state. The chapter continues with a discussion of the efforts of Mehmet 'Ali to establish a modern, Western-style country in Egypt and attempts by Ottoman rulers to stay competitive with the West through extensive top-to-bottom reform.

44. What interests did the Great Powers of Europe have in the Ottoman Empire?

The European powers began their encroachment into Ottoman territory in the late seventeenth century in the wake of the Ottoman defeat at Vienna. In answer to this question, we examine the designs on the Middle East—particularly the declining Ottoman Empire—of five European powers: Russia, Austria, Great Britain, France, and Germany.

In the late seventeenth and early eighteenth centuries, Czar Peter the Great of Russia (r. 1682–1721) had two national objectives that directly affected the Ottoman Empire. First, he sought a warm-water port for his icebound country. With Western technical assistance, he built up the Russian army and navy and challenged the Ottomans. Second, he aspired to assume the responsibility to protect Orthodox Christians within the empire. Both of his goals were later achieved by Empress Catherine the Great (r. 1762–96) through a successful war with the Ottomans (1769–74) and the subsequent Treaty of Kuchuk Kaynarja.

The Russians made significant advances into the Middle East under Peter and Catherine. Peter drove into the Caspian area in the 1720s and battled the Afghans, who had vanquished the Safavids in Persia. The Russians under Catherine defeated the Ottomans in the Black Sea area. By the terms of the Treaty of Kuchuk Kaynarja, the Russians obtained the Crimea and were granted the right to protect and exercise limited authority over Orthodox Christians residing in the Ottoman state. The latter provision indicated that the sultan had forfeited significant power to a foreign ruler. He had granted or would grant concessions—also known as capitulations—to other powers. The French gained the right to protect Roman Catholics in the empire; the British would safeguard Protestants. Soon, the capitulations extended to commercial privileges, extraterritoriality, and passports.

A third Russian goal also affected the Ottomans: the promotion of Pan-Slavism. The advocates of Pan-Slavism believed that all Slavic peoples should be united under Russian leadership and protection. The policy would inevitably lead to conflict with both the Austrians and Ottomans because both empires had large Slavic populations. The Ottomans were under extreme pressure to relinquish territory populated by Slavs, but they could not do so freely because they could not surrender any part of the Dar al-Islam. This commitment explains why the terms of the Treaty of Karlowitz (1699) and other concessionary treaties were a shock to the Ottoman state and the Islamic world.

Finally, in the nineteenth century, the Russians sought territory in eastern Anatolia to block the spread of pan-Turkic ideology into the Caucasus and Central Asia. They worried that Pan-Turkism would undermine their control over the Azeri, Turkmen, Uzbek, Kazakh, and Kyrgyz peoples of the Russian Empire.

The Austrians, ruled by the Hapsburg dynasty, sought to dominate commerce in the Danube River region and expand their empire in the Balkans. They also perceived themselves as the protectors of independent

Balkan states. Their expansion in the Balkans naturally led to conflict with the Russians, who were advocating Pan-Slavism. This rivalry between St. Petersburg and Vienna would culminate in World War I.

The British Empire's foremost concerns were securing the territory of its Indian colony, protecting the lines of communication between Britain and India, and opposing French and Russian expansion into the Middle East. Britain acquired India after it had defeated the French at the Battle of Plassey (1757), near Bombay, during the Seven Years' War. The British East India Company subsequently established stations at Aden, Muscat, Dubai, Bahrain, and Kuwait. The British government regarded the Ottoman Empire as the principal defender of its trade routes, both overland and by steamship, to India. Therefore, the British, in turn, protected the Ottomans. Britain's policy culminated in military and diplomatic actions during the 1850s and 1870s that saved the Ottomans from Russian expansion. In 1882 British forces invaded Egypt to protect the Suez Canal from a nationalist uprising known as the 'Urabi Revolt.

France's historic enemy was Great Britain. The French hoped to avenge their defeats at the hands of the British, regain territory lost in the Seven Years' War, and stay ahead of the British in the race for colonies. The French enjoyed a long involvement with the Ottoman Empire, and both states had a mutual enemy—the Austrians. The Ottomans and French engaged in diplomatic and cultural contact during the Tulip Era of the early 1700s, which witnessed increased contact between the Ottomans and Europe, and the French supplied the empire with its first Western military advisers. The French enjoyed close ties with the Catholic and Maronite populations of the Ottoman Empire and signed the first capitulations with the Ottomans in 1740. They gained a brief military toehold in the empire with Napoleon Bonaparte's invasion of Egypt in 1798. During the French occupation, Bonaparte launched a hearts-and-minds program: *la mission civilisatrice* (the civilizing mission). The French were eventually ousted by a joint British-Ottoman force in 1801. Mehmet 'Ali, the future autonomous ruler of Egypt, was a senior Ottoman officer during the campaign.

The French tried again to solidify their presence in Egypt with the construction of the Suez Canal. In 1854 they won the concession to build the waterway, which opened in 1869, but they were checked by the British, who eventually gained a controlling financial interest in the canal. With the British dominant in Egypt, the French focused on North Africa. They annexed Algeria in 1830 and eventually gained control of Tunisia and Morocco. France's ties to the Ottoman Empire were defined by culture, economics, religion, and competition with the other powers.

Following the proclamation of the German Empire in 1871, German Kaiser Wilhelm II (r. 1888–1918) sought closer diplomatic and economic ties with the Ottoman Empire, building on the existing Prussian-Ottoman military relationship. His overtures culminated in winning the contract to build a railway from Berlin to Baghdad. Begun in 1903, the railway would enable Germany to outflank the Suez Canal to reach the eastern world, increase its trade and influence in the Persian Gulf and greater Middle East, and strengthen its links to its colonies in Africa. A gulf dominated by Germany would directly threaten Britain's ties with India. The railway was unfinished by the outbreak of World War I in 1914.

45. How did the Ottomans and the European powers deal with the threat posed by Russia to the Ottoman Empire, an issue known as the Eastern Question?

Czarist Russia posed an existential threat to the Ottoman Empire during the years 1769 to 1914. Its desire for a warm-water port, concern for the welfare of Orthodox Christians in Ottoman lands, and support for Pan-Slavism unnerved the Western powers. Their fear of a rapid Ottoman collapse that would tilt the European balance of power in favor of the Russian Empire triggered both armed conflict and extraordinary diplomatic efforts in the latter half of the nineteenth century. The "Eastern Question"—a term coined during that century—refers to the paradox faced by the Great Powers as they weighed the advancement of their national interests in the Middle East against their concern for the territorial integrity of the Ottoman Empire. Since the early nineteenth century, the empire had been referred to in European capitals as "the Sick Man of Europe." With the powers concerned about Russian expansion into and influence over the Ottoman Empire, the Eastern Question had evolved into a balance-of-power issue.

On several occasions during the nineteenth century, the Great Powers came to the aid of the Ottomans when they were either pressured or invaded by the Russian Empire, which sought to increase its strength and influence vis-à-vis its European rivals at the Ottomans' expense. International rivalry over the empire came to a head during the Crimean War (1853–56), in which Britain, France, and the Kingdom of Sardinia thwarted Russian designs on Ottoman territory in the Balkans by defeating czarist forces in the Crimean Peninsula and other areas of the Black Sea region. The conflict was made famous by the nurse Florence Nightingale and Alfred Lord Tennyson's poem "The Charge of the Light Brigade." The subsequent Treaty of Paris (1856) restored Ottoman territory captured by Russia and elevated the Ottoman Empire to membership in the Concert of Europe. Two decades later, at the conclusion of the Russo-Turkish War of 1877–78, the Great Powers again rescued the empire—this time diplomatically. Russian troops had invaded the Balkans and established a large, pro-Russian independent Bulgaria. At the Congress of Berlin (1878), "Greater Bulgaria" was dismantled, and the Ottomans regained considerable territory in the Balkans. In these two interventions, the independence of the Ottoman Empire was preserved, and the balance of power was upheld.

46. What is the general nature of reform in the Middle East?

Before we examine the modernization in Egypt and reform in the Ottoman Empire, we need to consider the topic of reform in the Middle East. Historically, reform has taken place from top to bottom. Reform movements were usually led by the ruling class and social elites. Peasants and laborers were resistant to change, feeling they did not have the power to effect reform. There have been, however, a number of significant bottom-to-top reform movements or revolutions in the Middle East, such as those led by the Kharijites, 'Abbasids, and Wahhabis; the Iranian Revolution of 1979; and the Arab Spring of 2011. Most bottom-to-top reform movements or revolutions have been religious in character, rebelling against secular authority. The revolutions of 2011, on the other hand, were sparked and led by secular activists. Islamist organizations, such as the Egyptian

Muslim Brotherhood and Salafis, did not spearhead the demonstrations and got involved only after the revolutions were well under way; they capitalized on their existing political organizations to gain an advantage in the aftermath of Cairo's Tahrir Square demonstrations.

The Arabic-alphabet printing press, which was introduced in Egypt at the start of the nineteenth century, reproduced many Western works of literature and philosophy for an Arab audience. The writings of Karl Marx, Charles Darwin, and European nationalists were read and discussed in coffee shops and cafés. From Egypt, Mehmet 'Ali Pasha (r. 1805–48) sent an educational mission to Paris in 1826. Among those individuals accompanying the students was their Muslim chaplain, Rifa'a at-Tahtawi (d. 1873). He read Voltaire, Rousseau, and Montesquieu and, after returning to Egypt in 1835, established the School of Languages. His academic pursuits stimulated an Egyptian *nahdha* (renaissance) that flourished from the 1860s to 1940s. He is considered the father of Islamic modernism for his attempts to reconcile Islam with Western social justice theories and ethics. This era embraced the rise of political thinkers elsewhere who sought to reshape their countries. They include, among others, Giuseppe Mazzini (1805–72) of Italy and Sun Yat-sen (1866–1925) of China.

47. Why did Napoleon Bonaparte invade Egypt, and what is the legacy of the French occupation?

Any discussion of the emergence of a modern Egyptian state begins with the French invasion and occupation (1798–1801). Napoleon Bonaparte (1769–1821) informed the Egyptian people that he and his troops had come to their country to rescue them from the oppression of the Mamluks, but in reality he had come for a variety of political, strategic, and personal motives: The time was not right for him to seize control of the French government; he sought to cut the lines of communication between Great Britain and India; and he dreamed of emulating Alexander the Great by establishing a great empire in the Middle East.

Fresh from his victories in Italy, Bonaparte won the approval of the ruling Directory for his Middle East strategy; he then sailed for Egypt with more than 40,000 troops and hundreds of scientists. He seized control of Egypt by crushing the Mamluks at the Battle of the Pyramids—misnamed because it actually took place in a watermelon patch near the village of Imbaba, which is closer to downtown Cairo than to the Pyramids, but the "Little Corporal" was not about to pass up a chance to enlarge the significance of his victory. The French employed the fighting square tactic and superior firepower, inflicting a humiliating military defeat and major psychological setback on the fiercely proud and valorous Mamluk warriors.

To many Muslims, the French victory at the Pyramids proved that Islamic civilization was in decline compared to the West. Some Muslims called for Westernizing reforms while declaring that the problems facing the Muslim world could be traced to an erosion of the *umma*'s devotion to Islam. After he had occupied Cairo, Bonaparte hoped to win the support of the Egyptian people by reassuring them that he cared for their religion and culture. He sent the following message to the shaykhs at al-Azhar:

> O ye Egyptians, [the Mamluks] may say to you that I have not made an expedition hither for any other object than that of abolishing your religion; but this a pure falsehood and you must not give credit to it, but tell the slanderers that I have not come to you except for the purpose of restoring your rights from the hands of the oppressors and that I more than the Mamluks, serve God—may He be praised and exalted—and revere His Prophet Muhammad and the glorious Qur'an. . . . Further-more, the French at all times have declared themselves to be the most sincere friends of the Ottoman Sultan and the enemy of his enemies, may God ever perpetuate [H]is empire![1]

The Egyptians were suspicious of Bonaparte. They did not accept him because he was a foreigner and a non-Muslim, and they were completely unimpressed by a hot-air balloon demonstration. Shaykh al-Jabarti, a religious leader from al-Azhar, observed the failed experiment and offered the following: "Their claim that this apparatus is like a vessel in which people sit and travel to other countries in order to discover news . . . did not appear to be true. On the contrary, it turned out that it is like kites which household servants . . . build for festivals and happy occasions."[2]

Despite the unpopularity of the French occupation, Bonaparte can be credited with several noteworthy accomplishments. He established the first newspaper in Egypt, *The Egyptian Courier*, and founded the Institut d'Égypte, which studied all aspects of Egyptian geography, history, and society. The French-era in Egypt turned out to be a scientific bonanza, as the study of archaeology, botany, zoology, linguistics, and geography flourished. French soldiers in the delta unearthed the Rosetta stone, the tablet inscribed with three languages that unlocked the secret of hieroglyphics. His scientists published the twenty-three-volume *Description of Egypt*, which generated great competition among European scholars in the field of archaeology.

Bonaparte's invasion and subsequent occupation of Egypt was nothing less than a direct effort by a Western country to take over the heart of the Muslim world. Aside from the Crusades, previous contacts between Muslims and Europeans had taken place in peripheral regions, like the Balkans and the Caucasus, or through trade. On the negative side of the ledger, the French did little to improve the lives of the Egyptians. Their administration was harsh and heavy-handed—taxes were scrupulously collected—and French soldiers exhibited lewd and outrageous conduct. On the positive side, the French weakened the power of the Mamluks, exposed the Egyptians to Western ideas, and introduced the first printing press in Egypt. Of lasting significance, the work of Bonaparte's scientists marked the birth of Egyptology.

Bonaparte's adventure in Egypt initiated the great Anglo-French rivalry in the Middle East. The French fleet was destroyed by the British navy under Admiral Horatio Nelson (1758–1805) at the Battle of the Nile, stranding the French invaders in Egypt. The French were ultimately ousted by a combined Ottoman-British force in 1801. Despite the failure of his Egyptian adventure, Napoleon turned the defeat into a political victory in France. He seized power from the Directory, dismantled the republic, and proclaimed the First Empire. The French returned to Egypt mid-century to build the Suez Canal, which opened in 1869, but by 1882 their power and influence there had been overtaken by the British. Consequently, the French established dominance over Tunisia, Algeria, and Morocco in North Africa. In the years leading up to World War I, the two European powers recognized each other's territorial claims and spheres of influence in the Middle East and North Africa. The French invasion so weakened

Ottoman Mamluk power in Egypt that a governing vacuum ensued after the departure of British forces in 1802. The military strongman Mehmet 'Ali Pasha would fill the void.

48. How successful were the modernizing reforms of Egypt's Mehmet 'Ali in the nineteenth century, and how did he represent a threat to the Ottoman sultan?

The emergence of a modern Egyptian state began with the rule of Mehmet 'Ali, an Albanian Ottoman soldier of fortune who in 1801 fought with Ottoman and British troops to remove the French from Egypt. By 1805 he had assembled a military force and gained the allegiance of leading 'ulama and local notables. That same year, he removed the weak and despised Ottoman governor and, with the support of local Egyptian leaders and the approval of Sultan Selim III (r. 1789–1807), became governor and established a semiautonomous regime, maintaining the outward appearance of loyalty to his suzerain in Istanbul; he assumed the title pasha.[3] In 1811 Mehmet 'Ali systematically murdered several hundred Mamluks, removing them as rival sources of power. The Mamluks had been deposed by the Ottomans in 1517, but they continued to serve as military officers, governors, and administrators in the Egyptian government.

The core of Mehmet 'Ali's reform program was the creation of a standing Egyptian army. Providing his new army with food, uniforms, equipment, training, and medical care necessitated making major improvements in agriculture, industry, education, and medicine. Mehmet 'Ali began by vigorously improving the country's finances. He taxed *awqaf*, which infuriated tax farmers, the rural aristocracy, and *'ulama*, and placed most of the arable land under government control, creating a public agricultural monopoly. The government decided which crops the peasants would grow; supplied them with seeds, tools, and fertilizer; purchased their crops; and sold them for a profit. To facilitate the movement and sale of farm products, Mehmet 'Ali used Egyptian peasants to build new canals and roads. New irrigation works were also completed, expanding the country's farmland. He transformed agriculture from subsistence farming to cash crop production. The leading crops were tobacco, sugar, indigo, and long-staple cotton.

Using the revenues generated by the sale of cash crops, Mehmet 'Ali modernized the military, improved education and industry, and further developed in the agricultural sector. He took no foreign loans. He founded secondary schools, advocated basic education for girls, and established a medical school, military staff college, and technical schools. Hundreds of Egyptians went to Europe for technical and military training, and Western experts were brought to Egypt to carry out medical, engineering, and military training and develop new textbooks. He introduced an Arabic printing press for publishing textbooks and a government newspaper.

In 1818 Mehmet 'Ali established universal conscription, which was a radical measure because Egyptian peasants had not been drafted into the military since the Byzantine era in the seventh century. Peasants dreaded military service, yet they were whipped into a potent fighting force by their officers. Starting in the 1820s, Mehmet 'Ali established his own "military-industrial complex." He set up 300 factories with 40,000 employees, many of whom were drawn from the peasantry. He built textile factories to make uniforms and tents for the army, constructed foundries to produce weapons, and established a shipbuilding dockyard and arsenal in Alexandria. Through these actions, Mehmet 'Ali effectively restructured and advanced Egypt's economy, military establishment, and educational system.

In the early 1800s, Mehmet 'Ali deployed his army on behalf of Ottoman sultan Mahmud II to the Hijaz to defeat the Wahhabis, who had seized control of Mecca and Medina. Because the Hijaz was governed by appointees of the sultan, the Wahhabis were in effect threatening the Ottoman Empire. Egypt regained control of the holy cities in 1818. Three years later, the Egyptians moved south, subdued Sudan, and founded the city of Khartoum. Mehmet 'Ali's descendants, with the help of British troops, would battle the Mahdist uprising in Sudan from 1881 to 1898.

Mehmet 'Ali used his troops and navy to support the sultan in his effort to crush the Greek drive for independence. After the Great Powers destroyed Mehmet 'Ali's fleet at the Battle of Navarino in 1827, he sought revenge against his sultan. In 1831 an Egyptian army, commanded by Mehmet 'Ali's son Ibrahim (1789–1848), invaded Palestine and Syria. Within two years, Ibrahim Pasha gained control of the Levant and then drove deep into Anatolia. Mehmet 'Ali coveted Syria as compensation for the Greek fiasco. The Egyptian offensive challenged Great Power interests because an Ottoman defeat would create great instability in the Middle East. Nevertheless, only Russia came to the Ottomans' aid. The Ottomans and Russians launched a joint operation against Ibrahim in which they recovered some lost territory. By the Treaty of Kuhtaya (1833), which ended the conflict, the Egyptians had annexed Syria and Adana in southern Anatolia. In the aftermath of the Egyptian-Ottoman War, the Russians and Ottomans signed the Treaty of Hunkar-Iskelesi (1833). According to its terms, Russian ships won the right to transit the Turkish Straits, and the sultan would close the waterway to foreign shipping at the Russians' request. In return, the Russians pledged to uphold the territorial integrity of the Ottoman Empire. The treaty infuriated the British because it threatened their naval superiority in the eastern Mediterranean. (Jump to the present: Think about Russia's expansion into territories bordering the Black Sea and its growing military presence in Syria and the eastern Mediterranean.)

In 1839 Mahmud II challenged Mehmet 'Ali's control over Syria, but Ibrahim routed an Ottoman force at the Battle of Nezib. Ibrahim then advanced into Anatolia. He occupied Ankara, but his campaign was again thwarted by Great Power intervention. In 1840 a British-Ottoman relief force landed at Beirut, well to the rear of Ibrahim's line of advance. The Egyptians halted their offensive, came to terms with the new sultan, 'Abdulmejid I, and signed the Treaty of London (1841). By its terms, Mehmet 'Ali ceded Syria and the Hijaz, the Ottoman government recognized him as the hereditary governor of Egypt, and he agreed to enforce all Ottoman laws and treaties in Egypt. One of those treaties was the British-Ottoman Treaty of Balta Liman (1838), which placed a 9 percent tariff on British imports, including textiles, and a 12 percent tax on Ottoman exports to the British Empire. Thus Britain's mercantilist policies established a lopsided commercial relationship between the British and Ottoman Empires. The treaty wrecked Egypt's export trade, impeding further industrial development. Egypt instead became a major cotton producer. After Mehmet 'Ali had agreed to the Treaty of London, he became disheartened and grew disillusioned with his modernizing reforms.

Mehmet 'Ali's reform program is a superb example of top-to-bottom reform. Egypt became prosperous, especially in the agricultural sphere, but Mehmet 'Ali's program of industrial development challenged European interests. The European powers, mainly the British, would not brook any challenges to their naval superiority and commercial hegemony. Mehmet 'Ali's reforms also alienated Egyptian social elites and created social dislocations for many Egyptians.

49. How successful were the Ottoman rulers Selim III, Mahmud II, and 'Abdulmejid I in reforming the Ottoman Empire in the late eighteenth and nineteenth centuries?

The French Revolution of 1789 did not go unnoticed in the Ottoman Empire. In 1797 Sultan Selim III instituted the Nizam-i-Jedid (New Order). He was aware of his country's domestic problems and feared European designs on his country. His goal was to preserve and strengthen Ottoman society, not transform it, yet he planned a complete overhaul of the government, starting with the military. He instituted the first comprehensive program of military reform. Earlier measures had been piecemeal: some European advisers here and a few new weapons there. The Nizam-i-Jedid was another top-to-bottom reform effort. A European-style infantry corps, comprising Anatolian volunteers, was instituted. The corps was trained, outfitted, and equipped to European standards. Schools of artillery, military engineering, and navigation were established, and an extensive naval construction program was instituted. The Ottoman government established embassies in Paris, Brussels, Vienna, and London; Selim sought a healthy two-way dialogue with Europe.

Not everyone in the empire was happy with his reforms. The janissaries typically opposed every attempt at reform, viewing it as a threat to their independence. In this instance, the sultan managed to circumvent them to implement the Nizam-i-Jedid. In the end, they disapproved of his reforms but grudgingly tolerated them until 1805. The proverbial straw that broke the camel's back was the decree ordering the janissaries to wear Western-style uniforms and stipulating that soldiers for the new infantry corps would be recruited from outside their ranks. The janissaries were not the only opponents of reform. The *derebeys* (rural landlords) objected to the confiscation of *timars*, which Selim used to finance the Nizam-i-Jedid. The *'ulama* also opposed Selim's reforms because they were based on European models. They issued a fatwa declaring several of his actions contrary to Shari'a.

The years 1807–8 were a chaotic time in the empire. In 1807 the janissaries and other dissenters deposed and imprisoned Selim. He was briefly succeeded by Mustafa IV (r. 1807–8), and the new troops were cashiered out of the service. In 1808 the janissaries committed regicide, killing Mustafa and all his male heirs, except Mahmud II, who became sultan. Like Mehmet 'Ali in Egypt, Sultan Mahmud II (r. 1808–39) was a military reformer who recognized the urgent need to thwart political forces that challenged the central authority. He broke the power of the *derebeys* by ending the *timar* system and taxing the landlords. By abolishing the *timars*, he also eliminated the feudal *sipahis*, who were replaced by a salaried, professional cavalry. He ordered the creation of a European-style army, and his Imperial Naval Arsenal built the mammoth ship-of-the-line, the 128-gun *Mahmudiye*. As expected, in 1826 the janissaries rebelled, but Mahmud was ready for them. He surrounded their barracks and banquet hall and slaughtered them with modern artillery. He effectively abolished the janissaries, whose demise became known as the "Auspicious Event."

The Western reforms could have gone faster but the *'ulama* continued to oppose innovation, refusing to turn their backs on twelve hundred years of Islamic tradition. Mahmud hoped to rein them in by moving the office of shaykh al-Islam into the state bureaucracy and creating the Ministry of Religious Endowments to administer the *waqf* and provide government oversight. He streamlined tax collection and established a modern cabinet to manage the affairs of state. He tried to effect tax reform but was unsuccessful; every attempt resulted in less revenue.

After the Ottomans' disastrous defeat in the Greek War for Independence, they turned to Prussian, French, and British military officers for technical assistance. In 1835 the Prussian officer Helmuth von Moltke (1800–1891) arrived to train the Ottoman army. The language barrier and religious differences made training difficult, and Ottoman soldiers, reveling in past military glory, were reluctant to take directions from a foreign officer. Senior officers showed von Moltke deference, but junior officers resisted his advice. Nevertheless, his tour in Istanbul established a link between the Ottoman and Prussian armies that would last through World War I. The fez became the standard headgear for the Ottoman army and bureaucracy. Mahmud established the Imperial War College and an army medical school; instruction at both institutions was conducted in French.

Mahmud's principal motives for reform were straightforward. First, he believed that the empire had to change or be overwhelmed by the West. And second, he was overly concerned about the preservation of central authority—especially his own. His top-to-bottom reforms did not constitute an assault on social values; they were technical in nature. He sought to implement change without causing social disruption, which had always been a major concern in Muslim society.

The Tanzimat era of Ottoman reform, which began under Sultan 'Abdulmejid I (r. 1839–61) and took its name from the Turkish word for reorganization, was driven by his highly competent, European-educated bureaucrats—the "French Knowers"—namely, Rashid Pasha (d. 1858), Fuad Pasha (d. 1869), and 'Ali Pasha (d. 1871).[4] The first reform document of the period was the Hatt-i-Sharif of Gulhane (Noble Rescript of the Rose Chamber, 1839). European supporters of the Ottomans, most notably the British, demanded liberal reforms in addition to economic concessions. In the nineteenth century, political liberalism included such concepts as constitutional monarchies, individual liberty, and laissez-faire economics.

The Hatt-i-Sharif was another top-to-bottom reform. The edict established a framework for legal reform and equal rights and provided a basis for government apart from Shari'a. It included educational restructuring, financial and governmental reforms, and improvements to infrastructure. A system of state-operated schools was established to produce government clerks; the provinces were reorganized so that each governor would have delineated duties and the assistance of an advisory council; roads, canals, and rail lines were improved; and a modern financial system was set up with a central bank, treasury bonds, and decimal currency. The edict also called for fundamental rights for all subjects, equal rights for minority groups, judicial reform, equitable taxation, and an end to slavery and tax farming. Ottoman society was in the midst of a remarkable period of change. The *'ulama* naturally objected, arguing that the edict threatened Ottoman society, but 'Abdulmejid's reform movement went forward.

In 1856 'Abdulmejid promulgated a new decree, the Hatt-i-Humayun (Imperial Rescript). It affirmed the provisions of the Rose Chamber Edict and included several improvements. Britain and France had pressured the Ottomans for additional reforms in the aftermath of the Crimean War (1853–56). The Imperial Rescript confirmed equal justice, equal opportunities for schooling and state employment, and equal obligations, such as military service, for all Ottoman subjects. It contained revised tax codes, a new commercial code, a new civil code (Mejelle), new secular courts, and a new system of recruitment and conscription for the military. Mejelle was based on Shari'a and informed by European legal codes. The rescript also established a national budget. Once again, conservative religious authorities opposed the new reform document as a violation of Shari'a, but it was not shelved.

During the Tanzimat era, several schools and colleges opened. The Civil Service School (1859) and Ottoman Imperial High School (1868) provided a high-quality education for civilians. A system of secondary schools was established under the Ministry of Education. Roberts College (1863), a Protestant secondary school was founded for the education of Christian Ottoman subjects. The Alliance Israélite Universelle set up several French-language schools for Jewish children throughout the Ottoman Empire, North Africa, and Persia in the late nineteenth and early twentieth centuries.

The two decrees aimed to create and advance the concept of Ottoman citizenship or Ottomanism. Throughout the Tanzimat era, the Ottomans sought to achieve national unity and strength in order to pacify the Balkans and to stand up to the Great Powers. Instead, minorities in the Balkans continued their fight for more power and freedom. Nevertheless, Western-educated Ottoman officers sought political reforms, human rights, and a European-style constitution. They were known as the New Ottomans.

In the early to mid-1850s, a major European war broke out, with France, Britain, the Kingdom of Sardinia, and the Ottoman Empire on one side, and the Russians on the other. The Crimean War was the result of competing Russian, British, and French interests in the empire. For example, the

British feared Russian hegemony over the Turkish Straits, and Russia's advocacy of Pan-Slavism worked to undermine the loyalty of the empire's Slavic minorities. Britain and France also feared Russian acquisition of Ottoman territory, particularly in the Balkans. Both powers had become the de facto guarantors of the territorial integrity of the Ottoman Empire. Russia's designs on the empire and the urgent need to prop up the sultan culminated in a major European war. (A dispute over control of the Church of Holy Sepulcher in Jerusalem between the Orthodox Christians and Roman Catholics was the actual spark that triggered the conflict.) British, French, and Sardinian forces defeated the Russians; the Treaty of Paris ended the war. The Ottoman Empire joined the Concert of Europe, and its final collapse was postponed for sixty years. Owing to the war's costs, the Ottomans became heavily indebted to European creditors.

The period of reform and high debt marked the start of the terminal decline of the Ottoman state. Effecting reform and waging war exacted a high cost. The first European loan to the empire was made in 1854 to finance the Crimean War. By 1875 the Ottomans owed 200 million British pounds for the principal and 12 million pounds for the service on the loans. That same year, the empire took in only 22 million pounds in revenue. The government was bankrupt, and by 1881 it had defaulted on many of its loans. The Commission of the Public Debt, also known as the Ottoman Debt Commission, was established. Its function in some ways foreshadowed the International Monetary Fund: A group of foreign bankers supervised nearly all Ottoman financial affairs and encroached on all aspects of the state from defense to foreign policy. A British commissioner supervised the expenditure of the loan, and other members took up positions in the Ottoman government. The commission became one of the largest organs of the Ottoman government and enjoyed near absolute authority over the Ottoman economy and budget. The Ottomans again suffered a loss of confidence and erosion of sovereignty.

It is difficult to understand modern Turkey without appreciating the Westernizing reforms of Selim III, Mahmud II, and 'Abdulmejid I. A member of NATO, the Republic of Turkey is on the front line in the war against ISIS. The Turks are extremely sensitive to issues of sovereignty to this day.

9

The Emergence of Nationalism in the Middle East

This chapter focuses on nationalism in the Middle East during the nineteenth and early twentieth centuries. We analyze its nature, identify factors behind its emergence, and investigate its application in Egypt, the Ottoman Empire, Persia, and the Arab world. Nationalism has had both positive and negative impacts on the history and politics of the region. We study three states—Egypt, the Ottoman Empire, and Persia—to understand how nationalism evolved within each country, how it affected political development, and how it influenced relations with the imperial powers. We also examine Arab nationalism and the considerable influence that World War I had on the drive for Arab independence in the early twentieth century. This period of early nationalism influences the politics and foreign relations of the region to this day.

50. What is nationalism, and what factors gave rise to nationalist movements in the Middle East?

A pair of Middle East scholars defines "nationalism as the desire of a large group of people to create or maintain a common statehood, to have their own rulers, laws, and other governmental institutions. This desired political community, or nation, is the object of that group's supreme loyalty." The "shared characteristics" of a people and their "shared resistance" to foreign governments, institutions, and individuals also contribute to a sense of nationalism.[1] Many historians trace the origin of nationalism to the emergence of nation-states in Europe in the seventeenth century; others argue that nationalism is a manifestation of the natural urge of humans to form groups based on common characteristics. Within Islam, nationalism was an alien concept because the *umma* was the sole object of a Muslim's political loyalty, and Islam—in theory—transcended all tribal and national differences. Accordingly, nationalism should not exist in the Muslim world, yet it certainly does, owing to the strength of tribalism and devotion to ethnicity.

The rise of nationalist movements in the Middle East in the nineteenth and twentieth centuries was driven in large part by what many Arabs, Turks, Persians, Kurds, and Armenians were witnessing on the European continent in the aftermath of the Napoleonic Wars, the Revolutions of 1848, Italian unification, and proclamation of the German Empire. Many young Arabs either studied abroad or were influenced by what they read about national identity and unity. In 1911 Arab students and intellectuals founded al-Fatat, the Young Arab Society, in Paris, the earliest Arab nationalist association, which two years later became the First Arab Congress. The Ottomans cracked down on the movement, but within the empire, military officers and scholars began researching the concept of Turkishness (or Turkism or Turanism). The Christian intellectual George Antonius (1891–1942), who wrote *The Arab Awakening* (1938), stimulated debate over what defines an Arab. The Druze leader Shakib Arslan (1869–1946), who authored *Our Decline: Its Causes and Remedy* (1944), was a leading advocate of pan-Islamism and the tying of Islam with Ottomanism. He argued that the revival of Islam would preserve the Ottoman Empire, which in turn would maintain the unity of the *umma*. Finally, two Arabs studying in Paris, the Maronite Christian Michel 'Aflaq and Sunni Muslim Salah al-Din al-Bitar, developed the Arab nationalist ideology of Ba'thism, which has influenced Arab politics from the mid-twentieth century to this day, particularly in Iraq and Syria. We will examine Ba'thism further in chapter 12.

51. How did the British gain control of Egypt in the early 1880s?

Egyptian nationalism began with the dynasty founded by Mehmet 'Ali. After the signing of the Treaty of Balta Liman in 1838, European economic interest in the Ottoman Empire—particularly Egypt—increased dramatically. Foreign businessmen descended on Egypt during the reign of Isma'il Pasha (r. 1863–79), Mehmet 'Ali's grandson. In 1863 Sultan 'Abdulaziz visited Egypt and bestowed the title khedive (viceroy) on Isma'il. The sultan also gave Isma'il permission to negotiate his own foreign loans. Egypt was enjoying an economic boom owing to the demand for long-staple cotton caused by the disruption of the American Civil War. Cash, generated by the high price of cotton, flooded into Egypt. Isma'il and Egyptian landowners became extremely wealthy, and ordinary farmers benefitted greatly.

Isma'il was enticed by Western bankers to take out huge loans at low-interest rates to finance large public works projects, most notably the construction of the Suez Canal. He rebuilt Cairo, modeling it after Paris; constructed hundreds of miles of rail and telegraph lines in Egypt and Sudan; fought wars in Ethiopia; and curried favor with France's Napoleon III (r. 1848–70) by sending Egyptian troops to Mexico to serve Emperor Maximilian (r. 1863–67). Following the surrender of the Confederacy in 1865, the bottom fell out of the cotton market, and Egypt found itself under a tremendous debt burden. To service the debt, the Egyptians needed to take out more loans but had to pay higher interest. Meanwhile, the French were building the canal across the Isthmus of Suez; they had won the concession in 1854 from Isma'il's predecessor, his uncle Sa'id (r. 1854–63). Isma'il was confident that the great enterprise would increase global communication, facilitate the movement of Egyptian goods to buyers overseas, and increase national revenue. The French company awarded him one-third of the shares in the canal, which opened in November 1869 amid lavish celebrations. The composer Verdi wrote the opera *Aida* for the occasion. Despite canal earnings and higher taxes, Egypt was so deep in debt by 1875 that Isma'il sold 44 percent of his stock to the British, who by 1881 held 41 percent of canal stock, gaining a controlling interest of this strategic waterway—the lifeline to British India. (If you are deployed to the Middle East and have an opportunity to transit the Suez Canal, take some time to reflect on the history of this strategic waterway.)

Egyptian debt ballooned from 3 million Egyptian pounds in 1863 to 93 million Egyptian pounds in 1879. In 1876, fearing Egyptian bankruptcy, European creditors set up the Public Debt Commission to manage Egypt's foreign debt. In 1878 European creditors went further and established a dual control system, under which British and French officials served in the Egyptian cabinet and oversaw government expenditures.

By 1879 Europeans were fed up with Isma'il's extravagant behavior and his attempts to undermine the debt commission. Members of the representative assembly were appalled by the huge debt and were critical of the government. But the most significant source of opposition was the officer corps of the Egyptian army. Many officers resented the khedive because he had blocked the promotion of officers of Egyptian peasant origin in favor of those with Turk and Circassian ancestries. Furthermore, the army chafed against European domination of the Egyptian government and intrusion into the country's domestic affairs. Isma'il took advantage of their discontent by dismissing the two European controllers and appointing his own liberal cabinet, which started drafting a constitution. The British and French were profoundly concerned about their interests in Egypt and worried that Isma'il would evict Westerners to preserve his rule. Consequently, they persuaded Sultan 'Abdulhamid II to dismiss Isma'il, who was succeeded by his son Tawfiq (r. 1879–92).

Did Isma'il improve the welfare of Egypt, or did his spendthrift behavior harm the country? We can argue that his construction of schools, courts, telegraph networks, roads, and railroads united the country and produced a strong sense of Egyptian identity and that his departure proved to be a setback for Egyptian nationalists. Near the end of his reign, Egyptian army officers joined with bureaucrats, members of the assembly, journalists, and progressive *'ulama* in calling for a liberal constitution that would ensure many of the rights and freedoms enjoyed by Europeans. The constitutional movement would not continue under the new khedive.

Tawfiq faced a population that was growing increasingly resentful of European meddling in Egypt, yet he decided to play it safe and side with the European creditors. He implemented repressive measures to maintain order and clamped down on reformers. He dismissed his liberal cabinet, restored the dual control, banned newspapers, and exiled agitators, including Jamal al-Din al-Afghani (ca. 1838–97), the influential pan-Islamist. He continued the economic austerity program initiated under Isma'il.

In 1881 protests erupted against Tawfiq and the dual control. The uprising was the first modern nationalist rebellion in the Middle East. The Egyptian nationalist movement began in the army, where officers had formed secret societies. Appearances to the contrary, Tawfiq may have been secretly encouraging the nationalists as a means to retake control of his country from its European masters.

Colonel Ahmed 'Urabi (1841–1911), the leader of the rebellion, was a product of a traditional education and had been influenced by Western thought while he served in the army. He demanded a constitution that would reconcile French revolutionary ideas with Islam and establish a constitutional monarchy. He insisted on a liberal cabinet, elected parliament, and larger, more inclusive army. He also sought the restoration of local industries under Egyptian control. In September more than two thousand Egyptian officers and soldiers surrounded the palace. They convinced Tawfiq to accept their demands. Consequently, a newly appointed cabinet drew up a constitution and held elections. The National Assembly declared that it, not the dual control, was in charge of the national budget. Mahmud Sami al-Barudi (d. 1904), an ardent nationalist, became prime minister, and 'Urabi became minister of war. By the middle of 1882, the army-led nationalist movement enjoyed vast popular support in Egypt. Britain and France had too much at stake to permit the revolution—and liberal reforms—to continue; they feared political chaos and widespread instability. When the French declined to participate in an armed intervention, the British attacked Egypt alone.

In June 1882, British troops landed in Alexandria and the Suez Canal Zone to restore order and protect the waterway. Tawfiq publicly supported the British intervention. He dismissed Barudi's cabinet; sent 'Urabi into exile; jailed hundreds of rebels; put several nationalists on trial for rebellion; suspended liberal reforms, including the constitution; banned nationalist newspapers; and reorganized the army.

The British achieved de facto control over the country. The occupation ended the Anglo-French dual control system. In its place, the British established a "veiled protectorate," in which Egyptians occupied positions of authority, while British officials called the shots from behind the scenes. The early nationalists proved to be weak and ineffective. Their party was divided into many factions: army officers resenting Turks and Circassians in the officer ranks, civilian reformers advocating parliamentary rule, and clergy advocating an Islamic revival.

52. What were the characteristics and accomplishments of British rule in Egypt?

Evelyn Baring, later Lord Cromer, who served as British consul general from 1883 to 1907, administered an efficient system of indirect rule in Egypt. The scion of a British banking family, Cromer had a management style resembling that of the U.S. Navy's Admiral Hyman G. Rickover (1900–1986), the Father of the Nuclear Navy, who personally interviewed and carefully scrutinized every officer and civil servant he hired. Cromer served as the shadow khedive, and all Egyptian ministries had a British shadow minister serving alongside and advising his Egyptian counterpart.

Cromer carried out land reclamation projects, improved communications, and expanded the Nile irrigation system, which was regarded as a means to raise agricultural output, increase state revenues, lower taxes, and reduce the public debt. Initially, Cromer was respected by the Egyptians and was considered a fair-minded administrator, and his tenure was considered a period of enlightened leadership. He did much to improve the lives of the average Egyptian, except in the area of education. He feared producing a large educated class of Egyptians that could challenge British authority and a sizable group of skilled industrial workers that could create products to compete with British goods on the world market. The British under Cromer succeeded in reducing taxes, improving the agricultural sector, and building new railroads, but Egyptians felt that they were being held down through the heavy-handedness of British rule. Nevertheless, in general, life was improving for Egyptians under Lord Cromer until the Dinshaway incident of 1906. Until then, he had faced little opposition or resentment.

Khedive 'Abbas Hilmi (r. 1892–1914) worked to subvert British rule from both within and outside the Egyptian political system. He sparred with Cromer over the right to appoint and dismiss ministers and control the Egyptian army. Cromer won the battles by bullying ministers and stationing more British troops, but he lost the trust of 'Abbas, who in an attempt to undermine Cromer's authority, built up a coterie of European and Egyptian supporters. One of 'Abbas's native supporters was Mustafa Kamil (1874–1908), who started out as a palace courtier but became the leader of a revived nationalist movement. He established a boys' school and a daily newspaper, *Al-Liwaa* (The Banner). He advocated a democratic constitution, but his primary goal was the removal of the British from Egypt. Still, Cromer failed to acknowledge the existence of an Egyptian nationalist movement.

As you read the remainder of this answer, reflect on how the brutal repression of dissent by the regime of Syrian dictator Bashar al-Asad in 2011 turned protesters into insurgents and fractured the country and how the anti-Sunni policies of the Shi'a Iraqi prime minister Nouri al-Maliki created conditions in northern Iraq that facilitated the stunning ISIS victory at Mosul in 2014.

At Dinshaway a hunting accident turned into a riot. A group of British officers was shooting pigeons in the delta when some errant shots wounded a woman in a nearby village and started a fire. The villagers attacked the officers; one died. Cromer responded with an iron fist. Fifty-seven villagers were tried, thirty-two were convicted, and four were hanged. Egyptians were outraged; many British and other Europeans were appalled. The incident produced widespread disaffection and hatred directed against Britain's oppressive authority in the country. British rapport with the local population crumbled.

Kamil exploited Egyptian anger to increase his popular support and hasten Cromer's departure from Egypt. Because the incident occurred on his watch, Cromer was severely criticized and his administration discredited; he was subsequently dismissed. The Egyptians were fed up with British paternalism, namely, the British belief that they knew what was best for Egypt.

The Dinshaway incident intensified Egyptian nationalist feelings, but the movement was not yet united. Kamil reestablished the National Party in 1907, but its members disagreed on tactics to evict the British.

Moreover, Kamil, the movement's most effective leader, died the following year. Cromer's successors sapped the nationalists' momentum by exiling several of their leaders and by wooing the support of 'Abbas Hilmi, conservative landowners, and peasants.

Britain declared war on Germany in August 1914. Later that year, the Ottoman Empire entered the conflict on the side of the Central Powers (Germany and Austria-Hungary) by declaring war on the Allied Powers (Britain, France, and Russia). In December Britain established a protectorate over and martial law in Egypt. The British worried that the Ottomans would try to reassert their sovereignty over Egypt. They were also concerned about the security of the Suez Canal—and rightfully so. In 1915 Djemal Pasha (1872–1922), a member of the Young Turk ruling triumvirate, launched an offensive to retake the canal. His attack through the Sinai was repelled by British and Egyptian defenders. This outcome surprised the Ottomans, who assumed that the Egyptians would welcome them as liberators. In reality, the Egyptians dreaded reintegration into the Ottoman Empire more than they disliked British control. They put their freedom—albeit incomplete—ahead of being part of a large Islamic empire. The British maintained 100,000 troops in Egypt during the war. The large military presence alienated the Egyptian population and led to open hostility toward the occupiers. In Egypt the nationalist uprisings of the 1880s and the movement's resurgence in the early 1900s were eclipsed by a mass uprising, led by the Egyptian nationalist leader Sa'd Zaghlul (ca. 1859–1927), after the world war.

This period in Egyptian history is key to understanding Egyptian leaders from Gamal Abdel Nasser to Abdel Fatah al-Sisi and even al-Qa'ida leader Ayman al-Zawahiri, all of whom were immersed in the struggle to assert Egyptian national identity.

53. Why did Ottomanism, the Constitution of 1876, the Young Turk Revolt, Pan-Turanism, and Pan-Turkism fail to reverse the decline of the Ottoman Empire?

By the 1860s, reformers in the Ottoman Empire were seeking to reconcile the ideals of the Enlightenment, the goals of the French Revolution, and the teachings of Islam to create a modern system of government that was compatible with their faith. Moreover, as independence movements proliferated in the Balkans, the Ottoman government became increasingly concerned with holding the state together and countering the growing influence of the Russian Empire, which openly encouraged uprisings among the Balkan minorities of the Ottoman Empire.

One group of reformers, the Young Ottomans, espoused the idea of Ottomanism—universal citizenship in the Ottoman state—as a framework by which all racial, linguistic, and religious groups could live equally and harmoniously in the empire. The Young Ottomans were intellectuals and civil servants, many of them graduates of the modern schools that had been set up under the Tanzimat. In the 1870s, they emerged as the leading advocates of reform in both the government and military. In addition to Ottomanism, they advocated a liberal constitution that would protect the rights and freedoms of all ethnic and religious groups, a constitutional monarchy with limited powers, and an elected assembly representing all peoples of the empire. Each of these reforms was to be achieved under the aegis of Islam.

In 1876 a liberal minister, Midhat Pasha (1822–83), and his supporters succeeded in removing Sultan 'Abdulaziz (r. 1861–76), who was extravagant and corrupt, and ultimately installing 'Abdulhamid II (r. 1876–1909).[2] That same year, the new sultan proclaimed a liberal constitution based on the Imperial Rescript of 1856. It restricted his powers to a limited degree and went into effect at the worst possible time because war between Russia and the Ottoman Empire was looming.

The provinces of Bosnia and Bulgaria rebelled against the Ottomans in 1875 and 1876, respectively. The Ottoman government suppressed the Bulgarian revolt, but Russia responded by declaring war on the Ottomans. In the ensuing Russo-Turkish War (1877–78), Russian forces drove into Bulgaria, captured Edirne, and imposed the punitive Treaty of San Stephano (1878) on the empire. Its most crushing provision was the establishment of a large, independent Bulgaria. With its policy of maintaining the balance of power in the Middle East upended by the Russian victory, Britain threatened war on Russia.

German chancellor Otto von Bismarck (1815–98) convened the Congress of Berlin in 1878 to address the division of Ottoman territory and prevent a general war in Europe. The Treaty of San Stephano was scrapped. "Greater Bulgaria" was scaled back, but the Ottomans lost substantial territory, nevertheless: Serbia's independence was internationally recognized; Montenegro, Romania, and a smaller Bulgaria became independent; Austria took over the administration of Bosnia; Russia gained Kars and Batum in eastern Anatolia; and Britain acquired the island of Cyprus.

Under the pressure—or guise—of war with Russia, 'Abdulhamid II did an about-face. He suspended the constitution and dismissed the National Assembly. He canceled reforms, imposed strict censorship, and muzzled the press. He suppressed and exiled Young Ottoman leaders, many of whom fled to Europe. He set up a spy network to root out subversive activities and governed as a despot for the next twenty years.

In the late 1800s, the Ottoman government developed a close relationship with Germany, which had sponsored the Congress of Berlin and did not participate in the debt commission. Kaiser Wilhelm II (r. 1888–1918) visited the empire in 1889 and 1898, and in 1902 the Ottomans signed a contract with a German company to build the Berlin–Baghdad railway. The railway revived the idea of an overland route to the East that could effectively bypass British-controlled territories and waterways in the Middle East. The British responded by establishing a protectorate over Kuwait to prevent it from becoming a terminus of the railway.

Exiled Young Ottomans regrouped in Paris in the late 1800s and early 1900s. To preserve the empire and curb the power of the sultan, they called for the restoration of the Constitution of 1876. They allied with civil servants, European-educated military officers, and military academy cadets; together the groups formed a secret revolutionary society called the Committee for Union and Progress (CUP). Its members became known as the Young Turks.

The Young Ottomans advanced the concept of Ottoman citizenship, but the idea did not satisfy many minorities, especially those in the Balkans who had their own national aspirations. Ottomanism gradually gave way to the ideology of Pan-Turkism (or Pan-Turanism), which championed the unity of all peoples sharing an ancestral link to Central Asia. It is worth pointing out that the eminent linguists Matthias Castrén (1813–52) and Ármin Vámbéry (1832–1913) investigated the Asian roots of the Finnish and Hungarian languages. In the early 1900s, many Turks in the empire warmed to the idea of a nation distinct from the one advocated by the Young Ottomans—a nation encompassing the Turkish-speaking world. This concept evolved into the ideology of Pan-Turkism.

As the thought of a Turkish nation was growing, other ethnic groups asserted their autonomy in the empire. At the end of the nineteenth century, the Greeks began a drumbeat for the conquest of Constantinople—a goal they christened the "Big Idea." The Serbs, who had achieved independence in 1835, sought more territory at the expense of the Ottomans. And a nationalist movement rose among the Armenians of the empire. Some developments were generating extraordinary pressure on the Ottoman state: the growth of nationalist movements, the financial collapse, and the weighty involvement of foreign reformers in Ottoman affairs.

In 1908 the Young Turks, led by officers from the Third Army in Salonika, rose up and demanded that 'Abdulhamid restore the constitution and reconvene the National Assembly. At first, many minorities rejoiced, but then they withdrew their support and continued to advance their nationalist causes. In 1909 the Young Turks thwarted an Ottoman counterrevolution led by common soldiers and theology students. They accused the sultan of fomenting and supporting the rebels and deposed him. Many scholars regard 'Abdulhamid as a cruel sultan, reactionary in his attitudes toward Westernizing reforms and devoted to the doctrine of Pan-Islamism as a means of holding on to the Arab and Turkish populations of the empire. To that end, he emphasized his role as caliph. Pan-Islamism caused alarm in the Russian, British, and French Empires, which were populated with millions of Muslim subjects.

The Ottoman Empire suffered great territorial losses under the leadership of the Young Turks. In 1911–12 the empire lost Tripolitania and Cyrenaica, in modern Libya, to Italy in the Italo-Turkish War. In the First Balkan War of 1912, the empire lost most of its Balkan territory to an alliance of Bulgaria, Serbia, Greece, and Montenegro. It retained Eastern Thrace. The Young Turks were removed by an army coup in 1912, but they regained power the following year. They governed the empire through 1918 under a triumvirate of generals: Talat Pasha (1874–1921), Enver Pasha (1881–1922), and Djemal Pasha. The empire bounced back militarily and defeated Bulgaria in the Second Balkan War (1913), regaining part of Thrace.

It was unclear what the Young Turks advocated. They gravitated from Ottomanism to Pan-Turkism because Anatolia was the undisputed core of the empire. Pan-Turkism would bring together all Turkish speakers under Ottoman leadership, just as Pan-Slavism meant uniting all speakers of Slavic languages under Russia. Because many Turks were Russian subjects, Pan-Turkism seemed an effective way to repay the czar for the problems he had caused the Ottoman Empire. The Young Turks' efforts to impose Turkish in the schools and offices of their Arab provinces stirred up local resentment, which further weakened the empire.

The Young Turks' influence on Central Asian Turks was minimal. Their attempt at ethnic and linguistic nationalism failed on a transnational scale but succeeded when concentrated on only the Turks of the Ottoman Empire. This new ideology became known as Turkism. The fundamental flaw of Turkism and other nationalist movements, such as Pan-Slavism, is that they place one ethnic group above others, frequently resulting in tragic, violent discord.

54. What difficulties did the Qajar shahs of Persia have in establishing and maintaining effective central authority and resisting outside interference?

The Qajars were a dynasty of Turkic origins. In 1794 Agha Mohammed Khan became the first Qajar shah. He brought all of Persia under his control and established his capital at Tehran. As Turkic rulers of Persia, the Qajars had to adopt the Persian language and assimilate into Persia's ancient culture. Under Qajar rule, Persia experienced decreasing autonomy in dealing with the European powers, and the country became an important part of the "Great Game"—the competition between Britain and Russia over the Middle East and South Asia. The history of Persia in the nineteenth and early twentieth centuries is essentially the story of struggles with and between the two imperial powers.

In 1814 Persia and Britain signed the Definitive Treaty, which contained several capitulations. Many government assets, including the collection of customs, were sold to British companies. From 1826 to 1828, Persia and

Russia fought a war that concluded with the Treaty of Turkomenchai, which forced the Qajars to pay reparations and set borders between the two countries. The Azerbaijanis—a *kizilbash* tribe—wound up on both sides of the redrawn Russian-Persian border.

The mid-1800s were a time of great social and religious ferment in Persia. *Ijtihad* and the question of the Hidden Imam bestowing legitimacy on political leaders were important issues. There were also significant developments regarding the Shi'a clergy. It was becoming increasingly hierarchical, and advancement was primarily determined by one's ability in *ijtihad*. Both clerical issues came to a head in the mid-nineteenth century. In 1844 Sayyid 'Ali Mohammed (1819–50) declared himself the Bab (Door)—the precursor—to the reappearance of the Hidden Imam. He was executed in 1850. Three years later, Mirza Husayn 'Ali (1817–92), one of his followers, proclaimed that he was a messenger from the Hidden Imam and took the name Baha'ullah (Glory of God). In subsequent revelations, he laid the foundation for Baha'ism, a religion that recognizes the spiritual truth revealed by the world's great religions and promotes peace and universalism. The Shi'a clerics considered the movement a heresy because there can be no new revelations. Mirza Husayn 'Ali went into exile, first to Baghdad and then to Haifa, which became and remains the world headquarters of the Baha'i faith.

Nasir al-Din Shah (r. 1848–96) started his reign as a reformer, but he sold more and more concessions to foreign entrepreneurs. He improved Persia's infrastructure and educational establishment but removed all progressive reformers from his government. In 1872 Baron Paul Julius von Reuter (1816–99), a British entrepreneur, sought a major concession covering the country's mining, railroad, and banking industries. The shah granted him a seventy-year concession. Persians rebelled, and the Russian government strenuously objected; the shah relented and canceled the concession, although Reuter retained the right to set up the Imperial Bank of Persia.

Because British colonial officials in London and Delhi were concerned with safeguarding India, the jewel of the British Empire, Persia, the gulf, and the adjoining territory were areas of keen strategic importance. Following the Anglo-Persian War (1856–57), Britain gained control of the

Afghan city of Herat on India's northern tier. Meanwhile, a series of wars between Persia and Russia resulted in Saint Petersburg's dominance over Turkmenistan and Uzbekistan north of Persia by the early 1880s. In 1879 a Russian-trained and Russian-led Persian Cossack brigade was established. Around the same time, Britain built a telegraph system through Persia to connect Britain with India; its citizens were also granted the right of extraterritoriality.

Concession mania reached its zenith with the Tobacco Regie (Concession) of 1890. Nasir al-Din granted a British company the monopoly over all aspects of the Persian tobacco industry; a small percentage of the company's profits would revert to the shah. The tobacco concession triggered national outrage, and diverse sectors of Persian society joined in common opposition. Bazaar merchants allied with mullahs, who united with progressives. Grand Ayatollah Mirza Hassan Shirazi (d. 1896) condemned tobacco use, in a fatwa (religious opinion), while the concession was in effect. The tobacco boycott combined popular, religious, commercial, and intellectual elements of Persian society and was very effective; even the shah honored it. After two years of widespread protest, the *regie* was canceled. The boycott was a successful bottom-to-top movement. In 1896 Nasir al-Din was assassinated; he was succeeded by Muzzafir al-Din Shah (r. 1896–1907).

Because a religious leader played a key role in the tobacco boycott, it is essential to note that Shi'a clergy in Persia enjoyed autonomy vis-à-vis the government in the late 1800s. Clerics were supported financially through *awqaf* and donations, which assured them a livelihood independent of the government. Clergy provided an effective vehicle for mobilizing dissent and opposition. Intellectuals recognized the power of the mullahs and joined forces with them during the constitutional crisis of the early 1900s. Today most Shi'a clergy in Iran are in effect government employees who lack the autonomy of their religious predecessors. This development is a consequence of Ayatollah Ruhollah Khomeini's views on Islamic government. We will discuss his views further in Question 81.

Around the turn of the century, a constitutional movement emerged in Persia. The movement was spurred in large part by Russian Azerbaijanis who, owing to unique circumstances, were privy to revolutionary ideas. In 1828 Persia ceded the northern half of Azerbaijan to Russia according to the terms of the Treaty of Turkomenchai. In 1874 the first major oil discovery in the Middle East occurred at Baku in Russian Azerbaijan; additional fields were discovered in the 1880s and 1890s. Baku became one of the most industrialized cities in Russia. Populated with industrial workers and an urban proletariat, it became a hotbed of political ideas. In 1905 two events rocked Russia and indirectly influenced political developments in Persia. First, Japan defeated Russia in the Russo-Japanese War. The humiliating loss shocked the Russian people and was a great embarrassment to Czar Nicholas II (r. 1894–1917). Second, a revolution erupted in February (March by the Gregorian calendar), and Baku became one of the centers of rebellion. The czar abolished the Duma, the legislative body, and forcefully suppressed the uprising. Despite his actions, revolutionary ideas persisted in Russia and spread to Persia.

In the aftermath of the Russian Revolution of 1905, newspaper censorship was briefly relaxed. The newspaper *Mullah Nasir al-Din* (1905–17) was published in Russian Georgia in Azerbaijani Turkish and Persian, sent to Baku, and then shipped to Persia. The newspaper contained satire and social and political commentary about the Qajars. Its ideas spread like wildfire through Persian coffee shops and helped instigate a series of protests against arbitrary government actions, such as beating merchants who had raised sugar prices. In 1906 several thousand protesters sought a *bast* (sanctuary or asylum) on the grounds of the British embassy. (A *bast* usually takes place in a sacred or special place, such as a mosque, and is often combined with political protest.) Political discontent became more intense, fanning a conflict that became the Constitutional Revolution of 1906. Mullahs who sanctioned constitutionalism, intellectuals, and merchants joined forces and pressured Muzzafir al-Din into adopting a liberal constitution and convening the Majlis, the national legislature.

Britain and Russia effectively thwarted a strong, liberal, and independent Persia, and in 1907 the two powers agreed to recognize each other's spheres of influence in the country. Britain would have primary influence over the southeast, close to India, and Russia earned the right to send troops into the heavily populated north, which included the Persian provinces of Azerbaijan and Khurasan and the capital of Tehran. In 1908 Persian Cossacks attacked the Majlis building and established martial law. With

Russian backing, the new shah, Mohammed 'Ali (r. 1907–9), suspended the constitution of 1906 and padlocked the Majlis. The constitutionalists were knocked back, but the movement remained a major source of opposition to the Qajar regime.

In 1909, with the aid of Azerbaijani rebels, insurgent Bakhtiari tribesmen, and dissident mullahs, the constitutionalists regained power and reopened the Majlis. That same year, Ahmed Mirza Shah (r. 1909–24) was installed in power, and the American Morgan Shuster (1877–1960) was appointed treasurer general and tasked with reforming the country's finances. The alliance between the mullahs and intellectuals, however, became strained and eventually broke. They disagreed over opposition to the Qajars. The intellectuals thought that the Qajars' political reforms were not moving far and fast enough. The mullahs, on the other hand, thought the revolution was becoming increasingly secular. In the wake of the dispute, the central government became paralyzed, and the tribes reasserted their independence, always an unwelcome development. In 1911 Russian troops occupied Tehran, ousted the constitutionalists from the government, and removed Shuster from office. That same year, British troops landed on the Persian Gulf coast to stabilize their sphere of influence. The foreign interventions effectively ended Persia's constitutional era.

In the years leading up to World War I, the United States was Great Britain's chief supplier of petroleum. The Royal Navy, which had converted its ships from coal-fired to oil-fired boilers, realized that this arrangement was not entirely reliable, so it sought a source of oil under direct British control. After the discovery of oil in large quantities in Azerbaijan, geologists descended on the Middle East and conducted surveys in several areas. In 1901 Muzzafir al-Din awarded to a British company the contract to explore for oil. After seven years of fruitless searching, a survey team led by William D'Arcy (1849–1917) discovered a huge deposit at Masjid-i-Suleyman, in the southwest corner of the country. In 1909 D'Arcy founded the Anglo-Persian Oil Company (later renamed the Anglo-Iranian Oil Company) to develop Persia's oil resources. The shah awarded the company a sixty-year concession; few changes were made to the arrangement until the 1950s. In 1914, with prodding from Winston Churchill, the British Admiralty purchased a controlling interest in the

Anglo-Persian Oil Company. That year, oil started flowing via pipeline to a refinery on Abadan Island at the top of the Persian Gulf. Britain now had a ready source of oil for its dreadnoughts.

A nascent Persian nationalist movement developed between the early 1870s and the years leading up to World War I. It can be argued that the movement began in earnest in 1892 with the tobacco boycott, but it can also be argued that it started twenty years earlier with the award of a huge railway, mining, and banking concession to a British company. The previous concession generated great popular opposition. Persian nationalism emerged in reaction to the threat of a Russian military takeover, growing dependence on the West, and the divisive effects of tribalism in the hinterland. It was facilitated by the spread of roads, telegraph lines, and public and private schools, but Nasir al-Din's policy of selling to the highest foreign bidder the rights to develop and control Persia's industries and resources elicited his subjects' ire. Reflect on the unfairness of these arrangements. Words such as "dignity," "oppression," and "humiliation" figure prominently in the history of the imperialist era in the Middle East.

55. Why is Arab nationalism such a complicated and challenging concept to define?

In answer to this question, we will formulate an explanation of Arab nationalism, examine how it evolved, and discuss how the nationalist movement survived and burgeoned under Ottoman rule.

The concept of Arab nationalism is complicated and difficult to define owing to the concept of 'Uruba (Arabness) and the corresponding lack of consensus within the Arab world over who can be considered an Arab. Many Arabs insist that an Arab must not only speak Arabic but also hail from the Arabian Peninsula. Taking this argument a step further, there are Arabs who contend that an Arab must be from the Najd region of the Arabian Peninsula. Restrictive definitions such as these exclude Syrians, Palestinians, Jordanians, Iraqis, Egyptians, and the Arabs of North Africa. Other Arabs argue that an Arab must be a Bedouin or the descendant of a Bedouin living in the Arabian Peninsula, not a city dweller, and some Arabs even distinguish between Arabs of the desert and those who inhabit the coast. Complicating our discussion even further are those Arabic speakers who do not regard themselves as Arabs, namely, Jews who lived in an Arab country or still do, the Copts of Egypt, and Lebanese Christians. While many of the definitions of an Arab presented here are exclusive, our definition will emphasize inclusiveness. Accordingly, we define an Arab as anyone who speaks Arabic as his or her native language, was brought up in Arab culture, and revels in Arab culture and history. Following up on this definition, we define Arab nationalism as the belief that the world's Arabs make up a single nation and that the Arab nation, stretching from the Atlantic Ocean to the Arabian Sea, should be politically united.

The era of Mehmet 'Ali's governance of Egypt and Syria witnessed a resurgence of Arab culture and literature. At the same time, American missionaries provided an effective vehicle for the growth of Arab nationalism. In 1866 Syrian Protestant College (later renamed the American University of Beirut) was founded; it was open to all Arabs. Nine years later, the Université Saint-Joseph opened in Beirut. By the turn of the century, graduates of these institutions were spearheading a literary revival. Philology (the study of language) of Arabic progressed as Arab linguists studied the origins of the language and worked to purge it of foreign words. Syrian Arab nationalists were a group distinct from Egyptian Arab nationalists. The former wanted to remain part of the Ottoman system and espoused an Arab-Turkish state, similar to the dual monarchy of the Austro-Hungarian Empire.

Until 1908 only the most ardent Arab nationalists advocated separation from the Ottoman sultan. Most Arabs were content living in the empire, which they regarded as a righteous Islamic state. They were also apprehensive that independence might put their country under the control of a European power, like Egypt was. By the early 1900s, however, a number of Arabs believed that the Arab nation commanded a strong identity and deserved greater political autonomy—ideas that informed the rise of Arabism. The movement first manifested itself as literary clubs, reform societies, and clandestine organizations throughout the Ottoman Empire. Eventually, cultural identity and political protest permeated these groups, which called for making Arabic an official language, the appointment of Arabs to senior posts in the provinces, and increased autonomy. At this point, Arab nationalists would accept living in a decentralized Ottoman Empire.

In the 1890s, 'Abd al-Rahman al-Kawakabi (ca. 1854–1902), a Syrian intellectual, advocated the revival of an Arab caliphate in Mecca. He argued that since the Ottoman sultans were not from the Prophet Muhammad's Quraysh tribe—and not even Arabs—they could not serve as successors to the Prophet or as true protectors of Islam.[3] Al-Kawakabi's campaign to purify Islam was supported by local leaders, such as the Egyptian khedive, for their own political purposes. In 1905 Negib Azouri (ca. 1870–1916), a Christian Arab, called for an Arab nation independent of the Ottoman Empire that would extend from the Tigris to Suez and from the Mediterranean to the Arabian Sea. Interestingly, he excluded Egypt from the Arab state because Egyptians—in his opinion—were not part of the "Arab race" and thus had "the germs of discord and destruction" that would undermine a unified state.[4] Already at this early stage, there was disagreement over the parameters of an Arab nation; nevertheless, the dream of an independent Arab state would gather momentum in the years leading up to World War I.

One early nationalist group al-Ahd (the Covenant), made up of Arab officers within the Ottoman army, promoted a joint Arab-Turk sultanate. Another organization, the Cairo-based Ottoman Decentralization Party, called for greater self-government and enhanced power for Arab notables. A third group, al-Fatat (the Youth), was a secret society of Arab students in Europe that sought equal rights and recognition of Arab language and culture in the empire. In June 1913, al-Fatat and the Ottoman Decentralization Party convened the first Arab National Congress in Paris. The delegates embraced an autonomous Arab nation similar to Azouri's model. The Committee for Union and Progress still negotiated with the Arab leaders of the empire because common ground existed. It adopted conciliatory measures, such as increased Arab representation in the assembly and more positions in the government. Despite the growth and influence of Arab nationalist movements, most Arabs remained loyal to the CUP.

Following the Italo-Turkish War of 1911 and Balkan crises of 1912–13, the Young Turks took advantage of the empire's security predicament to advance their ideology of Pan-Turkism and program of political centralization. Arabs felt threatened by the Young Turk government, which imposed the Turkish language in their schools and provincial government offices. Increasing numbers of Arabs became open to the idea of secession from the Ottoman Empire. In February 1914, the government arrested Arab nationalist leaders throughout the empire, sentencing several to death. This act poisoned the atmosphere between Turks and Arabs on the eve of the world war.

In upcoming chapters, we will study three twentieth-century expressions of Arab nationalism: the Arab Revolt of World War I, the political ideology of Ba'thism, and Nasserism.

56. How did the Hussein-McMahon correspondence, Sykes-Picot Agreement, and Balfour Declaration define the imperial goals of the Great Powers in the Middle East during World War I and sow the seeds of future conflict?

Before we begin our discussion of this small—but significant—collection of diplomatic papers, we will briefly review the course of World War I at several battlefronts in the Middle East. The Ottoman military suffered many setbacks, but its doggedness in combat and victory in critical battles permitted the empire to stave off defeat until the fall of 1918.

In the decades leading up to the war, the Ottomans cultivated a close relationship with the German Empire. Kaiser Wilhelm II visited the empire twice, Germany's engineers were constructing the Berlin–Baghdad railway, its military advisers were training the Ottoman army, and its financiers were bankrolling civil works projects. In 1913, in the aftermath of the Balkan Wars, General Liman von Sanders (1855–1929) and a group of German officers assumed key leadership posts in the Ottoman army. Enver Pasha, the minister of war, pushed for an alliance with Germany, arguing that if war erupted, an alliance would give the empire an opportunity to strike Russia and regain its lost territories. In August 1914, he signed a secret pact with Germany; publicly, the CUP still espoused neutrality. Although the Allies failed to prevent the Ottomans from joining the German camp, they held the Ottoman military in low esteem. More important, they had their own territorial ambitions vis-à-vis the shriveling empire. Britain and France were no longer committed to its preservation, and their wartime goals would lead to its demise.

In September 1914, it was still unclear publicly what action the Ottomans would take regarding the war. Nevertheless, the British seized two Ottoman warships under construction in Britain; in response, the Ottomans welcomed to Istanbul two German warships: the battle cruiser *Goeben* and light cruiser *Breslau*, which were trapped in the Mediterranean by the Royal Navy. The Ottoman government purchased and reflagged the ships and used them to bombard Russian ports in the Black Sea. In November the Ottoman Empire formally declared war on the Allied powers. The Ottomans sought to recover their lost territory in the Caucuses and regain control over Egypt. At the behest of his German and Austro-Hungarian partners, Sultan Mehmet V (r. 1909–18) proclaimed a jihad against Britain, France, and Russia, hoping to encourage millions of Muslims living in the Allied empires to rise up against their colonial overlords. His declaration proved to have a negligible effect on the course of the war.

Following Istanbul's entry into the war, the Allies pursued—often in concert—their strategic, imperial interests in the Middle East. The British sought secure lines of communication with India, the French wanted all of Syria and part of southern Anatolia, and the Russians coveted control of Constantinople and the Turkish Straits. In December 1914, the British declared a protectorate over Egypt to prevent the Ottomans from reasserting their authority. In early 1915, a Turkish army under Djemal Pasha crossed the Sinai and launched an attack to seize the Suez Canal, but a British-led force repulsed the assault.

In December 1914, the Turks, led by Enver, attacked Russian lines in the Caucasus and nearly succeeded in taking Sarikamish, but the Russians drove them back to Erzurum Fortress, inflicting a major defeat and securing, for a time, the Caucasus from further attack. Throughout 1915 and the first half of 1916, Ottomans and Russians battled in eastern Anatolia; the Russians pushed to Lake Van and Trabzon on the Black Sea coast. As the Russians advanced, thousands of Armenians joined their ranks, inflaming tensions between the Turkish and Armenian populations. In the summer of 1916, Ottoman forces, led by General Mustapha Kemal (1881–1938), staged a successful counteroffensive that halted the Russian advance. Meanwhile, the Ottoman government, fearing an Armenian fifth column within its territory, ordered the deportation of the Armenian population to Syria. Some 1.5 million Armenians perished during the removal process. To this day, the world debates whether this tragedy constituted a genocide perpetrated by the Ottoman government. The government of the Republic of Turkey, a NATO ally of the United States, steadfastly rejects the use of the term. The issue, however, persists as a policy dispute within the halls of the U.S. government and a source of disagreement between Ankara and many capitals.

In March 1917, Czar Nicholas II abdicated his throne, but the Provisional Government kept Russia in the war. In November the Bolsheviks toppled the Provisional Government, and the new Russian leadership promptly signed an armistice with the Ottomans and sued for peace with Germany. As a result, the Ottomans maintained a firm hold on Anatolia.

Two years earlier, the British and French devised a bold plan to increase the military effectiveness of their Russian ally by attacking and seizing the Turkish Straits. The Dardanelles campaign had several strategic goals: opening a conduit for vital supplies to Russia, severing the Berlin-to-Baghdad line of communication, and facilitating a major Russian offensive against Germany that would relieve pressure on the western front. An Allied naval attack of February–March 1915 failed to open the waterway. Ironically, it was halted when the Turkish batteries were down to a single day's supply of ammunition. In April the amphibious phase got under way, but by the time the Allies landed on the Gallipoli peninsula, the Ottomans had rearmed and prepared their defenses. Despite their numerical advantage, the Allied expeditionary forces, commanded by British general Ian Hamilton (1853–1947) and comprising British, Australian, New Zealand, and French troops, were unable to achieve a breakthrough. The Ottomans, assisted by their German advisers, fought valiantly and retained their hold on the peninsula. In January 1916, the Allied force suddenly withdrew, having spent eight months pinned to their small beachhead and suffering more than 300,000 casualties. Kemal, who rallied the Ottoman defenders, emerged as a great national hero. In the history of warfare, the Gallipoli campaign is a prominent example of a sound strategy undone by poor execution. The Allied failure, however, proved to be a godsend for the Ottomans, who faced the prospects of total defeat and the loss of the straits. By the terms of the secret Constantinople

Agreement of March 1915, Britain and France promised Russia postwar control of the vital waterway.

In 1915 a British-led army, consisting primarily of Indian troops and commanded by General Charles Townshend (1861–1924), landed at the head of the Persian Gulf, took Basra, and advanced northward toward Baghdad. The Ottomans stopped the British force short of Baghdad, and the British retreated to al-Kut. The Ottomans encircled the town and carried out a siege lasting several months. In April 1916, the British, with their supplies nearly spent, surrendered; 35,000 troops were taken prisoner. The next year, an expeditionary force under General Stanley Maude (1864–1917) captured Baghdad.

During the war, the final rupture took place between the Ottomans and Arabs of the empire. In 1915 the British opened negotiations with Sharif Hussein Ibn 'Ali (ca. 1853–1931), the amir (prince) of Mecca, through the offices of Henry McMahon (1862–1949), the British high commissioner in Cairo. In the ensuing Hussein-McMahon correspondence (July 1915–April 1916), London hoped to convince Hussein to lead a rebellion against his Ottoman masters, which would force Istanbul to maintain troops in the Hijaz.

By the outbreak of the war, Hussein was viewed as the de facto leader of the Arab nationalist movement, and through his son 'Abdullah (1882–1951), he maintained close contacts with nationalist societies in Syria. He believed the Ottomans were going to remove him; therefore, he offered his services to the British against the Ottomans. In return, he sought British recognition of an independent Arab state in the Fertile Crescent and Arabian Peninsula, excluding British-held Aden. McMahon responded that Britain would recognize and support such a state, but it would not include the coast of Syria, which would be reserved as a French sphere of influence, or Basra and Baghdad, which would be set aside in a British sphere. The British government's vision of an independent Arab state corresponded roughly to the Ottoman province of Syria and all of Arabia except Aden. Did McMahon intend to include Palestine in the independent Arab state? His wording was ambiguous, and Palestine is not specifically mentioned. Hussein claimed that the British offer did include Palestine, but the British later argued that Palestine was in the coastal enclave set aside for France. Britain also offered Hussein military and financial support, but in early 1916, negotiations floundered over the Hussein's objection to territorial exclusions.

In May 1916, the British diplomat Mark Sykes (1879–1919) and the French diplomat François Georges-Picot (1870–1951) concluded a secret accord to divide between them the Arab territories of the Ottoman Empire. The Sykes-Picot Agreement would create an area of British direct rule in southern Mesopotamia, an area of French direct rule over coastal Syria and southern Anatolia, separate British and French spheres of influence in the desert interior, and an international zone for the territory surrounding Jerusalem. The agreement was approved by the czarist Russian foreign minister, Sergei Sazonov (1860–1927), whose country had been promised the Turkish Straits a year earlier. The Bolsheviks made public the agreement; therefore, Hussein knew its terms before the war ended. He was outraged but continued to cooperate with the British for the duration of the conflict.

Meanwhile, several British politicians argued that support for Jewish immigration to Palestine and the establishment of a Jewish national home would earn the backing of international Jewry for the Allied war effort. This initiative took particular aim at the Jews living in the United States and Russia. Most significant, the British government hoped that Russian Jews could convince the Russian government to keep the country in the war. In November 1917, British foreign secretary Arthur James Lord Balfour (1848–1930) sent an official letter to an influential member of the British Jewish community, Walter Lord Rothschild (1868–1937) for further transfer to the Zionist Federation of Great Britain. Balfour's statement of British policy is quoted verbatim: "His Majesty's Government view with favour the establishment in Palestine of a national home for the Jewish people, and will use their best endeavors to facilitate the achievement of this object, it being clearly understood that nothing shall be done which may prejudice the civil and religious rights of existing non-Jewish communities in Palestine, or the rights and political status enjoyed by Jews in any other country."[5] The declaration advocates a Jewish national homeland in Palestine but not at the expense of the civil and religious rights of the Palestinian Arabs or the political rights of Jews living abroad. Significantly, it did not address the political rights of the population residing in Palestine. The Balfour Declaration planted the seeds of Britain's failed postwar administration in Palestine, the birth of the State of Israel, and the seven-decade-long Arab-Israeli conflict.

During World War I, the British government made conflicting pledges to the Arabs, Jews, and French. The Arabs and Jews believed that the Hussein-McMahon correspondence and Balfour Declaration, respectively, laid the foundations for their future independent states. The British also conceded certain Arab lands to French control. By doing so, they hoped to win French support for the preservation of their empire after the war. They put an extremely high value on their alliance with France, which outweighed the promise of an independent state to the Arabs.

57. What were the causes and outcome of the Arab Revolt during World War I?

The seeds of the Arab Revolt were planted decades before World War I. During the Tanzimat era and under the Constitution of 1876, Arabs of the Ottoman Empire enjoyed greater rights and opportunities, but in the aftermath of the Young Turk Revolt of 1908 and the movement's advocacy of Pan-Turkism and then Turkism, the Ottoman government favored the empire's Turkish population politically and socially over other national groups. As a result, after the outbreak of war, Arab demands for autonomy became calls for independence, yet it was going to take rich inducements to persuade Sharif Hussein, the amir of Mecca, to lead an uprising against the empire. One such inducement was British promise of support for an independent Arab state.

During the negotiations between Sharif Hussein and the British official Henry McMahon, which began in July 1915, the amir indicated that he was willing to lead a rebellion of Arab tribes against the Ottomans if in return the British government would support the establishment of an Arab state in the Fertile Crescent and Arabian Peninsula. McMahon replied that Britain could support an independent state but one with specific territorial exemptions, among them coastal Syria and lower Mesopotamia. Disagreement over the territorial definition of a proposed Arab state derailed negotiations in early 1916, but events in Syria again brought the two sides together. By May 1916, Djemal Pasha, the Ottoman governor, had arrested several Arab nationalists, charged them with treason, and hanged some two dozen. A month later, Hussein accepted the British pledge and proclaimed a rebellion, which forced Istanbul to station thousands of troops in Arabia to keep the region pacified and the Hijaz Railway secure. Furthermore, a jihad against the Ottomans, declared by Sharif Hussein, a direct descendant of the Prophet Muhammad, would dilute the impact of Sultan Mehmet V's proclamation of holy war against Britain, France, and Russia.

In 1917 the British-led Egyptian Expeditionary Force (EEF), commanded by General Edmund Allenby (1861–1936), and an Arab guerrilla force, led by Hussein's son Prince Faysal (1885–1933) and his British adviser T. E. Lawrence (1888–1935)—the fabled Lawrence of Arabia—advanced on Palestine from Sinai and northwestern Arabia, respectively. The EEF followed the Mediterranean coast, while the Arab forces pushed northward through the interior, attacking Ottoman lines of communication. The EEF captured Beersheba in October, Gaza in November, and Jerusalem in December. In September 1918, the EEF defeated two Ottoman armies in northern Palestine, effectively ending Ottoman military operations in the country. That same month, Bulgaria, also a member of the Central Powers, dropped out of the war, severing the land link between Berlin and Istanbul. On 1 October, EEF and Arab forces occupied Damascus, and by the end of the month, they had seized Homs, Hama, and Aleppo. Faced with the withdrawal of Bulgaria and the loss of Palestine and Syria, Istanbul realized it could no longer continue the fight; consequently, the government accepted the Mudros Armistice on 31 October. Less than two weeks later, on 11 November, at eleven o'clock in the morning, the guns on the western front fell silent. Four years of terrible war had ended.

58. How successful were the nationalist movements in Egypt, the Ottoman Empire, Persia, and the Arab world before and during World War I?

Having examined national movements in the Ottoman Empire, Persia, Egypt, and the rest of the Arab world, a few observations on the topic of nationalism in the Middle East are in order. First, while these movements failed to install durable, constitutional regimes, they planted the seeds for sturdier movements that would emerge during and after World War I. Second, the rise of nationalism in the early twentieth century did not increase the power, territory, or freedom of Egypt, the Ottoman Empire, or Persia or of Arabs living under the control or influence of others.

In the Ottoman Empire, the 1860s and 1870s witnessed the rise of Ottomanism—the idea of universal citizenship for all national and religious groups in the state—and the gradual and reluctant transformation of the Ottoman sultan into a constitutional monarch. Sultan 'Abdulhamid II proclaimed a liberal constitution in 1876 but suspended it two years later, while the empire was embroiled in a war with Russia. He ruled as a brutal dictator until 1908, when a group of military officers, the Young Turks, seized control of the government and restored the constitution. Ottomanism and the constitution spawned a proliferation of political parties based on the religious and ethnic diversity of the Ottoman state. Ottomanism was eventually challenged and supplanted by the ideas of Pan-Turkism—a unified Turkish-speaking world—and then Turkism—an Ottoman state based on its Turkish-speaking population. The sociologist and writer Mehmet Ziya Gökalp (1876–1924) spurned Ottomanism and espoused the concept of a Turkish national identity. His writings influenced the political ideology of Mustapha Kemal Atatürk, who would spearhead the creation of the Republic of Turkey out of the devastation wrought by the war.

From 1879 to 1882, Egypt experienced the 'Urabi Revolt, a nationalist uprising that sought to depose Khedive Tawfiq, who was governing with an increasingly repressive hand, and rid the country of European interference. Colonel Ahmed 'Urabi, a charismatic officer of peasant origins, rooted out elitist Turco-Circassian officers from the army and called for a liberal constitution, limited monarchy, and parliament elected by the Egyptian people. To the British, the revolt was a threat to their imperial interests, most notably, the Suez Canal. They abruptly terminated the nationalist reform program by invading and occupying the country in 1882. Their occupation lasted until 1956.

Two events shaped Persian nationalism during the latter years of the Qajar dynasty. The first was the nationwide tobacco boycott of 1890–92, which forced Nasir al-Din Shah to cancel the lopsided concession that gave a British firm control over all aspects of Persia's tobacco industry in return for a small royalty payment. The principal figure in the protest was Ayatollah Mirza Shirazi, whose fatwa banning the use of tobacco galvanized popular opposition and convinced the shah to rescind the concession. The second event was the Constitutional Revolution of 1906 and the subsequent proclamation of a liberal constitution, which established a constitutional monarch who would share power with an elected legislature and prime minister. Mirroring what occurred in the Ottoman Empire in 1878 and Egypt in 1882, the constitutional era in Persia was overturned by the armed intervention of Great Britain and Russia. In 1911 British forces landed on the gulf coast to safeguard their interests. That same year, Russian troops entered Tehran and forced the constitutionalists out of the government. The latter act ended Persia's constitutional era.

The Arab nationalist movement began in the nineteenth century and caught fire during World War I, but it was thwarted by the imperial ambitions of Great Britain and France, which established mandates over the Arab lands of the defeated Ottoman Empire. In early 1919, Arab, Egyptian, and other nationalist leaders from all over the world came to the Paris Peace Conference to argue for their peoples' independence. In nearly every case, the victorious powers—Great Britain, France, Italy, and the United States—sent the nationalists home empty-handed. The Western powers were not ready to give up their empires.

To appreciate the current map of the Middle East, it is imperative that we study the wartime agreements between the Allies as they relate to the disposal of Ottoman territories and the promises made to the Arabs and Jews. By doing so, we can connect the outcome of World War I to the turmoil that has plagued the region since the end of that conflict. For example, ISIS has used the Sykes-Picot Agreement to justify its effacing of the Iraqi-Syrian border. How different might the course of modern Middle Eastern history have been, and the current political environment be had the liberal reforms of the nineteenth century been permitted to flourish? We can only wonder.

The Middle East
between the World Wars

In this chapter, we focus on significant political developments in the Middle East in the two decades following the end of World War I. The chapter opens with a recounting of the establishment of League of Nations mandates in Syria, Lebanon, Iraq, and Palestine and the subsequent formation of independent states in the Fertile Crescent. We then investigate the creation of the Republic of Turkey, the Westernizing reforms of Mustapha Kemal Atatürk, and the career and modernizing reforms of Reza Shah Pahlavi of Iran. Finally, we discuss the successful efforts of 'Abd al-'Aziz Ibn Sa'ud to unify the Arabian Peninsula, create the Kingdom of Saudi Arabia, and transform it into a regional power.

59. What were critical political developments in Syria, Lebanon, Iraq, and Transjordan in the decades following World War I?

For several years following World War II, the Arab world labored under the yoke of European imperialism. In response to this question, we will examine postwar political developments in Syria, Lebanon, Iraq, and Transjordan; examine how the competing wartime claims of the Arabs, Jews, British, and French were implemented or ignored; and evaluate the efforts of Arab nationalists to create independent states in the lands of the former Ottoman Empire.

In January 1919, the peace postwar conference opened in Paris. Prince Faysal Ibn Hussein and T. E. Lawrence promoted the national aspirations of the Arabs, while the Allies, who were drawing maps for the postwar Middle East, had to deal with U.S. president Woodrow Wilson's Fourteen Points, which espoused self-determination, and the conflicting promises of the Hussein-McMahon correspondence, Sykes-Picot Agreement, and Balfour Declaration. In early 1919, the General Syrian Congress convened in Damascus to form an Arab government. The British and French, however, remained wedded to the terms of the Sykes-Picot Agreement, despite their postwar profession of support for an Arab state. Meanwhile, Wilson appointed his own commission to investigate the political situation on the ground in Syria. The King-Crane Commission found that the populace favored either independence or an American mandate if independence was not immediately forthcoming. The commission also predicted that fulfillment of the Balfour Declaration would lead to conflict between Arabs and Jews in Palestine. In Paris the British and French ignored the commission's report.

In March 1920, the Arabs in Damascus declared an independent state and installed Faysal as monarch; they also selected Faysal's brother 'Abdullah to serve as king of Iraq. A month later, at the San Remo Conference, the Allies established League of Nations mandates in the Fertile Crescent. (Under the mandate system, an Allied power was charged with the responsibility of preparing for independence a colony or territory formerly ruled by a defeated Central Power nation.) France was awarded mandates in Syria and Lebanon; Britain was assigned mandates in Iraq and Palestine, which included the future Transjordan; and an international zone was designated for Jerusalem and Jaffa. The Hijaz would be an independent kingdom.

The Arabs felt double-crossed by the San Remo declarations. They had contributed their blood to liberate Arab lands from the Ottomans, and the British, in return, had promised the Arabs an independent state with specific territorial exclusions. Coastal Syria, Basra, Baghdad, and Aden would not be included in the proposed state. Additionally, according to the Sykes-Picot Agreement, coastal Syria would fall under direct French control. French troops landed in the Levant in 1919 and defeated Arab nationalists at the Battle of Maysalun in July 1920, forcing Faysal to flee Syria. By early 1921, the British faced multiple crises in the Middle East: the turbulent aftermath of the French military victory in Syria, 'Abdullah's occupation of Amman east of the Jordan River, and a Shi'a insurrection in Iraq. To defuse the crises, Winston Churchill, the British colonial secretary, met with senior British officials in Cairo. At the Cairo Conference, it was decided that Faysal would become king of Iraq, and 'Abdullah would be named amir of Transjordan.

To govern Syria and Lebanon, the French used a divide-and-rule strategy. First, they enlarged Mount Lebanon (the future Lebanese state), which was dominated by Maronite Christians, the single largest religious community but not a majority in the new Lebanese entity. All Christian sects together constituted a slight majority in Lebanon. The French action resulted in the inclusion of Muslim-populated rural areas in the larger Mount Lebanon area. The Maronites, in communion with the Vatican and closely identify with Catholic France, gave Lebanon a unique identity within greater Syria. Second, the French created two mini-states within the remaining portion of Syria: Jebel Druze and an 'Alawi state on the coast. The French opened up the civil service and admission to the military academy to minorities, such as the 'Alawi. The French relied on the 'Alawi population to help govern Syria because the country's Arab elite refused to serve in the French colonial administration, and the minority 'Alawi community would generously use force to keep other Syrian ethnic and religious groups in line. The unique security apparatus in Syria, the Troupes Spéciales du Levant (Special Troops of the Levant), was augmented by French Foreign Legion and colonial troops. The mini-states lasted until 1942. Third, in the non-Druze and non-'Alawi remainder of Syria, which was majority Sunni, the French established the city-states of Damascus and Aleppo. In 1924 they were combined into the State of Syria. Unlike the mini-states and city-states of Syria, Lebanon has endured because the country was dominated by a small Christian majority determined to maintain its dominance in the face of an increasingly aggrieved Muslim population. It is important to note that Syrian Arabs frequently rebelled against French rule. The French put down a great revolt that erupted in 1925 and lasted until 1927. In 1939, following a plebiscite, France ceded a portion of coastal Syria, Alexandretta, to Turkey. The Syrian Arab Republic has not recognized the cession of Alexandretta to Turkey nor does it recognize a separate Lebanon. It regards both territories as part of Greater Syria. During the 1930s, the country inched toward democracy, but the French neither ratified a Syrian-drafted constitution nor set a date for independence.

In 1940, following Adolf Hitler's stunning defeat of France, the pro-Axis Vichy French regime inherited control of Syria and Lebanon. The British were exceedingly concerned because the Levant in Vichy hands would provide a strategic base for Axis operations in the Middle East. German-led forces could sever the British air bridge to Iraq, seize the Iraqi oil fields, and support the Axis drive into Egypt from Libya. A year later, Free French and British troops won control of Lebanon and Syria, and General Charles De Gaulle (1890–1970), the leader of Free France, grudgingly promised independence for both mandates. This time British support for Syrian and Lebanese independence overruled France's desire to retain its mandates indefinitely.

In 1943 Lebanon's leaders signed the National Pact (al-Mithaq al-Watani), which established the framework for governing the newly independent Republic of Lebanon. The pact was based on a complicated power-sharing arrangement between the country's major religious groups. It established a Maronite-led state, although the sect was not a majority of the population. Seats in parliament and ministerial posts were allocated among major religious groups according to their percentage in the population. In the parliament and cabinet, Christians would hold a six-to-five advantage over Muslims. The 1932 census, on which the pact was based, was the last national headcount ever conducted. Christians have blocked a new census because their percentage of the population has steadily declined. Despite its shortcomings, the 1943 pact held sectarian divisions in check until the 1970s. Syrians gained their independence in 1946.

The British governed Iraq as a mandate from 1920 to 1932. In 1920 Shi'a in the south launched an uprising against British authorities. The British put down the insurgency with the power of the Royal Air Force and the assistance of minority Christian Assyrian troops. The revolt also drew in Sunnis and Kurds opposed to the mandate. The uprising was a seminal moment in the development of a modern Iraqi identity.[1] In March 1921, at the Cairo Conference, British officials decided to make Faysal— recently evicted from Syria—the king of Iraq. The British needed a strong Iraqi leader to maintain order and stability, but this action meant a Sunni minority would govern a Shi'a majority. After securing popular approval through a British-orchestrated plebiscite, Faysal (r. 1921–33) assumed the throne. A year later, Britain and Iraq signed a treaty that granted limited independence to Iraq. By its terms, Britain retained responsibility for external defense, foreign relations, and international trade; the Iraqis would manage their domestic affairs. In 1932 the British mandate in Iraq came to an end, and the country became a member of the League of Nations, yet it was still denied full independence because Britain retained control over military and security matters. A small group of influential Iraqi officials dominated national politics, taking turns serving as prime minister, but they had little genuine power. In 1933 Faysal died and was succeeded by his son Ghazi (r. 1933–39). Three years later, General Bakr Sidqi (1890– 1937), a Kurd, mounted an Iraqi nationalist coup. It was followed by six more coups over the next five years, indicating that the army had become a major force in Iraqi politics. In 1939 Ghazi died in an automobile crash and was succeeded by his four-year-old son, Faysal II (r. 1939–58).

In 1941 Iraqi pro-Axis nationalists led by the politician Rashid 'Ali al-Gaylani (ca. 1892–1965) seized power. A group of senior military officers—all Sunni, pro-Nazi, and anti-British—backed Rashid 'Ali. It is essential to recall that the war was not going well for the British in 1941. France had been defeated, and many of its colonies were under control of the Nazi-puppet Vichy regime. Britain was still under German air attack, and the Axis maintained a significant presence in North Africa and the Mediterranean. Moreover, Hitler was secretly preparing to invade the Soviet Union. Iraqi officers saw the coup, which had been supported by the Nazis, as a fortuitous opportunity to achieve full independence. The Iraqi army surrounded British bases in the country, but fortunately for the British, the German Luftwaffe, which had planned to support the coup and subsequent military operations from bases in Vichy-held Syria, was thwarted by the British and Free French liberation of Syria and Lebanon.

A British relief force from Transjordan defeated the Iraqi military and installed a pro-British government, which ruled until 1946.

Transjordan, a largely tribal area, was originally part of Britain's Palestine mandate. After Prince 'Abdullah had fled Syria in 1920, he occupied Amman with a force from the Hijaz. From there, he threatened to raid French-controlled Syria. In March 1921, at the Cairo Conference, Churchill and other colonial administrators resolved to make 'Abdullah amir of Transjordan (r. 1921–46), which would be carved from the Palestine mandate. The British supported 'Abdullah and hoped that the tribes would accept him as their legitimate ruler owing to his descent from the Prophet Muhammad. To protect 'Abdullah's domain, the British organized the Arab Legion. Led by British officers, the legion was commanded first by Sir John Bagot Glubb (1897–1986), better known as Glubb Pasha. Owing to the recruitment of tribal warriors for its ranks, the legion provided a valuable unifying force in the country.

The British made Transjordan a separate mandate in 1928. In 1946 they granted Transjordan independence and elevated Amir 'Abdullah to king (r. 1946–51). There were now two Hashimite kingdoms in the Middle East: Iraq and Transjordan. In the 1948–49 war with Israel, the Arab Legion held on to the Old City of Jerusalem and most of the territory on the west bank of the Jordan River. Both territories were later annexed by Transjordan, and the name of the country was changed to Jordan. 'Abdullah entered into secret peace negotiations with the Israelis, but in 1951 he was assassinated in front of his grandson Hussein on the Temple Mount in Jerusalem by a follower of Hajj Amin al-Husseini, the mufti of Jerusalem. Talal, 'Abdullah's emotionally unstable son, assumed the throne but was soon removed. In 1952 sixteen-year-old Hussein Ibn Talal became king of Jordan (r. 1952–99).

After World War I, Sharif Hussein Ibn 'Ali of Mecca, embittered by the broken wartime pledges of Britain and France, soon became a hindrance to British interests in Arabia. In 1924 he proclaimed himself caliph following the abolition of the caliphate by the new Republic of Turkey. His declaration, however, was not recognized anywhere else in the Muslim world. He spurned offers of assistance from the British and waged a guerrilla war against them. Ultimately, tribal forces led by 'Abd al-'Aziz Ibn Sa'ud and encouraged by the British drove Sharif Hussein from the Hijaz and ended his short-lived kingdom.

As we conclude this response, we should evaluate the success of the Arab nationalist movement following World War I. During and after the war, Britain and France placed a high priority on maintaining their wartime alliance as a means of preserving their empires and protecting imperial interests. They were much less concerned with Arab independence and regarded President Wilson's idealism a naive hindrance. In the Arab world, several Arab states emerged from the terms of the Sykes-Picot Agreement and the San Remo Conference. Neither Arab nor Islamic history was a factor in the drawing of new borders. By and large, the nationalist movements of the early decades of the twentieth century neither increased the power and territory nor achieved the full independence of Arab nations, such as Syria and Iraq. Arab nationalists made some gains, but they did not establish fully independent regimes until during or after World War II. It took even longer to establish durable regimes.

60. How did the Republic of Turkey come into being following World War I?

World War I and the turmoil that followed were twin catastrophes for the Ottoman Empire. Twenty percent of Ottoman Muslims—approximately 2.5 million—died during the years 1914 to 1922. More than a million Armenians died, and the survivors of the deportation became implacable foes of the Turks. Hundreds of thousands of other minorities died. The economy was prostrate, the agricultural sector was devastated, and lawlessness swept through the countryside. The empire's involvement in the war ended with the signing of the Mudros Armistice in October 1918. According to its humiliating terms, Ottoman troops were demobilized, a joint British-French force took control of Istanbul and the Turkish Straits, France and Italy occupied zones in Anatolia, and the Allies were permitted unrestricted navigation through the straits. To heap insult on top of injury, a French general rode through Istanbul on a white horse that was a gift from Greek nationalists. The striking image of the mounted general humiliated the Turks.

The Ottoman dynasty was significantly weakened by the war. High government spending, crushing taxes, and severe inflation ruined many

Turkish families. Deeply concerned with retaining power, Sultan Mehmet VI (r. 1918–22) threw in his lot with the Allies and was prepared to do whatever they demanded of him. By the end of 1918, large numbers of Turkish veterans in central and eastern Anatolia had formed defensive organizations called Societies for the Defense of Rights. In May 1919, General Mustapha Kemal, who still commanded an Ottoman army, was sent by the Istanbul government to Samsun on the Black Sea coast to pacify the societies.

Before the war, Kemal founded two secret, anti-Ottoman societies that called for the abolition of the sultanate, establishment of a homogeneous ethnic state, equal rights for all citizens, a Western alphabet, and European dress. He had participated in the Young Turks Revolt (1908), but his relationship with them became strained after the victory at Gallipoli. They were increasingly envious of his fame and charisma. Kemal may have viewed his connection with the defense societies as an opportunity to forge a new nation. Instead of quashing the societies at Samsun, he joined them, took charge, and soon formed a proto-nationalist government.

That May another fateful landing in Turkey took place: the Greeks deployed an army to the Aegean Coast of Anatolia. To balance Italian forces on the southern Anatolian coast and maintain order, the Allies permitted a Greek force to occupy Izmir and the coast. Several Greek nationalists advocated the Big Idea, which called for the revival of the Byzantine Empire, including possession of Constantinople, Anatolia, and the straits. Greek prime minister Eleftherios Venizelos (1864–1936) was one of the leading advocates of the Big Idea, and King Constantine I (r. 1913–17, 1920–22) supported it.

After landing at Samsun, Kemal came to the forefront of the Turkish nationalist movement. He resigned from the army and soon became the leader of two rebellious congresses: the Erzurum Congress in July and the Sivas Congress in September. At Erzurum the delegates elected Kemal as their chairman and drew up the National Pact, which would serve as the founding document of a future Turkish state. The pact called for the political and economic independence of ethnic Turks, sovereignty over those portions of the empire with a majority Turkish population, an elected government, the end of foreign privileges, protection of minorities, self-determination for Arabs and inhabitants of the eastern provinces, and international supervision of the straits.

At Sivas Kemal was declared leader of the nationalist struggle. The congress rejected any foreign protectorate or mandate over Turkey and demanded replacement of the weak Istanbul government with an elected one. Of major significance, Kemal called for national resistance to Turkey's foreign enemies: the French in the straits, Adana, and Cilicia; Italians in Antalya; British in the straits and Kurdistan; Greeks in Izmir and Thrace; and Armenians in northeastern Anatolia. Meanwhile, the nationalists won the parliamentary elections and dominated the Ottoman government in Istanbul. In January 1920, Kemal convened a nationalist-led government that was determined to implement the National Pact within the boundaries set down by the armistice. In March, the Allies occupied Istanbul, dissolved the nationalist government, and installed a compliant Ottoman government in its place. Many nationalist deputies escaped to Ankara, in the heart of Anatolia, safely beyond the range of Allied battleships. In April Kemal called the Grand National Assembly into session.

No peace settlement for the Middle East was worked out in Paris in 1919. At the San Remo Conference, in April the following year, the Allies divided most of the prewar Ottoman Empire into British, French, Italian, Greek, and Armenian zones. San Remo also established direct British and French control over Iraq, Palestine, Syria, and Lebanon. Four months later, the Allies forced the feeble Ottoman government to sign the Treaty of Sevres. The treaty rivaled the Treaty of Versailles—the German peace treaty—in the degree of humiliation it meted out. It formally dismembered the empire and established the League of Nations mandates. According to its terms, the Ottomans retained independent control over a small portion of Anatolia; their control over Istanbul was contingent on respect for minority rights; Arab lands were detached from the empire; the British protectorate in Egypt was recognized; Arab rulers in the Persian Gulf were independent but subject to the terms of treaties with Great Britain; mandates were established in accordance with the agreement at San Remo; the Balfour Declaration would be implemented; France and Italy were awarded territory in southern and southwestern Anatolia, respectively; Greece would occupy Eastern and Western Thrace and take over the administration of Izmir; Armenia was granted its independence;

an autonomous Kurdistan was proposed; international administration of the straits was established; the Ottoman army was limited to 55,000 troops; capitulation treaties were restored; and the debt commission was revived.

In September the Grand National Assembly declared itself the legitimate government of Turkey, directly challenging the sultan and assembly in Istanbul, which it regarded as Allied lackeys; the Ankara government also renounced the Treaty of Sevres. The nationalists then set out to remove or defeat Turkey's enemies one at a time. The conflict became known in Turkey as the War of National Salvation. The Turks pushed the French back to Aleppo; both belligerents then signed an armistice. Both the Turks and Soviets fought the Armenians; the Turks seized one half of the Armenian Republic, while the Soviets took the other; and the Italians negotiated a withdrawal from Antalya.

The bloodiest fighting took place between the Turks and Greeks. In the winter of 1920–21, Greek forces advanced toward Ankara, but the rural population put up stiff resistance. The peasants, who flocked to support the nationalists, revived the old *ghazi* tradition of loyalty to faith, land, and group. The Greeks pushed too far and soon tangled with the nationalist army. Britain and France withdrew their support for the Greeks when they advanced beyond their designated zone of occupation. The Turkish army, under the command of Kemal and supported by a talented cadre of field generals, halted the Greek advance at the Sakarya River after a three-week battle in August and September 1921. The Turks then commenced a counterattack that lasted a full year. The offensive turned into a rout of the Greeks, who conducted a scorched earth strategy and committed several atrocities as they retreated to the Aegean. After violent action, the Turks expelled the Greek army from Izmir (Smyrna). The harried evacuation was completed by mid-September 1922. In the aftermath of the Greek defeat, Britain's position in Turkey became untenable. The following month, it arranged an armistice—the Mudanya Armistice—between Greece and the Grand National Assembly. The Turks retained Eastern Thrace and won a pledge from the Allies to convene a conference to renegotiate the Treaty of Sevres.

In September 1922, the Grand National Assembly declared that henceforth the Ottoman sultan would only act as caliph, leaving him with no political authority. The Ankara government, which was determined to be the only Turkish ruling entity attending the upcoming peace conference in Lausanne, Switzerland, voided all Ottoman-era laws. The conference opened in December, and in July the Treaty of Lausanne was signed by the nationalist government and Allies. It recognized Turkey as an independent state; established and guaranteed the country's modern borders, except for Mosul, which was awarded by the League of Nations to British-controlled Iraq; recognized the territorial integrity of ethnic Turkey; canceled all foreign privileges, capitulations, debt, and prewar concessions; divided up the Aegean Islands among Turkey, Greece, and Italy; ceded Eastern Thrace to Turkey; and gave Turkey control of the straits, which were demilitarized and governed by an international convention.

The Republic of Turkey was proclaimed on 29 October 1923. The Grand National Assembly elected Kemal the republic's first president, abolished the caliphate, and declared the country a secular state. The Western-style constitution, which was adopted in April 1924, created a parliamentary system of government, a unicameral legislature, and an independent, secular judiciary. The new government was based on universal manhood suffrage and nonhereditary leadership. A single-party, Kemal's Republican People's Party, governed until 1950. In three astonishing years, the Turks negated the Treaty of Sevres, won their independence, secured international recognition, and established a durable system of government.

61. What were the significant reforms of Mustapha Kemal Atatürk?

Mustapha Kemal's reform agenda—a program of intense, rapid Westernization—was known as Kemalism. It comprised the following six principles, or Arrows: republicanism, the belief that the county's leaders should be drawn from the population and not take power through a hereditary system; nationalism, the conviction that the people are devoted to the glories and aspirations of the Turkish nation; populism, the concept that the sovereignty of the state resides with the people and government works for the common welfare; statism, also known as state capitalism, the principle that the government takes a leading role in the country's economic growth; secularism, the tenet that religion must not hold sway over the state's political, social, and cultural sectors; and reformism, the notion that the people and their government are dedicated to peaceful modernization of the nation.

In the early years of the republic, Kemal and the Grand National Assembly acted vigorously to advance secularism. Kemal was influenced less by the U.S. Constitution than by the French Revolution, which removed all references to religion from the state. The assembly abolished the caliphate, the office of shaykh al-Islam, madrasas, Shari'a, religious courts, *awqaf*, Sufi orders, and *millets*; prohibited clergy from serving in the assembly; and banned polygamy. It also decreed that the Qur'an be translated into Turkish, and Turkish would also be used in the Muslim call to prayer. The country adopted the Western calendar, and Sunday became the day of rest.

The assembly named Ankara the capital of the republic, a step that emphasized the country's Turkish majority. A new law code, based on the Swiss Civil Code, replaced Shari'a and Tanzimat statutes. Rights for women were advanced and guaranteed; they were assured of equal rights in marriage, divorce, and inheritance and were granted the right to vote and run for public office. In 1935 eighteen women won election to the assembly. Women were also appointed to the judiciary. Compulsory, free education was provided for the population. Co-educational schools were established throughout the country, and a secular curriculum was implemented.

Kemal promoted commerce and industry. He recognized that Turkey was bereft of a commercial class because so many Greeks and Armenians had fled the country starting in the late 1800s, so he sought to overturn the traditional attitude that trading was unbecoming of a Turk. The government pursued statist policies in the 1930s, emulating the economic strategies used by Stalin to expand industry in the Soviet Union. It took measures to enlarge several industries, namely, railroads, mining, textiles, steel, cement, glass, and paper. Soviet economists and technicians advised the Turks. The country eventually became an exporter of agricultural products and manufactured goods. The government also carried out tax reform to ease the burden on peasants and workers.

The Hat Law of 1925 mandated Western clothing for men; henceforth, they were required to wear hats with a brim and prohibited from wearing the turban, fez, or any article of clothing that designated social rank or religious affiliation. Kemal encouraged women not to wear the veil. In 1928 he announced plans to adopt a new alphabet of twenty-nine letters based on the Roman alphabet. This astonishing act dramatically improved the country's literacy rate, increasing it from 10 percent in 1923 to 35 percent in 1950 to well over 90 percent today, and made it easier for Turkish speakers to learn European languages. It caused, however, a sudden break between the Turkish people and their Ottoman past. In 1934 the Grand National Assembly decreed that every Turk was required to adopt a surname. The assembly bestowed the title Atatürk (Father Turk) on Mustapha Kemal. Titles, such as pasha, were abolished.

In one fell swoop, Atatürk reoriented Turkey from the Muslim-Arab world to Europe. He devoted the last fifteen years of his life to changing Turkey from the bastion of Islam to a secular nation-state. Through Kemalism, Turkey was swept into the twentieth century.

To implement these far-reaching reforms, Atatürk ruled as an autocrat within his rapidly modernizing state. He allowed only single-party government and suppressed rivals when necessary. Turkey was not a totalitarian regime to the extent of Italy, Germany, or Spain, but Atatürk realized that to achieve rapid reform there could be no internal debate: Carry out reform first and then permit democracy and multiple political parties. If persuasion failed, he imposed changes by force. The republic officially became a multiparty democracy in 1945; an opposition party took power five years later.

Atatürk died on 10 November 1938. He is deeply admired and greatly revered by the Turkish people. Every year, on that date, the entire country comes to a standstill to commemorate the exact time of his passing. Portraits, photographs, and statues of Father Turk are found all over Turkey. His rescue of the nation from calamity, establishment of the republic, and far-reaching reforms fostered great pride in the Turkish nation. At the beginning of every school day, Turkish students recite: "Ne mutlu Turkum diyene" (How happy is the person who can say "I am a Turk"). Mustapha Kemal Atatürk was succeeded by General İsmet İnönü (1938–50). Today, Turkey's political Islamists have a complicated relationship with Atatürk's legacy. They admire him for leading the country to independence but abhor his dismantling and undermining of Islam in Turkey's public life.

62. How did Reza Shah come to power in Persia, and what were his major reforms?

During World War I, Russia and Britain expanded their power over Persia, but the Bolshevik Revolution of 1917 eliminated Russian pressure from the north and cleared the way for Britain to take the upper hand in Persia. At war's end, the British could claim several strategic successes in the Middle East and Asia: India was secure, Egypt and the Suez Canal were safe, and Palestine and Iraq were under British control.

After the armistice, British foreign policy was driven by imperial concerns. The British were obsessed with protecting their oil interests and establishing linkages between far-flung parts of the empire. The government sought a "Cairo-to-Calcutta axis" to complement the existing "Cairo–to–Cape Town axis." Egypt was connected to the Palestine and Iraq mandates, which were not connected to India; the missing link was Persia. The British hoped to bring Persia into the imperial system, which would establish imperial control from Egypt to India. In 1919 Sir Percy Cox (1864–1937), the chief British diplomat in Tehran, attempted to place Persia under a protectorate, as it had done with Egypt, but the Majlis refused to ratify the treaty. The Russians were no longer an immediate threat to Persia; thus, there was no impetus to establish a protectorate. The British eventually withdrew the treaty, in part because of the postwar downsizing of the armed forces.

In 1920 the Soviet Republic of Gilan was established with Bolshevik help on the Caspian Sea coast of Persia; it was overthrown a year later by Persian forces. In 1921 Persia signed a Treaty of Friendship with the newly established Soviet Union. It abolished the Russian sphere of influence in Persia and canceled all Russian capitulations, except those governing Caspian fisheries. It did, however, grant Moscow the right to send troops into Persia if its security and interests were threatened by a third party. Compared to the Ottomans, the Persians had less to fear from Russia. Whereas a near constant state of war had existed between Russia and the Ottoman Empire since the late 1700s, this was not the case for Persia and Russia, as Persia enjoyed better commercial relations with Russia than did the Ottomans. Except for Azerbaijan, there was no Russian ethnic or religious connection to Persia, and there was nothing comparable to a "straits issue."

In 1921 a military strongman, Reza Khan (1878–1944), began his rapid ascent to power in Persia. He was born into a peasant family near the Caspian Sea and became an officer in the Persian Cossack Brigade, which was trained, equipped, and led by Russian officers. After the war, he rose to prominence in the brigade and helped oust its Russian commander. He organized a secret military society that opposed British and Russian control of the Persian military. A mutiny led to the dismissal of all Russian officers from the brigade, and Reza took command of the unit and its four thousand cavalrymen. He seized national power in stages from 1921 to 1925. In 1921 he led a military force into Tehran to put down anti-foreign demonstrations and then forced Ahmed Mirza Shah to appoint a new prime minister, Sayyid Ziya' ud-Din Tabatabai (ca. 1889–1969), who in turn made Reza commander of the army. From that position, he helped consolidate the power of the central government by defeating rebellious tribes. Reza became prime minister in 1923 and spent the next two years consolidating his power, which, because of his autocratic leanings, he did not want to share. In 1923 he sent Ahmed Mirza Shah out of the country on a long vacation. He later persuaded the Majlis to depose the shah and abolish the Qajar dynasty. In December 1925, the Majlis elevated Reza to the throne.

Reza Shah (r. 1925–41) instituted a comprehensive set of social reforms. He modeled his efforts on the work of Atatürk but did not go as far in his Westernization program because of the firmly held religious and cultural convictions of the Persian people and because of the clerical establishment's steadfast resistance to his reform efforts. For example, he did not change the alphabet because the people regarded it as the alphabet of God and treasured their poetry.

Reza enjoyed several major accomplishments. He supported the rediscovery and revival of pre-Islamic Iranian culture, changing the calendar to the ancient Persian solar calendar; adopting the dynastic name Pahlavi, which was also the name of the pre-Islamic Persian language; and renaming the country Iran (Land of the Aryans), which emphasized its Indo-European origins. He rid the country of foreign troops in the early 1920s; united the country by defeating rebellious tribes; restored order and made the country safe for commerce; created a professional army of more than

100,000 troops; streamlined finances and tax collection; built more than 15,000 miles of roads and a railroad system; circumvented religious courts by instituting a French legal system; confiscated clerical property; imposed Western dress, including a ban on the wearing of the chador (the traditional, usually black head-to-foot garment worn by women); established secular schools; and initiated compulsory primary education.

Three of Reza's reforms have endured: Iranian self-sufficiency, education, and breaking of the nomads' power. The Trans-Iranian Railway, which links the Caspian Sea and the Persian Gulf, was completed in 1938. It remains a testament to self-reliance, with all funds for construction coming from higher tariffs and taxes on tea and sugar. Regarding education, Reza built new elementary and secondary secular schools that instilled Iranian nationalism in their students. He opened Teheran University in 1935, and during his reign, thousands of young Iranians studied in the United States. To crush the Qashqai and Bakhtiari tribes, who had defied central authority in the mid-1920s, he unleashed his larger, better-equipped army.

Reza had little tolerance for clerical criticism of his policies. In 1935 he ordered his troops to fire on peaceful demonstrators who were protesting his imposition of Western dress; more than one hundred people were killed. He drove many dissident mullahs underground or forced them to flee to holy cities, such as Qom. He infamously ordered the beating of a cleric who had spoken out against Reza's wife appearing in Western attire in Qom. Among the clerics frustrated by Reza's heavy-handed reforms was young Musavi Khomeini, who later, as Ayatollah Ruhollah Khomeini, would lead the 1979 Iranian Revolution to topple Reza's son.

An important factor in Iran's modernization, which distinguished it from Turkey, was its vast oil reserves. Reza managed to cancel all foreign concessions in Iran except two: the Russian Caspian Sea fisheries and the Anglo-Iranian Oil Company (AIOC), the latter of which was far too important for British industrial and security interests. As a counter to British and Soviet influence, Reza hired German and American advisers, whom he believed were not heavily tainted by the poison of imperialism. Arthur Millspaugh (1883–1955), a former U.S. government official, attempted to reform the country's finances, but disagreements with Reza hampered his success.

Until World War II, the Americans had enjoyed a positive image in Iran. The British did not mind U.S. influence, but they were concerned about the Germans, who enjoyed cordial ties with Reza, especially in the commercial and banking arenas. After the outbreak of war in 1939, Reza declared his country's neutrality, but following Hitler's invasion of the Soviet Union in June 1941, the British could no longer bear his ties to the Third Reich. He also refused to allow the shipment of U.S. Lend-Lease war supplies through Iran to the Soviet Union. Consequently, the British and Soviets simultaneously intervened in Iran in August 1941.

Britain and the Soviet Union put enormous pressure on Reza, who ultimately abdicated in favor of his twenty-one-year-old son, Mohammed Reza Pahlavi (r. 1941–79). Reza went into exile in South Africa, where he died in 1944. Britain, the Soviet Union, and the United States, which oversaw the vital Persian corridor of Lend-Lease shipments, effectively took control of Iran. In chapter 12, we will investigate the political and social conditions in Iran during World War II, the career of Mohammed Reza Shah, and the era of Mohammed Mosaddiq.

63. How did 'Abd al-'Aziz Ibn Sa'ud establish the Kingdom of Saudi Arabia?

When we study the history and government of Saudi Arabia, the name of the country and the flag are good clues to what we will be dealing with, politically and religiously. The Kingdom of Saudi Arabia is named after and governed by the House of Sa'ud. The state and family are virtually one and the same. The words and sword on the national flag sum up the mission of the kingdom. The words are the *shahada*, and the sword under the *shahada* represents the defense of Islam. The color green, an ubiquitous Islamic symbol, is a metaphor for the lush gardens of paradise.

The House of Sa'ud—the ruling Saudi dynasty—can be described as a martial organization that possesses religious sanction. In 1744 Muhammad Ibn Sa'ud (d. 1765), the ruler of the town of Dar'iyya, in the desolate Najd region of central Arabia, and Muhammad Ibn 'Abd al-Wahhab (d. 1792), the founder of the Wahhabi religious movement, formed a political-religious alliance that in effect created the first Saudi state, known as the Emirate of Dar'iyya. The Wahhabis followed the strict and puritanical

Hanbali school of Sunni jurisprudence. They accused the Ottomans of a lack of piety, but because the Saudi-Wahhabi movement was based in the isolated heartland of Arabia, the sultan was not too concerned. The alliance subdued other tribes in central Arabia, and in 1804 the Wahhabis boldly wrested control of Mecca and Medina from the Ottomans. They were overpowered in 1818 by Mehmet 'Ali's Egyptian army, which returned custody of the holy cities to the sultan. The Wahhabi defeat marked the end of the emirate.

The second Saudi state, the Emirate of the Najd, emerged in 1824, when Turki Ibn 'Abdullah Ibn Muhammad al-Sa'ud (d. 1834) drove Egyptian forces from the area around the town of Riyadh. It was weakened by Saudi infighting and in 1891 the Rashid family of Ha'il, supported by the Ottomans, evicted the Saudis from Riyadh. They took refuge in Kuwait, where young 'Abd al-'Aziz Ibn Abd al-Rahman al-Sa'ud (ca. 1880–1953) vowed to regain Riyadh. He acquired a Machiavellian education under Shaykh Mubarak al-Sabah, the ruler of Kuwait (r. 1896–1915), who dispatched dissident elements into central Arabia to keep the region unstable and ripe for attack. 'Abd al-'Aziz revived the Wahhabi movement and used his reputation as its leader, his skill as a warrior, and his charisma to assemble a loyal following. Shaykh Mubarak sent 'Abd al-'Aziz and his warriors against Rashidi-held Riyadh in 1902. Later known as Ibn Sa'ud, 'Abd al-'Aziz formed a large tribal federation that united most of the Arabian Peninsula under his family.

Ibn Sa'ud married skillfully to cement peace with the tribes he had subdued. He married the daughters of tribal leaders, four at a time. His divorced wives did not suffer, and their families held no grudge, because the women returned home loaded with gifts. In an appendix of his book *The Kingdom*, Robert Lacey lists the forty-three sons of Ibn Sa'ud. His oldest, Turki, was born in 1900; his youngest, Hamoud, was born in 1947.[2]

Over the first half of the twentieth century, Ibn Sa'ud fashioned a huge ruling family. It is important to note, however, that being a citizen of Saudi Arabia does not mean that one is a member of the Sa'ud family. The last name al-Sa'ud indicates that a person is a member of the Sa'ud family; a Saudi Arabian or Saudi, on the other hand, is a citizen of the country named after the royal family. Ibn Sa'ud kept the tribes under control by organizing them into a fighting force called al-Ikhwan (Brethren). They were his shock troops—the core of his Muslim army— who were bound to him by their devotion to Wahhabi doctrine, which they were eager to spread through force of arms. In several instances, Ibn Sa'ud was forced to subdue the Ikhwan out of concern that they would attack the British mandates in Palestine and Iraq or the British protectorates in the Persian Gulf. He persuaded several warriors to settle down in *hujar* (agricultural communities), and for their benefit, he built mosques and sponsored farming projects. In 1927 several Ikhwan refused to be settled and rebelled against Ibn Sa'ud, who crushed the uprising two years later.

In 1902 Ibn Sa'ud began his conquest of Arabia by taking Riyadh, the al-Sa'ud ancestral home. Central and eastern Arabia fell under his control by 1913, the north by 1922, and the Rub al-Khali by 1925. Early Saudi expansion took place on the edge of the Ottoman Empire. During World War I, the British supported an Arab revolt, led by Sharif Hussein, against the Ottoman Empire. The British paid a subsidy to Ibn Sa'ud to maintain his neutrality and dissuade him from attacking the Hashimites, who were political and religious rivals of the Saudis. After the war, the British and French redrew the map of the Middle East. The League of Nations established French mandates in Syria and Lebanon and British mandates in Palestine, Iraq, and later Transjordan. The British installed Hussein's sons Faysal and 'Abdullah in power in Iraq and Transjordan, respectively. Furthermore, to protect their interests in the Middle East and India, the British considered making Hussein caliph. Hussein consented to the plan, believing that the British meant that he would wield both political and spiritual power; in reality, the British only intended that he have spiritual power. Undeterred, Hussein immediately proclaimed himself caliph in 1924, upon the abolition of the caliphate in Turkey, but his action was not recognized anywhere else in the Muslim world.

Because Hussein had proclaimed himself the monarch over all Arab lands—a designation that far exceeded the Allied-sanctioned title king of the Hijaz—the British feared that, if he took control of Arabia and linked up with his sons in Transjordan and Iraq, he would create a huge independent Hashimite state that could threaten British communications with India. The British now threw their support behind Ibn Sa'ud. The Ikhwan attacked the Hashimites in western Arabia; Hussein abdicated in 1924 in favor of his son 'Ali (r. 1924–25). By the end of 1925, Ibn Sa'ud's army had overrun the Hijaz; 'Ali fled to Iraq. In 1927 Ibn Sa'ud and Britain signed the Treaty of Jiddah, whereby the British recognized him as king of the Hijaz and sultan of the Najd. He also adopted the title Guardian of the Holy Places and, in 1932, renamed his state the Kingdom of Saudi Arabia.

Ibn Sa'ud enjoyed friendly relations with Great Britain and, later, the United States, and he established a modus vivendi between his kingdom and the West. William Alfred Eddy (1896–1962), the chief American diplomat in Saudi Arabia during World War II, wrote that Ibn Sa'ud sought the West's technical know-how but insisted that Europe and the United States not interfere with his country's traditional society and culture. He also reasoned with Wahhabi leaders to forge a compromise between tradition and modernity. For example, he successfully convinced the 'ulama that photography and the radio were not inventions of the devil. He agreed with them that sculpture and painting are blasphemous, but photography is good because the images it produces are composed of light and dark, which are essentially good. To demonstrate that radio was not the voice of the devil, he had a chapter of the Qur'an read and transmitted from Riyadh to Mecca. It was sent and received flawlessly, and afterward, he reminded the 'ulama that, according to the Qur'an, the devil cannot read the holy book; therefore, radio is not inherently evil. A tension between religious puritanism and modernity informs the relationship between the Saudi ruling family and the Wahhabi clergy to this day.

In 1933 Ibn Sa'ud awarded the Standard Oil Company of California (later renamed Chevron) a sixty-year concession to explore for oil. In 1938 the California Arabian Standard Oil Company (CASOC), a consortium of four American oil companies, including Chevron, was formed. Later that year, an American team led by the mining engineer Karl Twitchell (1885–1968) discovered oil in commercial quantities at Dhahran, in eastern Saudi Arabia. Full-scale production, however, was postponed until after World War II. In 1944 CASOC changed its name to the Arabian-American Oil Company (ARAMCO).

ARAMCO paid the Saudis a royalty of approximately six dollars for every five long tons of oil produced. In 1950 the Saudis and ARAMCO agreed to an even split of the profits. Saudi gross national product increased seventy-five times in ten years. The government used the windfall for development projects, such as building schools and colleges, roads and railroads, reservoirs, ports, telephone and telegraph lines, a postal system, and hospitals; for cradle-to-grave social services; for guaranteed annual income; and for investments in foreign corporations. The production and sale of oil drastically changed the economic, social, and cultural life of the Saudi population and made the House of Sa'ud the most influential government in the Arab world. Saudi profits and income steadily increased, and the amount of oil income was, and still is, astronomical. In the three decades following World War II, the once-marginalized Arab states of the Arabian Peninsula and the Persian Gulf attained some of the highest per capita incomes in the world.

In February 1945, three months before the unconditional surrender of Nazi Germany, Ibn Sa'ud and U.S. president Franklin D. Roosevelt (1933–45) met on board the cruiser USS *Quincy* in the Great Bitter Lake of the Suez Canal. They discussed basing rights and the question of Palestine. Roosevelt promised Ibn Sa'ud that he would not take any action regarding Palestine that would be detrimental to the Arabs. President Harry S. Truman, who succeeded Roosevelt in April, did not uphold his predecessor's pledge. Despite this policy reversal, Saudi Arabia and the United States have maintained a close relationship since World War II. In 1951 Saudi Arabia and the United States cemented their special relationship by signing a comprehensive, mutual-assistance defense agreement.

In 1953 Ibn Sa'ud, the founder of the Kingdom of Saudi Arabia, passed away; his sons have ruled the country ever since. His successors are Sa'ud (r. 1953–64); Faysal (r. 1964–75); Khalid (r. 1975–82); Fahd (r. 1982–2005); 'Abdullah (r. 2005–15); and Salman, who has ruled since 2015. Salman may be the last of Ibn Sa'ud's sons to serve as king because the current crown prince, Mohammed Bin Salman (b. 1985), is the son of the reigning king and a grandson of the kingdom's founder. Crown Prince

Mohammed, who already plays a major role in governing the country, faces a host of critical challenges, which include the civil wars in Syria and Yemen, political instability in Iraq, intra-Arab rivalry with Qatar, mollifying the Shi'a minority in the east, appeasing fundamentalist Salafi-Wahhabi clerics, and implementing his ambitious modernization plans. As of this writing, it remains to be seen if the crown prince will survive the international outrage over the murder of Saudi journalist Jamal Khashoggi (1958–2018), a U.S. resident alien who was killed in October 2018 inside the Saudi consulate in Istanbul, Turkey.

11

Egyptian Independence, the Zionist Movement, and the Creation of Israel

I n this chapter, we focus on two important developments in the first half of the twentieth century: Egyptian independence from Great Britain and the birth of the State of Israel. Our inquiry opens with an account of Egypt's nearly four-decade-long struggle for full independence following World War I, continues with an overview of the early history of the Zionist movement, and concludes with an assessment of the tortuous history of the British mandate in Palestine and establishment of Israel, including its victory in the 1948–49 Arab-Israeli War.

64. What were the significant events and developments in Egypt from 1919 to 1956 that resulted in full independence from Great Britain?

During World War I, Egyptian hostility toward the British was deep and visible, and nationalist fervor boiled over. Much of the popular anger was stoked by Sa'd Zaghlul (1859–1927) an Islamic modernist, progressive, and ardent Egyptian nationalist who had served as minister of education under the British administration. After the war, inspired by President Woodrow Wilson's Fourteen Points and its call for self-determination of subject peoples, Zaghlul hoped to take Egypt's case for independence to the 1919 Paris Peace Conference, but the British barred him from going to Paris out of concern for the security of the Suez Canal. In response, his Wafd (Delegation) Party toured the country, drumming up popular support for Egyptian independence. The British promptly arrested and exiled the leaders of the movement to Malta. In 1919 popular uprisings erupted throughout Egypt in support of the Wafd, Egyptian independence, and an end to the British protectorate. Muslims and Coptic Christians marched together against the British occupation. To restore order, the British high commissioner, Field Marshal Edmund Allenby, relented and allowed the Wafd to travel to Paris. Although the Wafd accomplished little of substance at the peace conference, it raised the national hopes of the Egyptian people. The Wafd and other nationalists, such as the Arabs' Prince Faysal Ibn Hussein and Vietnam's Ho Chi Minh, had gone to Paris believing in Wilson's advocacy of national self-determination.

The British and Egyptians could not agree on terms to end the protectorate; consequently, strikes and riots again broke out. The British cracked down on the unrest and initiated talks with the Egyptians, but they would not budge on the issue of the canal. As a result, Zaghlul boycotted the negotiations. In 1922 Britain granted limited independence to Egypt as a means of sapping the nationalists' popular support. The declaration contained conditions called the Four Reserved Points: the British maintained the right (1) to protect imperial communications in Egypt, namely, the canal; (2) to defend Egypt from aggression; (3) to safeguard minorities and foreign interests; and (4) to retain control of the Sudan. The British elevated Sultan Fuad to king, yet independence on British terms was still unacceptable to Egyptian nationalists.

King Fuad I (r. 1922–36) appreciated the power of the Wafd and hoped to use the party to counter the British. The party won the election of 1923, and Zaghlul formed a government under the new constitution. He immediately set out to revise the terms of independence but was thwarted by British refusal to cede control of the canal and Sudan. Fuad did not genuinely support the Wafd; he had only used the party to enhance his power. After the assassination of General Sir Lee Stack (1868–1924), the British governor general of the Anglo-Egyptian Sudan, by an Egyptian nationalist, Zaghlul opposed a series of punitive British demands and was forced from power. In 1930 the king promulgated a new constitution that established a system of indirect voting designed to keep the Wafd out of power. In 1936 Faruq (r. 1936–52) succeeded his father as king. The British called for a return to the 1923 constitution and free elections. After the restoration of the previous constitution, the Wafd won the election of 1936, and Prime Minister Mustafa al-Nahhas Pasha (1879–1965) formed a new government.

The new prime minister set out to renegotiate independence terms with the British. As it happened, the Italian invasion of Ethiopia moved the two sides together, and they concluded the Anglo-Egyptian Treaty of Alliance of 1936. It recognized Egyptian independence, granted Britain the right to defend communications in Egypt and use Egyptian bases in wartime, limited the number of British troops in the Canal Zone to ten thousand, placed Sudan under joint Anglo-Egyptian administration, permitted Egyptian membership in the League of Nations, and abolished capitulations, including mixed courts that favored Europeans living in Egypt. The treaty brought fifteen years of relative peace, but the unbalanced relationship between the Egyptians and British remained.

World War II had a significant impact on Egypt. Supplies staged in the country were for the exclusive use of the Allies, and Egyptians experienced social dislocations, high inflation, and a shortage of key food products. As a result, antiforeign sentiment intensified. By 1942 the British were concerned about the threat to Egypt posed by the Germans, Italians, and pro-Axis Egyptians. Germans and Italians were mounting an effective pro-Axis propaganda campaign in the Middle East, proclaiming that they were the liberators of Egyptians, Arabs, and other victims of the postwar peace settlement. European-style fascism was infecting Egypt, revealing itself in political parties such as Misr al-Fatat (Young Egyptians), whose members marched in green shirts, emulating Mussolini's Black Shirts and Hitler's Brown Shirts, and organizations such as the Muslim Brotherhood. General Erwin Rommel (1891–1944), the commander of the Wehrmacht's Afrika Korps, was preparing to invade Egypt, and Faruq's government, which had been led by pro-Axis prime minister 'Ali Maher Pasha (1882–1960) as late as 1940, was dogged by a series of weak coalition governments. The British were suspicious of Faruq, who hedged his bets by attempting to maintain positive relations with both the Allies and Axis. In early February 1942, the British government, represented in Cairo by Ambassador Sir Miles Lampson (1880–1964), undertook a bold step to strengthen its position in Egypt. British troops and tanks surrounded Abidin Palace, and Lampson forced Faruq to appoint an emergency Wafd-led government, under al-Nahhas Pasha, that would uphold the 1936 treaty. The Wafd was more anti-Axis than anti-British, thus, it was grudgingly acceptable to the British. The party was criticized for its cooperation with the British during the war, and Faruq's credibility was severely damaged as a result of the humiliating Fourth of February incident. It is important to note that the British position in Egypt was still insecure, as demonstrators on the streets of Cairo shouted, "Onward Rommel!" In October–November 1942, General Bernard Montgomery's Eighth Army defeated the Afrika Korps at the Battle of El Alamein. Egypt and the Suez Canal were safe from the threat of Axis invasion. In May 1943, the Allies drove the last of the Axis forces from North Africa.

After World War II, Egypt's severe domestic problems, foremost poverty, returned to the forefront. Because Faruq could not deal with the problems effectively, he guided the country into the international arena to deflect the people's attention from their difficulties. In 1945 he convened a conference of Arab leaders that established the League of Arab States. Arab nationalism became instantly overheated with the creation of Israel in 1948 and the subsequent war with the Jewish state. Faruq led Egypt into the first Arab-Israeli war for the wrong reasons. Egypt was a major belligerent, but he used the war to divert the public's attention from domestic problems and achieve Egyptian hegemony in the Arab world. Many Egyptian units fought bravely, but the country suffered a disastrous defeat. Several Egyptian officers blamed their king for the humiliating setback and labeled *him* the enemy. He had sent the army into battle with substandard equipment and enriched himself on kickbacks from military contractors. The public viewed him as immoral, corrupt, detached, inept, and incapable of challenging the British.

Unable to renegotiate the Anglo-Egyptian treaty, Faruq's government abrogated it in October 1951. The British condemned his unilateral act and refused to declare their intent to leave Egypt. Anti-British riots broke out in January 1952. The rioters attacked British troops in the canal zone, but the British fought back, killing fifty Egyptian police officers.[1] Then, on a day that has become known as Black Saturday, mobs in Cairo torched several Western businesses and cultural establishments. The British and U.S. governments and Egyptian military concluded that Faruq was rapidly losing control of the country. In July a group of young army officers called the Free Officers Movement, led by Lieutenant Colonel Gamal Abdel Nasser (1918–70) and supported by the Muslim Brotherhood, seized control of the government. The Free Officers formed the Revolutionary Command Council (RCC), which served as the supreme legislative and executive authority in Egypt. The RCC deposed Faruq, sent him into exile, abolished political parties, and promised elections under a new constitution. The officers sought to end imperialism, promote social justice, achieve economic progress, further human dignity, and advance the concept of Arab socialism, which would form the core of Nasser's ideology.

A significant socioreligious group in Egypt in the early 1950s was the Muslim Brotherhood (Al-Ikhwan al-Muslimun), which was founded in 1928 by Hasan al-Banna (1906–49), an Egyptian schoolteacher. The Muslim Brotherhood was and still is a fundamentalist religious-political movement. It called for a revival of Islamic norms and morality, advocated the interpretation of Shari'a to address modern circumstances, and advanced the Qur'an as the ultimate political authority. It advocated second-class citizenship for the People of the Book, that is, Christians and Jews who, had ruled large portions of the Muslim world, trampled its lands, and besmirched its honor.

The Muslim Brotherhood must be viewed within the context of a particular moment in its nine-decade history, which includes periods of violence, political compromise, and suppression by Egypt's rulers. Over the years, its program has alternated from a political form of Islamism—the idea that government and society should be guided by Islamic principles—to advocating compromise to a militance advocating violence. Today, it is regrettable that some opinion makers sensationalize the threat of the Muslim Brotherhood or conflate it with al-Qa'ida or ISIS. The Islamic State, for instance, denounces the Muslim Brotherhood, referring to it as the Murtadd (Apostate) Brotherhood. Also, we must not confuse the Muslim Brotherhood with "Salafi-Ikhwani," a term describing Salafist political parties, which believe that the Muslim world should be guided by the example and traditions of the faith's earliest believers. They charge the Muslim Brotherhood with not being sufficiently Muslim, and they promote a more fundamentalist political community. Salafi-Ikhwani Muslims are different from Salafi jihadis, who seek to impose an extreme interpretation of Sunni Islam through direct violent action and regard political activism as futile.

During the 1948 war with Israel, as many as seven thousand Muslim Brotherhood *fidaiyin* (irregulars or guerrillas) were armed by the government and fought in Palestine alongside the Egyptian army. They returned to Egypt humiliated and angry and refused to disarm, setting off a violent confrontation with the government that culminated with al-Banna's assassination in 1949, most likely carried out by the king's security forces. In 1954 the Brotherhood tried to assassinate Nasser and was subsequently outlawed. Whether functioning legally or thriving in the shadows, it has maintained a prominent position in the political and social fabric of Egypt and other Arab countries. In Egypt it operated an extensive social welfare program, and in 2012 its candidate, Mohammed Morsi (b. 1951), won the presidency, but the military removed him from office a year later. His imposition of Islamic norms on Egypt's diverse Islamic and non-Islamic population became untenable.

In 1954 Nasser deposed Egypt's first president, General Mohammed Naguib (1901–84), and assumed the office two years later. The son of a postal worker, Nasser personified the slogan "Egypt for the Egyptians." In the 1930s, he attended the military academy, which provided a means of upward mobility for middle-class families. At the beginning of his presidency, Nasser was on good terms with the British and Americans, and some Arabs even accused him of being too cozy with the West. He soon moved in other directions. Under heavy pressure from the United States, Britain and Egypt resumed negotiations over the status of the British in Egypt. In 1954 Britain agreed to a major revision of the 1936 treaty, which stipulated that British troops must leave the canal zone within twenty months. The British, however, retained the right to reoccupy the canal zone if an Arab League state or Turkey was attacked. The evacuation was to be completed by June 1956.

In early 1955, an Israeli raid into Egyptian-administered Gaza made it clear to Nasser that he needed a larger and more modern arsenal. He refused to purchase arms from the United States or Britain because of the strings attached, such as joining an anticommunist coalition or pledging not to attack Israel. That same year, the Bandung Conference in Indonesia marked the start of the Non-Aligned Movement; Nasser was one of the movement's founders.[2] It opposed Western domination and neocolonialism and sought to steer a course between the Soviet and Western blocs.

In 1955 Britain, Pakistan, Iran, Turkey, and Iraq signed the Baghdad Pact, a defensive alliance designed to block Soviet expansion into South Asia and the Middle East. Nasser refused to join and subsequently purchased arms from countries in the Soviet orbit. He espoused a policy of "positive neutralism," whereby he pursued friendly relations with both the East and West. He hoped to obtain arms from the Communist bloc and economic aid from the West. The United States attempted to influence Nasser's behavior by offering him technical and economic assistance and a huge loan to finance the building of the Aswan Dam. The United States opposed Nasser's policy of positive neutralism, condemned his threats against Israel and pro-West regimes in the Middle East, and denounced his recognition of the People's Republic of China. In July 1956, the U.S. government reversed its policy and canceled the loan for the Aswan Dam project. Nasser retaliated by nationalizing the Suez Canal, which was principally owned by Britain and France; the two powers began plotting to topple Nasser and get it back.

Britain and France had important reasons for stopping Nasser. Britain sought to preserve its imperial lifeline through Suez to Asia, and France wanted to halt Nasser's support for anti-French rebels in Algeria. In October 1956, the British and French, in league with the Israelis, invaded Egypt; the operation was codenamed Musketeer. This surreal episode in Middle Eastern history became known as the Suez Crisis. First, the Israelis invaded Gaza and Sinai and drove to the canal. Their stated reason for attacking Egypt was to halt Nasser's support for the *fidaiyin*. The British and French then intervened and took control of the canal zone, ostensibly to separate Israeli and Egyptian troops, but in reality to oust

Nasser and wrest control of the waterway. The United States and Soviet Union condemned the intervention and pressured the invading forces to halt their attack and leave Egyptian territory. The crisis marked the end for Britain and France as major powers in the Middle East. On the other hand, Nasser turned his major military defeat into a great personal victory; he became the dominant political figure in the Arab world. Israel bowed to international pressure and relinquished Gaza and Sinai, but it did not achieve peace with any of its Arab neighbors. The United Nations dispatched an observer force—the UN Emergency Force (UNEF)—to monitor strategic positions in the Sinai. In the end, the United States alienated its British and French allies and a friendly government in Israel yet earned little gratitude from the Arab world. Anticolonial sentiment still ran strong. Upon Great Britain's withdrawal of its troops, its seventy-four-year occupation of Egypt came to an end—finally.

65. What is Zionism, and how does it differ from political Zionism and other forms of the ideology?

Zionism is not a religious doctrine; it is a political ideology. It is the belief that the Jewish people make up a nation and have the right to establish a national home in Palestine. A Zionist is a person who supports that right. In the early years of the movement, the Jewish homeland did not necessarily have to be in Palestine, but by the end of the nineteenth century, its leaders agreed that the Jewish homeland should be in Palestine, the historic home of the Jewish people. The traditional Passover toast—"Next year in Jerusalem!"—calls for the return to the promised land. The notion of return has been a central theme for Jews since AD 70, when the Romans destroyed the Second Temple in Jerusalem, creating the Jewish Diaspora throughout the Middle East and Mediterranean world.

From the concept of a return to the Land of Israel, a variety of Zionist ideologies, political movements, and forms of expression have emerged. Political Zionism, advocated by the Viennese journalist and assimilated Jew Theodor Herzl (1860–1904), takes the establishment of a Jewish homeland a step further, combining the yearning of the Jewish people to return to the promised land with the creation and maintenance of a state in Palestine. Other Jewish leaders, such as the activist Leon Pinsker

(1821–91), espoused practical Zionism, which called for the settling of the land in Palestine as the most effective means to establish a Jewish presence on the ground. The chemist Chaim Weizmann (1874–1952), who served as Israel's first president, believed that the settlement of Jews in Palestine should be coupled with the political backing of the world's leading powers. His view was often referred to as synthetic Zionism. Advocates of cultural Zionism called for making an independent state in Palestine the center of Jewish culture, thus preserving Jewish identity and eliminating the need for assimilation in countries where Jews would be a minority. In the years leading up to the creation of Israel in 1948, proponents of revolutionary Zionism viewed the gathering of Jews in a Jewish homeland as nothing less than a radical undertaking.

During the British mandate, revolutionary Zionists engaged in armed attacks on both the British authorities and Palestinian Arabs. Among the ranks of the revolutionaries were revisionist Zionists, led by Vladimir Jabotinsky (1880–1940), who argued for a free market economy and a Jewish state that would include territory east of the Jordan River; the revisionists strongly opposed labor Zionism, which counted among its leaders David Ben-Gurion (1886–1973), Israel's first prime minister. The labor Zionists were influenced by European socialism and endeavored to establish a viable Jewish colony in Palestine that was democratic, egalitarian, and based economically on agricultural and industrial collectives.

Religious Zionism holds that the creation of the State of Israel is a religious duty commanded by the Torah and that human activity in the promised land will bring about the arrival of the Messiah. This belief is widely held today by Israeli settlers in the West Bank. After the Six-Day War of 1967, the extremist ideology of neo-Zionism took root. A contentious view in Israeli political discourse, it calls for the expulsion of Arabs from the West Bank followed by large-scale Jewish settlement. Christian Zionists assert that the creation of the State of Israel fulfills biblical prophecy and provides an essential precondition for the Second Coming of Christ. In 2007 the National Council of Churches of the United States resolved that Christian Zionism is a hindrance to both peace between Israelis and Palestinians and constructive relations between Jews and Muslims. The reestablishment of a Jewish state has never been a doctrine of the Roman Catholic Church. Acknowledging different Zionist ideologies will help us understand the political landscape of today's Israel.

It is clear from the preceding paragraphs that not all Zionists are Jews. It is also important to note that not all Jews are Zionists. Some Jews, namely, the ultra-Orthodox, consider Zionism a blasphemy and believe that only the Messiah can lead the Jewish people back to the promised land. Furthermore, many rabbis of the nineteenth century condemned the ideology as a form of self- or group-love that flew in the face of Judaism's great commandment: "You shall love the Lord your God with all your heart, and with all your soul, and with all your might" (Deuteronomy 6:5). On the other hand, many non-Jews support the right of the Jewish people to establish a homeland in Palestine. Every U.S. president since Harry S. Truman (1945–53) has pledged to uphold the security of Israel, and Evangelical Christians support Jewish migration to the Promised Land.

66. What role did Zionism play in the establishment of a Jewish homeland in Palestine?

The Zionist movement and the advocacy of Jewish leaders in Europe played a critical role in the formation of the State of Israel. Essential developments in the late nineteenth and early twentieth centuries were Theodor Herzl's writings, which explained the necessity of a Jewish state, and Chaim Weizmann's political activism, which culminated in a promise from the British government to establish a Jewish homeland in Palestine.

Before the late 1800s, Jews were concerned with maintaining their identity and traditions and surviving in the Diaspora. In Western Europe, they were treated as second-class citizens, living in ghettos and restricted to certain occupations, yet their status was better than it had been during the Middle Ages, when the Jews were expelled from Britain, France, and Spain and blamed for great plagues.

In the late eighteenth century, Jews began assimilating into European society and experiencing greater tolerance. Their improved status could be traced to the success of the Jewish Enlightenment (Hashanah), which grafted Western liberal ideals onto traditional Jewish culture. As a result, Jews could participate fully in society and be viewed as full citizens of the countries where they lived.

Many of the ideas of the European Enlightenment did not take root or find acceptance in Eastern Europe, where Jews were held in disdain by the local population and were frequently the targets of persecution. The Pan-Slavic movement of the late nineteenth century reinforced the notion that the Jews, along with other non-Slav peoples, were second-class citizens. Jews were often the targets of nationalists battling the Russian czar as well as scapegoats for his failed policies.

In the 1860s, the Russian government began authorizing pogroms (organized persecutions) aimed at Jewish communities. The pogroms resulted in the destruction of homes, farms, and businesses and sometimes the complete removal of an area's Jewish population. Jews were often blamed for the country's economic problems because they performed the unpopular work of collecting taxes and lending money. As a result of the pogroms, a growing number of Jews were calling for immediate migration to Palestine.

In 1862 Moses Hess (1812–75), a French-born Jewish philosopher and socialist living in Germany, wrote *Rome and Jerusalem: The Last National Question* (1862), urging Jews to move to Palestine and set up a socialist state, revitalize the land, and wait for the Messiah. Two decades later, Leon Pinsker, a Jewish Polish-Russian physician and founder of the Russian Zionist organization Chovevei Tzion (Lovers of Zion), authored *Auto-Emancipation: Warning to His Fellow People, from a Russian Jew*, arguing that the world's Jews would be subject to discrimination and repression—a circumstance he called Judeophobia—until they had a country of their own. In 1883 a Viennese student named Nathan Birnbaum (1864–1937) founded the student Zionist organization Kadima (Forward) and published the Zionist journal *Selbstemanzipation!* (Self-Emancipation!), which marked the first-known use of the term "Zionism." In 1882 the Lovers of Zion led the First Aliyah (migration; literally, "going up") to Palestine. The *olim* (migrants) of the First Aliyah aimed to create a socialist utopia in the promised land, but few *olim* remained in Palestine, which proved to be a difficult, unhealthy, and unfriendly place to live and work.

The Zionist movement gained momentum under the direction of Herzl. In 1894 he reported on the Dreyfus Affair in France. Captain Alfred

Dreyfus (1859–1935), a Jewish artillery officer on the French General Staff, was charged with spying for Germany. The French right-wing demanded justice to restore the nation's honor. Dreyfus was convicted on flimsy evidence and sentenced to confinement on Devil's Island in French Guiana.[3] Herzl was appalled by the strident anti-Semitism on display at the trial and concluded that Jews must have their own state to survive. In 1896 he published *Der Judenstaat* (The Jewish State), in which he argued for the creation of a modern country run by Jews but indicated no preference for its location. He proposed Kenya or Argentina, and the British government offered a tract of land in Kenya. A year later, Herzl and several participants of the First Aliyah organized the World Zionist Organization (WZO). Two branches of the movement—the Herzl-secular Zionists and the Hess-religious Zionists—met at the First International Zionist Congress, which convened in Basel, Switzerland. The religious Zionists gained control of the meeting and won passage of a resolution that called for a national home in Palestine, a colonization program, and efforts to secure official sanction and international support.

In 1901 Zionist leaders founded the Jewish National Fund. Money came from Jewish donors worldwide and was used to purchase land in Palestine. Managers of the fund were diligent in obtaining legal title to the land, but Ottoman property law worked against Palestinian Arabs. Most of the land was owned by absentee landlords, and Palestinian tenants paid rent in return for protection from obligations to the Ottoman Empire, such as paying taxes and performing military service. Thus, a feudal relationship existed between the peasants and their landlords. The peasants were attached to the land they rented, and the rental lease was hereditary. Land sales increased during World War I owing to the dislocation of many tenants. Landlords saw the war as a good time to sell. The Palestinians were shocked by the sales; in most cases, the land had been rented by a family for several generations.

The Russian Revolution of 1905, during which many Jews challenged the authority of the czar, spurred the Second Aliyah. The *olim* worked diligently to establish basic institutions in Palestine, such as schools, newspapers, factories, kibbutzim (communal farms), and political and labor organizations. They also founded the city of Tel Aviv, and the lexicographer

Eliezer Ben-Yehuda (1858–1922) revived Hebrew as a modern, spoken language. Inevitably, many *olim* left after a few years; those who remained became the founders of the State of Israel.

67. What were major events and developments during the British mandate in Palestine (1920–48)?

Under the post-Ottoman mandate system, Britain and France governed the Arab lands of the Fertile Crescent. Britain controlled Iraq and Palestine, including Transjordan; France governed Syria and Lebanon. The Third Aliyah brought approximately 40,000 Eastern European Jews to Palestine in the years following World War I. Because the Palestine mandate was binational—Arab and Jew—Britain's troubles began immediately. The British were committed to implementing the Balfour Declaration in accordance with the League of Nations, but on the ground in Palestine, they tilted toward the larger Arab community. During the war, the British made promises to both sides that they could not keep, and as a consequence, their policy vacillated terribly. In the end, the British succeeded in creating two well-armed, implacable foes.

British administrators in Palestine preserved the Ottoman *millets*—the self-governing Jewish, Muslim, and Christian communities—but retained the final say on who would lead each confessional group. Accomplishments of British rule include establishing a secular judiciary, comprised of lower criminal and civil courts and appellate and supreme tribunals; carrying out the censuses of 1922 and 1931, which gathered valuable demographic data; instituting the Palestine Police Force and introducing modern investigative and forensic techniques; and creating the Palestine Broadcasting Service, which during the years leading up to World War II became the BBC's Arabic Service, competing with Italy's Radio Bari and Radio Berlin, both of which had been flooding the Middle East with Axis propaganda. Another legacy of the mandate was a series of land studies, laws, and ordinances that divided the territory into zones. Attempts to regulate land sales along confessional lines, principally Jewish and Muslim, pleased neither side.

By 1920 Palestinian Arabs were already resisting the newest wave of Jewish immigrants by attacking Jewish businesses and raiding farms.

That same year, the Histadrut, a Jewish labor, industrial, and social organization, was formed; it created its own defense force, the Haganah (Defense). The force was of questionable legal status under the mandate, but the British permitted it to grow in the 1920s and 1930s, and many of its fighters served alongside other soldiers of the empire, fighting the Axis in Greece, the Middle East, North Africa, and Italy.

In 1921 Herbert L. Samuel (1870–1963) became the first British high commissioner in Palestine. He was a Zionist but endeavored to be fair to both sides. He encouraged the Arabs and Jews to set up their own civil institutions, such as labor organizations, representative governing bodies, and political parties, but only the Jews were prepared to do this immediately. That same year, Samuel appointed Hajj Amin al-Husseini (ca. 1896–1974), an Arab nationalist and anti-Zionist, as the mufti of Jerusalem, in the belief that bringing al-Husseini into the political process would moderate his views. In 1922 the Jewish Agency was established to administer the Yishuv, as the Jewish community in Palestine was known, and became a de facto Jewish government. By the mid-1920s, the Zionist movement had split into two rival groups: the labor Zionists and revisionist Zionists, described in the response to Question 65.

In the wake of Arab unrest, the British government promulgated the Churchill white paper (1922). It reaffirmed the founding of a Jewish national home in Palestine; rejected altering the ethnic makeup of the mandate; and argued that immigration should be limited to the "capacity of the country ... to absorb new arrivals."[4] As a result of the paper, both Arabs and Jews became suspicious of British motives and actions in Palestine. In the mid-1920s, during the Fourth Aliyah, more than 50,000 Jews, mostly from Poland, migrated to Palestine.

The window for compromise between Arabs and Jews narrowed considerably with the Wailing Wall incident of 1929. Disagreement over a public walkway and the placement of chairs near Jerusalem's Western Wall resulted in a violent anti-Jewish riot. The rioting spread to other cities; the Jewish and Arab communities each suffered more than a hundred fatalities. The British government dispatched the Shaw Commission to study the source of the violence. In its report, the commission acknowledged the validity of Arab complaints, recommended that Britain's obligations to the Arabs be spelled out clearly, and proposed that Jewish immigration be regulated. A parallel fact-finding mission, the Hope-Simpson Commission, also studied the incident and submitted its findings in the Passfield white paper (1930). It blamed Jewish land purchases for the turmoil and called for tighter immigration and the settlement of displaced Palestinian peasants. Jewish leaders were outraged by the findings of the two commissions; in protest, Chaim Weizmann resigned as chairman of the Jewish Agency. Embarrassed, the British nullified the Passfield white paper with a letter from Prime Minister Ramsay MacDonald (1924, 1929–35) to Weizmann. The MacDonald letter (1931) reaffirmed the Balfour Declaration; the Arabs dubbed it the "Black Letter."

In 1933 Adolf Hitler (1889–1945) and the Nazi Party came to power in Germany. Their draconian anti-Jewish laws and support for the harassment of Jews and the destruction of their property caused a flood of migration to Palestine. More than 170,000 Jews arrived in the mandate during the Fifth Aliyah. The Arabs questioned why they should lose their land and suffer social disruptions over the persecution of Jews in Nazi Germany. In 1936 local Arab resistance committees called a general strike to protest Jewish immigration and land purchases. The strike became a full-scale revolt, fueled by fears of rising unemployment and growing Jewish political strength. The strike and revolt spurred Arab leaders to establish a national organization, the Arab Higher Committee (AHC), and appoint al-Husseini as its president. Troubled by the revolt, the British dispatched the Peel Commission to study conditions on the ground; in return, al-Husseini called off the strike. The British commission recommended partition with most of Palestine going to the Arabs. The Jews reluctantly accepted the plan because it would give them a state. The Arabs rejected it, however, fearing the eventual loss of all of Palestine; they renewed their revolt. The British arrested and deported members of the AHC, and al-Husseini fled to Iraq. In 1939 the British Colonial Office brought Arabs and Jews together for a meeting in London in a long-shot attempt to negotiate a settlement to the dispute in Palestine. The three-way discussion, the London Roundtable, was a failure.

With a global war on the horizon, Britain realized the imperative of improving relations with the Arab populations of the Middle East, because doing so could enhance the security of imperial communications, particularly the Suez Canal, and access to petroleum resources. Consequently, in 1939 the British issued a white paper that effectively nullified the Balfour Declaration: "His Majesty's Government . . . now declare unequivocally that it is not part of their policy that Palestine should become a Jewish State. They would indeed regard it as contrary to their obligations to the Arabs under the Mandate, as well as to the assurances which have been given to the Arab people in the past, that the Arab population of Palestine should be made the subjects of a Jewish State against their will."[5]

Under the terms of the report, the mandate would end in ten years; immigration would be limited to 15,000 per year for five years, after which it had to have Arab approval; and land sales would be severely restricted. The Jews felt betrayed by the British and trapped by Hitler's anti-Semitic policies. The British policy inflamed Irgun, a radical group of Jabotinsky supporters led by Menachem Begin (1913–92). Al-Husseini, from exile, rejected the paper; he wanted immediate independence and an end to immigration. Most Arabs, however, viewed the paper as a measure of victory. While some Arab military and political leaders sided with the Axis Powers during the war, most Arabs remained neutral. On the other hand, the Jews, including Irgun, out of necessity, supported the British. David Ben-Gurion eloquently summarized the Jewish predicament during the war: "We shall fight the War as if there was no White Paper, and the White Paper, as if there was no War."[6] The menace of Hitler had elevated the Zionist sentiment of American Jews. More than ever, they realized that the Jews of Europe needed a safe homeland. In 1942 American Zionists adopted the Biltmore Program, which called for the cancellation of the 1939 white paper, open immigration, and the establishment of a Jewish state. The World Zionist Organization endorsed the program.

Over the course of the war, political conditions in Palestine became increasingly radical and violent. In 1941 al-Husseini traveled to Berlin, where he conferred with Hitler and set up an anti-British, anti-Zionist propaganda operation that would serve the Arabs of Palestine. Husseini went beyond advocating for Palestinian Arabs and assisted the notorious SS leader Heinrich Himmler (1900–45) in inciting anti-Jewish fervor. He also recruited Muslims in the Balkans to fight alongside the German army. In 1942 the Stern Gang, an extreme offshoot of Irgun, began attacking British authorities and any Zionist group that collaborated with British officials. The leader of the group, Avraham Stern (1907–42), opened a dialogue with the Nazis but was killed in a British raid that also killed or captured many of his followers. Survivors formed LEHI (the Hebrew acronym for Fighters for the Freedom of Israel), which assassinated Lord Moyne (1880–1944), the British colonial secretary, in Cairo. After the defeat of Germany in 1945, armed Jewish organizations, including Haganah, driven by the annihilation of 6 million Jews in the Holocaust and determined to liberate Palestine and establish a state, stepped up violence against the British. In 1946 Irgun blew up a wing of the King David Hotel, which served as the headquarters of the British administration in Palestine. In February 1947, with Jewish-British violence escalating and their stewardship of the mandate a shambles, the British handed the Palestine question over to the United Nations.

In the summer of 1947, the UN Special Committee on Palestine (UNSCOP) investigated conditions in Palestine, but its members could not agree on a common proposal. A majority favored partitioning Palestine into separate Arab and Jewish states and placing Jerusalem under international supervision; the minority favored a binational state. In September the British announced they would end the mandate and withdraw completely by May 1948. In the months leading up to the British departure, warfare between Arabs and Jews raged. Atrocities were committed by both sides, most notably the massacre of Jews at Gush Etzion and the slaughter of Arabs at Deir Yassin. In November 1947, the UN General Assembly approved the partition plan for Palestine. The Jews accepted the plan; the Arabs rejected it. On 14 May 1948, the British mandate expired, and Ben-Gurion, Israel's first prime minister, declared the country's independence. The first Arab-Israeli war began the following day.

68. What were key events and the outcome of the 1948–49 Arab-Israeli War?

Leading up to the UN vote, there had been growing pressure on U.S. president Harry S. Truman to back the partition plan. He supported it over the objection of his secretary of state, George C. Marshall (1880–1959), who argued that recognition of Israel would alienate the more populous Arab world and threaten access to Middle East oil. Truman was influenced by his religious convictions; his concern for a small, emerging democracy surrounded by hostile neighbors; and his awareness of the need for Jewish support in his upcoming campaign for a full term as president.

On 14 May 1948, the trouble-plagued British mandate in Palestine came to an end, and David Ben-Gurion proclaimed the independence of the State of Israel. He served as Israel's first and third prime minister (1948–54, 1955–63); Chaim Weizmann was selected as the country's first president (1949–52). The United States and the Soviet Union immediately recognized the new government. The Soviets did so to weaken Britain's position in the Middle East and court the favor of Israel, which it saw as a potential socialist ally in the region.

The next day, Israel's Arab neighbors—Egypt, Iraq, Lebanon, Syria, and Transjordan—attacked Israel. The war compelled hundreds of thousands of Palestinians to flee their homes. Some feared another massacre like that at Deir Yassin, while others were fooled by the Israeli army or seduced by their own leaders into believing that they would be able to return home soon. Many others were deliberately forced out of their homes by the Israelis.

UN-brokered cease-fires went into effect in June and July 1948. The Israelis used the stand-down to replenish their arsenal with arms from Europe and fortify their positions on the battlefield. During the fighting, the Israelis consolidated and expanded their control over the Galilee, Negev Desert, and parts of Judea. They gained territory beyond what had been allocated to the Jewish state according to the UN partition plan. They could not, however, wrest the Old City of Jerusalem or its Jewish Quarter from Transjordan's Arab Legion.

In 1949 on the Aegean island of Rhodes, Dr. Ralph Bunche (1904–71), the UN's chief mediator for the Palestine conflict, served as the go-between for Israel and its four Arab neighbors: Egypt, Transjordan, Lebanon, and Syria.[7] A year earlier, he had succeeded Count Folk Bernadotte (1895–1948), the victim of LEHI assassins. Bunche successfully negotiated a series of armistice agreements, reaching the last accord—between Israel and

Syria—in July 1949. He did not pursue an Israeli-Iraqi armistice because the two countries did not share a border. The armistice lines would serve as the de facto boundaries between Israel and neighboring Arabs until the Six-Day War of 1967. Since that conflict, the Arabs have steadfastly called for the armistice lines of 1949 to serve as a starting point in peace negotiations with Israel. The armistice agreements negotiated by Bunche were only a pause in the protracted Arab-Israeli conflict. The wars of 1956, 1967, 1973, and 1982 were continuations of that first conflict.

The Israelis and Palestinian Arabs—the local antagonists in the war—were fighting over land. Many Jews believed that their people had a biblical claim to the land of Palestine. An even larger number of Jews accepted the "half loaf" of the 1947 UN partition plan and were determined to fight for their new state. The Palestinians, on the other hand, argued that they were entitled to the land because Arabs had inhabited it for nearly two millennia, and during most of that period, Jews made up a small portion of the country's population.

The Arab countries that fought Israel had conflicting national goals. The Egyptian government hoped that a war would divert the attention of the Egyptian people from the country's dire domestic problems and ongoing British occupation. Egypt also aspired to be the leader of the Arab world, which could be achieved by spearheading the war that destroyed the new Jewish state. The Syrians sought to restore Greater Syria, which Arabs had governed during the early centuries of the *umma*. Establishing control over this territory had been a goal of Syrian nationalists since the 1920s. The Syrians also endeavored to thwart Egyptian and Hashimite designs on leading the Arab world. The Jordanians sought land, namely, fertile territory west of the Jordan River. King 'Abdullah also hoped to reestablish Greater Syria, but under Hashimite, not Syrian, leadership. He was opposed by other Arab leaders, especially Syrian nationalists, Egypt's King Faruq, and Saudi Arabia's King Ibn Sa'ud. Lebanon jumped on the bandwagon and joined the other Arab states in the war against Israel. Its contributions to the war effort were minimal. We must be aware of the divergent Arab interests in the war because the lack of a unified Arab front was arguably the most significant factor behind the Israeli victory.

The 1948–49 Arab-Israeli War was an extraordinary event that set in motion significant changes in the Middle East. For the Israelis, the struggle against the British, Palestinian Arabs, and neighboring Arab states culminated in their independence. For the Arabs, the defeat humiliated their armies and discredited their governments. Many Arab combatants vowed to remove the corrupt, incompetent governments that had ordered them to fight a war their larger Arab force should have won. Palestinian Arabs refer to the war as an-Nakba (the Disaster or Catastrophe). The war uprooted more than a half million Palestinians, who sought refuge in the Gaza Strip, the West Bank of the Jordan River, Jordan, Syria, and Lebanon. Many of the refugees emerged as ardent Arab nationalists bitterly opposed to Israel, its supporters, and Arab governments that dared to make peace with the Jewish state.

12

Turkey after Atatürk, Iran under Mohammed Reza Shah, and the Arab World after World War II

In this chapter, we trace major events and developments in the Middle East since the middle of the twentieth century. We begin with an overview of political, economic, and social changes in Turkey, from the death of Atatürk in 1938 to the present. We then examine the turbulent reign of Mohammed Reza Shah from his accession to the throne in 1941 to the months before his downfall in 1979. In the latter half of the chapter, we examine the Arab nationalist ideologies of Ba'thism and Nasserism and investigate key political developments in the Arab world from the conclusion of the 1948–49 Arab-Israeli War to the outbreak of the June 1967 Arab-Israeli War, a tumultuous period in intra-Arab relations ironically referred to as the Quiet Decade—quiet because no war erupted between Israel and its Arab neighbors.

69. What were significant political, economic, and social developments in Turkey following the passing of Atatürk?

The legacy of Mustapha Kemal Atatürk dominated Turkish politics throughout the turbulent 1940s. President İsmet İnönü continued the late leader's secularization program and carefully maintained the country's neutrality during World War II. To stave off invasion and occupation, he maintained diplomatic and commercial relations with both the Axis and Allies. Turkey received Lend-Lease material from the United States in 1941, and it imposed the Capital Levy of 1942 as a concession to the Axis powers. Pushed by Berlin, Ankara imposed a tax on property, savings, and investments as a means of penalizing Turks who were benefitting financially from the war. The tax burden fell disproportionately on non-Muslim businesses; Jews and Christians paid ten times the rate of Muslims, and many of them went bankrupt. People who could not pay the tax were sent to labor camps in Anatolia. The levy ended in 1944 with the waning of German power and influence.

As the German threat receded, Turkey tilted toward the Allied cause. It opened the straits to war matériel bound for the Soviet Union, and in February 1945, it declared war on Germany and, by doing so, became a charter member of the United Nations. After the war, Turkey joined the Western camp, supporting Washington's containment strategy against international communism. The Soviets soon pressured Turkey to cede control and governance of the straits and territory in eastern Anatolia. The Soviet demands led to a major U.S. policy declaration—the Truman Doctrine of March 1947—which extended U.S. aid to Turkey and Greece. (The Greek government was battling a Soviet-supported insurgency.) The Turkish armed forces were strengthened against the Soviet threat, and the crisis subsided.

Since the end of the war, the West had been pressuring Turkey to hold multiparty elections. In 1946 disaffected members of the ruling Republican People's Party (CHP), including Celâl Bayar (1883–1986), one of Atatürk's chief assistants, formed the Democratic Party (DP). The new party became a political home for a variety of individuals who had been shut out by Atatürk and the CHP over the past quarter century: businessmen and merchants who were opposed to state control of the economy, old rural landlords who opposed land appropriations, and religiously conservative peasants who were opposed to secularism and the emphasis on industrialization. The first multiparty election was held in 1946; the CHP won. Four years later, the DP was victorious. Bayar was chosen as president (1950–60); Adnan Menderes became prime minister (1950–60).

The new government rolled back some of Atatürk's reforms. First, it emphasized free market economics by privatizing industries and capital and building a major road network to facilitate commerce. Second, it relaxed secularism by reinstating the call to prayer in Arabic, permitting the reading of the Qur'an over the radio, and reestablishing the faculty of divinity at Istanbul University. Although the DP reversed many of Atatürk's policies, the Grand National Assembly in 1951 passed Law 5816, which made it illegal to insult the late leader or his legacy. The party would use the law as a bludgeon against any opponent of the government. Regarding foreign affairs, during the 1950s, Turkey's ties to the West grew stronger. It joined NATO in 1952 and contributed troops to the UN coalition fighting the communists in Korea.

The DP-led government was unable to deal with the severe economic and political problems that emerged in the late 1950s. High inflation caused salaries to decline in value, recession sapped the national economy, and the government incurred a huge foreign debt. Popular opposition, especially to the government's economic policies, grew. In response, the government became increasingly repressive. In 1957 the DP won a majority of seats in the assembly, avoiding a coalition government and effectively shutting the CHP out of the political arena. In 1958 press censorship was imposed. Two years later, a commission banned all subversive activities and employed the army to harass opposition politicians, including the former president, İsmet İnönü. Interfering in the election turned out to be the last straw; the CHP and army were outraged and moved against the DP.

In May 1960, a group of military officers, led by General Cemal Gürsel (1895–1966), overthrew the government. Gürsel served as both prime minister and president in the military-led government. In the Turkish political tradition, the military came to be viewed as the custodian of Atatürk's vision and legacy and supportive of Kemalism and democratic institutions. It seized power reluctantly and held it temporarily. The military-led government charged Bayar, Menderes, and other DP leaders with corruption and laxity in upholding Kemalism, especially the policies regarding statism and secularism. Bayar was imprisoned, Menderes was executed, and the DP was abolished.

In 1961 a new constitution was adopted that created the framework for a multiparty democracy. It provided for a bicameral legislature, the protection of individual rights, and the reaffirmation of secularism. That same year, the CHP returned to power in a coalition government, and İnönü was installed as prime minister (1961–65). The party represented a left-of-center constituency and held power in several coalition governments until 1980, when it was dissolved along with other political parties following another military coup. The Justice Party (JP), a center-right coalition led by Süleyman Demirel (1924–2015), won the election of 1965. The party was the successor to the DP. General Cevdet Sunay became president (1966–73), and Demirel served as prime minister from 1965 to 1971.

In the late 1960s, political liberalization coincided with economic liberalization. The remittances sent home by thousands of Turkish workers in Europe triggered an economic boom. By 1980 there were 1.8 million Turks living and working in West Germany alone. The huge influx of hard currency spurred expansion and generated a trade surplus. Political parties, including Marxist and Islamic groups, proliferated, and it became evident that small parties could interrupt the governing and legislative processes. Terrorism carried out by both the extreme left and extreme right escalated. In 1969 the JP won reelection.

In the early 1970s, governmental instability, a weakening economy, and political extremism plagued the country. Social unrest bred violent street demonstrations. The military pressured the government to solve these problems—especially the violence—or suffer the consequences, namely, another coup. The army's warning became known as the "coup by memorandum." The military threatened the government but did not take power. It did, however, exert influence on government decisions. It forced Demirel and several ministers to resign and replaced them with nonpartisan technocrats. The new government imposed martial law, which restored a modicum of order, but the crises continued because the government could do little to resolve the serious political and economic problems plaguing the country.

In 1973 Admiral Fahri Korutürk was elected president (1973–80), and independent politician Naim Talu served as prime minister (1973–74) in a caretaker government. In the October 1973 elections, the CHP, led by Bülent Ecevit (1925–2006), won the largest share of the votes and formed a coalition government with the National Salvation Party (MSP), a conservative religious party. It was a marriage of political convenience. Ecevit served as prime minister for most of 1974, the first of his four premierships. Meanwhile, social turmoil and political instability continued. In the summer of 1974, the Turkish government, fearing a merger between Greece and the Greek population of Cyprus, invaded the northern portion of the country to protect Turkish Cypriots, who comprised nearly a fifth of the island's population. The Turks established the independent Turkish Republic of Northern Cyprus, which has been recognized by only one government— the one in Ankara. The invasion drove a wedge between Greece and Turkey, both NATO allies, and strained relations between Washington and Ankara. In 2004 a UN-sponsored settlement was approved by Turkish Cypriots but rejected by their Greek counterparts. The Cyprus question still weighs heavily on the international community and remains unresolved.

In 1975 the JP formed a weak coalition government with Demirel as prime minister (1975–77). Two years later, the CHP formed another weak coalition government under Ecevit's premiership (1977 and 1978–79). Demirel served briefly as prime minister between Ecevit's terms. In 1979 the JP formed yet another weak coalition government, and Demirel returned as prime minister (1979–80). The country needed strong political leadership, but weak coalitions made governing difficult, if not impossible. Remittances were declining, and inflation was spiraling out of control. Moreover, instability and political violence were intensifying, and acts of terrorism were becoming more frequent. Domestic turmoil and severe economic problems—for instance, the inflation rate had reached nearly 120 percent—led the military to act. In September 1980, after clashes between left-wing and right-wing extremists had left hundreds of Turks dead, the military seized control of the government. The National Security Council, led by General Kenan Evren (1917–2015), imposed military rule over the country. Evren served as president until 1989.

The junta suspended the 1961 constitution, abolished all political parties, dissolved the assembly, and banned current politicians from political activity until 1987. It convened a constituent assembly, which drafted a new constitution that boosted the powers of the president, granting the officeholder the power to appoint government ministers and call the assembly into session, and limited the rights and freedoms of academics, labor unions, journalists, and politicians who had been active before 1980. Democracy was gradually restored over the course of the decade. In 1982 the people approved the constitution in a nationwide referendum. A small number of political parties were permitted to organize. The MSP, which had been abolished in 1980, was reorganized as the Welfare Party (RP) under the leadership of Necmettin Erbakan (1926–2011). The Motherland Party (ANAP), led by Turgut Özal (1927–93), was a coalition of Islamists, secular Turks, and free market liberals. It won the election of 1983, and Özal became prime minister (1983–89). A Massachusetts Institute of Technology–trained economist, he had served as deputy prime minister for economic affairs under the military government.

Özal and the ANAP were committed to reforming the economy through liberalization, free market principals, and integration into the global economy. Prosperity returned, and the country's triple-digit inflation rate sank to 75 percent. The party sought Turkey's entry into the European Community (later the European Union), which would integrate Turkey economically and politically into Europe. It also hoped to reconcile fundamental Islam with modernization. Political stability throughout the country was attained by 1987. Pressed by Western democracies, the generals lifted martial law and the limits on political freedoms. In 1989 Özal was elected president (1989–93). Two years later, the True Path Party (DYP), a faction of conservative, secular politicians led by Demirel, narrowly defeated the ANAP. It was the successor to the JP and DP. Business interests supported the ANAP; small business owners and farmers supported the DYP. Demirel served as prime minister until 1993, when he became president following the death of Özal. That same year, Tansu Çiller became Turkey's first woman prime minister (1993–96).

Following Iraq's invasion and occupation of Kuwait in 1990, Turkey supported the international coalition in Operation Desert Shield and Operation Desert Storm. It shut down Iraqi pipelines through Turkey and permitted the United States to launch air strikes against Iraq from Turkish bases. The country continues to seek membership in the EU. In December 2004, the EU announced that it would begin accession talks with Turkey in October 2005. At the time of writing, several developments and crises have distanced Turkey from membership in the union, namely, the eurozone crisis, the United Kingdom's vote to exit the union, the immigration and refugee crises facing Western and Central Europe, and the growing authoritarianism of the Ankara government. Furthermore, many Europeans object to Turkey joining the EU for cultural and economic reasons. They fear a large Muslim nation joining the union and worry that Turkey's economy is not as developed as the economies of Western Europe. On the other hand, many Europeans argue that Turkey could serve as a bridge between the West and the Muslim world. They also point out that the infusion of Turkish workers could help pay for the EU's growing social welfare obligations, as low birth rates are taking a toll on the future economic viability of several European nations. Since the collapse of the Soviet Union in 1991, Turkey has sought to carve out a major presence in Central Asia. It was the first country to recognize the newly independent Turkish republics of the former Soviet Union and continues to be a major supporter.

During the 1990s, Turkey suffered from several problems, some of which had troubled the country for years. The inflation rate was lower but was still very high, averaging 60 percent. Unemployment rose owing to the sell-off of factories. Remittances from Turkish workers declined owing to their displacement in German factories by workers from the former East Germany. National revenue fell after Iraq's invasion of Kuwait owing to the loss of $2 billion in annual oil pipeline payments; Iraq had been Turkey's largest trading partner. The violent conflict with Turkey's Kurdish population, which began as a rebellion in 1978 and evolved into full-scale war in 1984, continued claiming an estimated 50,000 lives over more than thirty years of fighting. Increasingly scarce water resources prompted the country to build dams on the Tigris and Euphrates Rivers, an action that strained relations with its two downstream neighbors: Syria and Iraq. Finally, the republic, officially secular, faced the problem of rising Islamic fundamentalism, seen as a backlash to the strict enforcement of secularism. In the election of 1995, the RP captured a plurality of the votes and formed a coalition government; Erbakan became prime minister (1996–97). In 1997 the military viewed Erbakan as a threat to secularism and pressured his party into quitting the government coalition. In its place, the military installed a government of secularists. The following year, the Constitutional Court banned the RP for infusing religion into its political activities and prohibited seven of its members, including Erbakan, from participating in politics for five years.

Mustapha Kemal Atatürk's vision continues despite ongoing challenges. Turkey remains committed to democracy, but on four occasions between 1960 and 1997, the armed forces stepped in to protect secularism and multiparty democracy. In 2002 Turkey suffered a financial disaster as the Turkish currency, the lira, dropped in value when liberalized banking policies fostered horrendous inflation. In 1985 the exchange rate was 100 Turkish lira to the dollar; seventeen years later, the exchange rate was 1.5 million Turkish lira to the dollar. In the elections of 2002, the Justice and Development Party (AKP), the moderate Islamist party currently under the leadership of Recep Tayyip Erdoğan (b. 1954), won a clear majority of the seats in the Grand National Assembly. The party's rise can be seen in large part as a response to the heavy-handed secularism of the late 1990s. Furthermore, its social welfare program was very popular with voters. The new government did not support the U.S.-led invasion of Iraq in 2003, yet it secured accession talks with the EU. 'Abdullah Gül, the nominee of the AKP, overcame strong secular opposition, was elected president by the assembly, and served from 2007 to 2014. The AKP was reelected in 2007 and 2011. In 2008 the assembly passed a constitutional amendment that overturned the ban on the wearing of headscarves in public universities. A year later, the Constitutional Court struck down the amendment. In 2010 the AKP announced that it would support any woman disciplined for wearing a headscarf at her university. The AKP's position on this issue was tantamount to an informal lifting of the ban.

In early 2011, several army officers were arrested, and a number of retired military commanders were detained for suspected involvement in Operation Sledgehammer, a plot to overthrow the government in 2003. More than three hundred officers went on trial. In the summer of 2011, the service chiefs resigned in protest and were replaced by officers chosen by Gül and Erdoğan. In September 2012, a court convicted 322 active and retired officers for their participation in Sledgehammer; the ringleaders of the plot—two retired generals and a retired admiral—were given life sentences. Thirty-four officers were acquitted. The apparent legal victory underscored the AKP's dominance over Turkey's military establishment, but in 2015 more than two hundred accused officers were acquitted after they had been retried, mainly because the court ruled that their initial convictions had been obtained through the use of phony evidence.

In August 2014, Erdoğan was elected president in the first popular vote for that office. In parliamentary elections held in June of the following year, the AKP maintained its plurality but lost its absolute majority in the Grand National Assembly; the party regained its majority in a snap election five months later. In July 2016, Erdoğan survived a coup attempt spearheaded by a faction of the armed forces that was alarmed by the president's growing authoritarian style; the erosion of secularism, democracy, and human rights; and the country's waning international reputation. AKP officials accused the coup leaders of being connected with the Sufi cleric Fethullah Gülen (b. 1941), a former Erdoğan ally living in exile in Pennsylvania. At the time of this writing, the Turkish government had accused the United States of harboring Gülen and was demanding his return to stand trial. Also, the AKP had earlier alleged that military officers and security officials were creating a clandestine nationalist cell, Ergenekon, named for a mythical land in the Altai Mountains of Central Asia. From 2007 to the acquittal of several officials in 2015, the AKP carried out McCarthy-like investigations aimed at destroying the reputations of military officers and security officials viewed as a threat to the government.

In April 2017, Turkish voters approved a set of proposed constitutional amendments to increase the number of seats in the assembly from 550 to 600 and would replace the parliamentary system of government with a presidential system, conferring on the incumbent enhanced executive powers. The office of prime minister will be abolished after the next general election.

As this work went to press, the effacing of rights and freedoms under Islamist AKP governments, the concentration of more power in the hands of a single person, and closer relations with Russia were matters of great concern for Turkey's allies in the West. Nevertheless, the Turkish economy continues to develop. The country is now one of Europe's leading shipbuilders and producers of automobiles, and its Vestel Group has become one of the continent's largest technology companies. Consequently, many European politicians and economists argue that Turkey's educated and skilled workforce and its agricultural and industrial sectors would contribute to the prosperity of the EU. On the other hand, considering the crises and developments mentioned above it appears that Turkey's march to become an integral part of Europe has stumbled.

70. What were critical elements of Mohammed Reza Shah's White Revolution, and why did his reforms generate domestic opposition?

Mohammed Reza Shah Pahlavi (1919–80) succeeded his father, Reza, shortly after Hitler's invasion of the Soviet Union. He spent his teenage years attending a boarding school in Switzerland. The ski slopes occupied much of his time, and he was regarded by many as a playboy. He also acquired a reputation for being weak and indecisive. Soon after he ascended to the Peacock Throne,[1] he concluded the Tripartite Treaty of Alliance with Britain and the Soviet Union. The Allies gained transit rights through Iran and reaffirmed Iran's independence, pledging to withdraw within six months after the end of the war. After it had entered the conflict, the United States also established a major presence in Iran, supervising the movement of critical Lend-Lease supplies to the Soviet Union through what became known as the Persian corridor.

World War II was a difficult time for Iran. The Allies effectively controlled the country, yet Axis agents roamed the land, and ordinary Iranians endured serious economic hardship. In November 1943, the Big Three—Roosevelt, Churchill, and Stalin—met in Tehran to discuss war strategy. The city was emptied of its population and sealed off for security and logistical purposes, and the shah was not permitted to host the conference. The Tehran Conference proved to be a humiliating experience for the shah and his people. The Allies operated the Middle East Supply Center to handle the shipment of Lend-Lease materials and other supplies to the Soviet Union. Hundreds of millions of tons of supplies and equipment flowed through Iran, but none of it found its way to the Iranian population. Moreover, all the matériel was removed from Iran after the war, further aggravating strong antiforeign sentiment.

British and American troops departed Iran soon after the end of hostilities, but Soviet troops remained. In what became known as the Iran-Azerbaijan crisis, the Soviets attempted to establish a communist state in Iranian Azerbaijan. In November 1945, Iranian communists proclaimed the People's Republic of Azerbaijan under the support and protection of the Soviet Union. President Truman protested and demanded that Stalin withdraw his troops. The Soviet leader did not expect the United States to get involved; he had anticipated a British response instead. Under pressure from the United States and the United Nations, the Soviets withdrew their forces from Azerbaijan, and the socialist republic collapsed.

Antiforeign resentment came to a head in 1951, when Mohammed Mosaddiq (1882–1967) became prime minister. He was of aristocratic Qajar stock, had earned his law degree in Switzerland, and had served as a college professor. He had had a long career in politics and was the leader of the National Front, an anti-Western political movement. The Front was composed of traditional and progressive members of the middle class, including mullahs and Western-educated professionals. They were united in their opposition to foreign influence. Mosaddiq had long struggled to bring constitutional democracy to Iran. He supported the 1906 constitution, opposed Reza Shah, and was placed under house arrest from the late 1930s until 1943. He vigorously opposed the terms of the concession that Reza had awarded the Anglo-Iranian Oil Company (AIOC) in 1933. Within two months of taking power, Mosaddiq nationalized the AIOC. His action generated international shock waves. Britain refused to purchase oil from the nationalized company; the United States supported the British boycott. Diplomacy and boycotts failed to resolve the crisis. Consequently, British intelligence and the Central Intelligence Agency (CIA) began plotting to remove Mosaddiq.

Mosaddiq and Mohammed Reza were at loggerheads for two years. Mosaddiq hoped to seize control of the government and impose constitutional restrictions on the shah; the Majlis had already taken charge of the army. Unable to oust Mosaddiq, the shah and his family left for vacation in Italy on 16 August 1953, fearing for his safety. Meanwhile, the two-year boycott of Iranian oil had weakened the country's economy and prevented Mosaddiq from carrying out many of his domestic reforms.

Furthermore, his political coalition was unraveling. The United States, which was determined to contain the spread of international communism, feared that the Marxist Tudeh Party might emerge as the strongest political force in Iran.

Kermit Roosevelt Jr. (1916–2000), President Theodore Roosevelt's grandson and head of the CIA's Middle East–Africa desk, engineered a coup—code-name Operation Ajax—against Mosaddiq three days after Mohammed Reza had left for Italy. The coup, carried out by pro-monarchy military officers and supported by a crowd of hired protesters, turned out to be an inexpensive covert operation, costing less than $500,000. (Its success encouraged subsequent CIA efforts to effect regime change, particularly in Latin America.) General Fazallah Zahedi (ca. 1892–1963) took charge of the government and arrested Mosaddiq and his supporters. Although the CIA played a leading role in the coup, it is important to note that the Iranian military, led by Zahedi, had been poised and ready to move against Mosaddiq. The shah returned to Tehran on 22 August 1953.[2] The following year, the oil dispute was resolved by a new agreement by which Britain and Iran agreed to an equal division of the profits. In dealing with Mohammed Reza, the Western powers hoped for a stable autocrat who was also mindful of human rights. For his part, the shah took steps to ensure that his throne would never be threatened again. He was not as strong or as independent a leader as either Atatürk or Nasser; arguably, his greatest attribute was his talent as an appeaser. He catered to those elements that could best serve his interests, namely, the West, the peasantry, and the military. He used patronage to win support and went to great lengths to improve Iran's standing with Europe and the United States.

Over the next twenty-five years, Mohammed Reza and the U.S. government enjoyed a close relationship. Iran emerged as a major American ally and supplier of oil to the United States. It became a leading recipient of military aid and purchaser of military equipment. Thousands of American military personnel and civilian technicians served in Iran. Unfortunately, a few of them displayed behaviors that offended and alienated the local population, a circumstance that would later be exploited by various anti-Shah factions.

In 1955 Iran became a charter member of the Baghdad Pact—later known as the Central Treaty Organization (CENTO)—which was established to block Soviet expansion into the Middle East and South Asia. A decade and a half later, Iran became the chief U.S. proxy in the Persian Gulf. The Richard Nixon administration had developed the "twin pillars" strategy to thwart Soviet encroachment into the region; the pillars were Iran and Saudi Arabia. The administration developed the strategy in response to Britain's withdrawal from the Persian Gulf that same year and out of consideration of U.S. involvement in Vietnam, which put a severe strain on American military assets. In 1972 U.S. president Richard Nixon (1969–74) granted the shah permission to purchase unlimited amounts of nonnuclear weapons. This policy continued until late 1978.

In the decade following the ouster of Mosaddiq, Mohammed Reza ruled as a pseudo-constitutional ruler, permitting elections and limited political activity. U.S. president John F. Kennedy (r. 1961–63), a steadfast advocate for the development of democratic institutions worldwide, had viewed Iran as an ally—but one without a tradition of democracy and respect for human rights. Consequently, he pressured the shah to enact reforms. Valuing the United States as an ally, the shah carried out a reform program to satisfy the Kennedy administration. In 1963 he unveiled the White Revolution, a collection of social and economic reforms that focused on land redistribution, educational reforms, and women's rights; it also included the privatization of industries, nationalization of state resources, and even profit sharing for workers.

Mohammed Reza ordered the breakup of large estates as a way of diminishing the power of the landed aristocracy and creating a new base of support among the peasantry and disadvantaged masses. The landowners resented the undermining of their centuries-old feudal authority. Most of the land grants, however, were too small to support self-sufficient farming. Furthermore, the introduction of modern farm machinery created a rise in rural unemployment. Consequently, many peasant families moved into the cities. The shah also appropriated and distributed *awqaf* land holdings, infuriating the mullahs. Under his literacy program, military conscripts spent fifteen months in rural villages, teaching elementary school during the day and conducting adult courses at night. In the long run, the literacy program undermined the shah's authority because a much larger number of disaffected people could now read. The White Revolution advanced women's social status by granting them the right to vote and to obtain a divorce and by opposing polygamy.

Mohammed Reza used his country's oil revenue to push industrial, educational, and health care expansion. The number of skilled factory workers increased sharply, but they earned low wages, while prices for consumer goods increased. Industrialization also harmed the traditional bazaar economy and undermined the handicraft industry. Elementary school enrollment grew from 1.6 million students in 1963 to 4 million in 1977, and coeducational classes were introduced. The expansion of the secular school system alienated the mullahs. Improved health care resulted in lower infant mortality. As a result, the population of the country grew from 26 million in 1966 to 33 million in 1976.

The White Revolution, an example of top-to-bottom reform, generated results that were the opposite of what Mohammed Reza had intended. Instead of reforming and modernizing Iran, it stimulated opposition among the mullahs, large landowners, merchants, the urban poor, and the middle class. Wealthy landlords who had supported the shah and mullahs who had consistently opposed him stood to lose considerable revenue owing to his land redistribution program. Another unintended consequence was that those Iranians who benefitted economically from the shah's reforms demanded the establishment of genuinely democratic institutions. National Front candidates campaigning in the early 1960s had criticized the White Revolution and encouraged strikes and demonstrations. Riots broke out in 1963, but they were crushed by the shah's security forces.

A leading opponent of Mohammed Reza was Ayatollah Ruhollah Khomeini (ca. 1902–89), a teacher in Qom. He resisted the redistribution of land, advancement of women's rights, and close ties with the West. He specifically opposed an agreement between the United States and Iran—a Status of Forces Agreement—that would exempt U.S. civilian technicians and military personnel from Iranian legal jurisdiction. He was exiled to Turkey in 1964, then to Iraq in 1965, yet he steadily gathered a cadre of dedicated supporters who would shape the future revolution. In 1969 he published *Hukumat al-Islami* (Islamic Governance), a collection of his sermons on politics. In it he outlined his vision of an Islamic state. Known for his fiery sermons, he referred to the shah as the Little Satan and the United States as the Big Satan. A new medium—audio cassettes—helped spread Khomeini's message. The cassettes were brought into the country through the Shi'a clerical network and circulated among cab drivers and people in the streets, bazaars, and mosques.

As the country's problems mounted, opposition became more intense, and Mohammed Reza's response became increasingly repressive. A new constitution consolidated his power and handcuffed the opposition. It established a token two-party system, but the parties were not independent of the shah, meaning that elections to the Majlis produced a rubberstamp legislature. In 1967 the shah staged an elaborate coronation ceremony for himself and his third wife, Empress Farah. Four years later, he celebrated the twenty-five-hundred-year anniversary of the Persian monarchy in a huge ceremony at Persepolis. Hundreds of international VIPs were invited, but few Iranians attended. Many Iranians disparaged the celebration for its ostentation and criticized the shah for his fixation with pre-Islamic Persian dynasties. His father had adopted the title Shahanshah (King of Kings); Mohammed Reza added the title Aryamehr (Light of the Aryans). Among Muslims two prominent negative role models from pre-Islamic history are Pharaoh (later a derisive term applied to Gamal Abdel Nasser, Anwar al-Sadat, and Hosni Mubarak) and Khusraw (one of the last Sassanian shahs; d. 628). Khomeini referred to Mohammed Reza as the New Yazid, recalling the Umayyad caliph who massacred the Prophet Muhammad's grandson Husayn and his followers at Karbala in 680.

Mohammed Reza became increasingly withdrawn from his subjects, isolated, and detached from reality. He neither gained genuine political legitimacy nor developed an authentic concern for the welfare of his people. These failings were magnified by the corruption and maladministration of his regime. Meanwhile, revenues skyrocketed, and the size of the national budget exploded owing to the oil windfall of the mid- to late 1970s. Revenues increased from $817 million in 1968 to $2.25 billion in 1973 to $20 billion in 1976, and the national budget underwent a more than tenfold expansion, increasing from $3.6 billion in 1963 to $45 billion in 1976. The country became increasingly dependent on foreign technicians to facilitate its development and modernization.

The extraordinary economic growth of the 1970s created great prosperity for a small and privileged group, while incomes for workers increased slowly if at all. Moreover, the number of schools and universities multiplied, turning out thousands of graduates that the developing economy could not absorb. Meanwhile, Mohammed Reza stepped up efforts against his opponents. SAVAK, his secret police, brutally suppressed opponents who became increasingly active during the 1960s and 1970s. In 1975, fearing a possible electoral challenge, the shah abolished the multiparty system and sanctioned only one party: the Rastakhiz (Resurgence) Party. He hoped that it would serve as a safety valve for dissent. The creation of a single-party system, however, served only to increase the totalitarian nature of his government. Henceforth, only the religious establishment would be capable of mounting an effective opposition.

A growing chorus of Iranian critics believed that Westernization was destroying Iran's soul. Jalal Al-e-Ahmad's (1923–69) book *Occidentosis* (*Westoxification*), published in 1962, exposed the corruptive influence of the West. Another popular term was "Gharbzadegi" (Weststruckenness). Conservative Shi'a clergy charged that the influx of Western businesses was weakening the traditional Iranian economy. For example, Kentucky Fried Chicken franchises posed a threat to local chicken businesses.

During the 1960s, the Iranian population, in general, admired the United States and its unrivaled level of prosperity; dissidents, on the other hand, were concerned about American influence eroding traditional Iranian values. Children of the upper class went to colleges in Europe and America, where they were exposed to new and controversial forms of expression, such as the popular but controversial musical *Hair* (1967). Consequently, ordinary Iranians were becoming repelled by Western art, entertainment, and perceived moral laxity.

In 1977 Mohammed Reza implemented an economic program to fight inflation. It removed subsidies and imposed price controls. It failed, however, as prices rose, unemployment increased, and life became more difficult for many, especially the poor. Again, a reform program advanced by the shah had results that were the opposite of what he hoped. The plan's demise increased opposition against the shah's regime, heaping greater anxiety and discontent on top of an already tense situation.

71. What are the principal beliefs of Ba'thism and Nasserism?

In this answer, we will investigate Ba'thism and Nasserism, two competing and now discredited Arab political ideologies of the mid-twentieth century. They sought to eradicate imperialism and establish economic opportunity, social justice, and Arab unity. Both movements created harsh, authoritarian states.

In the early 1940s, Zaki Arsuzi (ca. 1900–1968), a Syrian 'Alawi, founded the Arab Ba'th (Renaissance) Party, while Michel 'Aflaq (1910–89), an Arab Christian, and Salah al-Din al-Bitar (1912–80), a Sunni Muslim, began the Arab Ba'th Movement. In 1947 the two organizations merged as the Arab Ba'th Party. In the early 1950s the party merged with the Arab Socialist Party of Syria, becoming the Arab Ba'th Socialist Party. Branches were set up in other Arab countries, but only Syria and Iraq established Ba'thist governments. The founding Ba'thists were influenced by the liberal ideas of the French Revolution and by Italian and German nationalists who had forged unified states in the late nineteenth century. The Ba'thists advocated nationalism, socialism, secularism, and revolutionary activism. Specifically, they demanded land reform, public ownership of major industries, unification of the Arab world, and militant resistance to Israel and any remnant of Western colonialism. They rejected peace with Israel and the resettlement of Palestinian refugees in other Arab countries.

It is worth noting that 'Aflaq's writings reflected his disdain for Syrian communists, who were influenced by French communists, who in turn were dominated by the Soviet Union. He argued that Moscow's interests in the Arab world did not mirror Arab aspirations for a unified nation stretching from the Atlantic to the Tigris. Nevertheless, he and other Ba'th leaders believed that their goal of a united Arab state would be achieved through a progressive movement led by a revolutionary cadre or vanguard, an idea advanced by Vladimir Lenin before the Russian Revolution of 1917.

In a 1943 lecture, "In Memory of the Arab Prophet," 'Aflaq urged his audience of fellow Arabs to "revive the characteristics and acts that legitimize our lineage to our past and make that a real living entity. We must remove all obstacles of stagnation and degradation, so that our pure blood lineage will run anew in our veins." By doing this, the Arabs would revitalize their nature, strength, potential, and common bonds. Although a Christian, 'Aflaq recognized the powerful influence of Islam on Arab development, stating, "Islam constituted for the Arabs a dynamic earth-shaking movement that stirred the internal potential of the Arabs, imbued it with life, and enabled it to drive out the obstacles of imitation and the shackles of reform." He also credited the early conquests with shaping the character of the nascent Arab empire: "Before [the Arabs] ruled over other people, they had to rule over themselves, and learn how to control their temptations and to take charge of their will."[3]

Ba'thism has been compared with European fascism of the interwar period. Indeed, the Ba'thist regimes that emerged in Syria and Iraq exhibited some of the trappings of fascism. Both Syria's Hafiz al-Asad and Iraq's Saddam Hussein developed cults of personality, adopting the personae of fathers who kept their families (nations) safe and provided for their essential needs. Ba'thists also advocated the primacy of the Arab nation. Consequently, Syria and Iraq's non-Arab minorities suffered under Ba'thist governments.

Egypt's Gamal Abdel Nasser, who led the 1952 revolution that toppled the monarchy, built his political philosophy and compelling persona by defying Western imperialism and striving to reverse the humiliation that the West had heaped on the Arab world. These feelings of defiance and humiliation, along with a conviction that the Arabs could build a better future, led to the ideology called Nasserism. It contained three main elements: Pan-Arabism, positive neutralism, and Arab socialism.

Pan-Arabism was akin to Arab nationalism. It emphasized political unification to increase the wealth and power of the entire Arab world. Nasser achieved some degree of Arab unity in 1958 with the establishment of the United Arab Republic (UAR), a union of Egypt and Syria that lasted three years.

Positive neutralism was analogous to nonalignment. As we mentioned in Question 64, Nasser was one of the founders of the Non-Aligned Movement. He hoped to steer Egypt and other neutral states between the Soviet and Western blocs, promoting peace and a reduction of tension, while obtaining weapons from the East and economic aid from the West.

Nasser's Arab socialism is not easy to define. In large part, it evolved as a reaction to the economic system prevalent in the Arab world through the mid-twentieth century—a system in which foreign commercial interests owned a country's major industries and business enterprises; a small native elite controlled the land, buildings, and other sources of wealth; and workers and peasants lived in dire poverty and were exploited for their labor. To divide the national wealth more evenly, Nasser advocated public ownership of large industries and utilities, and to expand the nation's wealth, especially in the industrial and agricultural sectors, he called for central economic planning and the breakup of large private estates, giving the smaller plots of land to Egyptian farmers. In Egypt he lessened the influence of Islamic courts and gave women the right to vote and serve in the National Assembly, but his reforms did not create a secular state like that of Atatürk's Turkey. Despite his socialist tendencies, Nasser opposed Marxism over its call for class conflict and incompatibility with Islam. The Soviets still sought to influence the leading Arab state but realized that Marxism could not compete with the popularity of Arab socialism. The need for arms and economic aid nonetheless led Nasser and the Kremlin to an ever-closer relationship.

Nasser's charismatic personality and radical ideology dominated Arab politics from the late 1950s to 1967. A significant achievement of that period was the merger of Egypt and Syria into the UAR (1958–61). The stunning defeat of Egypt, Syria, and Jordan in the June 1967 Arab-Israeli War, also known as the Six-Day War, so discredited Pan-Arabism and the leadership of Nasser in Egypt and the Ba'thists in Syria that several Islamist movements, known collectively as as-Sahwa al-Islamiyya (the Islamic Awakening), emerged and would play a key role in the formation of radical Islamic organizations such as al-Qa'ida. In the decades since the Six-Day War of 1967, secular pan-Arabist movements have been replaced by a wide variety of Islamist political movements and jihadist organizations.

Anwar al-Sadat marginalized Nasserists in Egypt in the early 1970s, and the U.S.-led invasion of Iraq in 2003 eliminated Ba'thism in that country, leaving Syria as the only Ba'thist state. The purge of Ba'th officials from the Iraqi government robbed the country of essential governing know-how in the critical months immediately after the fall of Saddam Hussein's government. As of this writing, Syria's 'Alawi-Ba'thist elite is battling for its political survival in a horrific civil war that began in 2011. To improve its chances, Bashar al-Asad's regime has abandoned Ba'thist principles and relied instead on brutal repression and extreme sectarianism. The Syrian civil war has effectively ended Ba'thism as a political philosophy and irretrievably altered the composition of Syria as a nation-state.[4] In 2018 al-Asad's forces and their allies were poised to take Idlib, the last major city held by anti-government militias. In the next answer, we will consider political developments in the Arab world, including the extent to which Ba'thism and Nasserism dominated political discourse during the 1950s and 1960s.

72. What were the significant political developments in the Arab world from 1949 to 1967?

Several significant events or developments occurred in or affected the Arab world from 1949 to 1967. They include the armistice agreements signed by Israel and four Arab countries, the assassination of King 'Abdullah I of Jordan, the Egyptian Revolution, the Suez Crisis, the promulgation of the Eisenhower Doctrine, the rise of Ba'thism in Syria, the formation and dissolution of the UAR, the Iraqi Revolution, the first Lebanese civil war and U.S. intervention, the rise of Nasserism and Arab socialism, the Yemeni civil war, the Algerian war for independence, the Jordan River waters dispute, and the establishment of the Palestine Liberation Organization (PLO). Despite this impressive list, some historians refer to the years 1957 to 1967 as the Quiet Decade. How can that be? Very simply, during that period there was no war between Israel and its Arab neighbors. In the Arab world, the focus was on inter-Arab affairs instead of the conflict with Israel. The decade was dominated by Egypt's Gamal Abdel Nasser.

   The 1948–49 Arab-Israeli War caused a seismic shift in the region's history. For Israel, the victory of arms established an independent, democratic Jewish state. For the Arab states bordering Israel, the defeat humiliated their armies and discredited their regimes. For Palestinians— and most Arabs in general—the war was a catastrophe. It uprooted more than a half million Palestinian Arabs who sought refuge in the Gaza Strip, the West Bank of the Jordan River, Jordan, Syria, and Lebanon. The strident opposition of many refugees to both Israel and its supporters was matched only by their hostility toward those Arab governments that sought peace with Israel.

Around the globe, many people genuinely hoped that the armistice agreements would be the first step toward a general peace between Israel and its Arab neighbors. Unfortunately, discussions broke down before they got started. Israel demanded a comprehensive settlement, while the Arabs called on Israel to withdraw from all lands not allotted to the Jewish state under the 1947 UN partition plan.

Of the Arab states that fought Israel, the Hashimite Kingdom of Jordan was most affected by the outcome. When King 'Abdullah annexed the West Bank and Old City of Jerusalem after the war, a million Palestinians joined a half million Jordanians. 'Abdullah negotiated secretly with Israel, but when his actions became known, many Palestinians called him a traitor. In 1951 he was assassinated on al-Haram ash-Sharif (also called the Temple Mount) by a follower of Hajj Amin al-Husseini, the former mufti of Jerusalem. The killing took place in front of his grandson, the future King Hussein. Talal, 'Abdullah's emotionally unstable son, assumed the throne but was soon eased out. In 1952 sixteen-year-old Hussein Ibn Talal (1935–99) was crowned king. The country became stable and politically moderate during his reign. He developed close relations with the West and was increasingly supported by U.S. administrations.

The Syrian Nationalist Party (SNP), in power from 1945 until 1949, was determined to keep the Hashimites, who ruled Iraq and Jordan, from gaining control of Syria. The SNP advocated Arab unity but under the umbrella of the Arab League. It fought the 1948–49 war against Israel in alliance with Egypt but in competition with Transjordan. In 1949 a military coup led by General Husni al-Za'im (1887–1949) ousted President Shukri al-Quwatli (1891–1967), which ended the dominance of Ottoman-era politicians and the urban aristocracy. Two more coups occurred that year. General Adib Shishakli (1909–64), leader of the third coup, dominated Syrian politics for the next half decade, establishing the prototype of the all-too-familiar Arab populist dictator. Syria of the 1950s was politically unstable and strained by religious, ethnic, and regional contrasts, yet its leaders hoped to unite all Arabs against Zionism and Western imperialism. In 1954 Shishakli was removed from power, and the SNP won control of the government through free elections; the Ba'th won the second largest number of seats. Three years later, a coalition of Ba'thists and communists challenged the SNP over its failure to carry out much-needed economic and social reforms. The SNP retaliated and, by the end of 1957, had so weakened the Ba'th that it began working for union with Egypt as a means to survive politically.

Iraq fought against Israel but suffered far less from the defeat than any of the other Arab belligerent states. Its growing oil revenues were being invested in irrigation improvements and other projects that promised future prosperity, yet the country suffered from a host of problems. Cabinets changed with alarming frequency, minority problems festered, the socioeconomic gap between landowners and peasants widened, and the pro-Western monarchy was increasingly unpopular. In 1955 Iraq joined with Turkey, Iran, Pakistan, and Britain to form an anticommunist alliance, the Baghdad Pact. Relations between Baghdad and Cairo became strained, as both vied for hegemony in the fractious Arab world.

In July 1952, the Egyptian Free Officers Movement, led by Gamal Abdel Nasser, overthrew King Faruq, ending the dynasty of Mehmet 'Ali that had ruled Egypt since 1805. Egypt's defeat in the 1948 war with Israel, Britain's seemingly unending occupation of the country, and an array of serious domestic problems contributed greatly to the monarchy's downfall. Many Egyptians believed that only a strong, united Arab world could withstand the domination of the Western powers. They regarded Israel as a Western entity imposed on the Arabs as a means of maintaining Western influence in the region. At the same time, they did not favor communism, but because neither Russia nor the Soviet Union had controlled any part of the Arab world in the past, the Arabs felt no hostility toward the Soviets, an attitude that Moscow would soon exploit. Hoping to weaken the West's influence in the Middle East, the Soviets turned away from Israel and threw their support to the Arabs, turning the region into another field of competition during the Cold War.

Many U.S. government officials argued that an offer of diplomatic and military assistance might achieve for the United States greater support from Arab countries in the aftermath of the the Suez Crisis. In 1957 the Dwight Eisenhower administration announced a policy that became known as the Eisenhower Doctrine. It stated that the United States would come to the aid of any Middle Eastern state that sought help in defending itself from the threat of international communism. The first application of the doctrine took place in Jordan in 1957, when Ba'thist and pro-Nasser officers—none of whom were communists—threatened to seize King Hussein's palace. The king rallied loyal troops to his side and stared down the threat. U.S. secretary of state John Foster Dulles (1888–1959) announced that the preservation of Jordan's territorial integrity was a vital U.S. interest. In accordance with the Eisenhower Doctrine, the U.S. dispatched ships and Marines to the eastern Mediterranean as a show of support for the young monarch.

The Syrian Ba'th Party's proposal for union with Egypt went forward, and in 1958 Egypt and Syria agreed to a political merger, forming the United Arab Republic. While Syrian Ba'thists needed Nasser's support to maintain their political viability, the Egyptian leader hoped to advance Pan-Arabism and enhance his own power and prestige. Owing to the Ba'th's radical ideology, the presence of communists in the parliament, and the union with Nasser, many U.S. officials viewed Syria as a Soviet satellite, even though the country's leaders were mostly nationalists and socialists, not Marxists.

Establishment of the UAR elicited a variety of reactions in the Arab world. Saudi Arabia refused to join the UAR because it did not want to share its oil revenue with Egypt and Syria. In a countermove, Jordan and Iraq formed the United Arab Federation, which ended abruptly with the violent Iraqi Revolution in July 1958. Conversely, Yemen became a federated member of the UAR, and Palestinians were optimistic about the merger, believing that the Arabs now had the strength to liberate their homeland. Over the next three years, Nasser and Egypt's heavy-handed bureaucracy made inroads into Syria's economy and political system. Nasser believed that state planning and control of all major industries was necessary to fulfill his promise to double national income during the 1960s. Laws passed in 1961 nationalized all factories, financial institutions, and public utilities in Egypt and Syria; reduced to a hundred acres the maximum landholding; and imposed a cap on salaries. The new laws infuriated Syria's bourgeoisie. In September 1961, a military coup took place in Syria, and the UAR soon collapsed. The union dissolved because of disagreement over the composition of a joint military command and Syrian disapproval of Nasser's political and economic policies, namely, state control of the economy, nationalization of major industries, and absorption of the Ba'th Party into the Egyptian-led National Union Party.[5]

Despite the collapse of the UAR, pan-Arab sentiment remained strong; so much so, that Egypt retained the name UAR until 1971. After Syria's withdrawal from the union, Nasser pursued a new strategy: He would implement a successful socialist program at home, then export it to the rest of the Arab world. He was confident that if his policies promoted economic growth and social equality, other Arab states would follow suit, enhancing the chances of achieving unity.

Independent Algeria and the newly established Republic of Yemen were steadfast allies of Nasser. From 1954 to 1962, the Algerian National Liberation Front (known by the French acronym FLN) mounted a brutal guerrilla war against French authorities. Algeria, unlike Morocco and Tunisia, was a French settlement colony, making it an organic part of the French state. The Algerian war led to the collapse of the Fourth Republic (1946–58) and the return of General Charles de Gaulle to the political arena. Elected the first president (1958–69) of the Fifth Republic (1958–present), he took resolute steps to end the crisis and outlasted insurrections by French settlers—les Pieds-Noirs (literally, "the Black Feet")—mutinies in the armed forces, and attempted military coups. He unveiled measures to deescalate the conflict, modernize Algeria's economy, and provide for its self-determination. In March 1962, the Evian Accords implemented a cease-fire that ended the war and ensured Algerian independence. Voters in France and Algeria overwhelmingly approved the agreement, and on 3 July 1962, De Gaulle recognized the independence of Algeria.

In 1962 a group of pan-Arab army officers deposed Yemen's ruler, Imam Mohammed al-Badr (ca. 1926–96), and proclaimed the Yemen Arab Republic. Over the next six years, Nasser deployed tens of thousands of troops to Yemen in support of the republic in its struggle against royalist forces and their Saudi and Jordanian backers. The civil war soon became a stalemate, and Nasser's troops, which reached nearly 75,000, found themselves stuck in a quagmire. The war dragged on until 1970 with the republicans ultimately prevailing.

In 1963 Ba'thist coups in Iraq and Syria created the opportunity for a revived UAR, comprised of Egypt, Iraq, and Syria. The effort collapsed in a few days, however, because Nasser and the Ba'thists could not agree on how the state would be governed. Again, Nasser's political demands were too much for his potential confederates. The Egyptian president appealed to Arab hearts, not minds. His charisma and success in standing up to the West provided him a great deal of legitimacy. Not all Arabs, however, especially the conservative monarchies, agreed with his policies. In 1966 radical Ba'thists engineered a coup in Syria. Four years later, Hafiz al-Asad took power in the Great Corrective Movement, which installed a more moderate Ba'thist regime.

Despite Iraq's many problems, several Western leaders considered Iraq the model of a modernizing Arab state. Iraq's membership in the Baghdad Pact was a challenge to Nasser's leadership of the Arab world, but many Iraqis saw Iraq's participation in the pact as a sellout to the West. In July a violent military coup, led by General 'Abd al-Karim Qasim (ca. 1914–63), overthrew the pro-West government. King Faysal II (r. 1939–58), regent prince 'Abd al-Ilah (1913–58), and Prime Minister Nuri al-Sa'id (ca. 1888–1958) were violently murdered. Once in power, Qasim pushed for land reform, promoted Arab unity, established ties with the Soviet Union, and withdrew Iraq from the Baghdad Pact. In the view of several U.S. officials, it appeared as if extreme Arab nationalists and communists had taken control of Iraq; in reality, Qasim had forged a careful balance between both groups. Iraq under Qasim would stay out of the UAR, but the junta's second in command, Colonel 'Abd al-Salaam 'Arif (1921–66), did meet with Nasser to discuss a merger. The talks failed because Qasim refused to share Iraq's oil revenues and his power.

In 1958 Qasim brought the Kurdish leader Mustafa Barzani (1903–79) back from exile, but within three years, a full-scale Kurdish rebellion broke out. While the Qasim regime had improved the lives of ordinary Iraqis, many problems, notably the Kurdish question, proved to be no easier for the junta to resolve than they had been for the Hashimites. In 1963 the Ba'thists deposed Qasim, who was violently murdered and whose corpse was shown on Iraqi state television, and the new government joined Egypt and Syria in the unsuccessful attempt to form a united Arab state. A few months later, the military under Colonel 'Arif toppled the Ba'thist regime. In 1968 the Ba'th Party regained power, and a decade later Saddam Hussein (1937–2006) orchestrated an internal coup, taking control of both the party and the country.

In the 1940s and 1950s, Lebanon's national unity was held together by a complex political arrangement delineated in the 1943 National Pact. In accordance with the agreement, Christians would hold a six-to-five advantage in the allocation of seats in the Chamber of Deputies and positions in the cabinet, a Maronite Christian would occupy the presidency, a Sunni Muslim would serve as prime minister, and a Shi'a Muslim would wield the speaker's gavel in the Chamber. The government was outwardly democratic, but—more accurately—it was a "constitutional oligarchy" because the wealth and power of the country were concentrated in the hands of the leading families representing Lebanon's diverse religious communities. The influx of some 150,000 Palestinian refugees after the 1948–49 Arab-Israeli War complicated the delicate political balance among Christians, Sunnis, and Shi'a. Palestinian Christians were fully absorbed into the country's social and political fabric, but Palestinian Muslims were denied Lebanese citizenship. A new census would have shown that after 1948 a majority of Lebanese were Muslim. Amid the social and political strains caused by the growing Palestinian population, Lebanon's confessional leaders vowed to preserve Lebanon's independence and territorial integrity. Under the prevailing political structure, Lebanon appeared to be thriving, but in reality a small number of families controlled most of the country's wealth and power, and the army was too weak to protect the country or preserve order.

The National Front, an opposition movement, resisted the pro-Western government of President Camille Chamoun (1900–87). The front drew support from Palestinian refugees, disaffected Lebanese Muslims, Egypt, and Syria. Lebanon in the late 1950s was a haven for radical Arab ideologies that were popular with Muslims, Palestinians, the youth, and politicians excluded from the Chamoun regime. Two events propelled the country toward civil war. First, in the spring of 1958, a pro-Nasser newspaper editor was assassinated; the National Front quickly blamed the government. Second, Chamoun ignited a major political crisis when he proposed to amend the constitution to allow him to run for a second term. Shooting incidents in the countryside reignited ancient feuds, and the government responded with a curfew. The first Lebanese civil war had begun.

Chamoun feared that the political upheaval in Baghdad would inspire antiregime elements in Lebanon. A day after the violent overthrow of the Iraqi monarchy, he requested military assistance from the United States under the Eisenhower Doctrine. In July U.S. Marines landed unopposed in Beirut in Operation Blue Bat. They quickly secured the airport and harbor. Bolstered by the Marine presence, the Lebanese government restored order. Chamoun abandoned his idea of running for a second term, and General Fuad Shihab, commander of the Lebanese armed forces, became the new president (1958–64). After a deployment of three months, the Marines withdrew; they would return in twenty-four years.

In the late 1950s, Israel decided to build a national water distribution system, drawing from the Jordan River the volume of water allocated to it under the Jordan Valley Unified Water Plan, which had been negotiated by President Eisenhower's special envoy Eric Johnston (1896–1963). The plan would have divided the water among Israel, Jordan, Syria, and Lebanon. Israel and Jordan accepted their allocations, but other Arab states conspired to disrupt the operation of Israel's National Water Carrier by diverting the main tributaries of the Jordan. Israel immediately threatened air strikes against any effort to throttle the flow of water. In January 1964, Nasser invited Arab heads of state to Cairo for a summit conference to discuss the crisis. The Arab kings and presidents could not agree on a single course of action, but they agreed to hold additional summit meetings and approved the creation of the Palestine Liberation Organization. Formed with the emphatic backing of Nasser, the PLO would serve as the umbrella for all Palestinian societies, political organizations, and paramilitary groups. Its charter called for the armed liberation of Palestine and establishment of a secular democracy in place of Israel. The PLO began marshaling a conventional army made up of Palestinian refugees, principally in Jordan, but arguably the most effective fighting force within the PLO was the Fatah guerrilla movement, founded and led by Yasir Arafat.[6] In January 1965, Fatah conducted a raid on Israel's national water system. The Israelis responded with a devastating attack on the village of as-Samu' in the Jordanian West Bank. By the mid-1960s, it was evident that the Quiet Decade was rapidly drawing to a close; Israel and its Arab neighbors were on the path to war.

13

The Arab-Israeli Conflict,
1967–73

Much of this chapter chronicles violent modern warfare, extreme political ideologies, and small steps forward on the peace front. The chapter begins with an analysis of events and circumstances leading to the outbreak of war in June 1967 and a recounting of Israel's stunning victory over the combined armies of Egypt, Syria, and Jordan. Next, postwar diplomacy, specifically UN Security Council Resolution 242, is carefully examined. We then discuss the development of a viable Palestinian national movement that could take the leading role in the struggle for the establishment of an independent Palestinian state. In the two concluding responses, we examine the Jordanian civil war of 1970, fought between Palestinian guerrillas and forces loyal to King Hussein; Egyptian president Anwar al-Sadat's political and military strategy to break the diplomatic deadlock in the Arab-Israeli conflict; and the war of October 1973, which altered the dynamics of the Arab-Israeli conflict and initiated a peace process.

73. What were the causes and outcome of the June 1967 Arab-Israeli War?

In 1966 a radical faction of the Ba'th Party led by General Salah Jadid (ca. 1926–93) seized power in Syria. It clamored for military action against Israel and took special aim at Egypt's Nasser, goading him to resolve the crisis with Israel through force of arms and taunting him for "hiding" behind UN Emergency Force troops in the Sinai. Nasser was reluctant to square off against Israel, but he soon escalated his rhetoric against the Jewish state and joined Syria in a military alliance. By doing so, he hoped to satisfy the Ba'thists in Damascus and prevent them from leading the Arab world into war. For Nasser, this decision proved to be a grave miscalculation. It is also a superb lesson in how inflamed rhetoric and military posturing can be misconstrued and lead to an all-out conflict.

In the spring of 1967, Israel warned Syria that it would retaliate unless the firing on Israeli settlements in the Galilee stopped immediately. In May the Soviets informed Nasser that Israel was preparing to attack Syria. Nasser realized that he would have to take the initiative in the struggle with Israel to maintain his credibility and popularity throughout the Arab world. Although a significant portion of his army was bogged down in Yemen, the overriding pan-Arab issue for Egypt since 1948 remained the liberation of Palestine. Egypt called up its reserves, deployed tanks and troops to the Sinai, and threatened to blockade the Straits of Tiran, the opening to the Gulf of Aqaba.

Derided by Syria, Jordan, and Saudi Arabia for relying on the UN for the defense of his country against Israel, Nasser requested the removal of some UNEF troops from the Sinai. In an unexpected, unilateral decision, UN secretary-general U Thant (1909–74) pulled the entire force out of the Sinai. In May Egypt occupied Sharm al-Shaykh and sealed the Gulf of Aqaba, effectively cutting Israel's maritime trade with East Africa and Asia. This stunning act proved to be the immediate cause of the war.

Keeping the Gulf of Aqaba open had been a critical security concern for Israel since its reluctant withdrawal from the Sinai in 1957. Israel hoped that the Western powers would keep their post-Suez pledge to guarantee passage through the Straits of Tiran but soon realized that it would not receive any armed support from the United States or Europe to break the blockade. The United States was preoccupied with its escalating commitment in Vietnam, and Western European countries were importing an increasing amount of their oil from Arab producers.

The Arabs stepped up their strident anti-Israel rhetoric, Egypt and Jordan signed a mutual defense treaty, and the three frontline Arab states stood up the Unified Arab Command in Amman, Jordan, under the leadership of General 'Abdul Mun'im Riad of Egypt.[1] Meanwhile, a majority of Israelis were convinced that war was inevitable. Prime Minister Levi Eshkol (1963–69) of the Labor Party formed a national unity government that included Likud's Menachem Begin; General Moshe Dayan (1915–81) was named defense minister.

Compared to its adversaries, Israel faced many critical disadvantages at the start of the war. The Arabs had substantially more troops, tanks, aircraft, and warships than Israel and a huge advantage in national populations. The Arabs also enjoyed support from the Soviet bloc and developing world. On the other hand, President Lyndon B. Johnson (1963–69) counseled Israel that the United States would only intervene on its behalf if it absorbed the first strike, which to the Israelis was unacceptable owing to Israel's constrained geography and small population. Despite these circumstances, but perceiving grave and immediate danger, the Israeli government ordered a preemptive attack.

On 5 June, Israel launched a devastating strike on Egyptian air bases, gaining immediate air superiority. Israel also attacked and destroyed the Syrian and Jordanian air forces. The Israeli air force demolished approximately three hundred Egyptian, fifty Syrian, and twenty Jordanian aircraft, most of them on the ground. Israeli armor invaded the Sinai and captured the entire peninsula in four days. Israeli forces took al-Arish on the northern coast and outflanked heavy concentrations of Egyptian forces as they drove toward the Suez Canal. They occupied Sharm al-Shaykh and lifted the blockade of the Gulf of Aqaba.

Israel urged Jordan to stay out of the war, but King Hussein ignored their pleas and ordered his armed forces to shell West Jerusalem. He had to attack Israel to maintain his political standing in the Arab world and legitimacy at home. The Israelis launched an invasion of the Jordanian-controlled West Bank. They flanked around the Old City and attacked it from the east. Although the Jordanian Arab Legion fought determinedly, the Israelis wrested control the Old City and entire the West Bank in three days. The victory caused a new flood of Palestinian refugees, which dramatically altered the demographic landscape of the core Middle East. As you read this, think of the impact that Iraqi and Syrian refugees are having on the demographics of many countries of the Middle East and Europe.

On the fourth day of the war, Israeli forces attacked the strategic Syrian Golan Heights. The Israelis used a direct assault and took the plateau after three days of fighting. A UN-sponsored cease-fire, covering all three fronts, went into effect on 10 June. In six days, Israel occupied the Sinai, Gaza Strip, the Golan Heights, West Bank, East Jerusalem, and the Old City.

Several factors explain Israel's remarkable victory. First, the opening Israeli strike eliminated Arab airpower and permitted Israeli forces to overpower three Arab armies in succession. Second, tens of thousands of capable Egyptian troops were tied down in the five-year-long Yemeni civil war, resulting in a numerical advantage for Israel of well-trained troops on the Sinai front. Third, the Egyptian military establishment, led by Field Marshal 'Abd al-Hakim 'Amer (1919–67), was riddled with cronyism and incompetence and obsessed with the acquisition of personal power and fortune. A close confidant of Nasser and prominent Free Officer, 'Amer had climbed too high too fast and was ill-prepared to command a large, complex military operation. His shortcomings came to light when he panicked and ordered a retreat from the Sinai without a plan in place. The attempt at retreat turned into a rout as thousands of Egyptian soldiers abandoned their vehicles and equipment and fled toward the canal. Fourth, Israeli forces had advanced weaponry, superior communications, greater mobility, and skill in the use of combined arms. Fifth, Israel Defense Forces (IDF) members had considerably more technical proficiency, and 100 percent of Israeli soldiers were literate. Sixth, improvisation and egalitarianism were hallmarks of Israeli culture, giving the Israelis a huge morale advantage. Finally—and arguably most important—factionalism and distrust among Arabs undermined their combat effectiveness. Despite the establishment of a united command, there was little coordination between the Egyptian, Syrian, and Jordanian militaries.

Israelis were euphoric over their victory in the Six-Day War, achieved at the cost of some seven hundred lives. The Arabs, on the other hand, lost about 16,000 men. Israel now possessed the sacred Jewish sites in Jerusalem and controlled territories that under Arab control had posed a security threat since 1949. Israeli population centers along the Mediterranean coast were now out of the range of Arab artillery. The IDF acquired a myth of invincibility, and Israelis won much of the world's admiration. Many government officials, especially in the United States, believed that Israel could win any future conflict, so long as it remained well armed.

The Arabs referred to the crushing defeat as an-Naksa (the Setback). In its aftermath, they despaired over another defeat at the hands of the Israelis, engaged in soul-searching, and pointed fingers at leaders believed responsible for the debacle. Nasser immediately offered his resignation but was persuaded by popular acclamation to remain in office. 'Amer took his own life, and Egyptian military leaders took a deep inward look at their failures. In August, at an Arab summit in Khartoum, Sudan, the presidents and kings declared that they would not recognize, negotiate with, or sign a peace agreement with Israel. Instead, they demanded unconditional Israeli withdrawal from all territories captured in the June war.

Some Arab leaders became radicalized by the outcome of the war, but a significant exception was Nasser, who grew gradually more moderate *and* pragmatic regarding the conflict with Israel. He accepted UN Security Council Resolution 242, which we will discuss in the next response, and shortly before his death in September 1970, he accepted a cease-fire, brokered by U.S. secretary of state William P. Rogers (1913–2001), which ended the War of Attrition between Egypt and Israel, and negotiated a settlement between King Hussein and the PLO to end the civil war in Jordan.

After the war, the United States moved closer to Israel, while the Arab states turned away from the West. Many Arab governments severed diplomatic relations with the United States and strengthened their political, military, and economic ties with the Soviet Union. The Soviets helped the Egyptians and Syrians rebuild their militaries, while the United States loaned Israel increasingly larger amounts of money and sold it sophisticated weaponry, such as F-4 Phantom II fighter plane. The Arab-Israeli conflict was now a significant part of the Cold War.

The tripling of territory under Israel's control enhanced its security, but also created new problems. Israel now governed 1.5 million Arabs in the West Bank, Gaza, East Jerusalem, and the Old City. Three hundred thousand Palestinian refugees went to Jordan; 80,000 Syrians fled the Golan Heights for other parts of Syria. Arafat established a new headquarters for the PLO in Amman.

The Israelis were willing to trade land for peace with the Arabs, using the captured territories as a huge bargaining chip. They vowed not to repeat the mistake of 1957, when they gained nothing in return for their total withdrawal from the Sinai. Meanwhile, the Arabs had slammed shut the door to peace with their Khartoum Resolution of 1 September, which contained the "three nos": "no peace with Israel, no recognition of Israel, no negotiation with it, and insistence on the rights of the Palestinian people in their own country."[2] Also, an increasingly more visible and vocal Palestinian population sought its political rights. Are the national goals of the Israelis, on one side, and the Arabs and Palestinians, on the other, mutually exclusive, or is there room for compromise? Except for Israel's peace treaties with Egypt and Jordan, negotiations have failed to bridge the differences between the two sides.

The magnitude of the 1967 victory changed the mind-set of many Israelis. A growing number began to talk of retaining the territories not merely as bargaining chips, but as a tangible means to enhance security, provide more living space, and fulfill God's bequeathal of the land to Abraham and his progeny.[3] The Jewish settlements in the occupied territories are now a major impediment to achieving a peace agreement.

Within months of the cease-fire, Israeli's occupation of the West Bank, Gaza, and East Jerusalem became increasingly rooted. Israel carried out arrests, deportations, and house demolitions; built settlements; and unilaterally annexed East Jerusalem and the Old City. Meanwhile, Israel and Egypt dug in along opposite sides of the Suez Canal. Defeated and frustrated, many Arabs sought a solution to the crisis through the UN rather than dealing directly with Israel.

The June 1967 Arab-Israeli War created a new wave of Palestinian refugees; helped generate a distinct and more assertive Palestinian identity; discredited secular pan-Arab ideologies, such as Ba'thism and Nasserism; cemented the seemingly irreconcilable differences between Arabs and Israelis; and spawned the emergence of political and militant Islamist organizations. After the humiliation of 1967, many Arabs turned to Islam to make sense of what had happened and see what could be done. Slogans, such as "Islam is the Solution!" became commonplace. These slogans argued that the Arabs had tried all the isms of the age, such as nationalism, capitalism, and socialism; why not give Islamism a try? To understand the mind-set of al-Qa'ida's current leader, Ayman al-Zawahiri, we must appreciate the post-1967 environment in which he was raised.

74. What are the contents of UN Security Council Resolution 242, which outlined the principles for a Middle East peace settlement?

After five months of intense, high-level diplomacy, the UN Security Council unanimously adopted Resolution 242 on 22 November 1967. The statement underscored "the inadmissibility of the acquisition of territory by war" and set forth two principles for "the establishment of a just and lasting peace in the Middle East":

(i)   Withdrawal of Israeli armed forces from territories occupied in the recent conflict; [and]

(ii)   Termination of all claims or states of belligerency and respect for and acknowledgment of the sovereignty, territorial integrity and political independence of every state in the area and their right to live in peace within secure and recognized boundaries free from threats or acts of force.

The resolution also affirmed the need

(a)   For guaranteeing freedom of navigation through international waterways in the area;

(b)   For achieving a just settlement of the refugee problem;

(c)   For guaranteeing the territorial inviolability and political independence of every State in the area, through measures including . . . demilitarized zones.[4]

Syria and the PLO rejected the resolution, but Israel, Jordan, and Egypt accepted it. Nevertheless, the Arabs and Israelis held different interpretations of the wording regarding the evacuation of armed forces from the captured territories and resolution of the refugee issue. According to the Arabs, the resolution called on Israel to return *all* the lands it had taken in the war as a precondition for peace. On the other hand, Israel argued that the resolution called for the withdrawal from *some* of these lands because each country was to live peacefully within secure borders. Furthermore, the Arabs interpreted "a just settlement to the refugee problem" to mean Israel must readmit *all* displaced Palestinians wishing to return. Conversely, Israel maintained that the refugees should be settled in Arab countries or be compensated.

The resolution contained several noteworthy omissions. It was ambiguous and vague regarding the actual conditions for peace. It did not address arms reduction in the region. It ignored the practice of economic warfare, such as boycotts and embargoes. It failed to mention the Palestinians by name and ignored their rights and political aspirations. And it did not call for direct negotiations between Israel and the Arabs. With a document so diplomatically ambiguous, many observers believed that a new war was inevitable.

Six years later, UN Security Council Resolution 338, adopted on 22 October, attempted to halt the fighting in the 1973 Arab-Israeli War immediately. It affirmed the provisions of Resolution 242 and asserted "that immediately and concurrently with the cease-fire, negotiations start between the parties concerned under appropriate auspices aimed at establishing a just and durable peace in the Middle East."[5] The two resolutions provided the guiding principles for subsequent Arab-Israeli negotiations that produced the following accords and treaties: the Sinai and Golan Interim Agreements (1974–75), the Camp David Frameworks for Peace (1978) and subsequent Israel-Egypt Peace Treaty (1979), the Oslo I (1993) and Oslo II (1995) Accords between Israel and the Palestinians, and the Israel-Jordan Peace Treaty (1994).[6]

75. What accounts for the emergence of a viable Palestinian nationalist movement after the June 1967 Arab-Israeli War?

Following the war of June 1967, approximately 1.5 million Palestinians in the West Bank, Gaza, and East Jerusalem came under Israeli control. Another 300,000 fled to Jordan. Two years later, Yasir Arafat (1929–2004) was named the leader of the PLO. The first chairman, Ahmed al-Shuqayri (1908–80), was a respected lawyer from a prominent Palestinian family but was ill-suited to lead a revolutionary movement. Arafat, an engineer educated in Cairo, had founded the guerrilla organization Fatah in Kuwait in the late 1950s. Fatah under Arafat became the leading Palestinian guerrilla organization carrying out armed resistance against Israel.

In the wake of the Six-Day War, the Palestinian people and their leaders seized command of their own destiny. They had lost confidence in Arab leaders' ability to secure their political rights, and Arafat, who became the face of the Arab world's struggle against Israel, extolled the creation of a secular and democratic Palestine state. He deftly advanced his nation's cause by playing one Arab regime against another, exploiting the superpower rivalry, and using terrorism to strike at Israel and its supporters. He even secured observer status for the PLO at the United Nations. At the same time, Palestinians viewed themselves as a distinct people within the Arab nation, a group with a shared culture, history, and dreams. They rejected, as did many Arabs, the notion that they could merely be resettled in other Arab countries. They grew increasingly militant and were anxious to fight for their own liberation. They felt that the time had come to secure diplomatic support, build a stockpile of weapons, ramp up training, and begin the process of regaining their lands through armed means. Despite Arafat's charismatic leadership, the PLO did not enjoy unanimous support among Palestinians. Some organizations contested Arafat's authority, namely, the Popular Front for the Liberation of Palestine (PFLP), led by George Habash (ca. 1926–2008), and the Democratic Front for the Liberation of Palestine (DFLP), led by Nayif Hawatma (b. 1938). As Marxist-Leninist revolutionary movements, the PFLP and DFLP were concerned with the welfare of workers and peasants in addition to the liberation of Palestine. Arafat, on the other hand, remained focused on the struggle against Israel. In later decades, the PLO's hegemony would be challenged by radical Islamist movements, such as Islamic Jihad and Hamas.

The PLO and other organizations stepped up *fidaiyin* operations against Israel, challenged Israeli control of the West Bank, and accrued international backing. In March 1968, IDF troops crossed into Jordan and carried out a retaliatory raid on the village of al-Karama. PLO guerrillas and Jordanian troops fought side by side, valiantly and effectively. They killed or wounded nearly two hundred Israelis and destroyed four tanks. They regarded the battle as a great military victory. Politically, however, the PLO failed to gain permanent international acceptance of its belief that Zionism was equivalent to racism and fascism. The PLO covenant, which called for the destruction of Israel, also tarnished the Palestinian cause in the eyes of liberals in the West. Moreover, many Western governments considered the PLO and other Palestinian groups to be terrorist organizations. Nevertheless, in concert with its political and military activities, the PLO kept pressure on Nasser and other Arab leaders to support Palestinian independence.

The PFLP's Habash believed that the Palestinians could attain their goals only by first attacking Western governments, interests, and civilians to attract international attention to their cause. The PFLP was the first movement to use airline hijackings as an act of terrorism. Its terrorist activities often embarrassed Arafat and challenged his image as a revolutionary. He would, however, take more violent measures, such as authorizing the notorious terrorist attacks on the Munich Olympic Games in 1972 and the Saudi embassy in Khartoum the following year.

76. What were the causes and outcome of the 1970 Jordanian–Palestine Liberation Organization civil war?

The Jordanian-PLO civil war of 1970 was a brief, but violent, conflict that significantly affected the Palestinian cause and nearly ended the Jordanian monarchy. In September the PFLP hijacked four Western airliners and flew three of them to a deserted airstrip in the Jordanian desert. The fourth plane was flown to Cairo.[7] After the passengers had been safely removed from the airliners in Jordan, the PFLP blew up the aircraft. The spectacular operation was aimed at humiliating King Hussein and precipitating his downfall. It also marked the genesis of modern international terrorism. Political terrorism had been practiced for several decades in the Middle East, but the practitioners of the new brand of extreme violence sought to elicit greater public awareness, sympathy, and support for their causes.

By the start of the decade, several factors had foreshadowed a showdown between the Jordanian government and the country's sizable Palestinian population. First, deep divisions existed between Jordan's tribal population and Palestinian refugees over issues ranging from economic opportunities to the conduct of cross-border raids into Israel. Second, the Palestinians were increasingly defiant of governmental authority, especially inside their refugee camps. Third, Hussein was unable to halt Palestinian raids into Israel or Israeli-occupied territory, and—to make this matter far worse—the PLO was also losing control over many guerrilla groups. The Jordan-based attacks assuredly prompted harsh Israeli retaliatory strikes on Jordanian territory. Fourth, the Palestinian cause had become influenced by political rivalries within the Arab world. Over the years, Nasser's strident nationalist rhetoric influenced leftist groups, which called for the toppling of the Jordanian monarchy. Meanwhile, Syria and Iraq supported different Palestinian factions to subsume the Palestine liberation movement in either county's branch of Ba'thism and compete with Egypt's dominance of the pan-Arab movement. Finally, since June 1967, hundreds of armed clashes had occurred between Jordanian security forces and Palestinian guerrillas. The Palestinian presence in Jordan had, in effect, become a state within a state, with areas of the country and parts of Amman being "no-go zones" for Jordanian authorities.

To stave off a Palestinian takeover of his government, Hussein ordered his armed forces to root out and disarm all Palestinian guerrillas, not just the PFLP; Arafat fiercely resisted the king's order. The ensuing battle determined who would rule Jordan: the Hashimite monarch or Yasir Arafat. The radical Ba'th regime in Syria, which supported the Palestinian guerrillas, ordered an infantry division, supported by armored and mechanized brigades and commando units, to invade Jordan. General Hafiz al-Asad (1930–2000), the Syrian minister of defense, withheld air cover for the Syrian advance. Without air support, the Syrian invasion was halted by the Jordanian army and air force. According to declassified British documents, Hussein and the Israeli government maintained a secret conduit of communications throughout the crisis, and the king asked for assistance from the Israelis, who were ready to launch air strikes to stop the Syrian attack and save the Jordanian regime.[8] U.S. officials have confirmed this account. The crisis also prompted the movement of the U.S. Sixth Fleet and Soviet Fifth Eskadra (Squadron) to stations in the eastern Mediterranean, where they closely monitored the rapidly evolving crisis in Jordan. Soviet amphibious troops were deployed in case they were needed to support Syria, and a U.S. airborne division was placed on alert for possible use in Jordan.[9]

On 27 September, Hussein and Arafat met in Cairo and accepted a cease-fire brokered by Nasser, who died of a heart attack the following day. In less than two weeks of fighting, the Jordanian military cleared Amman of Palestinian fighters, and by June 1971, it had expelled the remaining guerrillas from the country. Palestinians refer to the bloody conflict as Black September, which claimed the lives of more than three thousand Palestinian guerrillas and civilians, over six hundred Syrians, and just under a hundred Jordanians.

The defeated PLO fighters moved to Lebanon, and Arafat established a new headquarters in Beirut. The huge influx of Palestinian militants into Lebanon quickly upset the precarious political balance and would contribute to the outbreak of civil war a few years later. In November 1970, al-Asad purged the radical Ba'thists from power in Syria in a political act he appropriately called the Great Corrective Movement. In 1971 Palestinian radicals formed Black September, a terrorist organization that carried out several notorious attacks in the early 1970s, including the murder of eleven Israeli athletes and coaches at the Munich Olympic Games in 1972 and the murder of two senior U.S. diplomats at the Saudi embassy in Khartoum in 1973.

77. What were the causes, events, and consequences of the October 1973 Arab-Israeli War?

The 1973 war between Israel and the states of Egypt and Syria was a defining event in the long, tragic history of the Arab-Israeli conflict. It ultimately led to a peace treaty between Israel and Egypt, but it did not lead to comprehensive peace and reconciliation between Israelis and Arabs. The war was unexpected, yet warning signs were present. The warnings were largely ignored.

After the June 1967 war, senior Egyptian military officers performed a soul-searching study of what had gone wrong during the war and how they could restructure their forces to stand up to Israel. The Soviet Union resupplied the Egyptian armed forces with advanced Soviet weaponry, and the Soviet presence in Egypt grew significantly. In October 1967, the Israeli destroyer *Eilat* was hit and sunk by Soviet-made cruise missiles fired from Egyptian patrol boats inside the harbor at Port Said. Forty-seven Israelis died in the attack; Israel retaliated by shelling Egyptian oil refineries at Port Suez. In March 1969, Nasser ordered his military to fire on Israeli positions along the canal, triggering a new round of fighting that became known as the War of Attrition. For a year and a half, Egypt hurled a steady barrage of artillery and missiles at the Israelis. Israeli forces stood their ground, returned fire, and launched a series of fighter-bomber raids deep into the Egyptian heartland.

In December U.S. secretary of state William Rogers unveiled a plan that would bear his name. It envisioned a lasting peace "sustained by a sense of security on both sides" with borders that "should not reflect the weight of conquest." It asserted that "there can be no lasting peace without a just settlement of the problem of those Palestinians whom the wars of 1948 and 1967 made homeless." And it maintained that "Jerusalem should be a unified city within which there . . . should be open access . . . for persons of all faiths and nationalities."[10] Nasser initially rejected the plan but accepted it the following year; Jordan quickly accepted it, while Israel reluctantly approved.

The deadly, but inconclusive, War of Attrition climaxed in July 1970, when Israeli and Soviet-piloted fighters clashed in an air battle near the Suez Canal. A cease-fire, brokered by Rogers, went into effect in August 1970. Nasser died the following month, and Vice President Anwar al-Sadat became the new president of Egypt (1970–81). In 1971 Egypt and the Soviet Union signed the Treaty of Friendship and Cooperation. That same year, the country adopted a new constitution and was renamed the Arab Republic of Egypt. Also that year, the Aswan High Dam was completed. It would have a huge impact on irrigation, agriculture, and industry in Egypt.

The War of Attrition gave the Egyptian military an opportunity to test new doctrines, practice new tactics, and experiment with reorganizing their forces. The Egyptians knew full well that they could not go head to head with the Israeli air force and sought to counter this advantage by installing a Soviet-built, advanced surface-to-air missile (SAM) defense system. On the ground, they conceded the superiority of Israeli armor, but held a numerical advantage in infantry. Using Soviet-built, wire-guided antitank missiles and heavy concentrations of rocket-propelled grenade (RPG) fire, the Egyptians hoped to blunt an Israeli tank attack in the next war.

Israeli intelligence maintained that Syria would launch a war only in concert with Egypt and that Egypt would go to war only if it were convinced it could effectively combat Israel in the air. This theory became ingrained in Israeli military thinking and contributed greatly to the country's general sense of security. Consequently, defense expenditures declined from their 1970 levels, the annual call-up of military reserves was reduced from sixty to thirty days, and the term of conscription was reduced from thirty-six to thirty-three months. Although Palestinian terrorism in the early 1970s became increasingly violent, Israelis felt relatively secure vis-à-vis their Arab neighbors. The success achieved by the Egyptians in reinforcing Israeli overconfidence in the years leading up to 1973 was an important lesson in the study of military deception.

On the other hand, Arab frustrations over the political deadlock were intensifying. Among the Free Officers who overthrew King Faruq in 1952, al-Sadat was regarded as the most ideological. Now, as president, he accused the Israelis of extreme intransigence, especially after they had rebuffed a peace overture he had unveiled in 1971. Moreover, the administration of President Richard M. Nixon was disinterested in the Middle East and did not pressure Israel to pursue peace. Nixon and his national security adviser, Henry Kissinger (b. 1925), were preoccupied with disengagement in Vietnam, détente with the Soviet Union, the opening of China to the West, and the reduction of strategic arms.

Al-Sadat figured correctly that the Israelis regarded the Arabs as too weak to launch an attack on Israel. He was also convinced that the Soviet Union was not acting in the manner of a loyal and helpful ally. The Soviets did not enthusiastically back al-Sadat's military preparations and had fallen behind in shipping offensive weapons to Egypt. In 1972 al-Sadat had had enough and ordered most of the Soviet advisers and technicians out of the country. By doing so, he was free to plan an attack on Israel.

He believed that a bold move was needed to break the diplomatic stalemate, revive Arab confidence, and prove to the world that the Arabs could combat Israel. In short, the Arabs needed war to make peace. Al-Sadat courted Syria's al-Asad as a military ally and King Faysal of Saudi Arabia as a political ally. The coordinated strategy would involve a joint Egyptian and Syrian invasion of Israeli-occupied territory and an oil embargo against Israel's supporters in the West.

Israel and its chief backer, the United States, would be caught off guard by the Arab surprise attack. Their intelligence services did not foresee an outbreak of hostilities having concluded that al-Sadat was in no position to launch a major offensive, especially after he had ousted the Soviet advisers and technicians. The Israelis were still flush with the victory of 1967 and heavily influenced by a sense of military superiority. The Egyptians reinforced this attitude by placing their least experienced units along the canal within sight of the Israelis. Moreover, the Israelis and Americans interpreted frequent Egyptian and Syrian maneuvers as routine training exercises. The Israelis also assumed that an Arab ground attack would be preceded by an air offensive to seize control of the skies. Instead, al-Sadat relied on his elaborate air defense system to cover the Egyptian army as it crossed the Suez and advanced into Israeli-held territory on the east bank.

Al-Sadat and al-Asad selected 6 October 1973 for the start of the war. It was a Saturday, the Jewish Sabbath, and it was Yom Kippur, the Jewish Day of Atonement. Furthermore, Ramadan, the Muslim month of fasting, had begun. Many intelligence officials believed that al-Sadat would not attack during Ramadan. Of note, the date marked the anniversary of the Prophet Muhammad's great victory at Badr in 624. Attacking on Yom Kippur produced one unintended consequence. On the High Holy Day, most Israelis were either worshipping in synagogues or relaxing at home. This situation facilitated the mobilization of IDF reserves because most reservists were easy to locate.

On Saturday afternoon, 6 October, Egypt and Syria launched simultaneous, coordinated attacks along the Suez Canal and in the Golan Heights. Only five hundred Israelis manned the massive sand-berm defense works, known as the Bar-Lev Line, along the east bank of the canal; furthermore,

only a single Israeli armored brigade was stationed near the canal. The
Israeli defenders faced withering fire from 2,000 Egyptian guns and an
assault by 80,000 troops of the Egyptian Second and Third Field Armies.
In the north, 1,500 Syrian artillery pieces signaled the opening thrust of
some 50,000 Syrian mechanized infantry and armored troops into the
Israeli-occupied Golan Heights.

The first three days of fighting on the Sinai front could rightly be
deemed a masterpiece of Egyptian tactics and innovation. Egyptian engineers erected floating bridges across the canal and blasted holes, using
water cannons, through the sand barrier, allowing ground troops to swarm
up and down the length of the canal. As the Egyptians secured their
bridgehead, the SAM umbrella kept them well protected, shooting down
several Israeli Skyhawk and Phantom jet aircraft. Similarly, the Israeli
tanks that responded to the front were met with saturation RPG and antitank missile fire. In the early phase of the war, the Israelis lost armor at an
alarming rate. The Egyptians soon halted their advance into the Sinai and
hunkered down under the protection of their SAM defense network. The
two Arab armies were better coordinated than in 1967, and their initial
attacks forced the Israelis to recoil on both fronts. In addition to their
overarching goals, Egypt and Syria were fighting for national objectives.
Syria sought to recapture the Golan Heights, and Egypt aimed to establish
a substantial presence east of the canal.

The Syrian assault in the Golan also overwhelmed the Israeli troops
stationed there. The Syrians were close to making a breakthrough that
would have given them an open path to the Mediterranean, splitting
Galilee from the rest of Israel. Observing the dire situation on the second
day, Israeli defense minister Dayan declared, "The Third Temple [the
State of Israel] is in danger."[11] He immediately ordered more troops and
aircraft to the northern front. If the Syrians had succeeded, it is believed
that Israel would have taken the extraordinary step of using its arsenal of
nuclear weapons to save the country.

In contrast to the 1967 war, the two superpowers were deeply involved
in this round of fighting between Arabs and Israelis. The Soviet Union
and the United States rearmed their respective allies and ordered naval
forces to the eastern Mediterranean.[12] The U.S. airlift of critical military

supplies and ammunition turned the course of the fighting in Israel's favor. The day after the United States began flying arms to Israel, the Arab oil-producing states announced that they would reduce production by 5 percent in October and that reductions would continue until Israel withdrew from all occupied territories and acknowledged the national rights of the Palestinians. Two days later, the Arab members of the Organization of the Petroleum Exporting Countries (OPEC) imposed an embargo on the United States and any other country that was overtly supportive of Israel. The Arabs also targeted the Netherlands.

The Egyptians and Syrians made significant advances in the early days of the war, but the Israelis regrouped and mounted a pair of counterattacks. They attacked the Syrians first, since the Golan was closer to major Israeli population centers. Israeli armor drove far beyond the heights, producing a huge salient that approached the outskirts of Damascus. As the Israeli attack progressed, al-Asad appealed to al-Sadat to restart the Sinai offensive to relieve pressure on the beleaguered Syrian troops in the north. Al-Sadat reluctantly consented, overruling the advice of the armed forces chief of staff, General Sa'd al-Din Mohammed al-Shazli (1922–2011), who was certain that Egyptian forces would be thrashed once they advanced beyond their SAM defensive shield. Al-Sadat's decision proved disastrous. Once the Israelis regained control of the northern front, they focused their attention on Sinai. Forward Israeli units found a weak spot between the two Egyptian armies, drove between them, crossed the canal, swung south, and surrounded the Egyptian Third Army.[13]

By the third week of the war, Egypt and Syria faced defeat. The Soviets invited Kissinger, now U.S. secretary of state *and* national security adviser, to Moscow to hammer out the terms of a cease-fire, which was officially promulgated as UN Security Council Resolution 338 of 22 October. The resolution, which passed with a single abstention, called for a cease-fire in place, the implementation of UN Resolution 242, and negotiations among the involved parties aimed at achieving a Middle East peace settlement. Incredibly, the cease-fire led to a dangerous confrontation between the United States and Soviet Union.

The cease-fire was not immediately observed because the trapped Egyptian Third Army kept attempting to break out and both sides continued to consolidate their positions. Fearing the complete destruction of an Egyptian army force, Moscow sent an ultimatum to Washington that called for a joint U.S.-Soviet force to monitor the cease-fire. If the Americans refused, the Soviets said that they would police the battlefront alone.

President Nixon responded to the ultimatum by ordering U.S. forces on high alert. It is widely speculated that he may have ordered the alert to distract the American public's attention from the Watergate scandal, which was consuming his administration, and focus it instead on the extremely grave situation in the Middle East. Declassified CIA documents indicate how dire the situation was and how it could have led to a dangerous military escalation. By 28 October, heavy fighting on the southern end of the Sinai front had ended, but only after two additional UN resolutions had been passed and the United States and Soviet Union had placed extraordinary pressure on their proxy forces. That same day, in a tent located at Kilometer 101 on the road from Cairo to Suez, Egyptian and Israeli representatives worked out a disengagement plan that provided relief to the encircled Third Army.

After the war, the United States saw a rich opportunity to advance peace in the Middle East. Kissinger organized an international peace conference that met in December in Geneva. The United States and Soviet Union served as cochairs, and all regional parties, except the Syrians and Palestinians, attended. The Syrians refused to meet directly with Israel, and the PLO was not invited. The delegates met only once; the conference achieved nothing substantial.

Egypt's presence at the conference indicated that al-Sadat was ready—with help from the United States—to deal with Israel. By January 1974, Israel was also ready to discuss terms with Egypt. With Kissinger acting as the lead negotiator, Israel and Egypt agreed to the Sinai I Agreement, which was signed later that month. Israel withdrew from the immediate vicinity of the Suez Canal, Egypt reoccupied the east bank in a zone that averaged six miles (ten kilometers) in width, and the UN Emergency Force was reestablished in the Sinai. The U.S. Navy led an international effort to clear mines and obstructions from the canal, which reopened with much fanfare in June 1975. Satisfied with Sinai I, al-Sadat helped persuade King Faysal to lift the oil embargo.

Syria also agreed to negotiate a disengagement of forces agreement with Israel. This agreement was much more difficult to achieve than Sinai I. By war's end, the Syrians held none of the territory they had gained during the opening phase of the fighting but hoped to emerge from the conflict with the perception that they had gained something tangible. Kissinger spent most of May 1974 in the region, shuttling between Jerusalem and Damascus. Ultimately, the Israelis agreed to give back to Syria the territory they had seized in the war. The UN Disengagement Observer Force (UNDOF) took up position along the eastern edge of the Golan Heights between Israeli and Syrian forces. The Syrians were back where they started on October 6; Israeli forces withdrew a short distance to the west, permitting the deployment of UNDOF.

The Sinai II Agreement of September 1975 fostered greater confidence between Israel and Egypt. Israel withdrew further to the east, giving up control of the strategic Sinai passes. UNEF took up positions there, and U.S. civilian technicians operated radar warning systems. Egypt also regained the Sinai oil fields, but Israel was permitted to purchase Egyptian oil. Israel could also ship nonmilitary cargoes through the Suez Canal. Sinai I and II were modest, confidence-building measures, yet Arabs and Israelis were beginning to believe that peace was achievable. Furthermore, the United States was regarded by both sides as a credible broker.

Although little Arab territory had been recovered from Israel, the 1973 war was a strategic and psychological victory for the Arabs. Israel was no longer seen as an invincible foe. Egyptian forces acquitted themselves well on the battlefield, and al-Sadat was hailed as the "Hero of the Crossing." After the war, he pursued important diplomatic and economic initiatives. He participated in the Geneva Conference and negotiated two interim agreements with Israel, which gave Egypt a modicum of honorable peace. He initiated infitah (opening), a move toward capitalism, which he hoped would expand the Egyptian economy by welcoming foreign investment and participating in the global economy.

Despite the Israelis' stunning comeback on the battlefield and the conclusion of three interim peace agreements, they felt vulnerable in the aftermath of the war. They would have to review their defense policies and intelligence procedures and implement appropriate reforms, but they would continue to depend on no outsider for their direct security. The war caused a shakeup in the Israeli government. Several ministers resigned over the preparations for and conduct of the war; they included Prime Minister Golda Meir (1969–74) and Defense Minister Dayan. Yitzhak Rabin became the new prime minister (1974–77, 1992–95). The war marked the beginning of a decline in power and influence of the Labor bloc; consequently, Menachem Begin and his Likud bloc would gain in popularity. Begin advocated peace through strength and advanced both religious and security arguments for holding the territories captured in the 1967 war. Likud emerged as the largest political bloc in the Knesset after its stunning victory in the elections of May 1977.

During and after the war, Arab oil producers reaped a huge financial windfall and amassed great international power and influence. The six-month oil embargo weakened the economies of the United States and Europe. Oil prices increased fourfold, from $2.74 per barrel in January 1973 to $11.65 per barrel in January 1974. The embargo and higher oil prices highlighted the vulnerability of Western economies, which suffered from deep recession, spiraling inflation, and high unemployment. Concerned with the well-being of their populations, many countries reduced their support for Israel and developed closer political and economic ties to the Arab world.

Although the United States had supported Israel during the war, it acquired new prestige throughout the Arab world. Several Arab countries restored diplomatic relations—broken since 1967—with the United States, which had used its power and influence to end the war and achieve diplomatic breakthroughs between Israel and two of its Arab neighbors. Kissinger's "shuttle diplomacy" had become legendary.

It can be argued that the Camp David Accords of 1978 were a direct result of the October 1973 Arab-Israeli War and that the path to the Israeli-Egyptian peace treaty began with the crossing of the Suez Canal. The Arabs could come to the peace table in a position of strength. The emergence of a right-wing group in Israel—Likud under Begin—and an Arab who wanted to discuss peace—al-Sadat—led to substantive peace negotiations. It is worth noting that the rise of Likud and its involvement in peace negotiations is analogous to a widely held belief in the United States that only Nixon, an ardent cold warrior, could visit the People's Republic of China. The Israeli people trusted Likud to make peace because they knew that Begin would give away very little in the process.

The October 1973 Arab-Israeli War shifted the economic and political center of gravity of the Arab world to the oil-producing states. The war had a tremendous influence on their budgets and politics. Increased oil revenue resulted in massive government spending on major infrastructure projects, expanded social welfare programs, and investment in foreign corporations. The oil producers used the wealth to influence foreign affairs. They bankrolled the PLO and frontline states, and they supported Iraq in the war against Iran.

Revolutionary Iran

This chapter focuses on late twentieth-century Iran, from the months leading up to the overthrow of Mohammed Reza Shah in 1979 to the death of Ayatollah Ruhollah Khomeini, leader and guide of the Iranian Revolution, in 1989. We examine the rise of political Islam; reasons for the shah's downfall; Khomeini's establishment of an Islamic government in Iran; the structure and powers of the government of the Islamic Republic that evolved from Khomeini's vision, particularly its unique system of checks and balances; and the causes, phases, and outcome of the eight-year Iran-Iraq War.

78. What accounts for the emergence of Islam as a political strategy in the Middle East?

Addressing this question requires careful, unemotional analysis. It also requires discernment of the differences between and among militant Islamists groups, such as al-Qa'ida and ISIS, and Islamist political parties and movements, such as Tunisia's Ennahdha Party and Turkey's Justice and Development Party (AKP). The emergence of Islam as a political strategy, one can argue, stretches back centuries and was typically shaped by regional crises. The first advocacy of political Islam is attributed to Taqi al-Din Ibn Taymiyya (d. 1328), a Sunni theologian and follower of the Hanbali school of jurisprudence, who lived in the aftermath of the Crusades and Mongol invasion. He castigated any

Muslim or non-Muslim who did not share his radical views. Centuries later, in *What Went Wrong* (2002), Bernard Lewis describes Napoleon Bonaparte's lopsided victory over a larger Mamluk force near Cairo in 1798 and the subsequent French occupation of Egypt, which prompted many Egyptians to ask themselves, How could something this humiliating happen to a major Muslim country and how can we prevent it from happening again? One remedy, according to some Muslim leaders of the era, was for Muslims to turn more zealously to their faith. British domination over India gave rise to Islamist accounts blaming Hindus for the loss of the Muslim Mughal Empire in the eighteenth century. Furthermore, in the nineteenth century, when Russia and Great Britain vied for control of South Asia, Islam and Afghan tribalism jelled into a potent force that repelled or blocked the invaders. The Afghans defeated a British army in 1842, and the British would later use Afghanistan as a buffer state against Russian encroachment into India. It is important to be skeptical of simplistic claims that Islam and its 1.6 billion adherents are collectively responsible for the grave problem of Islamist terrorism. Such notions have no place in a combat theater because they prevent us from making an earnest attempt to understand the human terrain and cultural nuances of the region and rob the United States of strategic as well as tactical options.

When we consider a description of an event or development in Islamic history, we should always appreciate the underlying reasons for that account. Is the account colored by social, political, or economic factors, foreign invasion, or a combination of some or all of these? A few examples illustrate this point: First, shortly after the start of World War I, the Germans used Islam to support their strategy against the Allies, persuading the Ottoman sultan to proclaim a jihad that would incite millions of Muslims to rebel against the Russian czar and their British and French colonial masters. The proclamation failed to spark a general Muslim uprising. Next, after the establishment of Israel and defeat of Arab armies in 1948, Islamist rationales proliferated to explain the shocking results of the conflict. A third seminal event was the June 1967 Arab-Israeli War, a defeat that so discredited secular Pan-Arabism and Arab nationalism that thousands of Arabs sought refuge in Islamist—including militant Islamist—ideologies.

After the 1967 war, Muslim activists argued that all the political isms had been tried and failed, and Islam should now be given a chance to serve as a governing model in the modern world. But simple, direct slogans such as "Give Islam a chance" did not address such critical questions as, In an Islamic state, which interpretation of Islamic law and practice will be dominant? Finally, some Arab leaders also exploited Islam to enhance their political legitimacy. In the early 1970s, Anwar al-Sadat reinvented himself as "President of the Faithful" to outmaneuver the Nasserists and leftists determined to remove him. Later, we will see how the dictator Saddam Hussein exploited Islamist politics to retain power in the aftermath of Operation Desert Storm.

A milestone year in the development of political Islam was 1979, which witnessed the Iranian Revolution, the siege of Mecca by Sunni extremists, and the Soviet invasion of Afghanistan. Repercussions from these three events reverberate to this day. The revolution demonstrated that radical Islamists could topple an American-backed regime. It produced a radical Shi'a regime that has challenged Saudi and other Sunni Arabs for leadership in the Persian Gulf, confronted the presence of Western powers in the Middle East, and endeavored to export its radical revolutionary ideology to other countries throughout the region. During the siege of Mecca, Wahhabi extremists, angered by the al-Sa'ud family's close ties to the West, took control of the Grand Mosque for more than two weeks. Commandos recaptured the site, and Saudi authorities subsequently assuaged the concerns of the country's clerical establishment by stiffening their religious zeal and imposing stricter mores on Saudi society. Following the Soviet invasion of Afghanistan on Christmas Eve, Afghan *mujahidin* (Muslim warriors or freedom fighters) used their faith to develop an effective political-military strategy that mired Soviet troops in a decadelong quagmire. During the Soviet-Afghan War (1979–89), thousands of Muslims departed their countries—in most cases to the satisfaction of the repressive, pro-West Arab regimes they left behind—and traveled to Afghanistan to join the jihad against the foreign occupiers.

After the U.S.-led toppling of Saddam Hussein's regime in 2003, the disbanding of the Iraqi army proved to be a huge mistake. The release of tens of thousands of combat-trained soldiers, with little prospect for civilian employment and unable to provide for their families, created an environment beneficial to al-Qa'ida in Iraq and its leader, Abu Mus'ab al-Zarqawi (1966–2006). The breakdown of authority in Iraq led to deadly sectarian conflict, with Muqtada al-Sadr (b. 1973) preaching militant Shi'ism and al-Zarqawi stoking Sunni Salafi-jihadi militancy. On the Shi'a side, militants, led by al-Sadr, targeted Sunnis and American combat forces in Iraq. Making matters worse, Prime Minister Nouri al-Maliki (2006–14) favored Shi'a over Sunnis, and this sectarian bias produced a set of circumstances that facilitated the expansion of ISIS into Iraq. As you read the questions and answers in later chapters of this guide, think about the ferment created by the Arab Spring, and see if you can determine which brand of political Islamism or militant Islamism exists in your geographical area of operation. Is it Sunni or Shi'a? Which Sunni school or branch of Shi'ism does it represent? And is it Salafi or Sufi? The use of religion to win votes, stir up emotions, or unify a population is neither new in history nor exclusive to the Muslim world.

79. What were the circumstances leading to the Iranian Revolution of 1978–79 and the overthrow of Mohammed Reza Shah?

In response to a previous question, we discussed the unintended consequences of Mohammed Reza Shah's White Revolution. His educational reforms increased the number of literate and college-educated Iranians, who became disillusioned with the regime, as it restricted civil freedoms and failed to create adequate opportunities for suitable employment. The shah's land reforms sought to produce a landed class of small farmers, but instead they generated a larger number of struggling farmers and landless peasants. Iran benefitted from the oil boom of the 1970s, but a considerable amount of its wealth remained in the hands of a small elite well connected to the monarchy. Iran's clerics increasingly sided with the country's aggrieved population.

In the mid- to late 1970s, American intelligence on Iran was badly flawed. In August 1978, the CIA predicted that the Pahlavi dynasty would last at least twenty-five more years. A few months later, the

CIA predicted that the shah would leave the country, a constitutional government would be established, and a temporary, protective role for the religious establishment would be set up. Why was U.S. intelligence so inaccurate? The primary reason is that the CIA was out of touch with what was happening inside the country. It had no human intelligence (HUMINT) resources on the ground; it had few Farsi speakers; it relied on SAVAK, the secret police, which was biased toward the shah, for its street-level intelligence; and it underestimated the clerics' influence.

Several significant economic and social factors contributed to the Iranian Revolution. Regarding the economy, the national budget increased threefold from 1972 to 1976, and the country's overheated development and growth led to a large increase in the number of dispossessed people, especially the urban poor, who moved to the cities seeking employment and once there were forced to live in squalor. They supported the revolution, having missed out on the gains of the White Revolution and the oil boom. When the oil bubble burst in 1978, revenues declined, the budget shrank, and popular discontent increased. In the social sphere, there was a large increase in enrollment in secondary schools, but opportunities for college-level and technical education did not keep pace. Many deserving young people could not attend college. Among those who did, many went to Western universities. While abroad, they noted considerable cultural differences between their country and the West; many clamored for Western-style reforms back home, where they had to face the reality that a university education was no guarantee of a good job. Meanwhile, conservative Iranians were concerned that rampant Westernization was corrupting their traditional way of life.

On New Year's Eve 1977, at a state dinner in Tehran, U.S. president Jimmy Carter (1977–81) toasted Mohammed Reza Shah: "Iran, because of the great leadership of the Shah, is an island of stability in one of the most troubled areas of the world."[1] This statement proved to be ironic. In January 1978, large anti-shah demonstrations broke out in the holy city of Qom. The protests began after the publication of a government-sponsored article in *Ettelaat* (*Information*), Tehran's leading newspaper, that criticized and disparaged Khomeini. Troops fired on the crowd, killing several demonstrators. A forty-day mourning period honored the martyrs, and subsequent demonstrations took place every forty days with mounting casualties. Khomeini encouraged public mourning because it focused the people's attention on the shah's repressive actions. The cycle of mourning reached its peak in December 1978 on the Shi'a holy day of 'Ashura. Nearly 2 million demonstrators marched in Tehran. They chanted for the return of the imam. Or were they chanting for the return of the Imam? Were the people calling for the Hidden Imam or for Imam Husayn or for Ayatollah Khomeini, referring to him as the imam? Regardless, the chanting unnerved the shah, his government, and the security apparatus. The shah had declared martial law in November and persuaded Saddam Hussein to banish Khomeini to Paris, where other exiled opposition leaders gathered around him. That same month, oil industry workers began a strike that Khomeini had encouraged. By the end of the year, the shah was panicked over the unrest in his domain.

On 16 January 1979, the shah and his family left Iran for a "vacation" of unspecified length. He appointed Shapur Bakhtiar (1914–91) of the National Front, a longtime political opponent and disciple of ousted Prime Minister Mohammed Mosaddiq, to the office of prime minister. The shah made the appointment to mollify the opposition, but it had no effect. Within weeks the revolution swept Bakhtiar out of office and neutralized the National Front as a political force. On 1 February, Khomeini returned from exile in Paris. The histrionic event was carried by news media around the world.[2]

Naturally, the shah wondered how such a turn of events could have happened—and so suddenly. He held firm to the belief that if the United States had kept its faith in him, his regime would not be in this position. Looking back, did the United States do the right thing in restoring the shah to power in 1953? This question is a compelling one indeed, especially with two and a half decades of hindsight. Thus, we should examine the following circumstances or developments that influenced U.S. policy toward Iran from 1953 to 1978: First, Mosaddiq was supported by the Left—most significant, the Iranian Communist Party. The United States viewed the political situation in Iran through the prism of Cold War–era anticommunism. Second, by 1970 many Western-educated Iranian intellectuals were satisfied with the shah's policies. This development was viewed positively by U.S. administrations. Mullahs, on the other hand, had substantial grievances against the shah, such as his emphasis on Iranian nationalism over Islam and his rampant program of Westernization. Third, prosperity soared until 1978, raising the expectations of all Iranians, yet most of that money was concentrated among a small, well-connected elite. Finally, the shah had always tried to do the right thing for his people, as King Louis XVI had done during the first phase of the French Revolution. Later, more extreme factions of the French National Assembly dominated the Committee of Public Safety, ushered in the Reign of Terror, and ordered the executions of the king, queen, and thousands of perceived enemies of the revolution.

In late October 1979, the shah, who was suffering from cancer, was admitted to a U.S. hospital. On 4 November, militant students occupied the U.S. embassy in Tehran and took several diplomats and staff members hostage; they demanded that the U.S. government return the shah to Iran to stand trial. On 27 July 1980, Mohammed Reza Shah died in Egypt; he was buried in Cairo. The students would hold the embassy and their hostages until 20 January 1981.

80. What were the steps in establishing the Islamic Republic of Iran?

Diverse groups supported the Iranian Revolution: clerics, the traditional and modern middle class, intellectuals, urban and rural poor, merchants, and communists. Many supporters, however, were mainly opposed to the rule of the shah and did not favor the establishment of an Islamic republic. After the collapse of the Pahlavi monarchy, several factions competed for control of the revolution, but within months the radical clerics triumphed.

In February 1979, Khomeini appointed Mehdi Bazargan (1907–95), an engineer and prominent intellectual, to head an interim government and charged him with forming an Islamic republic; Bakhtiar resigned a week later. While in Paris, Khomeini had established the Council of the Islamic Revolution (CIR) to oversee the revolution. It acted as a parallel government, passing its own laws, confronting leftists and secularists, and undercutting Bazargan's authority. Early on, the coalition of clerics and intellectuals enjoyed strong popular support, and the Tudeh Party was ascendant. The intellectuals, supported by the middle class and communists, called for a secular government that would be advised by the mullahs. On the other hand, the mullahs, backed by the peasantry and urban poor, were determined to establish a theocratic republic. The mullahs' base of support had grown over the years, largely through the wide circulation of Khomeini's recorded sermons.

The early months of the revolution were theatrical, unstable, and turbulent, and its future was uncertain. Nevertheless, a revolutionary organization gradually asserted itself on the streets and in the neighborhoods. Thousands of self-appointed *komitehs* (revolutionary committees) sprang up. Usually based near mosques, they worked to effect the goals of the revolution and exercised civil authority in many local areas. They operated under the direction of radical clergy. The Pasdaran (precursor to the Islamic Revolutionary Guard Corps, IRGC), comprised primarily of armed youth, battled counterrevolutionaries, and served as a counterweight to the regular armed forces. It functioned as the military wing of the Islamic Republican Party (IRP), which advocated a state modeled on Khomeini's concept of governance by Islamic jurist, which we will discuss in the answer to the next question.

In a March referendum, the Iranian people voted to replace the monarchy with an Islamic republic. At the polls, voters were asked if they wanted an Islamic state: yes or no? Naturally, millions of Iranians voted yes, confronted with such a stark choice. Furthermore, radical clerics declared that a no vote was a vote against Islam. On 1 April, the Islamic Republic of Iran was inaugurated, but few governing institutions were in place and functioning. Furthermore, the Shi'a clergy and secular nationalists competed vigorously for control of the government. They had opposing goals. The clerics sought a conservative Islamic state dominated by the Shi'a hierarchy; secular groups, on the other hand, supported an Islamic republic with a secular administration. According to the secularists, the clergy would provide moral oversight of the government—an important, but limited, role.

By the end of the year, the government of Iran had become radical. In November militant students seized the U.S. embassy and took the diplomats and embassy staff hostage, a gross violation of international law. They demanded the shah's return to Iran to stand trial. Acting at first without official backing, the students eventually secured Khomeini's support. The embassy takeover strengthened political hard-liners, who condemned the Jimmy Carter administration's resolute response to the crisis. The U.S. government had initiated steps to isolate Iran diplomatically. It dispatched an aircraft carrier task force to the Arabian Sea and froze more than $11 billion in Iranian assets. Occupying the embassy gave militant Islamists the high ground vis-à-vis their secular rivals; it neutralized the opposition of ayatollahs who disagreed with Khomeini's ideas on Islamic governance; and it discredited moderate, secular politicians, such as Bazargan. Shortly after the hostage crisis had begun, Bazargan resigned as prime minister, and the interim government was shorn of its power. The CIR governed the country until a newly elected Majlis was seated in early 1980. In December a new constitution, drafted by religious conservatives, was ratified by a nearly unanimous popular vote; Iran was officially a theocracy with many of the trappings of a republic. Article 56 states that sovereignty is the right of the people bestowed on them by God, but Article 110 grants the leader, the Islamic jurist, extraordinary power and authority compared to all other components of the government.[3] With the constitution in place, fundamentalist clerics had great strength, power, and political momentum.[4]

In April 1980, the United States severed relations with Iran. That same month, Carter approved a bold attempt to rescue the hostages. The mission, Operation Eagle Claw, was a tragic failure, costing the lives of eight American servicemembers. In September Iraq invaded Iran, initiating a deadly conflict that would last eight years. On 20 January 1981, 52 American hostages were freed after 444 days in captivity. The Iranians released them the moment Carter's term expired, subjecting the United States to one more humiliation.

The radical clerics had several advantages over their secular and religious rivals: common objectives, unified leadership, pithy slogans, popular support, a willingness to use violence, and the support of Khomeini. In late 1979, they initiated the ruthless suppression of their opponents, which included holdouts from the shah's government, rival political parties, antiregime guerrillas, democracy advocates, communists, moderate Islamists, and liberal and moderate secularists, the last of which included the incumbent, democratically elected president, Abolhassan Bani-Sadr (b. 1933), who was impeached and driven into exile. The struggle between and among Islamic factions was extremely violent. In the summer of 1981, the Mujahedin-e Khalq (People's Mujahidin of Iran), an anti-Khomeini, Islamic-Marxist organization, carried out two spectacular assassinations. In June it bombed IRP headquarters, killing the country's chief justice and four cabinet members. Two months later, a suitcase bomb killed the new president, Mohammed 'Ali al-Rajai (1933–81), and new prime minister, Mohammed Javad Bahonar (1933–81). Despite these horrific attacks, the radical Shi'a leadership and IRP consolidated their hold on power. During a reign of terror that lasted until mid-1982, more than four thousand opponents of the republic—actual or perceived—were executed; many others were jailed or exiled.

The lessons of the Iranian Revolution were not lost on other militant Islamists inspired by the success of a radical religious movement that toppled an authoritarian regime backed by the United States. The muscular Shi'a regime in Iran instantly posed an ideological and military threat to Wahhabi-influenced Saudi Arabia and the conservative Sunni monarchies of the Persian Gulf, a rivalry that has affected security issues in the Middle East to this day.

81. How does the system of checks and balances function in the Iranian government?

In the Islamic Republic of Iran, a parallel system of government exists: the governing institutions and an Islamic revolutionary organization. The Iranian model of government uses a system of checks and balances that gives the appearance of a government that is limited and answerable to the electorate. In theory, even revolutionary organs are subject to restraint. In reality, the system could not prevent the growing dominance of the IRGC over the social, economic, and political life of Iran. While checks and balances exist, what happens in actual practice is a different issue.

We will first examine the revolutionary organization, which consists of the following: the Vilayat-e Faqih (the Iranian cleric who exercises the governance of the Islamic jurist; the supreme authority in the state); Council of Guardians, which comprises twelve jurists; the Assembly of Experts, which is made up of eighty-six clerics; the Expediency Council; and the head of the judiciary.

Considering the Vilayat-e Faqih, a *faqih* is a Muslim jurist or legal expert; *fiqh* is the science of Islamic law or jurisprudence. Also referred to as the supreme leader, the Vilayet-e Faqih has powerful sway over the people and government. Ayatollah Khomeini, the first Vilayet-e Faqih, described the position in several sermons and lectures. Upon his death in 1989, he was succeeded by the serving president, Ayatollah 'Ali Khamenei (b. 1939). The Vilayet-e- Faqih is the highest authority in matters of religious jurisprudence and is charged with keeping the government on the true path. In the Islamic Republic of Iran, the fundamental principle of government is the rule of the Islamic jurist, who acts on behalf of the Hidden Imam.

In Islam, legitimate authority is based on the ability to interpret the law. Shi'a doctrine states that government rests with the Hidden Imam, and all governments are corrupt until his return; therefore, Khomeini's concept of Islamic government provided a dominant role for Shi'a clergy. The supreme leader, who is elected by the Assembly of Experts, is the head of state and commander in chief of the armed forces. He controls the intelligence and security apparatus, including SAVAMA (the secret police organization that succeeded SAVAK); approves major economic and foreign policies; and appoints half the members of the Council of Guardians and the heads of the judiciary, state media, and IRGC.

Khomeini established the Council of Guardians, a group of mullahs who review legislation and have the authority to throw out laws passed by the parliament that it deems in violation of Islam. The council also vets candidates for the Majlis, the presidency, and the Assembly of Experts. Typically, reformers and many women are blocked from running. Half of the members of the council are appointed by the supreme leader; the other half are nominated by the head of the judiciary and confirmed by the Majlis. Together the Vilayet-e Faqih and Council of Guardians make up the guardianship of the Islamic scholar. This arrangement ensures that the republic will be run by a religious hierarchy dedicated to the mainte-nance of an Islamic state.

The Assembly of Experts, which meets in Qom, decides crucial matters of state. It reviewed and revised the draft of the 1979 constitution. Candidates for the assembly are vetted by the Council of Guardians and are elected by the people. The assembly elects and monitors the performance of the supreme leader and has the power to remove him.

The Expediency Council, consisting of thirty religious and political leaders, advises the supreme leader and mediates disputes between the Majlis and the Council of Guardians.

The head of the judiciary, who oversees the country's court system, is appointed by the supreme leader. The head nominates half of the members of the Council of Guardians and appoints High Court (Supreme Court) justices and the chief prosecutor. The Iranian judiciary reviews all bills passed by the Majlis to ensure their conformity with Islam. Other tribunals include criminal and civil courts, national security courts, a revolutionary court, and a clerical court, which rules on crimes committed by clergy.

Governing institutions consist of the president, Council of Ministers (the cabinet), Majlis, and speaker of the Majlis. (The government originally included the office of prime minister, but it was abolished in the late 1980s.) Candidates for president and the Majlis are vetted by the Council of Guardians and elected by the people. The members of the Council of Ministers are nominated by the president and confirmed by the Majlis.

The president, who is the head of government, and Council of Ministers manage the day-to-day political and governmental matters. The Majlis, which consists of 290 members, drafts legislation, ratifies treaties, and approves the government's budget.

In *Islamic Government: Governance of the Jurist* (1969), Khomeini argues that an Islamic government is one headed by the Islamic jurist, who, along with the Council of Guardians, supervises the moral path of the state. Khomeini's manifesto resembles Plato's classic work *The Republic*, in which the Greek sage writes that the best government is one led by a philosopher-king who has the knowledge, wisdom, and experience to direct the state. Khomeini's ideas were not accepted by some prominent ayatollahs, such as 'Ali al-Sistani (b. 1930) and Mohammed Baqir al-Sadr (1935–80) in Iraq and Mohammed Hussein Fadlallah (1935–2010) in Lebanon. Understanding

Khomeini's governing philosophy and appreciating political differences within the Shi'a hierarchy can help in developing better informed U.S. foreign and security policies for the Middle East. Khomeini's philosophy is best considered a distinct form of Islamist political thought and is described as Khomeinism.

82. What were the causes, events and developments, and outcome of the Iran-Iraq War?

Iran and Iraq were political competitors in the Persian Gulf for decades, and the overthrow of the shah in early 1979 elevated their rivalry to a dangerous level. Iraqi leader Saddam Hussein viewed Iran's Shi'a fervor as a direct threat to his Sunni Ba'thist regime in Baghdad. Iraqi fears of radical revolutionary Shi'a ideology spreading from Iran were not unfounded given that 60 percent of the Iraqi population was Shi'a and had been dominated by a Sunni minority since the establishment of the British mandate.

As revolutionary Iran became increasingly unstable, Saddam prepared to attack his neighbor. His two principal goals were the toppling of the Khomeini regime and reasserting control over the vital Shatt al-Arab waterway. Before the 1975 Algiers Accords, Iraq had controlled most of the Shatt al-Arab. According to that agreement, Iraq would cede half of the waterway, and Iran would withhold support for rebellious Kurds in northern Iraq. Saddam believed that Iran's political turmoil and militarily weakness made it ripe for invasion and that the Arab population in the Iranian province of Khuzestan near the Shatt al-Arab would rise against the Islamic republic and support the Iraqi forces. (The Arabs on the Iranian side of the border refused.) In addition to these goals, victory over Iran would enable Iraq to acquire new territory; supplant Egypt, which had signed a peace treaty with Israel in 1979, as the leader of the pan-Arab movement; and increase its petroleum reserves by seizing Khuzestan.

On 22 September 1980, Iraq launched a surprise air attack, but the strike failed to destroy Iranian air assets on the ground. The next day, six Iraqi divisions crossed the border, chiefly in the south. Iranian fighter-bombers conducted deep strikes on Iraqi oil facilities, and AH-1 Cobra attack helicopters struck the advancing Iraqi forces. American-made Iranian F-14

Tomcat fighters downed several Soviet-built Iraqi fighters in the first three days of combat. The Iranians had the benefit of American arms, purchased by the shah, but their effectiveness was blunted by a lack of spare parts. The bloody, two-month battle for the Iranian city of Khorramshahr drained the momentum of the Iraqi offensive and gave the Iranian government the opportunity to mobilize the population. A successful propaganda campaign against Saddam Hussein unified the nation, which rallied to stop the Iraqi invasion. Hundreds of thousands of young Iranians volunteered for service with the Basij (Mobilization) irregular militia. Motivated by the Shi'a culture of martyrdom, they became infamous for their "human-wave" attacks against well-defended Iraqi positions. The mullahs also appealed to the Shi'a of southern Iraq to rebel against Saddam. (Like the Arabs of Khuzestan, they also refused.) Early setbacks on the battlefield discredited the leadership of Iran's secular, nationalist president, Abolhassan Bani-Sadr, who was impeached and exiled in June 1981.

By November 1980, a stalemate had descended on the front, and both sides had dug in. Combat soon resembled that on the western front of World War I but fought with late twentieth-century weaponry. Leading up to the invasion, the Iraqis made some serious miscalculations. They counted too heavily on Iran's internal instability and its inability to buy spare parts for its U.S.-built weapons, and they assumed they would acquire Western support as the hostage crisis in Tehran dragged on. In 1981 the Saudis and Arab gulf states formed a defensive alliance, the Gulf Cooperation Council (GCC); the gulf Arabs subsequently provided Iraq with considerable financing during the conflict, seeing it as a buffer against revolutionary Iran.

The Iranians went on the offensive in mid-1981. They attacked areas east of Baghdad and, by April 1982, had regained the lost territory in Khuzestan. In 1983 they launched human-wave attacks, deploying the Basij to clear minefields for advancing Iranian troops. The Iraqis introduced chemical weapons to thwart the mass attacks; later, they used chemical agents in an attempt to stamp out Kurdish opposition to the regime. Iraq called for a cease-fire in 1982, but Khomeini refused to halt the fighting unless Saddam surrendered power, admitted that Iraq had started the war, and paid an indemnity for the damages wrought by his country.

In 1984 a stalemate again gripped the front. As the war plodded forward, the United States and Israel desired to prevent a decisive victory by either side, a development that would tip the balance of power in the Middle East in favor of either Tehran or Baghdad and pose a greater threat to the security of the Persian Gulf region and the Jewish state. This strategy had risks. While a prolonged war could impoverish and weaken both countries, it might draw their backers into a wider conflict, endanger the shipment of oil out of the gulf, and weaken the economies of all oil-exporting states in the region.

Attacks on tankers and oil facilities began in 1984 and continued until the end of the war. Because Iraq's exports through the gulf were shut down early in the conflict, it relied on pipelines through Turkey and Saudi Arabia to export its oil. To prevent Iran from using its oil revenue to purchase weapons and other military equipment, Iraq attacked Iranian oil facilities on Kharg Island and its vicinity. As a result, Iran's revenue declined from $21.7 billion in 1983 to $15.9 billion in 1985 and to $7.3 billion in 1986. Iran retaliated by attacking the shipping of countries that supported Iraq. In early 1987, the Ronald Reagan administration reflagged Kuwaiti tankers as American vessels, and the U.S. Navy began escorting them through the gulf and Strait of Hormuz. In May the USS *Stark*, a guided-missile frigate performing radar picket duty, was inadvertently targeted by an Iraqi aircraft and subsequently hit by two Exocet missiles, which caused the deaths of thirty-seven sailors. In April of the following year, the USS *Samuel B. Roberts*, a ship of the same class, was severely damaged by an Iranian mine while escorting a convoy; miraculously, no crew members were killed. Both ships were saved through the heroic efforts of their crews. In retaliation for the mining that nearly sank the *Roberts*, the U.S. Navy launched Operation Praying Mantis, destroying Iranian oil platforms, sinking two Iranian warships, and heavily damaging a third. The daylong naval battle was the largest surface action since World War II.

Attacks on population centers began in March 1985. Iraq used aircraft and Soviet-built Scud surface-to-surface missiles to attack Tehran; Iran also hit Iraqi cities with long-range missiles and air strikes. In February 1986, the Iranians captured the Fao Peninsula on the Iraqi side of the

Shatt al-Arab. From December 1986 until February 1987, they assaulted the key Iraqi city of Basra, but the city escaped capture.

In 1987 the disclosure of secret U.S. arms sales to Iran prompted Congress to investigate a complicated scandal that became known as the Iran-contra affair. The Reagan administration had pursued Iran's assistance in freeing American hostages held by militant Shi'a in Lebanon in exchange for selling Iran SAMs and other desperately needed military hardware. The proceeds from the arms sales were then used to fund contras, Honduras-based guerrillas who were fighting the communist Sandinista regime in Nicaragua. All this was done to circumvent the will of Congress, which had banned lethal support for the contras. That same year, Iraq accepted a UN resolution calling for a cease-fire, but Iran refused. In 1988 Iraq launched a major offensive and recaptured considerable territory. The newly established and well-trained Iraqi Republican Guard Force spearheaded an attack on the Fao Peninsula, retaking it and then advancing into Iran. On 3 July, the guided-missile cruiser USS *Vincennes*, while on patrol in the Persian Gulf, accidentally shot down an Iranian civilian airliner that was flying from Iran to the UAE. The plane, which steadily approached the ship, was incorrectly identified as an Iranian F-14. That month, both Saddam and Khomeini accepted UN Resolution 598, which called for a cease-fire in the eight-year conflict. The supreme leader acquiesced for several reasons, namely mounting losses on the battlefield, declining morale, attacks on urban areas, growing international isolation, a weakening economy, and the shock of the *Vincennes* incident. He could have attained the same result in 1982 with far fewer losses for his country. In early August, after a few weeks of heavy fighting along the front, both sides withdrew to the international border, and the cease-fire took hold.

Fighting during the Iran-Iraq War was characterized by mass-wave attacks, poison gas, trench works, and economic warfare. Although accurate figures are impossible to come by, hundreds of thousands of soldiers and civilians were killed on both sides.[5]

15

Developments in
Egypt since 1973

This chapter and the three that follow address important political, economic, and social developments in the Arab world since the October 1973 Arab-Israeli War. In this chapter, we focus on Egypt, discussing the controversial reforms of Anwar al-Sadat; the cautious but corrupt governance of Hosni Mubarak; the political and social roles of Islamist groups, such as the Muslim Brotherhood; and the causes and consequences of the 25 January Revolution (2011). We conclude the chapter by investigating political Islam in the latter part of the twentieth century.

83. What were major political, economic, and social developments in Egypt from the end of the October 1973 war to the outbreak of the revolution in January 2011?

Anwar al-Sadat became president of Egypt upon the death of Gamal Abdel Nasser in September 1970. Many observers viewed al-Sadat as a placeholder until a stronger leader emerged. To the surprise of many, al-Sadat filled his predecessor's massive shoes and undid many of his policies. During his Corrective Revolution (1971), al-Sadat reinvented himself, calling himself Ra'is al-Muminin (President of the Faithful) and using Islamist politics to undermine Nasserists in the government and army as well as leftists on the streets of Egypt. By mid-1971 he had removed his political rivals and implemented a new constitution that formally abolished the United Arab Republic and established the Arab Republic of Egypt. The new regime exhibited the trappings of democracy and tolerated some modicum of dissent but remained firmly under the pervasive influence of the military, intelligence services, and police. Al-Sadat also took steps to privatize the economy. He halted the confiscation of private property, welcomed foreign investment, and promoted Egypt's entry into the global economy through his economic liberalization strategy known as the infitah (opening or open door).

Al-Sadat pursued many controversial measures. He recognized Islam as the principal source of law and dismantled many facets of Nasserism. He also ousted the majority of Soviet advisers and technicians, pursued war to break the gridlock of the Arab-Israeli conflict, and sought assistance from the World Bank and International Monetary Fund (IMF) to develop and modernize the economy. He was convinced that his vision of Egypt would be accepted by the people and would benefit the country. Infitah and the Camp David Accords were good examples of this thinking.

The World Bank and IMF attached restrictions to their development funds, such as cuts in government subsidies on oil, sugar, flour, rice, and tea. The reduction in subsidies caused prices to quadruple, causing severe hardship for the *fellahin* (farmers) and urban poor. Few meaningful jobs were created, and the gap between the elites and common folk widened because infitah primarily benefited a small group of wealthy entrepreneurs—a nouveau riche. Some Egyptians achieved great wealth; others became extremely poor. Agricultural production declined as people moved to the cities in the hope of finding high-paying jobs that did not exist.

The opening also brought Western influences. Some aspects of Western society, namely, drugs, alcohol, and a relaxed attitude toward sex, were seen by many Egyptians as threatening to Islamic civilization, harmful to the country's social norms, and detrimental to human dignity. Many Muslims worried that injurious Western values would be imposed on them—a form of cultural imperialism. Consequently, resentment and despair increased, and Islam became the voice of the poor and dispossessed. Militancy and popular discontent increased. In early 1977, food riots erupted, and crowds openly mocked al-Sadat, chanting, "'Hero of the Crossing,' where is our breakfast?" Al-Sadat believed that the riots stemmed from the people's lack of understanding of his policies; his ego prevented him from acknowledging any failure. He countered with repression, but the military drew a line with al-Sadat, refusing to use violence to suppress protesters. Nevertheless, arrests were carried out, and censorship was imposed. Al-Sadat did relent, however, and restored the subsidies for basic commodities.

Facing growing opposition, al-Sadat turned to the Arab-Israeli conflict to divert the public's attention. He made a dramatic trip to Jerusalem in November 1977, and in a speech to the Knesset, he made four key points: First, Egypt can no longer carry the burden of war. Second, he was sincere about seeking peace with Israel. Third, he would not negotiate a separate peace with the Israelis—one that excluded the Palestinians. Fourth, genuine peace between the Arabs and Israel must be based on the following conditions: an end to the Israeli occupation of Arab territories captured in 1967, the attainment of rights and self-determination for the Palestinians, the right of all states to live in peace within secure boundaries, the resolution of disputes through peaceful means, and an end to belligerency.

The main sticking point to any peace settlement was the status of the West Bank and Gaza, which Prime Minister Menachem Begin regarded as part of Eretz Israel, the Land of Israel. The Likud coalition platform of March 1977 proclaimed that "the right of the Jewish people to the land of Israel is eternal and indisputable" and "the establishment of a 'Palestinian State'. . . jeopardizes the security of the Jewish population, endangers the existence of the State of Israel, and frustrates any prospect of peace."[1]

A month after al-Sadat's visit to Israel, he and Begin met at the Egyptian city of Isma'ilia, where the Israeli prime minister unveiled a plan for Palestinian self-rule. He would support autonomy, not the establishment of an independent Palestine. Israel would retain control of foreign, defense, and agricultural policies. The Egyptian president, on the other hand, believed that the status of the occupied territories was negotiable. Despite their differences, Israel and Egypt both needed peace. The burden of military expenditures had become unbearable. Some

Israelis were moving to other countries because they were weary of high taxation, frequent military call-ups, and the stress of living in a hostile corner of the world. Egypt hoped to free up funds earmarked for the military to rebuild its economy.

In early 1978, Egypt and Israel attempted to keep their talks on track, but they soon reached an impasse, at which point President Jimmy Carter committed his administration to the arduous task of facilitating a peace agreement between the longtime adversaries. At the start of his presidency, Carter had attempted to convene a general Middle East peace conference but was unsuccessful. In September he invited al-Sadat and Begin to the presidential retreat at Camp David, Maryland, where twelve days of intense and difficult negotiations produced a pair of frameworks for peace, the Camp David Accords.

The Framework for Peace in the Middle East focused on the West Bank and Gaza. It called for the establishment of a self-governing Palestinian authority in the territories; the withdrawal of Israeli troops, excluding specified security zones; the commencement within three years of talks to determine the final status of the West Bank and Gaza; a transitional period for the territories of no longer than five years; and the realization of a Jordan-Israel peace treaty, based on the final status of the West Bank. For the sake of achieving an agreement with Israel, al-Sadat deferred a settlement on the occupied Palestinian territories to later rounds of diplomacy. At the same time, he hoped that the framework's approach would deflect Arab outrage over his pursuit of a peace agreement with Israel that did not include a resolution of the Palestine issue.

According to the Framework for Peace between Egypt and Israel, the parties would conclude a peace treaty within three months. The document contained the following important provisions: Israel would withdraw from the Sinai, and Egyptian sovereignty would be restored; the border of the old British mandate would serve as the border between Egypt and Israel; the right of free passage through the Suez Canal would be respected; and full diplomatic, commercial, and cultural relations between Egypt and Israel would be established. In March 1979, after months of intense negotiations, Carter officiated as al-Sadat and Begin signed a peace treaty on the White House lawn. Al-Sadat held a questionable referendum on the Camp David Accords; 99 percent of the voters approved. Egypt had regained all the Sinai by April 1982.

After the signing, many Arabs branded al-Sadat a traitor, accusing him of making a separate peace and selling out the Palestinian cause. Begin was lambasted for giving up the Sinai, but the treaty effectively removed Egypt from the Arab-Israeli conflict. The accord was a huge strategic victory for Israel. Henceforth, with Egypt diplomatically sidelined, other Arab countries would be extremely reluctant to combat Israel. Carter, the former U.S. Navy nuclear engineer, viewed the dispute between Egypt and Israel as a highly complex issue that he could resolve. The treaty enhanced his prestige in the short run and is arguably the greatest achievement of his presidency.

Since the late nineteenth century, Egypt has been the home of several Islamic modernist theorists and modernist movements, namely, Jamal al-Din al-Afghani, Muhammad 'Abduh, and the Muslim Brotherhood. In the twentieth century, Egyptians left their villages and moved to the cities in increasing numbers in search of better opportunities. The social fabric in a village is based on the extended family, but migrants to large cities—particularly single men—often lose that dependable support network. Consequently, religious organizations often serve as a substitute for the family. For example, the Muslim Brotherhood supports new arrivals with social welfare programs and a provides sense of belonging that they had enjoyed in their home villages.

Hasan al-Banna (1906–49), an Egyptian schoolteacher, founded the Muslim Brotherhood in 1928. Al-Banna called for a revival of Islam based on the practices of the Prophet Muhammad, his pious followers, and his earliest successors. The organization had established hundreds of lodges in Egypt by the end of the 1930s. Al-Banna opposed Western materialism and spoke out against values that corrupted Egyptian society, infected Islam, and facilitated the country's decline. He called for the centrality of Shari'a, arguing that many of Egypt's ills were caused by the substitution of Qur'anic principles with secular legal and political institutions. He believed that Islamic lands must rid themselves of foreign influence to attain complete freedom and that Egypt could revive through Islamic-based reforms and institutions. He was confident that Muslims could take advantage of the modern world without compromising their core religious values. One of his central tenets held that Shari'a should be interpreted to meet the needs and resolve the problems facing modern society.[2] Al-Banna was assassinated in 1949, most likely by King Faruq's security men. Five years later, Nasser outlawed the Brotherhood after it allegedly attempted to assassinate him, but not before it colluded with the Free Officers to topple the king.[3]

After the death of al-Banna, Hasan al-Hudaybi (ca. 1891–1973), a lawyer, took over leadership of the Muslim Brotherhood. His tenure witnessed the division of the Brotherhood into the moderate Hudaybiists (also called Bannaists) and the more violent Qutbists, named after the influential proponent of modern militant Islamism Sayyid Qutb (1906–66). In the late 1940s, Qutb studied education at Colorado State Teachers College (now the University of Northern Colorado), where he experienced—and one could argue sought out—the extremes and excesses of Western culture; he was appalled. He did admire, however, the power of Evangelical Christian media and the message of Christianity to undermine communist ideology. Back home, he criticized the dearth of morality in Egypt's government and society and was outspoken in his rejection of Western values, especially its blatant materialism and fascination with gratuitous sex and violence. He advocated the use of force to remove Western influences from Egypt and transform the state in accordance with his views of Islamic mores. He was opposed to Marxism and was critical of the Soviets, who in his opinion had carried out an ineffective program of social and economic development. He was especially appalled by Muslim hypocrites who touted Islam but did not practice what they preached. He expected Westerners to act the way they did but was critical of Muslims who did not live up to the tenets of their faith. He and his followers were opposed to Nasser's brand of socialism and argued that the purpose of government was to carry out God's laws. If the government enforces Islamic morality, the people must be obedient. Conversely, if the government does not act in accordance with Islam, the people are not bound to obey it. Furthermore, it was the people's duty to abolish an immoral government by whatever means available. In 1965 Qutb was arrested by the Nasser regime; he was executed a year later. The calamity of June 1967 discredited the leadership of secular Arab regimes in general and disgraced Nasser's revolutionary ideology in particular. Many Egyptians believed that the crushing defeat was due in large part to their country's weak adherence to Islam. Qutb's writings gained a wider following.

In the late 1970s, many Egyptians blamed infitah for introducing the corrupting influence of Western values and materialism into the country, and the political landscape became increasingly strained owing to a surge in radical Islamic fundamentalism. Before then, the principal Islamic movement in Egypt had been the Muslim Brotherhood. Since the mid-1950s, there had been varying degrees of tolerance of the Brotherhood by Egyptian authorities. Al-Sadat had reached an accommodation with its leader, 'Umar al-Tilmisani (1904–86), allowing its members to meet and publish a newspaper, but they were banned from politics. The agreement marked the end of the Brotherhood's militant—or violent—phase, which had peaked during the 1950s. A 1980 constitutional amendment declared Shari'a the primary source of legislation, but al-Sadat admonished people to go to the mosque for prayer, not political activity—an attitude that alienated many Egyptians. To accommodate and control the Islamists, he encouraged the formation of nonrevolutionary Muslim societies to counter Marxist, Nasserist, and radical Islamist ones, thus providing a permissive environment for clandestine militant Islamist groups to develop.

From 1979 to 1981, al-Sadat cracked down on dissent. He outlawed opposition parties because of their sharp criticism of the peace treaty with Israel and his economic program. In September 1981, he banned the Muslim Brotherhood's magazine, *Ad-Da'wa* (*The Call*), imposed censorship on mosque sermons, and jailed more than a thousand dissidents without trial. His actions generated a resurgence in more radical and violent political Islam and sowed the seeds of his demise.

On 6 October 1981, at the annual military parade in Cairo commemorating the crossing of the Suez Canal in October 1973, al-Sadat was brutally assassinated by the militant Egyptian Islamic Jihad (EIJ), consisting of former members of Al-Takfir wal-Hijra (The Apostasy and Migration), a group that had infiltrated the army and was led by Captain Khalid Ahmed al-Islambuli (1955–82). Plowing his way through high-ranking officials on the reviewing stand, al-Islambuli, reportedly shouted to them, "Get out of my way. I only want this son of a dog!"[4] Face to face with al-Sadat, he emptied his automatic rifle into the body of his president and exclaimed, "I am Khalid al-Islambuli, I have killed Pharaoh, and I do not fear death!"[5]

Vice President Hosni Mubarak, a former air force general, who was seated next to al-Sadat, succeeded him as president. He cast himself as a pragmatic ruler and set out to ease the social and political turmoil raging through the country. He declared a state of emergency and clamped down on universities and the press. He freed some of the political and religious dissidents that al-Sadat had jailed but used violent crackdowns when he thought they were necessary. He allowed the Muslim Brotherhood to operate politically in conjunction with other parties, such as the secular Labor and Wafd Parties. He restored a degree of public trust in the government by working for economic and social reforms. American aid boosted the economy and helped provide a social "safety valve." The U.S. government would forgive upward of $9 billion of debt in gratitude for Egypt's participation in Operation Desert Shield and Operation Desert Storm (1990–91).

Egypt regained the Sinai in April 1982, but Israel's invasion of Lebanon that summer turned the peace between the two countries frigid. Egyptians were also frustrated by Israel's subsequent occupation of southern Lebanon and its increasingly restrictive policies in the West Bank and Gaza. Meanwhile, Mubarak went forward with a carefully crafted foreign policy to reintegrate Egypt into regional affairs. Over the course of the 1980s, Egypt restored diplomatic relations with Jordan, aided Iraq in its war with Iran, supported U.S. military actions against Libyan dictator Colonel Mu'ammar al-Qaddafi (1969–2011), and resumed a dialog with PLO Chairman Yasir Arafat. With Arab governments having reestablished diplomatic ties with Cairo, Egypt was readmitted to the Arab League, and the league's headquarters returned to Cairo. Egypt would provide some 20,000 troops to the international coalition to evict Saddam Hussein from Kuwait, and Mubarak was viewed by Western governments and Israeli leaders as a major force in the peace process.

The Muslim Brotherhood modified its tactics during its quiet reemergence under Mubarak. It became a more grassroots and less nationally based organization, yet it took advantage of its restricted role in the political process by supporting various political parties, including secular ones, opposed to Mubarak's ruling National Democratic Party (NDP). Its candidates could not legally run for office as members of the Muslim Brotherhood but could compete as independents or with other legal parties. The Brotherhood continued to operate an extensive social welfare program that included hospitals, schools, and orphanages. Recent crackdowns by the current regime have somewhat depleted the Brotherhood's resources. The organization is an excellent example of a bottom-to-top reform movement. We will see that—aside from the army—it was the only Egyptian political institution left standing in the aftermath of the Arab Spring of 2011.

Since the mid-twentieth century, popular support for Islamist activism in Egypt had steadily increased. Owing to the country's rapidly expanding population, high school and college graduates experienced limited employment opportunities and were resentful that a qualified person needed the right connections to land a respectable job. A good education and poor job opportunities were a lethal mixture that spawned despair, discouragement, and anger. Furthermore, Islam had provided a social base for recent migrants from the village to the big city. Limited prospects for the future and social dislocation led many people to turn to Islamic groups, some radical, for a remedy to their troubles.

Islamist opposition to the policies of the Egyptian government and its Western backers was often expressed through acts of terrorism against government officials, the Coptic Christian minority, foreign tourists, Muslims critical of extremist ideologies, and secular writers. In 1977 a former minister of religious endowments, Shaykh Mohammed al-Dahabi, was brutally murdered by Al-Takfir wal-Hijra for his Islamic-based criticism of the organization. Two decades later, in November 1997, terrorists from the Islamic Group attacked the Temple of Hatshepsut near Luxor, killing sixty-two tourists. Reaction to the horrific act caused a split among militant Islamists and led to a suspension of hostilities directed against the Mubarak regime. In the 2005 parliamentary elections, the Muslim Brotherhood, running with other parties, captured eighty-eight seats, establishing itself as a viable political opposition movement. Five years later, it won only one seat in national elections. Mubarak and his ruling NDP had blatantly rigged the election to thwart opposition parties, causing great consternation among some of Mubarak's close advisers, including army generals. In 2011 Islamists were quiet during the lead-up to the 25 January Revolution, but participated more vigorously as the protests gained momentum and ultimately forced Mubarak from power. The Muslim Brotherhood and various Salafi political parties aggressively contested the parliamentary elections that took place between November 2011 and March 2012. The Islamists and their allies won 73 percent of the seats. In June 2012, Mohammed Morsi of the Freedom and Justice Party, an Islamist party that served as the political face of the Muslim Brotherhood, narrowly won the first free presidential election in Egyptian history. After only a year in office, he was removed from power in a military-led coup, mainly because of his attempts to legislate morality and impose it on the country, which appeased his base of supporters but alienated huge segments of Egyptian society, including the senior military leadership who presumed that he would impose his vision of Islam on Egypt.

84. What were the causes and outcome of the 25 January (2011) Revolution?

"Ayesh, hurriyah, adalah ijitimayiyah!" (Bread, freedom and social justice!) That was a popular chant of protesters in Tahrir Square in January 2011. It was turned into a hit song and became one of the unofficial anthems of the 25 January Revolution. Another mantra was "Ash-shaab yureed isqaat al-nizam!" (The people demand the downfall of the regime!). The protesters had been encouraged by the recent overthrow of the regime in Tunisia, but the Egyptian revolution was years in the making. In late 2010 and early 2011, factors came to a head that incited a popular uprising: repression, corrupt and ham-handed governance, and the unequal distribution of wealth.

A review of modern Egyptian political history provides a suitable prologue to the 2011 uprising. Following the 1952 revolution, the Free Officers did not have an articulated ideology but instead promised major political, economic, and social changes. Nasser later pursued a socialist restructuring of the economy. Until the 1970s, the political base of the regime had consisted of farmers, workers, and a growing middle class. On the outs were capitalists and Western investors. Al-Sadat's economic program, infitah, overturned the social underpinnings of the Cairo regime;

groups that had been on the outside were now in. From the mid-1970s to 2011, the Egyptian state was marked by phony democratic institutions, a semiauthoritarianism that afforded few genuine liberties and imposed many restrictions, and an intrusive state security system. In four national referendums, the electorate overwhelmingly affirmed Mubarak as president. Then in 2005 the first multiparty contest for that office took place. The electoral process was tightly controlled, and the laws favored the incumbent. Moreover, the regime played on fears of political instability and suppressed parties that called for repealing the emergency laws and introducing genuine democracy. After winning the election, Mubarak began grooming his unpopular son Gamal (b. 1963) to succeed him.

A handful of long-term factors contributed to the January 2011 revolu-tion. The country still suffered from several decades-old problems. Half the population was under the age of twenty-six, economic dislocations were worsening, and corruption was rampant in the government and society. Moreover, the assault on human dignity forced on the people by Mubarak's security forces generated a level of discontent that eclipsed all other problems. The Egyptian people were fed up with the relentless humiliation they suffered at the hands of their government.

Three principal factors compelled the Egyptian people to take to the streets and risk all in opposition to the Mubarak regime. First, the economy was very weak. The GDP was growing, but poverty, unemployment, and inflation were increasing. Labor protests often turned violent. The under-standing established between Nasser and college-educated Egyptians had long evaporated. According to this unwritten compact, every college graduate was guaranteed a job and was promised subsidies on utilities, food commodities, petrol, and housing. The economy would have to create hundreds of thousands of jobs each year to absorb the growing population, which by 2011 had reached nearly 83 million. As of 2018, the population had surpassed 95 million.

Second, police brutality and torture were rife in Mubarak's Egypt. In the summer of 2010, twenty-eight-year-old Khaled Mohammed Saeed was beaten to death by police in Alexandria. His senseless death galvanized protesters who exclaimed both in the streets and on social media, "We are all Khaled Saeed!" Mubarak's opponents, most of whom were young and proficient in the use of technology, exploited social media and the Internet to organize political events at light speed. The Internet permitted Egyptian dissidents to exchange information with activists who had brought down Serbian dictator Slobodan Milošević (1941–2006) and with pro-democracy nongovernmental organizations in Europe and the United States. Labor protests were organized and announced through social media, and street-level repression and abuse carried out by Mubarak's security forces and the police were captured on smartphones and spread worldwide on Twitter and YouTube. Within hours, the images appeared on hundreds of Arabic-language satellite channels, with Al-Jazeera leading the way. Protests in Tunisia that culminated in the exodus of President Zine El-Abidine Ben 'Ali (b. 1936) on 14 January galvanized the region.

Third, political fraud had been rife in the November–December 2010 parliamentary elections, which were rigged to the advantage of the ruling NDP. In the years following 9/11, the Bush administration had encouraged Mubarak to introduce a genuine multiparty system, but more than two decades of authoritarian rule presented Egyptians with only two political alternatives: the NDP or the Muslim Brotherhood. Other organizations, such as the grassroots Kefaya (Enough) movement and the secular New Wafd Party, were either too weak or insufficiently organized to challenge the NDP. Meanwhile, blatant electoral deceit was undertaken by Gamal Mubarak's cronies, which included billionaire businessman and politician Ahmed Ezz (b. 1959). Despite urgings from Mubarak's inner circle, including his intelligence chief, General Omar Suleiman (1936–2012), and defense minister, Field Marshal Mohammed Tantawi (b. 1935), to counter the commonly held belief that Gamal would succeed him and to deal with his corrupt associates, the Egyptian president did nothing, deciding instead to listen to Gamal and the interior minister, General Habib al-Adly (b. 1938). His party was the landslide winner in the sham 2010 elections. The Muslim Brotherhood, on the other hand, lost eighty-seven of the seats it had won in 2005 and was effectively shut out of power.

On 25 January 2011, massive demonstrations took place in Cairo and other Egyptian cities. Two days before, social media across the country had come alive, organizing rallies concurrent with developments in Tunisia. The 25th of June was also Police Day, and many protesters believed that the police would let their guard down in observance of the holiday. The choice of Police Day was also a political statement because the day had been created decades earlier when the public held the Egyptian police in high regard. The Mubarak regime was aware of the impending protests but underestimated the size, fervor, level of organization, and determination of the crowds. Several prominent opposition groups and individuals planned and participated in the demonstrations. Among them were the April 6 Youth Movement, which had led several labor protests in recent years; the National Association for Change, founded by Nobel Peace Prize laureate Mohammed ElBaradei (b. 1942); the Kefaya movement, which had participated in the 2005 elections; the New Wafd Party, the modern successor to the party founded by Sa'd Zaghlul; and the Ghad (Tomorrow) Party, founded by Ayman Nour (b. 1964), who had opposed Mubarak in the 2005 presidential election.

The early protests passed through multiple phases: mass demonstrations with government repression, organized chaos, determined resistance, government resignations, and lawlessness. Mostly unemployed and underemployed youths participated at the beginning, gathering on Cairo's Tahrir Square; by the third day, the Muslim Brotherhood had entered the square; after two weeks, Salafi political groups joined the throng. Actions by the NDP antagonized the crowd, as did Mubarak's refusal to step down. After increasing levels of violence, the army eventually sided with the protesters and deposed Mubarak. A group of two dozen generals, comprising the Supreme Council of the Armed Forces (SCAF), took the reins of power and ruled the country by decree until a new parliament was seated in early 2012.

A sense of profound optimism pervaded Tahrir Square. Protesters and activists maintained pressure on the caretaker military government to amend the constitution; hold free, multiparty elections; bring Mubarak, his sons, and other members of the regime to trial for corruption and the deliberate killing of protesters; abolish the emergency laws, which permitted indefinite detention without formal charges; and remove all vestiges of the old regime, including eliminating the Mubarak name from all public places. For example, Mubarak Station on the Cairo Metro was renamed Martyrs' Station. The protesters' spirit was reminiscent of the initial optimism felt for Nasser and the Free Officers when evidence of the Egyptian monarchy and British dominion was erased from public spaces.

The specter of fear that had cowered Egyptians for decades was shattered. People publicly told jokes about Mubarak and expressed themselves freely in a variety of media. The revolution produced notable songs, chants, raps, graffiti, cartoons, and YouTube clips that lampooned Mubarak, his family, and his cronies. Social media facilitated the mobilization of Egyptian protesters and allowed Arab youths from all over the region to "converge" or support the demonstrators in Tahrir Square, the eye of the anti-Mubarak hurricane. The sense of a new Egypt that transcended sect or social class emerged. Within the barricades, Coptic Christians protected Muslim worshipers engaged in prayer, and Muslims protected Copts celebrating a makeshift Mass. Tragically, human divisions, driven by insecurities, eventually supplanted these scenes of unity and commonality.

The 25 January Revolution was the culmination of a perfect storm of circumstances: a huge, youthful population; a disaffected citizenry; high unemployment, especially among college graduates; government corruption; the Khaled Saeed affair; the success of protests in Tunisia; new media; and a highly critical media, namely, Al-Jazeera. The Mubarak regime attempted to thwart the protesters by shutting down the Internet, mobile communications, and Al-Jazeera, but innovations such as Speak-2-Tweet circumvented efforts to stifle communications. The regime severely underestimated the strength, creativity, and determination of the protesters.

The Muslim Brotherhood maintained a low profile during the months leading up to the uprising but made its presence felt by the third day of the protests. It also dominated the subsequent parliamentary elections, held in two stages in late 2011 and early 2012. The Democratic Alliance for Egypt, led by the Brotherhood-affiliated Freedom and Justice Party, won 235 seats (46 percent) in the People's Assembly; the Islamic Block, led by the Salafist al-Nour (the Light) Party, which ran on a platform proclaiming that the Muslim Brotherhood was not sufficiently Muslim, won 121 seats (24 percent); and al-Wasat (the Middle), a moderate Islamist party offering itself as a compromise choice among secular and religious parties, won 10 seats (2 percent). Nearly three-quarters of the seats in the new parliament were won by an Islamist party. The secularists had been too fractured to organize an effective campaign. The country's high court later declared the newly elected parliament unconstitutional because a third of its members had been elected unlawfully.[6]

The Freedom and Justice Party had originally planned to sit out the upcoming presidential election but reversed its decision and fielded Khairat al-Shater (b. 1950) as a candidate. Al-Shater was ultimately disqualified by the SCAF on a technicality. The party then ran a second-tier candidate, Mohammed Morsi, who narrowly defeated Ahmed Shafiq (b. 1941), one of Mubarak's prime ministers and a former air force general, in June 2012. Morsi's tenure as president was a debacle. Brutes employed by the Brotherhood intimidated judges, and Morsi granted amnesty to radical Islamists and established relations with the militant Palestinian organization Hamas, actions that outraged Egypt's military hierarchy. The generals were concerned about Palestinian encroachment from Gaza into the Sinai. Morsi boldly convened the illegal parliament, ordered it to write a constitution, and declared that until a new constitution was enacted his actions were not subject to judicial review. The Brotherhood-influenced constitution was approved by referendum in December, but it outraged many Egyptians because it subtly defined the Brotherhood's version of correct Islamic behavior. For example, women had the right to work, so long as it did not impinge on their domestic duties, and citizens enjoyed freedom of speech, unless their expression violated Islamic norms. Constitutional articles, such as these, prompted many Egyptians to ask, Who determines whether a woman is fulfilling or has fulfilled her domestic duties? Who determines when Islamic norms are violated? Could the answers to both questions be the Muslim Brotherhood? The Tamarrud (Rebellion) movement circulated a nationwide petition expressing opposition to Morsi's government and requesting that the military intervene. They reportedly acquired more than 17 million signatures, which exceeded the vote total Morsi had garnered the year before. On 3 July 2013, one year after he had taken office, Morsi was deposed in a military-led coup. In the aftermath of the Morsi presidency, it is important to question the central underpinning of any effort at Islamic governance: Whose interpretation of Islam serves as the basis for that government? Basing a system of government on a particular interpretation of Islam marginalizes all other interpretations and is unsustainable because it will lead to argument and division.

Field Marshal Abdel Fatah al-Sisi (b. 1954), Morsi's defense minister, retired from the army and won the next presidential election, effectively placing the military and security services back in power. The new regime purged the leadership of the Muslim Brotherhood and declared it a terrorist organization. These steps might someday backfire on the government because at least one-third of the electorate is sympathetic to some form of Islamist rule, and the generals cannot suppress their way to domestic stability and calm. Meanwhile, the army and security forces skirmish almost daily with Ansar Bayt al-Maqdis (Supporters of Jerusalem), an ISIS affiliate that proclaimed a ministate in the Sinai. In March 2018, Al-Sisi again won the presidency by 97 percent in an election tarnished by the intimidation of challengers, low voter turnout, and a feeling among many voters that liberty can be effaced in the effort to secure some semblance of security. At the time of this writing, Egyptian powerbrokers are looking to the example of China and amending the Egyptian constitution to abolish presidential term limits.

America's insistence on genuine democratic institutions in Egypt, despite a lack of appreciation that Morsi might use them to legislate his version of Islam, and its acknowledgment of the Egyptian military's and the public's concerns that Morsi's presidency could produce civil strife have left the United States distrusted by the ruling establishment and Muslim Brotherhood supporters alike. Egypt's military government cannot wish away the influence of Islamism among the electorate. The number of Egyptians who will become supporters of political Islam in the years ahead remains to be seen. An Islamist backlash should not come as a surprise and must be strategically managed or contained to avoid further destabilization of the region.

85. Why has Islam proved to be a successful strategy for challenging secular authority in the Middle East?

In recent decades, extreme religious ideology and violent tactics have combined to form a militant version of Islamism, which in its simplest form believes that government and society should be founded on and guided by

Islamic principles. There are several circumstances common to political Islamism and its militant form that account for its emergence and growth. They include the existence of failed secular regimes, advocacy of a "return to Islam" in the aftermath of national humiliation or trauma, the rise of antiregime and anti-Western reactionary movements, and the growth of religiously inspired nationalistic movements opposed to foreign influence and control. Islamist political organizations and militant groups also have many shared goals, such as Muslim self-determination, the establishment of Islamic governments, and restoration of Muslim self-esteem. There is little agreement among Islamists on what form an Islamic government or social order should take. Moreover, political and militant Islamists disagree on the means of achieving their goals, with the former working within the established political system and the latter willing to use violence aimed at Muslims and non-Muslims alike.

History has shown that religion can be an effective vehicle for stirring people to achieve a political or social aim. While Islam's attempts in challenging secular authority is well documented, the post–Arab Spring political environment provides evidence of Islamist groups' trying to establish a fundamental social order that denies the legitimacy of other forms of Islamic expression. Former Egyptian president Mohammed Morsi, the candidate of the Muslim Brotherhood's Freedom and Justice Party, attempted to impose his political and social beliefs while facing opposition from secularists, Coptic Christians, Sufi Muslims, ultrafundamentalist Salafi political groups, and the military. Dealing effectively with these factions required a level of political skill that he did not have. In Tunisia the moderate Islamist party Ennahdha compromised with secular groups to stave off civil strife in the country. In Saudi Arabia, the imposition of Wahhabism—a form of Salafism—on the population has produced a generation of disenfranchised Shi'a and younger Saudis who feel held back by Wahhabi norms. Their dissent can be seen most vividly on social media and the Internet. A violent Saudi crackdown could foment instability in the Shi'a-populated Eastern Province of Saudi Arabia, where the bulk of Saudi oil reserves are located.

When a secular government is oppressive in the Middle East, the face and voice of protest are often expressed in Islamic terms. In that sense, religious expressions of justice pose a challenge to authoritarian regimes, which often use the facade of democracy to placate the international community. Iraqi strongman Saddam Hussein used the secular Ba'thist ideology to create a dictatorship based on fear and Arab supremacy. The Syrian Ba'thist regime, led by the al-Asad family, has exploited the secular nationalist ideology to hold on to power for over four decades. The language of Ba'thism hides the cruel reality that minority groups, such as the 'Alawis and Kurds, are extremely vulnerable and are reduced to the status of outsiders in their own country. The history of Shi'ism, which contains the central story of Imam Husayn's rebellion against Umayyad authority and his subsequent martyrdom in the face of an overwhelming force, has advanced the view that religion can serve as an effective medium of political opposition. In the language of revolutionary Shi'ism, the *mustadafun* (oppressed) must oppose the *mustakbirun* (oppressors).

Mustapha Kemal Atatürk borrowed an extremist concept from the French Revolution in his mission to secularize Turkey: the enforcement of laicism, the belief that religion has no place in the public square. After having lived for decades in Atatürk's secular state, the Turkish electorate swept the moderate Islamist Justice and Development Party (AKP) into office in 2002. The party has used the ballot box and populism to retain its hold on power ever since.

Each time a militant Islamist group forcefully imposes its social order or whenever an Islamist party attempts to legislate its definition of morality, that action transgresses the religion of more than 1.6 billion practitioners of Islam. Furthermore, because many Islamist political organizations and militant groups cannot agree on a common vision, strategy, or set of tactics, they are often in conflict. For example, al-Qa'ida and ISIS are existential threats to non-Muslims and Muslims alike and are fierce rivals in the world of Salafi jihadism today.

16

National Tragedies in Lebanon and Syria

In this chapter, we study the terrible history of the Lebanese civil war, examining its causes, the violence wrought by the warring factions, and its ultimate resolution. We then trace the recent history of Syria, highlighting the brutal strategies used by father-and-son dictators, Hafiz and Bashar al-Asad, to preserve their hold on power and the appallingly violent upheaval that has racked the country since the Arab Spring of 2011.

86. How did the Lebanese National Pact of 1943 maintain the political balance of power in Lebanon until the early 1970s?

The French played a leading role in laying the groundwork for the disastrous Lebanese civil war. They altered the ethnic makeup of Lebanon during the mandate period, using a divide-and-rule strategy that established mixed Muslim and Christian zones in Syria and Lebanon. They expanded the size of the original Mount Lebanon, which had been a semiautonomous Christian enclave in the Ottoman province of Syria since the mid-nineteenth century. As a result of French gerrymandering in Lebanon, the Maronite Christians came to govern a country with a sizable Muslim minority. Another religious minority group, the 'Alawi, acquired significant power in Syria. The al-Asads of Syria are members of the 'Alawi minority that dominates a much larger Sunni majority.

The French were criticized by the League of Nations for not moving fast enough to prepare Lebanon for independence. They were determined to maintain their empire, which was a source of pride, power, and prestige. After Hitler's swift conquest of France in 1940, the French military in Syria and Lebanon pledged its loyalty to the Vichy government, the Nazi puppet regime that ruled over unoccupied France. The British were anxious about an Axis-friendly regime in the heart of the Middle East that could threaten strategic oil reserves and the Suez Canal. Consequently, they pressured General Charles de Gaulle (1890–1970), the leader of the Free French, to promise independence for Syria and Lebanon if their people would support him, not Vichy France, which they did. In the summer of 1941, British and Free French forces liberated the two mandates, and De Gaulle kept his promise. Lebanon and Syria gained their formal independence in 1943 and 1946, respectively.

During World War II, Lebanese leaders established the country's governing institutions. From 1943 to 1975, Lebanese politics were based on family connections and client-patron relationships, political parties were extensions of family networks, and a small cadre of political godfathers managed the governing networks. They might have disagreed on issues but always reached a compromise in the end. They were also effective at keeping their "troops" in line. This was commonly known as the "za'im system." A za'im is a political boss or strongman, similar to the caudillos in Latin America, but in Lebanon the za'im represented a specific religious community and provided services and protection to that community in exchange for loyalty. This personal brand of politics predates the Lebanese state, going back to the Ottoman era. Among the notable za'im families were the Jumblatts, who represented the Druze community, and the Chamouns, who represented Maronite Christians. Each family had its own militia, and some were involved in smuggling and racketeering.

The Lebanese National Pact (al-Mithaq al-Watani) of 1943 established a plan for governing the independent Republic of Lebanon. Based on the 1932 census taken by the French, it created a system of confessional power-sharing among the country's major religious groups. According to the pact, the president would be a Maronite Christian; the prime minister, a Sunni Muslim; the speaker of the Chamber of Deputies, a Shi'a Muslim; the deputy speaker, a Greek Orthodox Christian; and the army chief of staff, a Druze. Members of the Chamber of Deputies would be elected with a ratio of six Christians to five Muslims. Other elements of the pact required the Muslims to abandon their hope of reuniting with Syria and the Christians to accept the reality of being part of an Arab nation. The confessional formula, however, could not maintain the political equilibrium for long because the Muslim birth rate was higher than that of Christians and the country had experienced an influx of Palestinian refugees. By the early 1970s, Muslims outnumbered Christians in Lebanon. Nevertheless, the bosses kept the system intact and functioning as long as they could. Was Lebanon a time bomb waiting to explode? It is important to remember that the pact was a onetime fix and other factors and actors had much to do with the fragmentation of Lebanon.

In the years following World War II, Lebanon prospered, and its capital, Beirut, was acclaimed as the "Paris of the Middle East." The country survived the civil war of 1958 and remained intact until the mid-1970s. We will briefly review that first civil war.

In the mid- to late 1950s, Lebanese Muslims clamored for more autonomy and a larger share of national political power. In 1958 President Camille Chamoun tainted the political atmosphere by seeking an amendment to the pact that would permit him to serve a second term. External pressures, particularly Gamal Abdel Nasser's pan-Arab nationalism and the fallout of the bloody Iraqi revolution that toppled the monarchy, worried Lebanon's ruling elite. In July civil disorder broke out but on a relatively small scale; nevertheless, the West endeavored to prevent a leftist takeover. In response to Chamoun's request for assistance under the auspices of the Eisenhower Doctrine, the U.S. government dispatched U.S. Marines to Lebanon to prop up Chamoun's government. The Marines, a disinterested party to the conflict, landed in Beirut, helped establish order, and withdrew a few months later. General Fuad Chehab, the commander in chief of the armed forces, worked closely with the Americans. He reaffirmed the governance of the *za'ims* and their traditional power network. Owing to the Lebanese spirit of compromise, the leaders agreed to several political understandings, and the civil war was brought to a quick resolution. Shihab was elected president and emerged as a conciliatory leader who boosted the power of the central government.

In the 1960s and 1970s, the political situation in Lebanon began to unravel. Pan-Arab and leftist movements sought to undermine the pro-Western government, and the creation of Israel led to the swelling of Palestinian refugees in Lebanon. Palestinians settled there in three waves: after the 1948 war, following the 1967 war, and in the aftermath of the 1970 Jordanian-PLO civil war. After Black September, Yasir Arafat set up a new headquarters for the PLO in Beirut. The organization brought a well-equipped army into Lebanon and assembled a base for guerrilla attacks on Israel that they launched with or without the approval of the Lebanese government. The Israelis retaliated by hitting PLO bases in Lebanon. The Palestinians became a state within a state in Lebanon, which started to resemble late 1960s Jordan.

The sizable Palestinian presence in Lebanon and PLO raids into Israel created friction between the Maronite ruling elite, whose political primacy was under assault, and Muslim leftists, who supported the guerrillas. Reprisals by Israel further undermined the fragile central government, which was too weak to confront the Israelis. Meanwhile, leftists, who attempted to use the PLO to alter the prevailing political structure, cautioned the government to refrain from acting against the PLO. In 1973 Israeli commandos raided downtown Beirut to strike at PLO guerrillas. The Lebanese National Movement (LNM), a coalition of Muslim leftists led by the Druze leader Kamal Jumblatt (1917–77), demanded that the government retaliate against Israel. The government, led by President Suleyman Franjiya (1970–76), struck back at the PLO instead. The LNM was outraged, but a cease-fire between the Lebanese army and the PLO was arranged. The National Pact was unraveling, and Lebanon stood at the brink of catastrophe.

87. What were the causes, significant developments, and outcome of the Lebanese civil war (1975–90)?

Full-scale fighting broke out in Lebanon in April 1975 when Palestinians shot up a Maronite church in East Beirut, and militiamen from the

Phalange, a right-wing Maronite party, retaliated by attacking a bus carrying Palestinians. Combat between the PLO and Maronite militias continued until June. Two months later, fighting erupted between Christians and Muslim militias. The PLO reentered the conflict in late 1975, followed by the Lebanese army. In January 1976, militias of the Lebanese Front, a Christian coalition, massacred hundreds of Palestinian Muslims in the East Beirut neighborhood of Karantina. In response, PLO fighters attacked the Christian village of Damour. That summer the Lebanese Front laid siege to and attacked the Palestinian refugee camp at Tel al-Zaa'tar, near Beirut; thousands of Palestinians were killed. Lebanon was now in the grip of a civil war between the PLO and LNM, on one side, and Christian factions and the Lebanese army, on the other. Lebanon's Shi'a were not yet involved in the conflict.

In 1976 the Lebanese army's combat effectiveness collapsed because of Muslim soldiers' desertions, and the Green Line was drawn in Beirut to separate its Muslim and Christian populations. Victory by the PLO and LNM appeared imminent, but in May Syria intervened militarily to save Franjiya's government and prevent a PLO-LNM takeover in Beirut. Syria's president, Hafiz al-Asad, worried that a PLO victory would lead to Israeli intervention and war with the Jewish state. Furthermore, he wanted to thwart a stronger, more independent PLO that could contest his leadership of Greater Syria, a swath of territory comprised of Syria, Lebanon, Jordan, and Palestine. To keep Arafat under control, al-Asad supported disaffected factions of the PLO. In October a cease-fire brokered by the Arab League took effect, and the 40,000 Syrian troops in Lebanon were designated the Arab Deterrent Force (ADF). The Syrians wanted to control Lebanon, not rule it. After they had settled in, the Syrians gradually shifted their support to the LNM and PLO.

From 1976 to 1978, life in Lebanon slogged forward despite sporadic fighting on several fronts. Politically, the Christian population separated into two distinct groups: centrists, who supported Franjiya, backed Syria, and advocated reconciliation and compromise with the PLO and LNM, and the right wing, which included the Gemayel and Chamoun families and Christians opposed to the PLO and Syria. The Phalange emerged as the dominant Christian faction. It had been founded by Pierre Gemayel

(1905–84), who modeled the organization after Generalissimo Francisco Franco's fascist movement in Spain. Phalange members, who identified as Lebanese, not Arabs, were ultranationalist Christians. A coalition of the Phalange and other rightist Maronite parties formed the Lebanese Front under the leadership of Gemayel's son Bashir (1947–82). The Lebanese Forces, the front's military arm, were supplied with arms by Israel and posed a direct threat to Syrian troops in Lebanon. A confrontation between the Christian right and Syria was only a matter of time.

In early 1978, fighting broke out between the Syrian army and armed Lebanese groups, and PLO raids into Israel and artillery attacks on Galilee escalated. In February the Hundred Days' War broke out between several Christian militias—including the Phalange, Tigers Militia, and Army of Free Lebanon—and the Syrian-led ADF. The Christian forces drove the ADF out of Beirut and shattered the fiction that the ADF was a neutral party in the civil war. In response to PLO aggression, Israeli prime minister Menachem Begin launched Operation Litani in March to clear PLO bases near the Israel-Lebanon border. The Israelis drove ten kilometers into Lebanon. After a partial withdrawal, they established a "security zone" patrolled by Major Sa'd Haddad (1936–84), a cashiered Lebanese army officer, and his Christian Free Lebanese Militia, later renamed the South Lebanese Army (SLA). UN peacekeepers—the UN Interim Force in Lebanon (UNIFIL)—took up positions in the south.

In the summer of 1978, the Shi'a of southern Lebanon became active. They opposed the Palestinian presence in the country because PLO attacks on Israel provoked Israeli counterattacks on southern Lebanon, causing the Shi'a great suffering. Imam Musa al-Sadr (1928–78), a Shi'a leader and the founder of the Amal (Hope) political movement, struggled to prevent Lebanon's deeper descent into civil war. He sought reconciliation between the various Lebanese factions but failed. He disappeared while visiting Libya that summer. He was most likely murdered by the regime of Mu'ammar al-Qaddafi, but conflicting reports still abound about the imam's fate. He may have been killed by Qaddafi at the behest of Arafat or al-Asad, or the Libyan dictator may have ordered the imam's execution after the two men had a bitter theological disagreement.

Over the course of 1981 and 1982, the fragmentation of Lebanon continued at an alarming rate, and the country hurtled toward full-scale war, a conflict that would undoubtedly draw in Syria and Israel. The Lebanese Forces fought the PLO and Syria, the Syrians supported the Shi'a against the PLO and the Lebanese Forces, and the Shi'a supported Israel at this point in the civil war. Israel, following its partial withdrawal from southern Lebanon in 1978, ignored UNIFIL and attacked PLO strongholds. Typically, the raids were done in reprisal for PLO attacks, but Begin reserved the right to hit terrorists without provocation. In 1981 Syria installed surface-to-air missile batteries in the Bekaa Valley to deter Israeli reconnaissance of Syrian forces. Israel threatened to destroy the missiles, provoking an international crisis. Meanwhile, the PLO-Israel conflict escalated; Palestinians fired rockets into northern Israel, and Israeli warplanes pounded the cities of Sidon and Tyre. In July Israeli planes bombed Beirut, killing hundreds of Palestinians and Lebanese. That month U.S. special envoy Philip Habib (1920–92) arranged a cease-fire between Israel and the PLO and defused the missile crisis, yet at this point neither the PLO nor Israel was willing to support a long-term cease-fire. PLO rocket attacks on the Galilee continued, despite the presence of the SLA and UNIFIL. In May 1982, Israel bombed a Palestinian base near Beirut. The PLO responded by shelling northern Israel, murdering an Israeli diplomat in Paris, and severely wounding the Israeli ambassador to Great Britain. The Israeli government had had enough and used the attack on the ambassador as the pretext for a massive invasion of Lebanon.

Begin's government launched Operation Peace for Galilee on 6 June 1982. Its ostensible goal was to eliminate PLO guerrillas in southern Lebanon, but Begin had other objectives. First, he sought the political and military destruction of the PLO by driving it out of Lebanon, decapitating its leadership, and demolishing its military infrastructure. The Israelis allied with Bashir Gemayel's Lebanese Front. Second, he wanted to establish a stable, friendly government in Lebanon. After that, he hoped to conclude a peace treaty with Lebanon.

Approximately 78,000 Israeli troops, supported by some 30,000 Christian fighters, invaded Lebanon. At first, the Shi'a welcomed the

Israeli invasion, hoping it would deliver them from the turmoil instigated by the Palestinians. The United States and United Nations pressed all parties to cease fire immediately. Habib, who a year earlier had negotiated the PLO-Israeli cease-fire and resolved the SAM crisis, returned to the region and engaged in Kissinger-style shuttle diplomacy. He arranged a truce between Israel and Syria on 11 June 1982, but by mid-June the Israeli army had advanced well beyond its declared forty-kilometer limit. It surrounded West Beirut, trapping thousands of PLO combatants. In August Habib negotiated a second Israeli-PLO cease-fire agreement, which provided for the evacuation of 14,000 PLO fighters from Beirut and safe transfer to several Arab countries. The operation was completed by early September under the supervision of a multinational force that included U.S. Marines and troops from France and Italy. The PLO set up a new headquarters in Tunis.

In late August, Gemayel was elected president of Lebanon but, before he could take office, her was killed by a massive car bomb planted by a Syrian agent at Phalange headquarters in Beirut. Immediately after the assassination, the Israelis moved into West Beirut. In retaliation for the assassination, the Lebanese Forces massacred thousands of Palestinians at the Sabra and Shatila refugee camps in southern Beirut. The act was done right under the nose of the IDF, which occupied the city and permitted the Lebanese Forces to enter the camps. Following the massacre, public outrage and condemnation were directed at the Israelis. The Israeli government formed the Kahan Commission to investigate the circumstances surrounding the massacre. It found the Phalange directly responsible and the Israelis indirectly responsible for the attack on the camps. Begin and Defense Minister Ariel Sharon (1928–2014) were vilified by the commission's report.

The multinational force returned to prop up the national government, now led by Amin Gemayel (1982–88), Bashir's older brother. On 17 May 1983, Israel and the Gemayel government signed a peace treaty, but it was promptly condemned by Syria and most Lebanese and was never implemented. Still, Israel and Lebanon maintained diplomatic contact for several months. Burdened by the camp massacres, growing unpopularity of the war, and passing of his wife, Begin resigned as prime minister in

October; he was succeeded by Yitzhak Shamir (1983–84, 1986–92). That same month, Israeli troops searching for Palestinian guerrillas angered Shi'a when they disrupted an 'Ashura commemoration in southern Lebanon.

During the Lebanese war, the Islamic Republic of Iran sent a detachment of revolutionary guards to Lebanon to train Shi'a in unconventional warfare. The guards recruited Shi'a youths who were willing to sacrifice their lives in the effort to drive the Israelis and their perceived allies, the U.S. Marines, out of the country. Hizballah (Party of God) emerged as the principal Shi'a political and guerrilla organization in Lebanon. Amal, the political movement founded by Musa al-Sadr, supported the Lebanese state and sought political rights for Shi'a within the country's multiconfessional system. Hizballah, which viewed Amal as insufficiently militant, endeavored to create an Islamic state—modeled on Iran—in Lebanon. Israel and the United States soon emerged as Hizballah's chief enemies. In 1985 the Israelis redeployed their troops to their "security zone" in southern Lebanon. They would keep forces there until 2000 to guard against attacks on Israel by residual PLO guerrillas and Hizballah fighters.

Operation Peace for Galilee was a strategic failure for Israel; Lebanon proved to be its Vietnam. The Israelis broke the military power of the PLO, but the organization retained its political and diplomatic efficacy. In the years following the withdrawal of Israeli troops from the vicinity of Beirut to the south, Lebanon descended into a dystopian state resembling Thomas Hobbes' view of the state of nature: "During the time men live without a common power to keep them all in awe, they are in that condition called war; and such a war, as if of every man, against every man."[1] Because the Gemayel government could hardly strike awe into the heart of anyone, many Lebanese joined and supported militias to stay alive. Terrorist bombings, engineered by Hizballah's military operations chief, 'Imad Mughniya (1962–2008), were directed against U.S. interests and forces during 1983–84. The U.S. embassy was bombed in April 1983, killing sixty-three, including seventeen Americans. In October the horrific suicide car bombing of the U.S. Marine barracks at the Beirut airport killed 241 American servicemembers. Eleven months later, the U.S. embassy annex was bombed; twenty-four people were killed, including two American military personnel. The U.S. Marine contingent of the multinational force hunkered down at the airport, where it was targeted by snipers and artillery. The heavy loss of American lives sapped the will of the peacekeeping mission. By early 1984, Reagan saw the handwriting on the wall and ordered the Marines to redeploy to ships offshore.

America's policy in Lebanon failed for several reasons. First, the United States tried to restore order but was naive about its chances for success. It thought that its 1980s intervention would be a repeat of the 1958 deployment: help restore order and then withdraw after a few months in country. Second, Lebanese Muslim groups viewed the United States as an adversary for its support of the Christian Phalange-dominated government. Third, it did not acknowledge the reality that few of the country's political and religious fractions recognized the legitimacy of the Lebanese government and that its sovereignty did not extend beyond the Christian neighborhoods of East Beirut. Fourth, by supporting the government, the United States forfeited its neutrality. The Marines became just another armed group—another "militia"—in the civil war. Finally, U.S. policy could not cope with the intense political and religious factionalism in Lebanon. Consequently, the Marines were caught in the middle of an increasingly chaotic and exceedingly violent conflict.

The Shi'a—especially Hizballah—arguably deserve the lion's share of the credit for driving Israeli and Western forces out of Lebanon, and they capitalized on this accomplishment politically. The major factor in Shi'a success was their willingness to sacrifice their lives for their cause; they were inspired by the teachings of Ayatollah Ruhollah Khomeini, the example of Imam Husayn, and the culture of martyrdom. In the mid- to late 1980s, West Beirut fell under the control of Shi'a and Druze militia. Fighting raged throughout the country, and the Gemayel government was incapable of restoring order. American and other foreign nationals were kidnapped and held hostage by Shi'a groups, greatly contributing to the Middle East's reputation as a region synonymous with terrorism. In the latter half of the decade, in what became known as the War of the Camps, Hizballah repeatedly attacked Palestinian refugees in Beirut and southern Lebanon.

If the Lebanese were to have peace, the warring factions would have to revise the constitution and disarm their militias, and foreign troops would have to leave. In the summer of 1988, the Chamber of Deputies could not convene safely in Beirut to elect a successor to Gemayel, whose six-year term as president was about to expire. Lebanese military commander General Michel Aoun (b. 1933) demanded that all Syrians leave the country and opposed the pro-Syrian caretaker government. In 1989 the Saudis invited the deputies to meet in Taif to elect a new president. They chose René Moawad (1925–89), a moderate Christian acceptable to Syria, but he was assassinated seventeen days after taking office. The deputies then elected Iliyas Harawi (1989–98), a politician who was also acceptable to Syria. That same year, the deputies agreed on a framework—the Charter for National Reconciliation, or the Taif Accords—to address the underlying political causes of the civil war. The agreement, which dramatically changed the National Pact of 1943, contains the following key provisions: the government should be founded on the principle of equal power sharing; Christians and Muslims have equal representation in the Chamber of Deputies and on the Council of Ministers; proportionality of representation within faiths is to be assured (for example, Muslim deputies should be divided among Sunnis, Shi'a, and Druze); geographic proportionality (for example, interior versus seacoast) is to be guaranteed; and greater executive power is granted to the president, prime minister, and Council of Ministers. The Taif Accords, which were approved by the Chamber of Deputies by the end of the year, restored parliamentary, republican government in Lebanon.

The confessional ratios established by the 1943 pact no longer reflected the demographic reality in Lebanon in the late 1980s. Between 1940 and 1980, the Shi'a population had doubled, and the Maronite population had declined by 25 percent. The steadfast refusal of the Maronite community to revise the pact in light of obvious demographic changes led to a horrific, fifteen-year civil war. In 1990 the Aoun and Harawi Maronite factions fought bitterly; Aoun had rejected the Taif Accords. In October Harawi's Syrian-backed troops crushed Aoun's militia, and Aoun went into exile in France. Syria redeployed its troops to the Bekaa Valley.

In 1991 Syria and Lebanon signed a pact giving Damascus substantial influence over Lebanon's foreign and military affairs. That same year, the remaining U.S. and British hostages in Lebanon, abducted during the civil war, were released. The Syrians also pledged to leave Lebanon but would not do so until 2005, in the wake of the international outrage over the Syrian government's suspected involvement in the assassination of former Lebanese prime minister Rafiq Hariri (1944–2005). The slain leader, who had done much to rebuild the country's economy, had vehemently opposed Syria's presence and influence in the country. Today, while many Lebanese are strongly opposed to Syrian involvement in their country, the Syrians and Iranians continue their support of Hizballah as a means to confront Israel.

In 2000 the Israelis withdrew from southern Lebanon, but Hizballah persisted in lobbing rockets at Israeli population centers in the Galilee. In July 2006, Israel responded to a series of attacks by launching a huge air assault on Hizballah targets in southern Lebanon. Israel also closed the port of Beirut and destroyed the runway at the Beirut airport to prevent the flow of military equipment into the country. A brief Israeli incursion into Lebanon in August led to a UN-brokered cease-fire—Security Council Resolution 1701—that was accepted by Hizballah, the Lebanese government, and Israel. The Lebanese army and a reconstituted UNIFIL deployed to the south. Hizballah, which, according to the cease-fire, was able to keep its weapons, remains a potent political and military force in the country. The Lebanese population, both Christian and Muslim, supported Hizballah during the Israel-Hizballah war.

In January 2011, Hizballah ministers walked out of the government led by Sa'd Hariri (b. 1970), the son of Rafiq Hariri, and forced the appointment of a caretaker government. They were protesting the government's refusal to condemn in advance the report of the UN's Special Tribunal for Lebanon. The report indicted current members of Hizballah for their involvement in the Hariri assassination. A year later, the Shi'a organization took the unprecedented step of deploying combat units outside Lebanon, to Syria, where they would operate in concert with the Bashar al-Asad regime, Iran, and Russia to help the Syrian dictator combat a huge civil insurgency and retain his hold on power. Moreover, the current conflict in Syria has spilled into Lebanon stoking sectarian strife. In August 2017, Hizballah fighters and the Syrian army, along with the Lebanese armed forces, operating separately, cleared ISIS and other militant Islamists from the Syria-Lebanon border area. That November Hariri suddenly resigned as prime minister, accusing Iran and Hizballah of undue influence both in Lebanon and throughout the region. Today, Hizballah maintains a fighting presence in the Syrian civil war, allying with the Islamic Revolutionary Guard Corps and the Russian armed forces to prop up the brutal al-Asad regime.

88. How does the al-Asad family maintain power in Syria, and what are its strategies for holding on to that power during the civil war that erupted in 2011?

In April 2018, the United States, the United Kingdom, and France launched air strikes against targets in Syria in response to the government's use of chemical weapons against its own population. In the paragraphs that follow, we examine the history of the al-Asad regime, which has retained power since 1970. Hafiz al-Asad ruled Syria from 1970 until his death in 2000. A member of the ʿAlawi community, he was a career air force officer who rose to the rank of general and served as defense minister. He participated in the 1963 Baʿth Party coup and the 1966 internal Baʿth coup, which brought the radical Baʿthists to power. Following the Great Corrective Movement of 1970, an internal coup that replaced the radicals with more moderate members of the party, al-Asad emerged as the dominant political figure in Syria. He became president in 1971. The ʿAlawis, an offshoot of Shiʾism that makes up about 12 percent of the population, thus came to govern a majority Sunni population. The al-Asads constantly reminded Syria's religious minorities—the Druze, Christians, and ʿAlawis—that if the regime fell, the Sunni majority would persecute them without mercy.

Since 1970 the governance of Syria and the direction of its economy have been an al-Asad family operation. Hafiz was president, and his brother Rifaʾat (b. 1937) was security chief. The latter commanded a special guard force known as the Defense Companies. Hafiz's oldest son and heir apparent, Basil (1962–94), was killed in an automobile accident, and his youngest son, Maher (b. 1967), commander of the Republican Guard, was passed over because of his erratic, brutal behavior. Consequently, his second son, Bashar (b. 1965), an ophthalmologist by profession, succeeded him in 2000. Other family members and 'Alawi loyalists have held important posts in the government, armed forces, intelligence and security services, and major business concerns. The UN investigation into the brutal assassination of former Lebanese prime minister Rafiq Hariri in 2005 implicated members of the al-Asad family.

The principal focus of the Syrian Ba'th Party since 1967 had been the conflict with Israel and recovery of the Golan Heights. This was an effective mobilization strategy because it took the public's mind off domestic problems, vicious internal politics, and repression. Moreover, challenging Israel supported the Ba'thist goal of galvanizing Arab unity. In October 1973, al-Asad joined Anwar al-Sadat of Egypt in a surprise attack on Israel. The Syrians temporarily regained territory on the Golan Heights, but their forces were thrown back by a devastating Israeli counteroffensive. In 1974 al-Asad agreed to a disengagement agreement with Israel. According to the agreement, which was negotiated by U.S. secretary of state Henry Kissinger, Israel gave up part of the territory it had captured in the 1973 war and permitted the establishment of a demilitarized zone, patrolled by UN peacekeepers, in a slice of the Golan Heights bordering Syria.

Over the years, the al-Asad regime faced opposition from the Sunni Muslim community. In the 1970s, the Muslim Brotherhood spearheaded a popular protest movement that sought to remove the regime and establish an Islamic state. In February 1982, the Syrian military and Rifa'at's Defense Companies crushed a Muslim Brotherhood–led uprising in Hama, flattening entire neighborhoods of the city. An estimated 20,000 members of the Brotherhood were slaughtered. The Hama massacre confirmed Syria's reputation as a brutal security state that the al-Asads ruled through patronage, intimidation, sectarian fear, and the outright elimination of opponents. All this was done under the veneer of Ba'thism, an expression of Arab nationalism, yet when the regime faced an existential threat, it relied on its small 'Alawi base to uphold its authority—often violently.

From 1976 to 2005, Syria maintained a significant military presence in Lebanon. It became the de facto ruler of the country and pledged to withdraw its troops in accordance with the Taif Accords of 1989, but its forces remained until 2005. The Syrians finally departed under extraordinary international pressure, including a UN Security Council resolution, in the aftermath of the assassination of Hariri. Some within Bashar al-Asad's inner circle considered the withdrawal a sign of weakness that would undermine the dictator's power as he confronted opponents during the Arab Spring and violent civil war that followed.

The al-Asad family also used cult-of-personality imagery to promote national unity and maintain its grip on power. Hafiz al-Asad was pragmatic and deliberate in the application of Ba'thist principles, which were infused into the population at all levels of education. He also used fear—the stick—and the need to fight Israel and recover the Golan Heights—the carrot—to curry popular support. Peace with Israel might weaken the regime because it would remove a means of mobilizing the population. Furthermore, the Israeli occupation of the Golan Heights gave the al-Asads a reason to occupy Lebanon for three decades, calling the deployment of tens of thousands of troops a national security measure.

In March 2011, large protests erupted in cities all over Syria, demanding an end to the al-Asad regime. They began as peaceful demonstrations, but the government brutally repressed every act of dissent, effectively transforming pockets of protest into a nationwide insurgency. The demonstrators used increasing amounts of force to confront the regime, presaging an armed rebellion. In November the Arab League suspended Syria's membership in the organization after al-Asad had refused to withdraw his military forces from cities and enter into dialogue with his opponents. Since the spring of 2011, more than 400,000 Syrians have died in the conflict, and millions of people have fled the country, creating a refugee crisis in the Middle East and Europe.

The Ba'thist-'Alawi regime in Damascus maintained a roster of foreign and domestic enemies to rally popular support and influence its moderate neighbors—Lebanon and post–Saddam Hussein Iraq—but that influence has declined as a result of the government's involvement in the assassination of former Lebanese prime minister Hariri and the brutal repression of its citizens with the outbreak of the civil war.

Ethnic and confessional strife has intensified in Syria, demonstrating that establishing and maintaining a state with a diverse population is difficult for any government—authoritarian or democratic. National groups seeking their own states are a threat to the Ba'thist regime in Syria. According to one of its tenants, Ba'thism provides a theoretical solution to the issue of national identity by creating a pan-Arab identity. But according to this idea, where do non-Arabs fit in? In short, they do not, as Ba'thism upholds Arabness and imposing it on non-Arabs. Under the best of circumstances, countries with a principal ethnic identity regularly face this issue because anyone outside that ethnic group is automatically the "other," even though he or she is a citizen. We have seen this in Turkey—land of the Turks—where the Kurds for many decades have been referred to as "Mountain Turks."

Iraq from the Rise of Saddam to the Fragile Beginnings of Democracy

I n this chapter, we cover the recent history of Iraq, investigating Saddam Hussein's rise to power, scrutinizing his reasons for invading Kuwait in 1990, and examining U.S. policy toward Iraq, from the run-up to the 1991 Gulf War to the election of a constitutional government after the fall of Saddam and his Ba'thist regime.

89. How did Saddam Hussein take control of the Ba'thist regime in Iraq and retain power for nearly a quarter century?

The answer to this question has been the subject of many studies of modern Iraq and biographies of Saddam Hussein 'Abd al-Majid al-Tikriti. Saddam was born in 1937 in the tiny hamlet of al-Awja, near the city of Tikrit, north of Baghdad. He was born into extreme poverty, and it is believed that his mother, Subha Tulfah (d. 1982), attempted to terminate the pregnancy. Saddam's father disappeared before his birth, and rumors abound that he was murdered. Young Saddam lived with his maternal uncle, Khayrallah Tulfah (d. 1993), until the age of three, when his mother married an abusive man, Ibrahim al-Hasan (nicknamed "Hasan the Liar"). When he was ten, Saddam ran away and lived with his uncle, who was an officer in the Iraqi army and participant in the failed effort to evict the British from the country in 1941. With his uncle's support, Saddam attended school and even pursued college-level training in the law. The lure of Pan-Arabism, however, enticed him to abandon his studies and join the Ba'th Party.

In 1958 the monarchy of King Faysal II was overthrown in a violent military coup led by General 'Abd al-Karim Qasim. The king, members of his family, and senior government officials were brutally murdered. Qasim, whose father was a Sunni Kurd, was an ardent Iraqi nationalist, but he was surrounded by Ba'thists who loathed his improving relationship with Iraqi communists. The communists in turn opposed a union with Nasser's Egypt. Saddam made his name within the Ba'th Party by orchestrating a failed attempt in 1959 to assassinate Qasim. Saddam fled to Cairo, where he lived until 1963, studying law off and on, organizing clandestine cells of Iraqi dissidents, and plotting his return to Iraq. That year Qasim was deposed and killed in a violent coup engineered by Ba'thist army officers.

Saddam returned to Iraq and spent time in prison until he escaped in 1967. Meanwhile, his cousin Ahmed Hasan al-Bakr (1914–82) was elected leader of a clandestine cell within the Iraqi Ba'th Party that undermined the successive presidencies of 'Abd al-Salaam 'Arif (1963–66) and his brother 'Abd al-Rahman (1966–68); Saddam served as al-Bakr's deputy. In 1968 Ba'thists overthrew the 'Arif government in a bloodless coup. Al-Bakr became president, and Saddam was installed as deputy secretary of the Regional Ba'th Command in Iraq, a post that permitted him to oversee internal security and enforce party unity through a combination of rewards and strong-arm tactics. It gradually became apparent that Saddam—the enforcer—was the power behind al-Bakr's presidency.

In 1976 Saddam became the de facto leader when it was announced that President al-Bakr's health had declined. Saddam required cabinet ministers to see him before they met with the president, and he used Michel Aflaq, one of the founders of Ba'thism, to secure his appointment as leader of the Regional Ba'th Command. In 1979 Saddam, who had for years maintained a subservient posture toward his cousin, removed the ailing leader and assumed the presidency. According to one report, al-Bakr was allegedly contemplating a union with Ba'thist Syria in which he would be president and Syrian leader Hafiz al-Asad would be his deputy. This would have diminished Saddam's power. Saddam had been working since the late 1960s to insert his loyalists in every corner of Iraq's bureaucracy and armed forces. Within days of his takeover, he assembled all Iraqi Ba'thist leaders and denounced sixty-eight of them for treason, disloyalty, and conspiracy. He achieved near total loyalty through one terrifying act of grand political theater, going so far as to have those not accused demonstrate their loyalty by serving as the firing squad for those named as traitors. Ba'thist ideology provided the veneer of political legitimacy for Saddam's regime, giving it unbridled power. Iraqi author Kanan Makiya (b. 1949) aptly described his country under Saddam as the "Republic of Fear."

In Iraq the presence of three sizable and distinct ethnoreligious groups has long challenged the central government's ability to rule the country. The Ottomans divided the territory that makes up present-day Iraq into three separate provinces: Mosul, in the north, home to the Kurds; Baghdad, in the center, the Sunni Arab heartland; and Basra, in the south, an area dominated by Shi'a Arabs. Since the establishment of the British mandate in 1920, history has shown that an authoritarian regime or single-party state has had the best chance of maintaining Iraqi unity. Until the early 2000s, the minority Sunni Arabs formed Iraq's ruling class. The British used them to govern the country during the mandate period, and they held power until Saddam's Ba'thist regime was deposed in the U.S.-led invasion in 2003, which handed power to the Shi'a majority.

For decades, Syria and Iraq each regarded itself as the epitome of a Ba'thist state. Consequently, a fierce war of words and an intense rivalry ensued, and each regime took steps to undermine the other. The founders of the Ba'th movement left Syria and took up residence in Iraq, which proved to be a great public relations coup for Saddam's regime. He also benefitted from the oil boom of the 1970s, which saw Iraq's oil revenue increase from $476 million in 1968 to $26 billion in 1980. What could Iraq do with that huge cash windfall? It could be used to improve education and health care, build highways and other infrastructure, and increase the electrification of towns and villages, or it could be wasted on the purchase of luxury goods, expensive palaces, and vast quantities of military equipment. Saddam did both. He rearmed the military after the Iran-Iraq War, even though his government was heavily in debt, and the country's rate of GDP growth remained stagnant.

Saddam used several strategies to mobilize national unity. During the 1980–88 war with Iran, government propaganda painted the Islamic republic as a resurrected Persian Empire, bent on reclaiming lost territory in Mesopotamia. The invasion of Kuwait and subsequent Gulf War, which we will discuss in the next few responses, provided Saddam with another opportunity to boost national unity. He had accused the ruling al-Sabah family of stealing oil from his war-ravaged country and then declared the emirate the nineteenth province of Iraq. During the war, he used Islam as a unifying measure, a remarkable step for a secular Ba'thist ruler, but not surprising for a ruthless political opportunist. He prayed publicly and ordered "Allahu Akbar" (God is great) added to the Iraqi flag. Finally, Saddam exploited the Palestinian-Israeli conflict to forge national cohesion. He fired Scud missiles at Israel during the Gulf War and made cash payments of $10,000 to $25,000 to the families of Palestinian suicide bombers during the second Palestinian uprising, which began in 2000. His tangible support for Palestine earned him considerable respect and credibility in the Arab world—acquired at the expense of other Arab leaders and rivals.

In April 2003, Saddam's regime was toppled by the U.S.-led invasion of Iraq—Operation Iraqi Freedom. He went into hiding around Tikrit but was captured eight months later by special operations troops of the U.S. Army's Fourth Infantry Division.[1] He stood trial in an Iraqi court for ordering the destruction of a village following a failed assassination attempt, was found guilty, and was hanged in December 2006. One of the witnesses smuggled in a smartphone and recorded the event, during which chants of "Muqtada! Muqtada! Muqtada!" could be heard from supporters of the Shi'a cleric and Jaysh al-Mahdi (JAM, also known as the Mahdi Army) leader Muqtada al-Sadr. Saddam's execution also took place during 'Id al-Adha, in contravention of the Iraqi constitution, which prohibited the carrying out of a death sentence on a holy day for Shi'a, Sunnis, and Christians. Furthermore, the spectacle of Saddam's execution tarnished America's image in the Arab world in the aftermath of the 2003 invasion because Saddam had been transferred from U.S. military custody to Iraqi control.

90. What were Saddam Hussein's motives for invading Kuwait in August 1990 and attacking Iraqi Kurds and Shi'a?

In July 1989, Iran and Iraq signed a peace treaty formally ending their devastating eight-year war. During the conflict, Saddam managed his country's finances shrewdly: Iraq earned revenue from oil exports, transported via pipelines, and at the same time, it had received aid from many Arab leaders, who sided with Saddam against the radical Shi'a regime in Tehran. Nevertheless, Iraq finished the war nearly $100 billion in debt, half of which was held by oil-producing Arab countries in the Persian Gulf; Kuwait alone advanced Iraq more than $15 billion. Saddam, on the other hand, adamantly believed that his fellow Arabs owed him and his people an immeasurable obligation, and their debt should be written off. After all, Iraqi blood and treasure had stood as the bulwark against the spread of revolutionary Shi'ism from Iran into the Arab world.

After the war, Saddam's Arab allies halted their financial support, seriously undermining Iraq's economic well-being, which to a large degree was dependent on foreign grants and loans. Making matters worse for Iraq, world oil prices slumped, and the Kuwaitis called in their loans, which they claimed Saddam had used not for military purposes, but for new palaces and other luxuries. By the start of the new decade, Iraq desperately needed greater oil revenue to rebuild its war-ravaged economy, resettle thousands of returning Iraqi soldiers, and meet its foreign debts, but increased oil income could be attained only by increased production or higher prices. Aggressive oil sales at cut-rate prices by Arab oil producers, principally Kuwait and the UAE, and their refusal to approve an increase of Iraq's production quota thwarted its economic recovery. In July 1990, Saddam demanded financial assistance from Kuwait, but the emirate refused, arguing that it had been a major creditor for Saddam during the war. Saddam also accused Kuwait of tapping Iraq's share of oil from their jointly owned Rumayla oil field and plotting to deliberately impoverish Iraq by overproducing oil to drive down its price on the world market. Efforts at mediation by the Arab League, King Fahd of Saudi Arabia, and

Egypt's Hosni Mubarak failed to satisfy Saddam's complaints, although Mubarak elicited from Saddam a questionable pledge not to invade Kuwait. Several Western intelligence services reported that Saddam was massing troops on the Kuwaiti border, but few expected him to invade his oil-rich neighbor.[2] In late July, Saddam summoned the U.S. ambassador to Iraq, April Glaspie (b. 1942), to ascertain the U.S. government's position on the Iraq-Kuwait dispute. Glaspie stated that the United States did not have an opinion on disagreements between Arab states. Saddam concluded that he could attack Kuwait with little American opposition.

On 2 August, Saddam ordered his army to invade Kuwait. The Kuwaiti royal family and government officials fled to Saudi Arabia. The Saudis and many Western leaders feared that Saudi Arabia—and its oil-rich eastern province of al-Hasa—would be attacked next. King Fahd acknowledged his kingdom's vulnerability to Iraq's armor and massed infantry and consented to an American request to deploy forces in what would be the buildup phase of Operation Desert Shield. On 5 August, U.S. president George H. W. Bush (1989–93) condemned the invasion, declaring, "This will not stand, this aggression against Kuwait."[3] His administration immediately set out to assemble an international coalition to protect Saudi Arabia and, if necessary, eject Iraqi forces from Kuwait. A huge military force of Western and Arab countries was soon organized; countries that did not provide troops, such as Japan, pledged billions of dollars to support the military buildup.[4] The U.S. government also froze Iraqi and Kuwaiti assets in American banks. On 8 August, Saddam annexed Kuwait, asserting that he was merely recovering territory that the British had wrongfully taken from the Ottoman Empire before World War I. When the British fixed the borders of their Iraq mandate in 1921, they excluded Kuwait, an act that left Iraq with almost no access to the Persian Gulf. Since then Iraqi regimes have argued that Kuwait was illegally carved from Iraqi territory.

Iraq's largest demographic groupings are Shi'a Arabs (approximately 60 percent), Kurds (as high as 20 percent), and Sunni Arabs (upward of 15 percent). The Kurds and Shi'a were constantly threatened and politically disenfranchised under Saddam Hussein, which produced conditions ripe for agitation and rebellion. Kurdish aspirations ranged from being suitably represented in Baghdad to autonomy to outright independence. Moham-med Reza Shah supported Kurdish insurgent movements in northern Iraq, while Saddam stoked uprisings among the Sunni Arabs of south-west Iran. In 1988, during the last months of the Iran-Iraq War, Saddam attacked a rebellious Kurdish village, Halabja, with chemical weapons, a vile act that he also committed against Iranian human-wave assaults. In early 1991, a Shi'a uprising erupted after the Iraqi army's eviction from Kuwait and President Bush's inarticulate call for the removal of Saddam. The Kurds, who had launched the National Uprising against the regime, were pursued by Saddam's forces deep into the mountains of northern Iraq, where the U.S.-led coalition established a safe haven protected by friendly aircraft. During the Shi'a uprising in the south, the prominent cleric Ayatollah Muhammad Sadiq al-Sadr (1943–99) exhorted his core-ligionists to cease the practice of *taqiyya* (dissimulation, the act of deny-ing one's faith for self-preservation) and fight injustice openly.[5] Saddam, however, maintained the upper hand, using helicopter gunships to crush the Shi'a insurrection. A year later, the coalition established a no-fly zone in southern Iraq to safeguard Shi'a Arabs from attacking Iraqi aircraft. The absence of tangible, immediate American support for the Kurdish and Shi'a uprisings and the Iraqi regime's brutal riposte produced extreme reluctance on the part of ordinary Iraqis to challenge Saddam.

91. What were the phases of the 1990–91 Persian Gulf crisis, the outcome of the war, and the conflict's impact on the Middle East?

After the Bush administration had convinced King Fahd that Saudi Ara-bia was in grave danger of an Iraqi invasion, it initiated a huge multination military buildup in the kingdom in the late summer and fall of 1990. The buildup was given the code name Operation Desert Shield, and by the end of October, there were more than 200,000 American troops in the kingdom. The following month, the United States doubled the number of its troops in the region, shifting from a defensive to an offensive pos-ture. By February 1991, the U.S.-led coalition had massed over 900,000 troops in Saudi Arabia and the Persian Gulf. In addition to the United States, several other countries committed sizable military forces, namely,

Saudi Arabia, Great Britain, Egypt, France, Syria, Morocco, Free Kuwait, Oman, Pakistan, Canada, the UAE, Qatar, Bangladesh, Italy, Australia, the Netherlands, and Argentina.

Saddam underestimated the reactions of the United States and Soviet Union to his invasion of Kuwait. He was confident that the United States would not intervene because of its experience in Vietnam and believed that the Soviet Union would remain on the sidelines, having completed its withdrawal from Afghanistan. The Soviets did not directly participate in the coalition, but they did not stand in its way, and Moscow ceased military sales to Iraq.

Syria, Egypt, and other Arab countries supported Operation Desert Shield as a means to contain Iraq while ignoring popular opposition to Saudi and U.S. policies. Jordan and Yemen, on the other hand, supported Saddam because of their economic ties with Iraq and did so at the risk of offending their Arab neighbors and the Western members of the coalition. Palestine Liberation Organization chairman Yasir Arafat also backed Saddam. Most Palestinians—neglected by the West, oppressed by the Israelis, and abused by other Arabs—supported and admired the Iraqi dictator, buying into his blustering rhetoric and call for Arab and Muslim unity against the West.

The UN Security Council passed a series of resolutions calling on Iraq to withdraw immediately and unconditionally from Kuwait and imposing economic sanctions against Iraq until it did so. Saddam ignored the resolutions and refused to pull out of Kuwait. Finally, on 28 November, the Security Council passed Resolution 677, which authorized "Member States . . . to use all necessary means to uphold and implement . . . relevant resolutions and to restore international peace and security in the area."[6] Saddam still refused to back down, and on 17 January 1991, the coalition commenced air strikes on Baghdad. The attack was code-named Operation Desert Storm.[7]

Two days later, Iraq fired Scud missiles at Israel. Saddam hoped to drive the Arab countries out of the coalition by drawing Israel into the war, but pressure and reassurance from the Bush administration kept Israel from retaliating. Saddam made a connection between the war against Iraq and the Israeli-Palestinian conflict. He announced that he would withdraw from Kuwait if Israel withdrew from occupied Arab territory. Many people in the "Arab street" agreed with Saddam and accused the United States of a double standard with regard to occupied territories, doing nothing for Palestine but going to war for Kuwait. Meanwhile, the Soviet Union advanced proposals to end the crisis-turned-conflict, but Bush and the other coalition leaders demanded that Iraq accept all resolutions and leave Kuwait unconditionally.

On 24 February, the ground war commenced, and the Iraqi forces were quickly routed. Three days later, a cease-fire went into effect, ending the Hundred-Hour War. The coalition had evicted the Iraqi armed forces from Kuwait. The decision to halt the war at that point has been hotly debated. It allowed thousands of Republican Guard troops to escape from Kuwait, but many world leaders thought that advancing on Baghdad would produce a much higher number of casualties and cause more problems than it would solve. Regime change in Iraq was not a goal of the UN-sponsored action. On 3 March, General Norman Schwarzkopf (1934–2012), commander of the Allied coalition, met Iraqi generals at Safwan, in southern Iraq. He permitted the Iraqi military to fly armed helicopters as part of the cease-fire terms. The Iraqis deceivingly insisted that helicopters were necessary to reach areas of Iraq made inaccessible by the destruction of bridges and roads. Schwarzkopf's decision turned out to be a grave mistake.

A Shi'a uprising in the south and a Kurdish rebellion in the north erupted shortly after the cease-fire. At first Bush encouraged the uprisings, but the coalition offered no direct support. In the early stages, it appeared that the Shi'a and Kurds would seize considerable territory. It has been a topic of speculation that the United States did not fully support the rebellions out of fear that they could destabilize the region. Saddam used the Republican Guard and attack helicopters to brutally suppress the Shi'a and Kurdish revolts. Thousands of Kurds and Shi'a were killed or displaced; several Shi'a clerics—notably, a younger generation of religious leaders—were murdered. The United States, France, Great Britain, and other countries established no-fly zones in northern Iraq in 1991 and southern Iraq in 1992. The no-fly zones would contain Saddam and protect the Kurdish and Shi'a populations.

During this period, Usama Bin Ladin (1957–2011) began his open criticism of the United States and attacked the Saudi royal family for its dependence on Western infidels to defend the kingdom. In late 1991, Bin Ladin had fled Saudi Arabia and settled in Sudan, where he organized the international terror network that would become al-Qa'ida. Meanwhile, Saddam increasingly favored Sunni Islam and advocated Islamist policies to enhance his political viability in his war-shattered country, but his efforts polarized Iraqi society. His attempts to play the political Islamist card in the late 1990s included building the "Mother of all Mosques" in Sunni-dominated western Baghdad and supposedly having an entire Qur'an written in his own blood, which he donated over a period of two years. In reality he kept a mistress and stocked his palaces with cases of Mateus medium-sweet rosé wine.[8] Meanwhile, his psychotic older son, 'Uday, owned a hoard of liquor, indulged in fine wines, abused drugs, committed sexual assaults, and kept a private zoo of exotic animals.

92. How did U.S. policy toward Iraq evolve from the end of the 1991 Gulf War to the terrorist attacks of 11 September 2001?

In 1998 the U.S. Congress passed the Iraq Liberation Act (1998), a law that sanctioned the removal of Saddam Hussein from power. Standing in the way of this goal was Saddam's *mukhabarat* (intelligence bureau), which was among the most ruthless in the region. It rewarded people for denouncing their neighbors and children for informing on their parents. In the wake of the suppression of the Shi'a and Kurdish uprisings of 1991, no viable domestic opposition movement could remove Saddam. Shi'a groups occasionally rose up, but they were not held in favor by U.S. policymakers, owing to the relationship between Iraqi Shi'a and the Iranian government. Ayatollah Muhammad Sadiq al-Sadr, who had urged a general uprising in 1991, was murdered by Saddam's security forces in 1999. Meanwhile, throughout the 1990s, the United States and Great Britain enforced no-fly zones in northern and southern Iraq, yet with each passing year Saddam's air defense network increasingly challenged coalition aircraft. In the north, under the protection of friendly air cover, the Kurds carved out an autonomous region that survives to this day.[9]

Through an interlocking series of government bureaucracies, Saddam ruled Iraq with absolute power. He fancied himself the successor of ancient Mesopotamian despots, brutally crushed Shi'a and Kurdish uprisings, and did not shrink from killing close relatives for political reasons. His two sons-in-law, Hussein Kamil al-Majid (1954–96) and Saddam Kamil (1965–96), defected to Jordan in 1995, along with their families. The two were coaxed back to Iraq and immediately executed. Saddam relied on a carefully selected clique of family and friends from his hometown of Tikrit to implement his policies. In the last years of his rule, he delegated some authority to his two sons, 'Uday (1964–2003) and Qusay (1966–2003), both of whom were killed by U.S. forces.

With Saddam firmly in power, the coalition focused on enforcing the UN-mandated destruction of Iraq's nuclear, biological, and chemical weapon programs. UN Security Council Resolution 687 (1991) mandated the demarcation of the boundary between Iraq and Kuwait; the establishment of a demilitarized zone; the complete destruction of Iraq's chemical and biological weapon and long-range ballistic missile systems; the total cessation of the country's nuclear, biological, and chemical weapon research programs; the return of all seized Kuwaiti property; and an accounting of all Kuwaiti prisoners of war. To enforce the resolution, sanctions on Iraq would remain in place with the exception that the government could purchase food, medicine, and humanitarian supplies. For more than a decade, the sanctions impoverished the Iraqi people without really affecting Saddam's regime. It is estimated that more than a million Iraqis, especially infants and children, died because of the deprivation wrought by the sanctions.[10]

The UN Special Commission on Iraq (UNSCOM) was established to implement Resolution 687. Despite a campaign of Iraqi deceit, concealment, harassment, and obstruction, UNSCOM succeeded in destroying 38,000 chemical devices, 690 tons of chemical agents, 48 operational missiles, 60 fixed Scud launch pads, 30 special missile warheads for chemical and biological weapons, and hundreds of pieces of equipment used in the production of chemical weapons. Despite these accomplishments on the part of UNSCOM, Saddam made the fatuous claim that he had won the war—after all, George H. W. Bush lost his bid for reelection in 1992, and Saddam rebuilt his army, threatened Kuwait in 1993 and 1994, and continued to hinder UN inspectors. In 1998 the UN unilaterally halted its inspection program and abruptly withdrew its inspection teams from the country. Iraq's weapons of mass destruction (WMD) program was an intelligence-collection black hole until the 2003 U.S.-led invasion. In December 1998, in response to Saddam's record of deliberate obstruction and the sudden UN withdrawal, President Bill Clinton (1993–2001) ordered a military strike, code-named Operation Desert Fox; Great Britain also participated. The four-day air campaign hit military installations and suspected research facilities supporting Saddam's effort to produce, store, maintain, and use WMDs. Saddam attempted to sustain his WMD programs in the years immediately following the war, but he later abandoned them, while maintaining great uncertainty about their scope and lethality.

In 1996 Saddam accepted an "oil-for-food" program that permitted Iraq to sell $2 billion worth of oil every six months. With that revenue, Iraq could purchase food and medicine. The cap was soon raised to $5 billion and then removed altogether. By 2001 a decade had passed since Iraq's eviction from Kuwait, and sanctions fatigue had set in. Most Arab countries, Turkey, and Iran were trading with Iraq as if the sanctions were no longer in effect. In the weeks leading up to the terrorist attacks of 11 September, the George W. Bush (2001–9) administration attempted to set up a "smart sanctions" protocol that would exclude only specific items from Iraq.

93. What were the factors leading to the U.S.-led invasion of Iraq in 2003, and what are the prospects for post-Saddam Iraq?

Over the twelve-year interval between Desert Storm and the U.S.-led invasion of Iraq in 2003, Saddam faced a pair of existential challenges: first, how to manage Iraq's WMD programs while under UN sanctions, and later, how to maintain a credible threat to his neighbors, including Israel, and the West without being exposed as a fake. Defectors described his WMD programs, but were their reports accurate or was Saddam conducting an elaborate deception campaign directed at his neighbors? Either way, a perceived, credible threat would limit U.S.

military options and intimidate the countries of the region. Therefore, Saddam had to maintain a credible threat while keeping the truth about his abandoned WMD programs under wraps. He fooled his neighbors, the United States, and the United Nations into believing that he was secretly maintaining some level of WMD capability. In the wake of the 9/11 terrorist attacks, that perceived threat led to an American-led invasion and his downfall.

Between 1998 and 2002, the UN Monitoring, Verification and Inspection Commission (UNMOVIC), which had replaced UNSCOM, did not conduct a single inspection in Iraq, and the international community grew increasingly weary of abiding by and enforcing the sanctions. The horrific terrorist attacks of September 2001 completely changed the Bush administration's Iraq policy. According to the so-called Bush Doctrine, the United States would take preemptive military action against a perceived threat to the security of the country. In November 2002, the UN Security Council passed Resolution 1441, which called for the enforcement of all existing provisions of UN resolutions regarding Iraq, including Resolution 687. Saddam had to abide by the resolutions, or he would face unspecified consequences.

After 9/11 the Bush administration grew increasingly concerned with Saddam's challenge of the no-fly zone, alleged connections to al-Qa'ida, suspected WMD programs, and prior use of chemical weapons against his own Kurdish population and the Iranian army. The administration made the case that Saddam presented a threat to U.S. national security, but in the end, there was no connection between Saddam and al-Qa'ida, and there were no WMDs. The administration's critical intelligence source had been an Iraqi refugee named Rafid Alwan al-Janabi (b. 1968), better known by his CIA code name: "Curveball." He provided erroneous information about mobile WMD production laboratories in exchange for asylum in the West. Another questionable source was the Iraqi Shi'a dissident Ahmed Chalabi (1944–2015); he enjoyed connections with Iran and had been charged with bank embezzlement in Jordan. Meanwhile, the drumbeat for war only got louder, as Congress abdicated its role of oversight of the U.S. intelligence community and the American news media failed to scrutinize the administration's rationale for attacking Iraq.

Specifically, Congress and the media could have rigorously challenged the evidence of WMDs and existence of a Saddam–Bin Ladin connection and raised the alarm that a war to remove Saddam Hussein would deflect valuable resources from the war in Afghanistan and divert attention from the hunt for Usama Bin Ladin and destruction of al-Qa'ida. Another critical flaw in Operation Iraqi Freedom was highlighted by Army chief of staff General Eric Shinseki (b. 1942), who warned Congress that more than a half-million American combat troops would be required to stabilize Iraq in the aftermath of the invasion. His prescient comments proved embarrassing to the administration.

On 17 March 2003, President Bush declared Saddam to be in violation of existing UN resolutions and gave him forty-eight hours to leave Iraq or face removal by force; Saddam refused to comply. Two days later, Bush ordered air strikes on Iraq and announced the start of Operation Iraqi Freedom. U.S., British, and Australian forces commenced air strikes and a ground invasion. The fiercest Iraqi resistance came from the Fidaiyin Saddam insurgents, not the regular military. Iraqi resistance—organized or otherwise—largely ceased after 9 April, and by the end of the year, Saddam and many of his chief deputies had been captured or killed.

The U.S.-led Coalition Provisional Authority (CPA) governed Iraq for more than a year but did little to stabilize the country, a situation made far worse when Ambassador L. Paul Bremer (b. 1941), the CPA administrator, issued two decrees: the first abolishing the Ba'th Party and the second disbanding the Iraqi army. The former robbed the country of experienced bureaucrats and technicians when it needed them most; the latter placed tens of thousands of armed, military-trained, and now unemployed men on the streets and in the countryside, contributing to a sharp rise in lawlessness and violence. The CPA's policies created the perfect environment for militias and insurgent organizations, such as al-Qa'ida in Iraq (AQI), to take root. Chalabi was placed in charge of the de-Ba'thification effort. A Shi'a, he used his authority to remove Sunnis from government positions; the program became in effect one of de-Sunnification, which further stoked sectarianism in Iraq.

In June 2004, the CPA transferred sovereignty to a UN-selected Iraqi interim government; the Shi'a political leader Iyad 'Allawi (b. 1944) served as the caretaker prime minister. The new Iraqi government faced critical challenges, especially a violent insurgency. In January 2005, Iraqis elected a new interim government, which would be charged with drafting a constitution; Ibrahim al-Ja'fari of the Shi'a ad-Da'wa Party became prime minister 2005–6). In October Iraqis approved a new constitution. Two months later, Iraqis elected a permanent, constitutional government. In April 2006, a new government under Nouri al-Maliki (2006–14), also of ad-Da'wa, took power. Oil again flowed from Iraq, but the industry's infrastructure was often the target of Sunni insurgents. Furthermore, political turmoil spurred the proliferation of Iranian-backed Shi'a militias and Sunni Salafi-jihadi factions, which in turn prompted the rise of Abu Mus'ab al-Zarqawi (1966–2006), the founder of AQI, and Muqtada al-Sadr, who led the militant Shi'a group JAM. In this unstable environment, Abu Du'aa, a Sunni incarcerated in the U.S.-run Camp Bucca detention center in southern Iraq started a new movement. In 2010 he would become the leader of AQI and rebrand himself Abu Bakr al-Baghdadi (b. 1971) before going on the lead ISIS (formerly AQI).

Despite the fracturing of Iraq along ethnoreligious lines, the United States never supported partition of the country into separate states. Instead, it favors a federal solution. For the country to hold together, there must be a healthy political balance among the Arab Shi'a, Kurdish, and Arab Sunni communities. Ottoman rule was a relatively peaceful period in Mesopotamia, as each group had its own province, but the Ottomans were outsiders who retained ultimate sovereignty. The United States served as the outside power in Iraq from 2003 to 2011, sacrificing much blood and treasure to keep the Iraqi state intact.

In early 2007, in response to the spiraling violence between Sunnis and Shi'a, Bush ordered the deployment of 20,000 troops to Iraq to secure major population centers and give the Maliki government an opportunity to establish effective control. The surge, as it became known, largely succeeded. Contributing to its success was the decision by Sunni tribal leaders in Anbar province to switch their support from the insurgents to the U.S.-led coalition. Their effort to defeat the insurgency, which became known as the Awakening, precipitated the collapse of the Islamic State of Iraq (ISI)—formerly AQI—in 2008.

Approximately 20 percent of the Iraqi population is Kurdish. Politically, the Kurds are divided into two main factions: the Patriotic Union of Kurdistan (PUK) and Kurdistan Democratic Party (KDP). The PUK, which was founded by Jalal Talabani (1933–2017), the former president of Iraq, has at times enjoyed close relations with Iran. It represents urban Kurds. The KDP is led by Masoud Barzani (b. 1946), current president of the Kurdistan Regional Government (also known as Iraqi Kurdistan). It represents tribal Kurds. The PUK and KDP have experienced times of both conflict and harmony over past decades. Half of the provinces of Kurdistan are ruled by the PUK, the other half by the KDP.

Approximately 60 percent of the Iraqi population is Shi'a Arab. They live primarily in the south and in and around Baghdad. They have close historical ties to Iran owing to their shared religion, but the Shi'a of Iraq and Shi'a of Iran belong to different ethnic groups. Therefore, the former has no interest in forming a firm political union with Iran. After Saddam's regime had suppressed the Shi'a uprising of 1991, it embarked on an aggressive program to drain the marshes of southern Iraq, aimed at destroying the livelihood of the Shi'a Marsh Arabs, who had inhabited the land of southern Mesopotamia for centuries, and eliminating the environs as a place of refuge. Since Saddam's fall in 2003, the marshes have made a remarkable recovery.

There is no consensus among the Iraqi Shi'a over who should lead them; their opinions range from secularist to Islamist. Since 2003 six major Shi'a groups or individuals have emerged: ad-Da'wa Party; the Supreme Council for Islamic Revolution in Iraq (SCIRI), later renamed the Islamic Supreme Council of Iraq (ISCI); Grand Ayatollah 'Ali al-Sistani (b. 1930); Muqtada al-Sadr; al-Fadhila Party; and secularists, most notably Ahmed Chalabi and Iyad 'Allawi. Ad-Da'wa was founded by devout Shi'a in 1958 and competed with the Ba'th and communist parties. Primarily an urban party, its heyday was the 1960s and 1970s. It does not insist on clerical rule but advocates its interpretation of Islamic law and a Western-style economy. In the wake of the Iranian revolution, Saddam cracked down on all Shi'a dissent. He executed several ad-Da'wa leaders, including Muhammad Baqir al-Sadr, who was killed in 1980 and had advocated a consultative rule for clerics. Many surviving Shi'a leaders fled to Iran.

SCIRI, which was organized by exiled Shi'a leaders in Iran in 1982, served as an umbrella Shi'a political organization that, for a time, included ad-Da'wa. Ayatollah Muhammad Baqir al-Hakim (ca. 1939–2003) became the organization's leader in 1984. He favored an Iranian-style, mullah-led government and sought to carry out a Khomeini-style insurgency in Iraq. SCIRI carried out a guerrilla campaign against Iraq in the 1980s. Many Iraqis, however, viewed this action as traitorous because Iraq was at war with Iran at the time. Muhammad Baqir al-Hakim was killed by a car bomb in August 2003. His brother and successor, 'Abd al-'Aziz al-Hakim, had close ties to both Iran and the United States. SCIRI was represented on the Iraqi Governing Council, which advised the CPA. SCIRI adopted the name ISCI after Saddam's fall. The organization advocates a two-stage political strategy: participate in and support a pluralistic, parliamentary system and then replace that system with a Shi'a government. 'Abd al-'Aziz al-Hakim died in 2009; he was succeeded as leader of ISCI by his son 'Ammar al-Hakim (b. 1971).

Older, nonpolitical Shi'a follow Grand Ayatollah Ali al-Sistani. He came to Iraq from Iran in 1951 and is recognized as Iraq's principal Shi'a religious leader. He favors a government that makes a distinction between religion and state. He follows the Najaf tradition, which is quietist with regard to politics; believes that there should be no clergy in government; and argues that Shi'a should keep out of sight and survive. He insisted on a constitution drafted by elected individuals; called for direct, early elections; and demanded that the United States withdraw from Iraq as soon as feasible, but he did not issue a fatwa against the occupation. In summary, he supports elections, parliamentary government, and the will of the people. In April 2003, he said, "Iraq is a Muslim country and is inspired by Islam in its laws, ethics and course of action."[11] For the January 2005 elections, Sistani forged a unified Shi'a list—the United Iraqi Alliance—to ensure that Shi'a won a substantial number of seats in the 275-member National Assembly. (Parliamentary seats are assigned to parties based on their percentage of the vote.)

Younger, more radical Shi'a follow Muqtada al-Sadr, the son of Grand Ayatollah Muhammad Sadiq al-Sadr, a prominent Iraqi Shi'a cleric who was murdered, along with two of his sons, by Saddam in 1999. The younger al-Sadr emerged as a galvanizing political figure who rejected the U.S.-led occupation of Iraq and demanded an American withdrawal. He declared that peaceful protests had become useless and in April 2004 urged his followers to terrorize their enemy. The CPA issued an arrest warrant for al-Sadr, but he was never apprehended. In 2004 heavy fighting took place between al-Sadr's JAM and U.S. military forces. His movement stayed out of the January 2005 elections but soon joined the political process, espousing a Khomeini-style government. He left the country to study theology in Iran but returned following the 2010 parliamentary elections.

'Abd al-Majid Khoei, a prominent Shi'a clergyman who had returned from exile in London, was stabbed to death at the shrine of Imam 'Ali in Najaf in April 2003. Ayatollahs Sistani and al-Hakim had refused to meet with him because they viewed him as too close to the United States and Britain. Followers of Muqtada al-Sadr are suspected of culpability in his murder.

Al-Fadhila (the Islamic Virtue Party), which follows Ayatollah Muhammad Ya'qubi (b. 1960), a disciple of Muhammad Sadiq al-Sadr, is a branch of the Sadrist movement but is a rival to the faction led by Muqtada al-Sadr. The party participated in the 2005 elections as part of Sistani's United Iraqi Alliance.

The United States tacitly wanted a secularist to take power in Baghdad or have significant influence in the Iraqi government. Early on, the secular politician Ahmed Chalabi was held in high regard by Pentagon leadership, but eventually he fell out of favor with the Bush administration over allegations that he fabricated intelligence on Saddam and his inability to compromise with Sunnis and other political adversaries. Iyad 'Allawi, the leader of the Iraqi National Alliance, became interim prime minister upon transfer of sovereignty to Iraq in June 2004. 'Allawi's list won the largest number of seats in the 2010 election, but he was unable to form a governing coalition.

The Kurds and Shi'a dominated the 2005 parliamentary election and won the largest number of seats in the National Assembly. The United Iraqi Alliance won 47 percent of the seats, the Kurdish Alliance won 25 percent, and the Iraqi National Alliance won 14 percent. Sunnis boycotted the elections. Ibrahim al-Ja'fari of ad-Da'wa became the first

democratically elected prime minister of Iraq, and Kurdish leader Jalal
Talabani was selected to serve as the president. The National Assembly
assembled a committee to write the constitution. Sunnis were given
adequate representation on the committee even though they had boycotted
the political process. The assembly endorsed the draft constitution, which
contained modifications to assuage the Sunni population. The constitution
was ratified by the public in October 2005, garnering nearly 80 percent
approval. A majority of Sunnis voted no, but the no vote exceeded 67
percent in two of four majority Sunni provinces. The first constitutional
government was elected in December 2005. The United Iraqi Alliance
won the largest share of the seats in the National Assembly. After months
of political deadlock, Iraqi political leaders agreed on a broad-based,
national unity government. In April 2006, Nouri al-Maliki, a senior
ad-Da'wa leader, replaced al-Ja'fari as prime minister.

A second parliamentary election was held in March 2010. Al-Maliki
ran with Sunni partners in a cross-sectarian coalition called State of Law.
A new Shi'a coalition, the National Iraqi Alliance (NIA), opposed him.
It included ISCI, Muqtada al-Sadr's faction, al-Fadhila, Chalabi, and
al-Ja'fari. Al-Maliki was also opposed by a Sunni-dominated coalition,
al-Iraqiyya (the Iraqi), led by Iyad 'Allawi. Al-Iraqiyya captured more seats
than State of Law, but 'Allawi could not form a government. After eight
months of wrangling, al-Maliki managed to stitch together a governing
coalition with the NIA. He reached out to 'Allawi, who agreed to head a
newly formed security council.

Operation Iraqi Freedom officially became Operation New Dawn on
1 September 2010. The United States withdrew the last of its troops in
December 2011. In the wake of ISIS's rout of Iraqi forces in the first half
of 2014, al-Maliki stepped down as prime minister. He was replaced by
Haider al-'Abadi (b. 1952), another ad-Da'wa stalwart. Al-Sadr's Saairun
(Forward) coalition won the largest block in the 2018 parliamentary
elections and had a major voice in the formation of the new Iraqi
government.

The prospects for Iraq's future depend on whether the country's
leaders can establish and maintain a multisectarian, multiethnic representative polity that permits Shi'a, Sunnis, and Kurds to share political

power, allocate national resources, vent their grievances, and defend the country as Iraqis. The likely alternative is that Iraq will fracture and become a battleground for sectarian militias and insurgent groups backed by regional powers, such as Iran and Saudi Arabia, and outside powers, namely, the United States and Russia. If history—from ancient times to the present—is our guide, then it is important to acknowledge that the location of Mesopotamia—later Iraq—and the larger Fertile Crescent have made the area a coveted prize for many great empires, starting with Akkadians in the third millennium BC. When American combat forces set foot on Iraqi soil, they found themselves bivouacking and fighting on the very landscape where Babylonians, Persians, Macedonians, Romans, Byzantines, Arabs, Ottomans, and British had previously fought.

The Israeli-Palestinian Conflict and Peace Process since the Late 1980s

In this chapter, we trace the course of the Israeli-Palestinian conflict over the past three decades and the attempts to achieve a peaceful resolution to the dispute. We also investigate the two Palestinian uprisings, intifadas, which began in 1987 and 2000.

94. What were important developments in the Israeli-Palestinian conflict and the Arab-Israeli peace process from the outbreak of the first intifada in 1987 to the collapse of the Camp David talks of 2000?

December 1987 marked the beginning of the intifada, which means "shaking off" in Arabic. The intifada was a low-level uprising of Palestinian youths against the Israeli occupation in East Jerusalem, the West Bank, and Gaza. The uprising was sparked by outrage over an Israel Defense Forces (IDF) traffic incident in which a group of Palestinians was killed. The Palestinians proved to be coordinated in their opposition to the Israeli occupation and effective in refuting Israel's claim that they were happy and prosperous under Israeli rule. The uprising did not settle down until 1991, with the convening of the post–Gulf War Madrid Conference.

Several signs of trouble existed in the Israeli-occupied Palestinian territories in the 1980s. There was great tension and little peaceful coexistence between Israelis and Palestinians. A key event just before the intifada was the Arab summit meeting held in Amman in November 1987. At the conference, the heads of state paid lip service to the Palestinian cause but authorized member states to resume diplomatic relations with Egypt. The unstated message to Palestinians was that the Arab world had forgiven Egypt and that the Palestine Liberation Organization (PLO) should stop expecting unlimited diplomatic and military support.

The uprising was not under the control of Chairman Yasir Arafat and the PLO leadership based in Tunis. It was led by Palestinians in the West Bank and Gaza and proved to be a battle between David and Goliath. In 1948 the Israelis were David, and the Arabs were Goliath. Four decades later, the roles were reversed.

The Palestinian protesters were not armed with modern weapons. They used rocks, slingshots, and burning tires against Israeli soldiers, tanks, attack helicopters, and fighter-bombers. Local Palestinian leaders took charge of the rebellion and quickly gained respect from other Arab leaders and the international community. They called for general strikes, and the Palestinians shuttered their shops in East Jerusalem and boycotted Israeli goods. Palestinian laborers stayed home instead of working in Israel. Meanwhile, the PLO in Tunis viewed the uprising as a means to achieve foreign recognition and international legitimacy.

In July 1988, King Hussein renounced Jordan's claim to the West Bank, clearing the way for future Palestinian sovereignty in the territory, and in November the Palestinian National Council, the Tunis-based Palestinian legislature-in-exile, proclaimed an independent Palestinian state and accepted UN Resolution 242 as a basis for ending the Palestinian-Israeli conflict. In December, at a special session of the United Nations in Geneva, Arafat publicly renounced all forms of terrorism and recognized Israel's right to exist. In response to Arafat's pronouncements, President Ronald Reagan (1981–89) directed his administration to begin a dialogue with the PLO.

Some Israelis vehemently rejected the idea that the PLO represented a government-in-exile and could be treated as a suitable negotiating partner. Other Israelis argued that the way to resolve the Palestinian-Israeli conflict was through a two-state solution. Many hard-line Palestinians opposed efforts to make peace with Israel, which they viewed as their oppressor. Palestinian acts of terrorism continued.

The fall of the Iron Curtain in 1989 marked the beginning of a massive wave of immigration of Soviet Jews to Israel. In July 1990, President George H. W. Bush's administration suspended dialogue with the PLO following a terrorist incident in Israel. At the time of the suspension, the administration was trying to persuade Israel to allow local elections in the Palestinian territories.

During the intifada, the Palestinian Islamist organization Hamas (the Arabic acronym for Islamic Resistance Movement) burst onto the scene. The organization, an offshoot of the Egyptian Muslim Brotherhood, was supported by local leaders disillusioned by and opposed to the secular PLO. Many Middle East analysts contend that Israel facilitated the emergence of Hamas as a rival to the PLO; its goal was to split the Palestinian movement. The two organizations had significant differences. The PLO was a secular nationalist movement. Hamas provided an Islamist component to the Palestinian struggle. It sought to eliminate Israel and create its version of an Islamic state in Palestine. Arafat recognized a role for Islam, but the Gulf War broke out before he could reach an accommodation with the Islamists. Hamas continued to carry out terrorist attacks in Gaza and the West Bank.

In August 1990, Iraq invaded Kuwait. Iraqi leader Saddam Hussein insisted that any negotiations over a withdrawal from Kuwait must include discussions about the Palestinian-Israeli conflict. He also provided financial awards to the families of Palestinian suicide bombers. During the war, Saddam fired several Scud missiles at targets in Israel with the goal of breaking up the international coalition arrayed against him. None of the missiles caused great damage, but they did generate a high degree of panic. Some Scuds were partially intercepted by the U.S.-supplied Patriot anti-missile defense system. The attacks demonstrated how ballistic missiles might be used in a future war in the Middle East.

After a series of successes in the late 1980s, Arafat's approval rating among Palestinians declined. To return to the forefront of the Arab-Israeli conflict, he made the fateful decision to support Saddam during the war. The Saudis were furious and cut off his financial assistance. Forced to readjust his strategy, he moved toward negotiations with Israel.

The Gulf War dramatically changed Israel's relationship with the Palestinians and its Arab neighbors. Also, during the war, the Soviet Union revised its Middle East policy. It did not oppose the U.S.-led coalition against Iraq, it allowed its Jewish citizens to immigrate to Israel, it restored diplomatic relations with the Jewish state, it stopped arming Syria and other frontline states, and it assisted the United States in convening a postwar peace conference.

The Arab oil-exporting states realized that the most serious threat to their security came from Iraq or Iran, not Israel. The credibility of Jordan and the PLO among the oil states was damaged by their support of the Iraqi dictator. Both suffered diplomatically and economically from their war policies and had few viable options for the future; therefore, they agreed to negotiate with Israel. Syria was also willing to join peace talks if it stood a reasonable chance of regaining the Golan Heights.

The Madrid Conference was a direct consequence of the Gulf War. Its chief organizer was U.S. secretary of state James A. Baker (b. 1930), who had made a pledge to the Arab members of the coalition that the United States would use its offices to convene an international conference on Middle East peace. In July 1991, Jordan, Lebanon, Syria, and the Palestinians—both local officials and PLO leadership—agreed to peace talks with Israel. Israel and the United States experienced a significant policy disagreement in the months leading up to the conference. It concerned whether the Bush administration would authorize $10 billion in loan guarantees with which the Likud government of Prime Minister Yitzhak Shamir could finance the resettlement of Soviet Jews, including the expansion of Jewish settlements in the West Bank. The administration elected to delay action on the loan guarantees to avoid undermining the upcoming Middle East peace conference. Since Israel's allies in Congress did not have the votes to prevent the delay, the Shamir government approved Israel's participation in the Madrid Conference.

The conference, which convened in October 1991, did not produce any breakthroughs, but it set the stage for direct Israeli-Palestinian negotiations. Multilateral, working-group meetings were held on a variety of issues, such as water, refugees, economic development, and arms control. Most of the meetings were held in Washington. After the June 1992

elections in Israel, Yitzhak Rabin of the Labor Party became prime minister. His more conciliatory position regarding the occupied territories
won out over Shamir's hard-line approach. Secret talks began in Norway
between representatives of Israel and the PLO; the Norwegian foreign
minister facilitated the talks.

After news of the secret talks leaked out, the Norwegians relinquished
their role as chief mediator to the United States. The subsequent Oslo
Accords of 1993 and 1995 established a framework for a permanent settlement. On 13 September 1993, a signing ceremony was held at the White
House. President Clinton, Rabin, Israeli foreign minister Shimon Peres
(1923–2017), and Arafat were the chief participants. The handshake
between Rabin and Arafat was the highlight of the ceremony. The principal parties signed two documents: The first was a statement of mutual
recognition; the second was the Declaration of Principles on Palestinian
Self-Rule, better known as Oslo I. The declaration established the Palestinian National Authority, more commonly known as the Palestinian
Authority (PA); Arafat became its first president. The Palestinians were
granted authority over Gaza and the area in and around Jericho; Israeli
forces would begin a gradual withdrawal from Palestinian population
centers in the West Bank; Jewish settlers would remain under Israeli protection; and bilateral talks would start no later than the third year of a five-
year transition period, during which the parties would determine the final
status of Jerusalem, Palestinian refugees, Jewish settlements, and borders.

Since the Oslo I Agreement left many issues unsettled, the parties
became more rigid in their positions, which undermined the negotiating process. The Israelis began removing their troops from territories
not settled by Jews and permitted Arafat to return to Palestine and begin
building governing institutions. The PA established a police force, but it
evolved into a Palestinian militia that would combat Israel. Foreign governments withheld much of the $2 billion they pledged to the PA because
Arafat insisted on full control over the money without public scrutiny.
Consequently, economic and political conditions worsened in the West
Bank and Gaza. Oslo I brought neither independence nor prosperity to the
Palestinians, but it opened the door for other agreements between Israel
and a handful of other Arab states. In October 1994, Jordan signed peace

treaties with Israel. Moreover, Morocco and Tunisia established consular ties with Israel, and several of the Gulf States established economic relations with Israel. Sabotaging the peace effort were terrorist attacks carried out by Hamas and Palestinian Islamic Jihad (PIJ), violence by Jewish settlers against the Palestinian population, and the heavy-handedness of Israeli security forces.

In September 1995, Rabin and Arafat signed the Oslo II agreement. The agreement delineated an intricate plan for Israel's gradual withdrawal from the West Bank, setting up three distinct zones: Zone A, comprised of eight West Bank cities where the PA would provide civil authority and security, except for the parts of Hebron containing Jewish settlements; Zone B, consisting of other West Bank towns and villages where the PA would provide civil authority, but Israel would provide security; and Zone C, encompassing Jewish settlements, unpopulated areas, and lands that Israel viewed as vital to its security. In this third zone, Israel provided civil authority and maintained security, pending the outcome of the final status talks. The redeployment of Israeli troops would occur in six-month intervals, Israel and the Palestinians would form joint patrols where appropriate, and Israel would build bypass roads for settlers and security forces.

Events in Israel and actions by Palestinian extremists—from Islamists to leftists—combined to upset the peace process. Many Palestinians opposed what looked like the creation of small pockets of their territory in the West Bank. Hamas opposed both Oslo agreements, demanding instead a Palestinian state in all of historic Palestine. In their view, territory in the Dar al-Islam could not be surrendered. The secular, nationalist PLO did not want an Islamic state but did not criticize the views of Hamas. Arafat was under heavy criticism for the slow progress of the peace process and rife corruption within his administration.

Meanwhile, conservative Jewish West Bank settlers vowed that they would never relinquish their sacred land to the Palestinians. In their view, they were fulfilling God's covenant. On 4 November 1995, a Jewish theological student, Yigal Amir (b. 1970), shot and killed Rabin. His death was a huge setback to the peace process, but by the time of the assassination, the peace process had already stalled. Rabin was succeeded as prime minister by Peres. In spite of the tragedy, the Clinton administration made several attempts to launch the final status talks. Unfortunately, Peres did not enjoy the same level of popular support as Rabin, and Hamas became stronger and more assertive. Many Palestinians began to regard Hamas as a viable alternative to Arafat and the PLO.

In early 1996, two deadly suicide bombings in Israel were attributed to Hamas. In May the Israelis voted narrowly to replace Peres' Labor government with Likud, which was led by Benjamin Netanyahu (1996–99, 2009–present), who vowed to slow down the peace process and promised voters a stronger hand in dealing with Palestinian violence. Netanyahu suspended permanent-status talks but indicated that he would carry out Israel's commitments under Oslo II. Meanwhile, Iran's support for Hizballah and Hamas further undermined the efforts of Israel and the Palestinians to advance the peace process. In April 1996, Hizballah's attacks across the Israel-Lebanon border triggered a sixteen-day Israeli response known as Operation Grapes of Wrath. In January 1997, Netanyahu agreed to withdraw approximately 80 percent of the Israeli troops from Hebron but refused to give back other areas of the West Bank because of bombings, which he blamed on Arafat. The Palestinians grew more frustrated with a peace process that offered them no hope for freedom or even gainful employment. They also resented the Israeli policy of creating, over the objections of the international community, new Jewish settlements in the occupied territories, especially East Jerusalem.

In October 1998, the Clinton administration convened an Israeli-Palestinian summit at Wye Mills on Maryland's Eastern Shore with the aim of renewing Israeli's commitment to Oslo II and allaying its fears over security. Under the supervision of Clinton and other senior U.S. officials, an agreement was reached. According to the Wye River Accords, named after a Chesapeake Bay tributary, Israel would withdraw from another 13 percent of West Bank territory, the PLO would affirm its rejection of terrorism, and the CIA would monitor security on the ground. The agreement weakened Netanyahu's standing within his party, and in the May 1999 elections, Labor made significant gains and formed a coalition government that included small splinter parties and enjoyed the tacit support of Israeli Arabs. Ehud Barak (1999–2001), a former commando in the IDF, defeated Netanyahu in the first popular election for prime minister.

Barak, with Clinton's help, hoped to make peace with both the Palestinians and the Syrians. In early 2000, high-level talks took place between Syria and Israel in Shepherdstown, West Virginia. The effort failed because Syrian leader Hafiz al-Asad, who passed away soon afterward, refused to negotiate with Israel unless he was promised in advance the return of the entire Golan Heights.

In a dramatic move, aimed at boldly advancing the peace process between Israel and the Palestinians, Clinton hosted a summit between Barak and Arafat at Camp David in the summer of 2000. Barak proposed the creation of Israeli security corridors in the West Bank, offered Gaza and most of the land in the West Bank to the Palestinians, and was willing to compromise on East Jerusalem, but he would neither cede all the West Bank and East Jerusalem nor agree to readmit Palestinian refugees from the 1948 war. He was also concerned that the PA had pledged to crack down on terrorism, yet attacks on Israelis continued. Arafat turned down Barak's offer of most of the West Bank, all of Gaza, and shared administration of the sacred Temple Mount or al-Haram ash-Sharif. Arafat knew that he would be profoundly criticized by the Muslim world for not obtaining complete control of al-Haram ash-Sharif. He proved not to be much of a politician and compromiser because, being an old revolutionary, he could not abandon the struggle. Camp David II, as it became known, subsequently collapsed. Barak's generous proposal to Arafat was unprecedented, and Arafat drew criticism from several U.S. officials, most notably President Clinton, for not accepting it. Meanwhile, Israel continued to build new settlements and expand older ones. At Taba, in the Sinai, in January 2001, Clinton, Barak, and Arafat made another attempt to reach an agreement. Barak was more conciliatory on the refugee issue, but Arafat again refused to accept the offer. Meanwhile, a second and more deadly intifada had erupted throughout Israel and the Palestinian territories.

In 2002 the United States, Russia, the United Nations, and the European Union formed a diplomatic group known as the Quartet for the Middle East, dedicated to achieving a negotiated resolution to the Israeli-Palestinian conflict. A year later, the Quartet promulgated a "Roadmap for Peace," but the parties to the dispute never seriously took it up. Over the next three years, the Middle East witnessed the death of

Arafat, Israel's unilateral withdrawal from Gaza, and Hamas' landslide victory in Palestinian parliamentary elections, the last of which prompted the United States and European Union to suspend aid to the West Bank and Gaza through those agencies administered by the Hamas-dominated Palestinian Authority. It is important for observers of the Middle East to watch for signs of internal political conflict among both Palestinians and Israelis and to gauge the impact of those fissures on the peace process. For example, Fatah and Hamas continue to compete for political primacy in Palestine, and Hamas is locked in a struggle against Islamist groups, such as the Islamic State, which is trying to establish a viable presence in Gaza. Meanwhile, on the Israeli side, the influence of hard-liners, who are loath to compromise, and the inaction of government officials, who are unable to balance diplomacy and force, have perpetuated the futility in achieving a solution to the Israel-Palestine conflict.

95. What are the prospects for a peace settlement between the Israelis and the Palestinians?

In September 2000, Likud leader and candidate for prime minister Ariel Sharon (1928–2014) visited the Temple Mount, or al-Haram ash-Sharif, for his campaign. He was severely criticized for unnecessarily stoking tension between Israelis and Palestinians, especially in the aftermath of the failed Camp David summit. In response, he said, "I came here to the holiest place of the Jewish people to see what happens here and really to help the feeling that we are now ready to move forward." Arafat condemned Sharon's visit as a "dangerous step."[1] Borrowing from the Old Testament prophet Hosea, Sharon's provocative act served to "sow the wind"; over the next few years, Israelis and Palestinians would "reap the whirlwind" (Hosea 8:7).

Sharon served in the IDF from 1942 to 1973 and led the stunning counterattack across the Suez Canal during the October 1973 Arab-Israeli War. He entered politics after he had retired from the military and was a strong supporter of Menachem Begin. He served as Begin's defense minister (1981–83). During his watch, the Israeli invasion of Lebanon and massacres at the Sabra and Shatila refugee camps took place. A national inquiry found Sharon negligent for enabling the massacres to take place. Because he was considered a murderer by many Arabs, his visit to al-Haram ash-Sharif sparked a Muslim uprising in Jerusalem, in Arab areas of Israel, and in the occupied territories that would persist for several years. Palestinians attacked settlers with rocks and firearms and launched a wave of suicide bombings. Instead of joint police action by Israelis and Palestinians to quell the uprising, the Israelis responded unilaterally with massive force, destroying houses, uprooting olive groves, shooting protesters with live ammunition, and drenching whole villages with tear gas. Thousands of Palestinian workers who were employed in Israel suffered the loss of their livelihoods when Israel sealed the border crossings to the West Bank. The intifada won the support of nearly all Arabs, who demanded that their governments cut all diplomatic and commercial ties with Israel. Only Egypt and Jordan maintained formal relations with Israel. More than nineteen hundred Palestinians and seven hundred Israelis died in the uprising. Arafat was unable and perhaps unwilling to contain this violence.

As the intifada and suicide attacks continued, the Israelis considered their very survival was at risk. Heated debates took place in the Knesset over what many politicians thought were the overly generous offers made by Barak at Camp David. Barak agreed to early elections; his challenger for the premiership was Sharon. The Likud leader presented himself as the one leader who was tough enough to achieve peace between Israel and the Arabs. In the election held in February 2001, Sharon won by twenty percentage points, but he was forced to form a broad-based coalition government that included Labor leader Peres. It was difficult for Sharon's government to devise a unified policy toward the Palestinians or to attain its stated goal of a peace settlement with the PLO.

Meanwhile, radical Palestinian groups seized the initiative from Arafat, who was seen by a growing number of Palestinians as inept and corrupt. Violence increased in the West Bank and Gaza, and armed groups, such as Hamas, Islamic Jihad, and al-Aqsa Martyrs' Brigade, stepped up suicide bombings in Israel. The most horrific attacks took place at a Sbarro Pizza restaurant in Jerusalem in August 2001 and during a large Passover seder (ritual feast) in Netanya in March 2002. Since the perpetrators of the suicide bombings had come from the West Bank, the Israelis retaliated by invading and reoccupying the territory in the spring of 2002. The military offensive was called Operation Defensive Walls. The Israelis also targeted Palestinian leaders. Arafat was trapped in his headquarters compound in Ramallah and was nearly killed when the IDF attempted to demolish the building in which he had taken shelter. Intense international pressure convinced the Israelis to halt its destruction. Two leaders of Hamas, Shaykh Ahmed Yassin and 'Abd al-'Aziz al-Rantisi, were assassinated in March and April 2004, respectively.

The Israelis commenced the erection of a barrier that would permanently separate Israelis from the Palestinian population in the West Bank. The Palestinians refer to the barrier as the "wall." It is universally condemned, has been declared illegal by the International Court of Justice, and has disrupted the lives of thousands of Palestinians, but it has reduced the number of terrorist attacks on Israel to a fraction.

Arafat died in December 2004, and Mahmud 'Abbas (b. 1935), a former Palestinian prime minister, was elected president of the PA the following month. He had a reputation as a pragmatic politician.

Sharon's government successfully carried out the evacuation of all settlements from Gaza and four settlements in the West Bank in the summer of 2005, but the unilateral action did not advance the peace process. Subsequent events demonstrated that the withdrawal was an isolated development that enhanced the prestige of Hamas and further radicalized the conflict. That fall Sharon formed a new, centrist party, Kadima (Forward), to buttress his efforts to resolve the Palestinian dispute. Netanyahu split from Sharon over the issue of disengagement from Gaza and became the leader of Likud in December. Sharon suffered a debilitating stroke in January 2006; Ehud Olmert, the deputy prime minister and former mayor of Jerusalem, became interim prime minister. In the March 2006 election, Kadima won twenty-nine seats, the largest total of any party; Likud won only twelve seats. In May Olmert officially became prime minister (2006–9).

In January 2006, Hamas won a majority of seats in the election for the Palestinian Legislative Council. The following year, a factional war broke out between Fatah and Hamas, and Hamas took control of Gaza. The Palestinians thus faced a bifurcated rule: the PA, dominated by the PLO, governing the West Bank, Hamas governing Gaza. In May 2011, Hamas and Fatah accepted an Egyptian-brokered reconciliation pact, but the two sides could not reach an agreement on the composition of a caretaker government or a schedule for national elections. The Doha Agreement of 2012, signed by the Fatah and Hamas leaders, also failed to establish a timetable for elections. From June 2014 to June 2015, Fatah and Hamas ministers formed an interim national unity government under 'Abbas but were unable to carry out elections. In late 2017, Egyptian-brokered negotiations between Fatah and Hamas produced an agreement to hold general elections by the end of 2018. At time of writing, the Palestinian elections have not taken place.

By mid-decade the Arab population of Israel and the occupied territories had surpassed the number of Jews in those combined areas. According to a 2004 U.S. Department of State report on human rights, the total number of Palestinians living in Israel, the Gaza Strip, East Jerusalem, and West Bank stood at more than 5.3 million, while the corresponding Jewish population numbered 5.2 million.[2] The Palestinians have a higher birth rate than the Israelis. The security barrier might delay, but will not resolve, the tremendous demographic reckoning that looms over Israel.

Olmert ordered two controversial military operations to halt rocket attacks on Israeli population centers carried out by Hizballah, based in southern Lebanon, and radical Islamists in Gaza: what Israelis call the Second Lebanon War (the Israel-Hizballah war) in 2006 and the Gaza war (Operation Cast Lead) in 2008–9.[3] He was roundly criticized, both domestically and internationally, over his handling of the two operations. In November 2007, he and 'Abbas participated in the Annapolis Peace Conference, during which for the first time the two-state solution was articulated as the agreed upon means to resolve the Israel-Palestine conflict. In 2008 Olmert, who was under investigation for corruption, announced that he would not seek reelection as the leader of Kadima. Foreign Minister Tzipi Livni (b. 1958) became the party's new leader.

In the February 2009 election, Kadima won twenty-eight seats; Likud, twenty-seven seats; Yisrael Beiteinu (Israel Is Our Home), fifteen; and Labor, thirteen. Livni was unable to form a government so President Shimon Peres (2007–15) then turned to Netanyahu, who fashioned a governing coalition of right-wing parties and the Labor Party and succeeded Olmert as prime minister in March 2009. Ehud Barak was named defense minister, and Avigdor Lieberman (b. 1958) of the ultranationalist Yisrael Beiteinu was named foreign minister.

Owing to the increase of Islamist militancy after the outbreak of the Arab uprisings of 2011 and the seemingly interminable civil war in Syria, which frequently flares up near Israel's border, the prospects for a peace settlement are not good. Post–Arab Spring politics has polarized Palestinian and Israeli societies, marginalized the PA, and provided an opening for Hamas and other violent and less compromising Islamist movements, such as ISIS and PIJ, to compete for Palestinian hearts and minds. Hamas may gain a foothold in the West Bank through the electoral process, further undermining the governance of the PA. It is important to note that Hamas's attempt to expand into the Sinai during Mohammed Morsi's brief tenure as Egyptian president alarmed Egypt's military and security establishments and contributed to Morsi's removal. The Israeli blockade and severe restrictions on the movement of the people of Gaza and tight controls on the Egypt-Gaza border have created the conditions for extremism and violence.

The political climate in Israel is increasingly uncompromising, and Israeli society is finding itself more and more separated—"walled off" might be an apt phrase—from the chaotic aftermath of the Arab Spring, fostering the belief that peace with the Arabs is not as essential as it once was. As a result, actions such as the building of Jewish settlements in the Israeli-occupied Palestinian territories continue unchecked, making a negotiated peace settlement increasingly difficult to achieve. In the elections of 2013, an alliance between Likud and Yisrael Beiteinu won thirty-one seats and formed a coalition government with three other parties: Yesh Atid, which won nineteen seats; Habayit HaYehudi, twelve; and HaTnuah, six. Netanyahu remained prime minister. Two years later, Netanyahu and Likud turned back a challenge from the Zionist Union—a Labor–HaTnuah coalition. Likud won thirty seats and formed a government with Kulanu (ten seats), Habayit HaYehudi (eight), Shas (seven), and Yehadut HaTorah HaMeuhedet (six).

On the other hand, there are Palestinians who advocate a one-state solution to the Palestinian-Israeli conflict, arguing that in the spirit of human rights and decency, Palestinians should be accorded Israeli citizenship, which would grant them passports and the right to travel and the opportunity to lead ordinary, dignified lives. On its face, this argument might have some appeal, until one recalls that a majority-Palestinian state would effectively efface Israel's identity as a Jewish nation unless the Jewish population manages to retain its hold on power through an unacceptable system of political apartheid.

Egyptian president Abdel Fattah al-Sisi has called for renewed talks between Israelis and Palestinians. Stability in the Sinai is linked to stability in Gaza, and both Israel and Egypt have interests in seeing a Gaza that is competently governed and not radicalized. There appears to be transition from a general intifada to an "individual" or "stabbing" intifada, in which lone assailants, many fueled by social media, stab, shoot, or mow down Israelis with vehicles. In response, the Israeli government has suspended tens of thousands of permits for Palestinian workers, and some political leaders encouraged Israelis to arm themselves. In turn, ISIS exploits Israeli actions such as these to incite its followers. Usama Bin Ladin's son Hamza (b. 1989) has inflamed militant Islamists by speaking out on the Palestinian issue. Eruptions of violence in Jerusalem's holy places have divided members of the international community, with France calling for the deployment of international observers and the United States calling for restraint on both sides. In December 2017, U.S. president Donald J. Trump (2017–present) formally recognized Jerusalem as the capital of Israel, a controversial measure that upended the decades-long American policy that the final status of Jerusalem would be decided through negotiations between Palestinians and Israelis. Trump's decision, which was celebrated by Israelis and roundly condemned throughout the Arab world, will undoubtedly complicate efforts to achieve a final peace settlement. Furthermore, the Trump administration's decision to cut U.S. funding for Palestinian aid programs and to close the PLO's office in Washington threatens to exacerbate the humanitarian crisis in the Palestinian territories and increase anti-American resentment throughout the Arab world.

If Palestinian and Israeli leaders are unwilling to sit together and negotiate a peace settlement, no amount of outside pressure can bring them together and halt the cycle of violence. It *was* possible in the 1990s and *can* happen again today with courageous leaders in place on both sides.

19

Understanding Islamist Extremism in the Twenty-First Century

In the final two chapters of our guide to the Middle East, we examine the critical subject of Islamist extremism, an issue that concerns the American public and influences U.S. policy in the region. In this chapter, we discuss the rise of militant jihadism and analyze the origins and ideologies of militant Islamist organizations, such as al-Qaʾida and ISIS.

96. What accounts for the rise of militant jihadist movements in the world today?

It is difficult for scholars and students of the Middle East to identify a specific era or event that marks the emergence of violent jihadism. Did it occur as a reaction to the Crusades, or was it inspired by the writings of radical Islamist theorists, such as Ibn Taymiyya (ca. 1263–1328) or, more recently, Sayyid Qutb (1906–66)? One thing is sure, however. With the collapse of the Soviet Union in 1991, the United States stood alone as a superpower. Consequently, it became the leading target of global discontent, splattered with unrelenting criticism for not doing enough to alleviate complex problems, such as extreme poverty, economic downturns, mass violence, and damage to the environment. Victimization is appealing to many individuals and groups because it enables them to shift responsibility for their plight. We begin our examination of this question a dozen years before the end of the Cold War, when the Soviet Union invaded and occupied the fiercely independent and fractious country of Afghanistan.

When Soviet forces invaded Afghanistan on Christmas Day 1979, it triggered a conflict that lasted nine years and spawned numerous jihadist organizations. The Soviet-Afghan War became a significant event of the last years of the Cold War, with the United States, Pakistan, and Saudi Arabia and other Arab states providing funds and equipment to *mujahidin* (jihadists, guerrilla fighters) factions fighting the Soviet occupation. During the war, the West viewed the *mujahidin* as "freedom fighters", and President Jimmy Carter's national security adviser, Zbigniew Brzezinski (1928–2017), while visiting a *mujahidin* camp along the Pakistan-Afghan border, invoked the name of God in the struggle against the communists. Several Arab leaders, including President Hosni Mubarak of Egypt and King Khalid of Saudi Arabia (r. 1975–82), viewed the war as a golden opportunity to rid themselves of Islamist militants and political activists who challenged their regimes by sending them to fight the Soviet Fortieth Army and hoping they never came back—a strategy that proved to be a major miscalculation. Pakistan and parts of Afghanistan were inundated by thousands of Arabs arriving to fight the Soviets. The militant Palestinian cleric Shaykh 'Abdullah Yusuf 'Azzam (1941–89) noted the endemic disorganization in the camps and set up several induction centers, called Maktab al-Khidmat lil-Mujahidin (the Services Office for Jihadists), to regulate the arrival and training of would-be jihadists, who became known as Arab Afghans. 'Azzam urged a wealthy, young Saudi, Usama Bin Ladin (1957–2011), to come to Pakistan and help run the centers. Bin Ladin funded the training program, indoctrinated new warriors, and connected 'Azzam with wealthy Arab donors.

Meanwhile, a new Soviet leader, Mikhail Gorbachev (b. 1931), came to power in 1985. He pursued a nonconfrontational foreign policy, which included improved relations with the United States and the withdrawal of Soviet troops from Afghanistan. The withdrawal was completed in early 1989. The Soviet-Afghan War produced tens of thousands of Soviet and *mujahidin* casualties and millions of Afghan refugees and displaced families on both sides of the Afghanistan-Pakistan border. It also affected the lives and outlook of the Arab Afghan jihadists. Some remained in Afghanistan and Pakistan, many returned to their home countries, others took on new battles in Bosnia and Yemen, and several sought political asylum in the United States and other Western countries, where at the time they were held in esteem as persecuted anticommunist warriors and freedom fighters. Bin Ladin returned to Saudi Arabia, where he sharply criticized the government for its overdependence on the United States for the country's defense following Iraq's invasion of Kuwait in 1990. The Saudis placed Bin Ladin under house arrest, but he fled in 1991 and ultimately relocated to Sudan.

Following the assassination of 'Azzam in 1989, Bin Ladin gradually took charge of his organization and, while living in Sudan, built it into a global network that took advantage of the Arab-Afghan diaspora. He named the organization al-Qa'ida al-'Askariyya (the Military Base)— known simply as al-Qa'ida—but the name may have derived from 'Azzam's sermons, in which the cleric called for *al-qa'ida al-sulba* (firm foundation), which is both physical *and* moral. Bin Ladin and his deputy, Ayman al-Zawahiri (b. 1951), disagreed strenuously with 'Azzam over the direction of the Arab Afghan movement and are suspected of plotting his assassination.

Before Bin Ladin's ascent to notoriety, militant Islamist theorists adhered to the concept of defeating the "near enemy" (corrupt, repressive Arab regimes) before attacking the "far enemy" (the United States and the West). Bin Ladin and al-Zawahiri, on the other hand, argued that it was futile for militant Islamists to try to topple local regimes so long as they were backed by the United States. Instead, they should lure the United States into an exhausting, unwinnable regional conflict that would compel it to quit the Middle East and abandon the discredited Arab regimes, which in turn would become vulnerable prey for their detractors. To fulfill this strategy and retaliate for decades of U.S. policy in the Middle East that it reviled, including support for oppressive governments, al-Qa'ida bombed U.S. embassies in Kenya and Tanzania (1998), attacked the USS *Cole* in Aden (2000), and carried out the horrific attacks of 11 September 2001. Whereas most terror groups had excelled in one or two forms of violence, such as hijackings, bombings, or hostage taking, al-Qa'ida exhibited the ability to carry out spectacular attacks on land, at sea, and in the air.

Weakened by the post-9/11 war on terror, al-Qa'ida was reassessed by counterterrorism experts and designated al-Qa'ida Associated Movements (AQAM). Its senior leadership was based in Pakistan, and it maintained several "franchises" or "affiliates" throughout the Middle East, South Asia, and Africa, including al-Qa'ida in Iraq (AQI), which became ISIS and was denounced by al-Qa'ida's senior leadership in 2014; al-Qa'ida in the Arabian Peninsula (AQAP); al-Qa'ida in the Islamic Maghreb (AQIM); al-Shabab (the Youth) in Somalia; and Jabhat al-Nusra (the Victory Front) in Syria, which was created by AQI as its Syrian affiliate in 2011 but split from the organization in 2012 to preserve its independence and concentrate on the struggle against Bashar al-Asad's regime. AQAM's ostensible leader is al-Zawahiri, who succeeded Bin Ladin after he was killed by U.S. Navy SEALs in 2011. Al-Zawahiri, who lacks Bin Ladin's charisma, attempted to rein in the violence unleashed in Iraq by AQI but failed, and his organization is now battling AQI's successor, ISIS, for preeminence in the global jihadist movement. The 2015 appearance of Hamza Bin Ladin (b. 1989), Usama's son, in AQAM media may represent an attempt by the organization to appeal to millennials and unify the militant Islamist movement under its umbrella, particularly with the collapse of the physical ISIS-led "caliphate" in 2017.

In the wake of 9/11, a significant majority of Muslims worldwide—even Iranians—expressed sympathy or solidarity with the United States and backed the U.S.-led invasion of Afghanistan—code-named Operation Enduring Freedom—which aimed to destroy al-Qa'ida and topple the harsh Taliban regime that had provided it a safe haven. Unfortunately, this period of good feelings was short-lived, upended by President George W. Bush's "axis of evil" speech, which singled out Iran, Iraq, and North Korea for their support of international terrorism, and the U.S.-led invasion of Iraq in 2003.

In the run-up to the invasion, the Bush administration claimed the existence of a link between al-Qa'ida and Saddam Hussein. Although the accusation was proved false, notoriety helped produce a new generation of jihadists, one of whom was the Jordanian Abu Mus'ab al-Zarqawi, the leader of AQI. Independent, brash, and prone to extreme levels of violence, he declared war on foreign entities and Iraq's Shi'a population, fomenting a vicious sectarian conflict that nearly wrecked the country. In 2006 he was killed by a precision U.S. air strike and was succeeded as amir of AQI by Abu Ayyub al-Masri (1968–2010) of Egypt and then by Abu Omar al-Baghdadi (1959–2010) of Iraq. They renamed AQI the Islamic State of Iraq (ISI), which was soon taken down by Sunni tribesmen and the surge of U.S. combat troops; both leaders were killed in a raid conducted by Iraqi and U.S. forces. Meanwhile, an obscure ISI figure, the Iraqi-born Abu Du'aa (b. 1971), while in the Camp Bucca detention facility, recruited a network of jihadis that left him well-positioned to take over leadership of ISI following his release and the deaths of al-Masri and al-Baghdadi. After taking the reins of ISI in 2010, he rebranded himself as Abu Bakr al-Baghdadi and came to lead ISIS. We should note that the life cycle of ISIS evolved from insurgency, to the seizure of territory, to collapse, to insurgency again. In the answer to Question 99, we will dig deeper into the origins of ISIS.

Another influential jihadi strategist is Abu Mus'ab al-Suri (b. 1958), a native Syrian who holds Spanish citizenship. In the aftermath of 9/11, the United States hardened its defenses and committed itself to a global offensive to eradicate terrorism. As a result, al-Suri developed the concept of leaderless resistance, by which individuals and cells, inspired by al-Qa'ida, would carry out attacks without central direction. His theories brought us the age of "lone wolf" and independent cell terrorist attacks, which are extremely difficult for intelligence and law enforcement agencies to prevent, especially if the conspirators have no criminal records. The cooperation of the Muslim community is essential to identifying and thwarting these threats. Likewise, it is vital that a partnership between the private and public sectors defeat increasingly complex modes of encryption that facilitate terrorist recruitment, planning, and operations.

97. What are the origins and goals of the militant jihadist organization al-Qa'ida?

The roots of al-Qa'ida can be traced to the Maktab Khidmat al-Muja-hidin, established by the militant cleric 'Abdullah 'Azzam during the

Soviet-Afghan War. Aside from pouring the foundation for al-Qa'ida, 'Azzam introduced Bin Ladin to the theater of war and elevated him from money courier and fundraiser to leadership of Maktab al-Khidmat. Following 'Azzam's death and the Soviet withdrawal from Afghanistan, Bin Ladin brought together Arab Afghan jihadists and advanced the argument that they should not attempt to topple hated Arab regimes until they exacted a heavy toll on the United States, which supported them. If the United States withdrew from the region, its departure would hasten the fall of those governments and pave the way for the establishment of Bin Ladin's vision of a caliphate. Neither the Qur'an nor hadith ordains any form of government, including a caliphate, but among militant Islamists and some Islamist political groups, the revival of this institution became an essential element of their ideology.

Al-Qa'ida achieved extraordinary success as a terrorist organization, owing to its deadly, innovative tactics; ability to operate transnationally; and transition from a structured to a decentralized organization after 9/11. Al-Qa'ida's franchises in Iraq, Yemen, and North Africa came to operate with considerable autonomy, much to the frustration of Bin Ladin and al-Zawahiri.

In May 2011, after incalculable hours devoted to intelligence collection, prisoner interrogations, and painstaking analysis by the men and women of the U.S. intelligence community and meticulous planning by U.S. Special Forces, Seal Team Six entered Bin Ladin's compound in Abbottabad, Pakistan, and killed the world's most notorious terrorist. President Barack Obama (2009–17) was not completely certain that Bin Ladin was in Abbottabad, but he accepted the risks, took the gamble, and ordered the mission. The killing of Bin Ladin validated the innovative leadership of General Stanley McChrystal, former commander, Joint Special Operations Command (JSOC), who put intelligence analysts in the field, where they worked shoulder to shoulder with special operators, permitting the latter to react immediately to actionable intelligence. This groundbreaking concept was the basis for the "find, fix, and finish" doctrine, which has facilitated the killing or capture of many of the world's leading terrorists. Nevertheless, it is just one component of a broader strategy to counter militant Islamist groups such as al-Qa'ida and ISIS.

Today, AQAM must compete in the world of radical jihadism with other more militant organizations, most notably ISIS, which AQAM ironically denounced in 2014 for its extreme brutality. One of the most dangerous AQAM affiliates targeting the United States is AQAP, based in Yemen. One of its leading clerics and propagandists, the American-born Anwar al-Awlaki (1971–2011), inspired Major Nidal Hasan (b. 1970), a U.S. Army psychiatrist, to carry out a mass shooting at Ft. Hood, Texas, in 2009, in which thirteen military personnel and civilians were killed, and 'Umar Farouk 'Abdulmuttalab (b. 1986), the infamous "underwear bomber," to try to blow up an airliner over Detroit on Christmas Day that same year. Thankfully, the bomber was unsuccessful. What is particularly important for Americans to appreciate is that militant Islamist groups, like AQAM, its affiliates, and ISIS, present a grave threat to Muslims and non-Muslims alike, and blunting the attraction of these radical groups and foiling their deadly plots cannot be done without the partnership of concerned Muslims in the United States, in Europe, and around the world. Militant Islamist groups reject all other faiths and have no tolerance for a diversity of beliefs and practices, even accusing Muslims who oppose their ideology of being apostates and calling for their elimination. They stand for a bankrupt ideology that can be maintained only through fear, intimidation, and death. It is vital that we maintain the cooperation of Muslims in combatting the challenge of militant Islamists groups and their ideologies. Our Muslim partners must never be considered part of the problem; instead, they must always be held in esteem as part of the solution.

98. How does Usama Bin Ladin's concept of jihad differ from others?

Jihad, a controversial and often misunderstood concept, has multiple meanings; therefore, to address this question accurately, we need to consider its broadest and narrowest meanings. Most commonly, jihad means striving, struggling, or persevering to live the best possible Muslim life. In the Qur'an, this idea is revealed as following the path to righteousness: "Those who strive in Our (cause),—We will certainly guide them to Our Paths: For verily Allah is with those who do right" (29:69). In short, jihad is the inner struggle to maintain piety, reject temptation, and do what is moral in the eyes of God. This struggle, according to the Prophet Muhammad, is the greater, or spiritual, jihad. In a much narrower sense, jihad can mean fighting the enemies of Islam. Muhammad deemed this form a lesser, or armed, jihad. Thus, jihad has a range of meanings, from leading a virtuous life and endeavoring to correct a social injustice to confronting with force those who seek to harm the *umma*.

While the great majority of Muslims struggle daily to keep to the right path, among militant Islamists, such as Usama Bin Ladin, jihad means armed conflict. For them, there is no broader definition. In a May 1998 interview, Bin Ladin repeated a call for war against the United States and its allies that he had made earlier in the year:

> The call to wage war against America was made because America has spear-headed the crusade against the Islamic nation, sending tens of thousands of its troops to the land of the two Holy Mosques [Saudi Arabia] over and above its meddling in its affairs and its politics, and its support of the oppressive, corrupt and tyrannical regime that is in control. These are the reasons behind the singling out of America as a target. And not exempt from responsibility are those Western regimes whose presence in the region offers support to the American troops there. We know at least one reason behind the symbolic participation of the Western forces and that is to support the Jewish and Zionist plans for expansion of what is called the Great Israel [*sic*]. Surely, their presence is not out of concern over their interests in the region. . . . Their presence has no meaning save one and that is to offer support to the Jews in Palestine who are in need of their Christian brothers to achieve full control over the Arab Peninsula which they intend to make an important part of the so-called Greater Israel.

Bin Ladin also singled out one of his near enemies—the House of Sa'ud— for destruction:

> The fate of any government which sells the interests of its own people and, betrays the nation and commits offenses which furnish grounds for

expulsion from Islam, is known. We expect for the ruler of Riyadh the same fate as the Shah of Iran. We anticipate this to happen to him and to the influential people who stand by him and who have sided with the Jews and the Christians giving them free reign over the land of the two Holy Mosques. These are grave offenses that are grounds for expulsion from the faith. They shall all be wiped out.[1]

From a redoubt in Afghanistan and—later—from a comfortable villa in Abbottabad, Pakistan, Bin Ladin advocated jihad in its simplest, narrowest form: holy war. In militant Islamist literature from the late thirteenth century to the present, the persona of the Prophet Muhammad has been reduced to a warlord. The teachings of Islam—and of any religion, for that matter—are ignored or made irrelevant when an extremist group believes that the end justifies its actions.

While in Islam warfare is justified in defense of the *umma*, rules regulate its practice. For example, force is the option of last resort; women, children, the elderly, and infirm must not be harmed; trees must not be cut down; fields must not be destroyed; people in places of worship must not be disturbed; and a boy must have the permission of his parents to join a military campaign. The difference between *fard kifaya* (an obligation for the whole community that can be assumed by a few), such as participation in an offensive conflict or the Muslim prayer over the dead, and *fard ayn* (an obligation for all Muslims), such as daily prayer or participation in a defensive conflict, is blurred by militant Islamist ideologues who portray all warfare as defensive and justify the participation of all. Shaykh 'Azzam, Bin Ladin's mentor during the Soviet-Afghan War, synthesized fragments of Muslim scholarship to subvert the Muslim doctrine of just war, going so far as to claim that armed jihad should be a pillar of Islam—more important than prayer and fasting.

99. What are the origins and goals of the Islamic State of Iraq and Syria (ISIS)?

To better understand the origins of ISIS, we must review the history of AQI, which rose out of the turmoil following the U.S.-led invasion of Iraq. AQI used brutal Ba'thist-like methods of population control, taking the militant Islamist movement to unprecedented levels of violence. Al-Zarqawi, a native Jordanian, started out as a street tough, hustling prostitutes, dealing drugs, and committing other acts of thuggery. He traveled to Afghanistan, but the Soviets were in the process of completing their withdrawal, and he never got into the fight. Instead, he became embroiled for a time in the fighting between Afghan *mujahidin* warlords. He then returned to Jordan, where he conspired to topple the Hashimite monarchy. He was arrested and sent to prison, where he muscled up, cut out his tattoos, and studied militant Islamist ideology under the Palestinian-born Abu Muhammad al-Maqdisi (b. 1959). He was released from prison under an amnesty announced by Jordan's new king, 'Abdullah II (r. 1999–present), and returned to Afghanistan, where he launched a bloody campaign against the country's Shi'a population, an extreme move that caused Maqdisi to distance himself from his pupil.

During the early stages of Operation Enduring Freedom, he eluded coalition forces, fled the country, and resettled in northern Iraq. There, he bided his time until U.S. secretary of state Colin Powell (b. 1937) propelled him into the limelight. In early 2003, while laying out the Bush administration's case for the use of military force against Saddam Hussein, Powell mentioned al-Zarqawi in connection to an alleged link between the Baghdad regime and al-Qa'ida. Al-Zarqawi took advantage of his newfound fame and the chaos that followed the U.S.-led invasion of Iraq to establish the militant group Jama'at al-Tawhid wal-Jihad (Organization of Monotheism and Jihad). In 2004 he renamed it al-Qa'ida fi bilad al-Rifidayn (al-Qa'ida in the Land of the Two Rivers), which became known as al-Qa'ida in Iraq. At the onset of the U.S. occupation of Iraq, AQI carried out a series of spectacular terrorist attacks within the country and in Iraq. Those attacks included the bombing of UN headquarters in Baghdad (2003), which claimed the life of Sergio de Mello, the world body's senior envoy; murdering Shi'a who were observing the holy day of 'Ashura in Karbala (2004); bombing three hotels in Amman (2005); and bombing al-'Askariyya mosque in Samarra, one of the holiest sites in Shi'ism and destroying its golden dome (2006).

Al-Zarqawi's goals were to incite a Sunni-Shi'a war and make the United States the remaining foreign presence in Iraq. He would achieve the latter by targeting all other outside entities, such as the UN and members of the coalition. He pioneered the grotesque practice of posting on YouTube footage of hostage beheadings and improvised explosive device (IED) explosions under U.S. military vehicles. The clips were designed to strike fear into his enemies *and* persuade young Muslims to join his jihad. In 2006 he died in a U.S. air strike. His legacy consists of the skilled use of broadband technology, spectacular acts of violence, strident sectarianism, refusal to compromise with other jihadi groups, and the founding of a state based on his own brand of militant Islamist ideology. These features became hallmarks of ISIS and attracted a new generation of "hashtag jihadis" and "ISIS fanboys" who years earlier would have been acolytes of al-Qa'ida.

Al-Zarqawi's war on the Shi'a and his proclivity for extreme brutality troubled his nominal superiors, Bin Ladin and al-Zawahiri. Al-Zarqawi scoffed at their concerns and rejected their advice yet retained the al-Qa'ida label. From 2006 to 2010, AQI was led by Abu Ayyub al-Masri and Abu Omar al-Baghdadi, who were originally from Egypt and Iraq, respectively. They advanced a distorted view of Shari'a to justify extreme violence against non-Muslims, Shi'a, and Sunnis who did not share their beliefs. AQI seized large portions of Anbar province, including the cities of Falluja and Ramadi, and took on a new name: the Islamic State of Iraq (ISI). A surge of more than 20,000 U.S. combat troops and the Sons of Iraq movement, a coalition of disaffected Sunni tribes in Anbar who despised ISI and the violence it had wrought, soon regained control of the province. A battered ISI reverted to being a terrorist insurgency organization under its former name AQI. In 2010 al-Masri and al-Baghdadi were killed in a joint U.S.-Iraqi raid targeting their safe house. During this interval, an obscure ISI official, Abu Du'aa, was incarcerated at Camp Bucca in southern Iraq, where he built a clandestine network of AQI fighters, ex-Ba'thists, and former Iraqi military officers and noncommissioned officers (NCOs) that left him well positioned to take the reins of AQI after his release from prison and the deaths of al-Masri and al-Baghdadi. In 2010 Abu Du'aa was named the leader of AQI, and he changed his name to Abu Bakr al-Baghdadi. He remains the leader of ISIS (formerly ISI/AQI) at the time of this writing, but the caliphate had collapsed by 2017. His terrorist movement has fallen back to leading an insurgency in Iraq and Syria.

Meanwhile, in Syria the merciless response by President Bashar al-Asad (2000–present) to the protests of the Arab Spring transformed popular demonstrations into a nationwide insurgency, which in time presented AQI with an extraordinary opportunity to expand across the border. After it had seized considerable territory in eastern Syria, including the city of Raqqa on the Euphrates, AQI refocused its attention on the strident sectarian regime of Iraqi prime minister Nouri al-Maliki (2006–14), whose pro-Shi'a policies were so threatening to the nation's Sunni Arab minority that an alliance of convenience united AQI, dozens of Sunni tribes, and radicalized former Ba'thists who sought to regain their dominance over the country. In the spring of 2014, AQI routed Iraqi forces and captured Mosul, a city of nearly 2 million inhabitants, after which it rebranded itself the Islamic State of Iraq and Syria (ISIS). The stunning victory provided ISIS with thousands of tons of captured U.S.-supplied weapons, equipment, and ammunition that had been abandoned by the Iraqi army. It also tilted the theater of war in its favor, particularly in northern Iraq, and if not for timely U.S. military intervention, the militant organization would have made inroads into the autonomous Kurdish region of northern Iraq and placed the Iraqi government in great peril. That summer al-Baghdadi proclaimed a caliphate over the area under his control, a vast swath of territory stretching from northwest Syria to the outskirts of Baghdad and containing some 8 million people, many of whom were forced into servitude. He changed the name of ISIS to the Islamic State (IS; in Arabic, al-Dawla al-Islamiyah) and adopted the name and title of Caliph Ibrahim the First, an act of hubris and narcissism that outraged most Muslims, including many Salafi jihadis.[2]

A significant difference between ISIS and AQAM is the former's willingness to attack not only non-Muslims and Muslims with whom it disagrees, but also Salafists with whom it differs over ideology and tactics. Even Salafi-jihadi theorists who have been scathing in their criticism of ISIS, such as al-Maqdisi, have been denounced and targeted for assassination. ISIS has even called for the murder of certain Saudi Arabian Salafi Wahhabi clerics—a line al-Qa'ida never crossed. Furthermore, ISIS pushed violence to an unimaginable level—carrying out mass beheadings, burning or drowning caged prisoners, and even using children as executioners—and then posting the sickening images on the Internet and social media to gain greater media attention, intimidate enemies, and recruit young Muslims who might be attracted by its propaganda and brutality. ISIS at its height following the capture of Mosul boasted an estimated 30,000 foreign fighters, mainly from Arab countries but also some 6,000 combatants from Western Europe, Russia, and the United States. Moreover, the organization was well financed through the extortion of funds from the population under its control, oil smuggling, antiquities dealing, and looting. As of this writing, the caliphate had been rocked back on its heels by an eclectic host of regional and global players—ranging from the United States and Russia to the Iraqi and Syrian governments to Kurdish and Shi'a militias—resulting in the loss of nearly all its territory in Syria and Iraq and a significant degrading of its combat effectiveness. In July 2017, ISIS lost Mosul and its de facto capital of Raqqa, and in December Iraqi prime minister Haider al-'Abadi (b. 1952), who succeeded al-Maliki in 2014, boldly declared victory over ISIS and proclaimed the border between Iraq and Syria free of Islamic State fighters. Nevertheless, Islamist insurgency will continue throughout the Middle East, ISIS will become more focused on global terrorism, and like al-Qa'ida, it will become increasingly decentralized, with far-flung branches or provinces in Libya, the Sinai, Yemen, Somalia, the Philippines, Nigeria, Afghanistan, Saudi Arabia, and the Caucasus region of Russia. It will also rely on lone-wolf attacks.

While al-Qa'ida's leadership was forged and tempered by the Soviet-Afghan War, the leaders of ISIS were born in the convulsion of Operation Iraqi Freedom. The first and second Battles of Fallujah, the Battle of Tal Afar, the Battle of Ramadi, and the collapse of ISI in 2008 were formative events for the men leading ISIS. As we conclude this chapter, think of where the next charismatic jihadi leader will emerge. Will he be a veteran of the 2017 battles for Mosul and Raqqa? Will he emerge from the Sinai or somewhere in Africa or even the Philippines? What is the future of a virtual ISIS caliphate, where the fantasy is lived out on the Internet? What is certain is that the United States and its partners must continue their pursuit of militant jihadists around the world. In late 2017, four U.S. Army Green Berets were ambushed and killed while fighting an ISIS affiliate in Niger, demonstrating America's resolve to combat, degrade, and ultimately defeat this deadly threat.

20

Combatting Islamist Extremism in the Twenty-First Century

This chapter follows our investigation in chapter 19 of the origins and beliefs of militant Islamists. In this chapter, we identify a number of strategies aimed at defeating the radical jihadi movement and evaluate the likelihood of achieving liberal Islamic reform.

100. What are effective strategies for combatting militant Islamist organizations?

The U.S. intelligence community and armed forces have developed a remarkable ability to locate and kill or capture militant Islamists and disrupt their attack planning and operations. Together, sound intelligence and military expertise make up only one component—albeit vital—of a multifaceted, nuanced, and long-term strategy that the United States and its global partners must devise and implement to weaken and ultimately defeat radical, militant Islamists and restrain Islamist political groups. To that end, we advocate a strategy that contains these additional elements.

First, the United States and its allies must take great care not to formulate any policy that alienates the overwhelming majority of the world's Muslims, who disavow extremism and violence. At the same time, they must acknowledge and embrace the remarkable diversity of belief and practice within Islam, while carrying out a public information campaign that reminds the citizens of the world that militant Islamist groups from al-Qa'ida to ISIS have no tolerance for beliefs and practices different from their own and have killed many Muslims who have opposed their worldview. They pose a threat to Muslims and non-Muslims alike, but their victims are predominantly other Muslims.

When, for example, European legislatures or American school boards attempt to regulate or even ban religious dress, such as the wearing of the hijab, they make the issue a cause célèbre and create a more sympathetic environment in which militant Islamists can thrive. In the United States, we must not alienate through prejudice or fear-mongering the very population whose help is needed to counter militant Islamist ideology and watch for militant Islamist cells forming in our communities. Muslims who oppose militant Islamists must be viewed as an essential part of the solution and not merely part of the problem. By including these Muslims, we affirm our cherished belief that a country that values religious freedom can accommodate a diverse collection of faiths and practices. We are assuredly not at war with Islam, much less Salafi Muslims who pine for a return to Islamic traditions that existed during the time of the Prophet Muhammad and the earliest leaders of the *umma*, but we *are* at war with Salafi jihadis, who have demonstrated a readiness to kill anyone opposing them on the battlefield and a willingness to attack any Muslim rejecting their ideology.

Second, it is necessary that we understand the differences between militant Islamists, Islamist political groups, and the Muslim world at large. Militant Islamists seek to impose through coercion—including the use of violence—their vision of a political-social order. Islamist political groups aim to achieve the same but through political means, including the ballot box. Meanwhile, the world's 1.6 billion Muslims, who have a variety of histories and cultures, manifest a rich diversity of religious expression that ranges from nonpracticing to fundamentalist. Therefore, we must use tailored methods to challenge militant Islamists and their political counterparts, while maintaining the support and cooperation of the world's Muslims, many of whom have suffered at the hands of militant Islamists. The world must deal with militant groups in a threefold manner: through the careful application of force, by undermining their ideology, and with the clear and constant message that they are a threat to non-Muslims *and* to a majority of Muslims. On the other hand, the first step in containing political Islamists groups, including sanctioned political parties, is closely monitoring their pronouncements and aims. Any Islamist proposal that threatens individual liberties or political rights or mandates how Muslims are to practice their faith must be publicly denounced and vigorously opposed through political—and other means—including the careful application of military power. Such a political development took place during the short-lived presidency of Egypt's Mohammed Morsi, the candidate of the Muslim Brotherhood, whose policies pushed the country to the verge of civil war and led to the intervention of Egypt's armed forces.

Third, Islamic-based arguments and counternarratives that target groups like al-Qa'ida and ISIS must saturate the Internet, social media, and satellite channels. Muslim criticism of extremist groups is found in numerous media where young Muslims, seeking their religious identity, can participate in constructive and well-informed discourse. Today, concerned Muslims are using modern media to reproach al-Qa'ida, ISIS, and Salafi jihadis.

Fourth, the strategy to protect the American public and thwart the allure of militant Islamists must have at its forefront the values of religious freedom and individual liberty. Under the U.S. Constitution's guarantee of religious freedom, an individual Muslim has the right to lead a secular life or practice Islam in any form, be it Sunni, Shi'a, or Sufi, or even as a Salafi preacher or politician. What is *not* protected by the First Amendment is an individual's decision to cloak him- or herself in religion and then conspire to commit or carry out an act of terrorism. Salafis living in the United States enjoy considerable liberties compared to their colleagues in the Middle East. They can sustain their religious freedom by being vigilant and identifying and denouncing Salafi jihadi cells operating in their neighborhoods.

Since the world's Muslims are not in complete accord regarding the practice of their faith or implementation of Shari'a, any attempt to impose a caliphate, which ISIS attempted, or write Islam into a country's constitution, which many Muslim countries have done, raises the question: Whose Islam will be the one afforded legal primacy? Because the brand of Islam embraced by a religious government, whether elected or not, takes precedence over others practiced in the country, this circumstance will—at best—generate popular opposition or—at worst—set off a violent response. Two recent examples illustrate this point. In Egypt, shortly after the Muslim Brotherhood's Mohammed Morsi (2012–13) was elected president as a Freedom and Justice Party (FJP) candidate, he reconvened the Islamist-dominated parliament that had been disbanded by the supreme court, annulled constitutional amendments that had limited presidential powers, and issued a proclamation that permitted him to rule by decree until a new constitution was in place. Many Egyptians, including a majority of Muslims, feared he would impose strict Islamic practice and undermine the rights of the Christian population. After months of grassroots protests, including a massive social media campaign and a petition drive that demanded his removal from office, he was ousted in a military led-coup after only one year and four days in power. In Turkey, since the early 2000s, the Justice and Development Party (AKP), a mainstream Islamist political organization, has sought through legislative means to overturn or erode many of the republic's secular features, an effort that has alienated a sizeable portion of Turkish society, spurred antigovernment demonstrations, and prompted an unsuccessful coup attempt in 2016 against the Islamist president, Recep Tayyip Erdoğan (2014–present).

Fifth, the strategy must accurately define the Islamist threat. It is not terrorism, which is a tactic; nor is it Shari'a, which is subject to a range of interpretations; and it certainly is not the religion itself, which has 1.6 billion diverse adherents. We define the militant Islamist threat as any attempt by any group to infringe individual liberties and impose its religious views or ideology through coercive means, including the use of violence or threatening acts of violence.

In the United States, an individual can choose to be, for example, a white supremacist and enjoy the right to gather with like-minded persons. That individual even has the right to express his or her views peacefully in the public square. What white supremacists in America do not have the right to do is conspire to shoot up a church, burn down a synagogue, or bomb a mosque. Serious questions we must ask ourselves—as citizens concerned with the health of our republic—and discuss with others include the following: When does hate speech cross over to a call for violence? Is expressing support on the Internet or social media for al-Qa'ida and ISIS and cheering their acts of terror protected speech? Has the criminalization of hate speech provided extremist groups with a claim to victimhood? And where is the balance between protecting civil liberties and carrying out surveillance of people suspected of plotting terrorist acts? Answers to questions such as these will require informed public debate, not knee-jerk passion, incendiary sound bites, or political sloganeering. That debate must include input from ordinary citizens, the media, academia, the legal profession, and many layers and organs of government. Hopefully, such an effort would construct a sensible and effective strategy that both protects the homeland and upholds our civil liberties.

Finally, whenever you hear worn-out statements, such as "Islam is an evil religion" or "Islam is a religion of violence and oppression," the first question that should pop into your mind is, How do these views help us develop policies to protect America, remain true to our values, and preserve our liberties? They certainly do not. While militant Islamists despise religious diversity, we must celebrate it, draw inspiration from it, and refuse to follow others into the abyss of intolerance.

101. Can a liberal Islamic reform movement succeed in the world today?

Liberal Islamic reform movements, calling for an end to violent jihad and standing for secular governance, human rights, religious freedom, and social equality, do exist and have existed in the past. But before we discuss and evaluate the chances for effective reform within Islam today, let us travel back to the late nineteenth century, when two Muslim modernist thinkers, Jamal al-Din al-Afghani (ca. 1838–97) and Muhammad 'Abduh (1849–1905), maintained that Islam was compatible with modern ideas, institutions, and technology and that religious law and practice could be adapted to meet modern circumstances.

Originally from Persia, al-Afghani went to Cairo, where he taught at al-Azhar, but he was exiled by Khedive Tawfiq for supporting Ahmed 'Urabi's uprising and eventually settled in Persia. There he led protests against the tobacco concession and was exiled again, living out his life in Istanbul. He preached a message of Islamic modernism, advocating the reform of Islamic practice—namely, the rediscovery of the true principles of the faith—and calling for Sunnis to revive *ijtihad* as a source of law. He viewed Islamic modernism as a process of self-criticism—an effort to redefine Islam to meet modern situations. He also advocated the selective adoption of Western ideas and technology. A proponent of Pan-Islamism, al-Afghani opposed European imperialism and argued that a unified Muslim world was the best way to resist and ultimately eliminate Western influence. He also hoped to heal the Shi'a-Sunni divide. Al-Afghani's message was a dual-edged sword, calling for the removal—through violence if necessary—of Muslims who had enabled the European colonizers. Islamist radicals, as well as Muslim reformers, were inspired by him. He had important disciples, namely, Muhammad 'Abduh and Sa'd Zaghlul, who embraced his liberal ideas; and Rashid Rida (1865–1935), a Muslim reformer who adopted his anticolonial and Pan-Islamist ideologies. Rida inspired Hasan al-Banna, the founder of the Muslim Brotherhood.

'Abduh, an Egyptian, was also exiled by Tawfiq but returned to Egypt, serving as mufti during the last years of his life. He extended al-Afghani's concepts of Islamic modernism, developing the belief that reason and the fundamentals of the faith are compatible. His ideology took flight as the Salafiyya movement, whose name is derived from the Arabic word *salaf* (ancestor). This movement differed significantly from that of today's Salafi jihadis. 'Abduh's movement asserted that study of the early *umma* provides the surest guide to divinely approved behavior because the basic requirements of Islam, as found in the Qur'an and hadith, were most faithfully observed during the life of Muhammad and the era of the Rashidun caliphate. Practices adopted since were influenced by reason to meet new social and political circumstances.

Al-Afghani and 'Abduh broke from the traditional Islamic thinking by seeking to reconcile Islam with Western ideas and differed from other reformers, such as the Wahhabis, who regarded the Qur'an and hadith as the sole sources of Islamic law, and sought to transpose those teachings to modern life. The two thinkers had an immense impact on the Muslim world at the time and influenced other modernist movements, such as the Muslim Brotherhood, which we discussed in chapter 11. To modern Salafis, however, the neo-Salafism espoused by al-Afghani and 'Abduh is heresy. We mention this to make American troops aware of the difference between neo-Salafism and Salafi jihadis, who engage in hashtag warfare in 280 characters or less.

The authors of this work, however, are doubtful that a liberal reform movement can succeed in the near future. The reality is that many countries of the Muslim world are still struggling to establish genuine democracies—meaning polities that not only describe themselves as democratic but also contain genuine democratic institutions, such as free elections, an independent press, the rule of law, and checks on the power of government. Most Muslims live in autocracies or illiberal democracies, dictatorships with democratic window dressing, which have trampled civil liberties to such a degree that it is challenging for either democratic or Islamic reform movements to take root.

In the 2000s, Turkey demonstrated that an Islamist-based party, the AKP, could govern a modern republic and maintain the balance between religious expression and individual liberty. Under Prime Minister Erdoğan (2003–14), the founder of the AKP, Turkey reformed its economy, expanded the industrial and high-tech sectors, implemented several legal reforms, secured accession talks with the European Union, and emerged as a regional power. In recent years, however, the party and Erdoğan, who was elected president in 2014, took steps to strengthen their hold on power and silence their critics. The AKP's assault on democratic institutions, disregard for civil liberties, and damage to the country's international reputation generated popular opposition and division within the party and culminated in July 2016 with the unsuccessful attempt by a faction within the armed forces to remove Erdoğan and seize control of the government. If Turkey's recent past can serve as prologue, then the AKP will exploit the failed coup to stifle its opponents further.[1]

During Hosni Mubarak's three-decade-long presidency (1981–2011), conservative, secular Egyptians and foreign supporters regarded him as a bulwark against militant Islamists, some of whom were vocally expressing the need to impose a theocracy in Egypt. Governance by a liberal party or coalition of parties—a third option—was not feasible. Liberal political groups were viewed as threats to the regime; therefore, they were constrained, repressed, or victimized by fraud to the point where they had no political viability. That left the Muslim Brotherhood as the only group capable of getting out the vote in elections held after Mubarak's ouster. In the parliamentary elections of 2011–12, Islamists won 356 out of 508 seats in the lower house. The results of the election were soon invalidated by Egypt's high court, but Morsi called the assembly back into session shortly after he had assumed the presidency, openly defying the high court's ruling.[2] In 2013, at the behest of a sizable percentage of the Egyptian electorate, Morsi was removed in a military-led coup. Egyptian military and security forces later carried out a brutal clearing of Rabi'a al-'Adawiyya Square, where Morsi supporters had encamped; hundreds of protesters were killed. The interim government declared the Muslim Brotherhood a terrorist organization, and the following year, Egyptian courts blocked members of the Brotherhood from running for elective office and ordered the shutdown of the organization's political party. In stark contrast to the 2011–12 parliamentary elections, in 2015 Islamists won only 11 seats out of 596, a loss of 345. With the Muslim Brotherhood driven underground, analysts fear that some Egyptian Islamists will join more militant jihadi groups, including the ISIS affiliate in the Sinai: Ansar Bayt al-Maqdis. Egyptian leaders must confront the reality that a large number of Egyptians are either Islamist or sympathetic to some form of political Islam. The Egyptian government must face the reality that it cannot "jail" or "suppress" its way to acceptable levels of political stability and domestic harmony.

In contrast to the experiences of political Islamists in Turkey and Egypt stand those of Tunisia, where Ennahdha (Renaissance) is the leading Islamist political movement. Its cofounder and leader, Rachid al-Ghannouchi (b. 1941), spent time in exile writing on Muslim economics and constitutionalism and reconciliation of Islam and modernity. What distinguishes him as an Islamist leader is his willingness to compromise with secular politicians to advance his party's agenda and preserve national unity. For an Islamist party to succeed in Tunisia, it must recognize the country's history of organized labor and advancements in women's rights. Ironically, the compromising nature of Islamist politics in Tunisia may explain why Tunisia has furnished a relatively high number of foreign fighters to ISIS. Unwilling to meet halfway, many Tunisian Islamist militants would rather seek change through coercion and violence. Hatred of political compromise may also explain why ISIS refers to the Muslim Brotherhood, which has enjoyed electoral success in Egypt, as the Murtadd (Apostate) Brotherhood and why it scathingly attacks the AKP, which plays an important role in the anti-ISIS coalition.[3]

In January 2015, President Abdel Fatah al-Sisi of Egypt delivered a powerful address to the shaykhs of al-Azhar University, challenging them to lead "a religious revolution" to remove militant extremists from Islam:

> I say . . . that we are in need of a religious revolution. You imams are responsible before Allah. The entire world is waiting on you. The entire world is waiting for your word . . . because the Islamic world is being torn, it is being destroyed, it is being lost. And it is being lost by our own hands. . . .
>
> We need a revolution of the self, a revolution of consciousness and ethics to rebuild the Egyptian person—a person that our country will need in the near future. . . .
>
> It's inconceivable that the thinking that we hold most sacred should cause the entire Islamic world to be a source of anxiety, danger, killing and destruction for the rest of the world. . . . I am not saying the religion—I am saying this thinking. . . .
>
> This [thinking] is antagonizing the entire world. It's antagonizing the entire world! Does this mean that 1.6 billion people [Muslims] should want to kill the rest of the world's inhabitants—that is 7 billion—so that they themselves may live? Impossible![4]

Al-Sisi's message notwithstanding, Muslim reformers in general must cope with autocrats, on the one hand, and militant and political Islamists, on the other. As a result, they must carefully navigate between state security organs and extremist groups, both of which pose an existential threat to advocates of reform. A few recent examples illustrate this point. The Egyptian academic Faraj Foda (1946–92), a staunch defender of secularism and human rights and vocal critic of Islamic fundamentalism, was accused of blasphemy by the clerics of al-Azhar and murdered by the Islamic Group. The Egyptian scholar Nasr Abu Zayd (1943–2010), an authority on the Qur'an and opponent of political Islam, was declared an apostate by a religious court in 1995; death threats forced him to take refuge in Europe. An egregious case involved Mahmoud Taha (ca. 1909–85), a Sudanese intellectual and political leader whose provocative commentaries on the Qur'an resulted in his arrest for apostasy and execution at the hands of the Islamist regime in Khartoum. A current example involves Raif al-Badawi (b. 1984), a Saudi Arabian blogger who decried the influence of Wahhabi clerics over the day-to-day affairs of the country, criticized their symbiotic relationship with the Sa'ud family, and wondered aloud if Wahhabism is capable of reforming itself to deal with the complexities of the twenty-first century. He was charged with slandering Islam and apostasy and sentenced to a term in prison that includes public lashings. His wife and children live under political asylum in Canada. It remains to be seen how well the Wahhabi clergy will react to King Salman's declaration permitting women to drive and the proposed reforms of Crown Prince Mohammed Bin Salman to liberalize the Saudi economy.

In addition to Salafi jihadis, the world faces two competing Islamist systems: first, ultrafundamentalist Wahhabism, which is based on an expression of Islam that succeeded in the austere deserts of seventh-century Arabia, has been the sanctioned religion of the Saudi dynasty since the eighteenth century, and has provided a model for such political-religious entities as the Taliban of Afghanistan, al-Qa'ida, and ISIS; and second, revolutionary Twelve-Imam Shi'ism, which has manifested itself in Khomeinism and the Islamic Republic of Iran and has sought to influence a number of regimes in the Middle East, including Lebanon, Syria, Iraq, and Yemen. The rivalry between the two has ranged from a hostile war of words, to support for warring regional proxies to a battle for new adherents fought online and through satellite media. Reflecting on the Sunni-Shi'a conflict that shook Iraq in 2006–7, American foreign affairs journalist and commentator Fareed Zakaria urged Islam to "make space for differing views about what makes a good Muslim. Then it will be able to take the next step and accept the diversity among religions, each true in its own way."[5]

Islamic reform needs intellectual soil in which to take root. The Internet and social media can provide space for spreading opinion and hosting a vibrant debate, but—as we know all too well—those media are sources of both marvelous *and* repulsive content. From the 1950s through the 1980s, most Muslims lived in a media world consisting of state-controlled television, radio broadcasts, and newspapers. If an individual had a shortwave radio, he or she could access independent news and a variety of political opinions. Today, the Muslim world, with a larger and more youthful population, has at its disposal the Internet, social media, and hundreds of satellite television and radio channels. Before the advent of the World Wide Web and digital media, Muslims could live unaware of differences in religious thought and practice. Today, modern media deliver to a Muslim's home computer and cell phone information ranging from the well-reasoned postings of reformers to the efforts by militant Islamists to shock the public and troll for recruits—and everything in between.

The reality that intellectual diversity exists within the Muslim world cannot be understated. If a person believes that all Muslims think alike, he or she will be unable to appreciate the opportunities and challenges that Islamic reformers face. U.S. military personnel deploying to the Middle East must be aware of the diversity within Islam; otherwise, they will enter their area of operation without genuinely appreciating its human terrain and might fall into the trap of labeling everyone in the country as the enemy, thus defeating the very purpose of their deployment.

Islamic reform is possible but will be difficult to attain. For it to succeed, a conducive environment must be cultivated first within individual Muslim nations, then throughout the Muslim world, and finally around the globe. Let us end this question, this chapter, and our guide on a note of optimism. In December 2015, thirteen activists from a variety of countries and backgrounds gathered in Washington, DC, where they announced the formation of the Muslim Reform Movement. Here is the preamble to its declaration:

We are Muslims who live in the 21st century. We stand for a respectful, merciful and inclusive interpretation of Islam. We are in a battle for the soul of Islam, and an Islamic renewal must defeat the ideology of

Islamism, or politicized Islam, which seeks to create Islamic states, as well as an Islamic caliphate. We seek to reclaim the progressive spirit with which Islam was born in the 7th century to fast forward it into the 21st century. We support the Universal Declaration of Human Rights, which was adopted by United Nations member states in 1948.

We reject interpretations of Islam that call for any violence, social injustice, and politicized Islam. Facing the threat of terrorism, intolerance, and social injustice in the name of Islam, we have reflected on how we can transform our communities based on three principles: peace, human rights, and secular governance. We are announcing today the formation of an international initiative: the Muslim Reform Movement.

We have courageous reformers from around the world who have written our Declaration for Muslim Reform, a living document that we will continue to enhance as our journey continues. We invite our fellow Muslims and neighbors to join us.

The declaration closes with an appeal for global, multidenominational action: "We stand for peace, human rights and secular governance. Please stand with us!"[6]

The authors of this work are honored to have been given the unique opportunity to share these 101 questions and answers with their fellow citizens, particularly the brave men and women of the U.S. armed forces who will deploy to distant stations in the Middle East, Africa, and Central and Southwest Asia, where they will serve on the first line of our nation's defense. Good luck and godspeed.

Notes

Chapter 1. The Physical and Human Geography of the Middle East

1. "International Energy Statistics," U.S. Energy Information Administration, last modified September 21, 2018, https://www.eia.gov.
2. Barack Obama, "Text: Obama's Speech in Cairo," *New York Times*, June 4, 2009, accessed December 9, 2017, http://www.nytimes.com/2009/06/04/us/politics/04obama.text.html.
3. Marshall G. S. Hodgson, *The Classical Age of Islam*, vol. 1 of *The Venture of Islam: Conscience and History in a World Civilization* (Chicago: University of Chicago Press, 1977), 60–61.
4. CENTO (1955–79) was a military alliance established to check Soviet expansion into South Asia and the Middle East. Member states included the United States, the United Kingdom, Iran, Iraq, Pakistan, and Turkey. The alliance is also referred to as the Baghdad Pact and the Middle East Treaty Organization (METO). CENTO is generally regarded as the least effective of all anti-Soviet Cold War alliances.
5. U.S. Central Command, "U.S. Central Command History," accessed October 11, 2017, http://www.centcom.mil/ABOUT-US/HISTORY/.
6. U.S. Department of State, "Near Eastern Affairs: Countries and Other Areas," accessed October 10, 2017, http://www.state.gov/p/nea/ci/.
7. Central Intelligence Agency (CIA), "Middle East," *The World Factbook*, last modified September 29, 2017, accessed October 10, 2017, https://www.cia.gov/library/publications/the-world-factbook/wfbExt/region_mde.html.
8. Middle East Institute, "*Middle East Journal*: Submissions," accessed October 10, 2016, http://www.mei.edu/mej/submissions.
9. Middle East Studies Association, "About," accessed October 10, 2017, http://mesana.org/about.
10. Yassin Al-Haj Saleh, *Impossible Revolution: Making Sense of the Syrian Tragedy* (Chicago: Haymarket Books, 2017), 114.
11. Organization of Islamic Cooperation, "History," accessed October 10, 2017, http://www.oic-oci.org/page/?p_id=52&p_ref=26&lan=en.
12. World Bank, "Middle East and North Africa," accessed October 10, 2017, http://www.worldbank.org/en/region/mena.
13. CIA, "Middle East."
14. Abu Amar, "Our Life in the Zaatari Refugee Camp: No Electricity, No Place to Sleep, No Escape," *Guardian*, last modified September 14, 2015, http://www.theguardian.com/commentisfree/2015/sep/14/life-refugee-camp-syrian-family-jordan-escape.

15. "World Oil Transit Chokepoints: Strait of Hormuz," *EIA: Beta*, last modified July 25, 2017, https://www.eia.gov/beta/international/regions-topics. cfm?RegionTopicID=WOTC.

16. Roger Allen and Shawkat M. Toorawa, eds., *Islam: A Short Guide to the Faith* (Grand Rapids, MI: William B. Eerdmans, 2011), 4.

17. Pew Research Center, Forum on Religion and Public Life, "Mapping the Global Muslim Population," October 7, 2009, http://www.pewforum.org/2009/10/07/ mapping-the-global-muslim-population.

18. Pew Research Center, Forum on Religion and Public Life.

19. CIA, "Middle East"; Tom Heneghan, "Syria's Alawites, a Secret and Persecuted Sect," *Reuters*, January 31, 2012, http://www.reuters.com/article/us-syria-alawites-sect-idUSTRE80U1HK20120131.

20. Heneghan.

21. Eliza Griswold, "Is This the End of Christianity in the Middle East?" *New York Times Magazine*, July 22, 2015, http://www.nytimes.com/2015/07/26/magazine/is-this-the-end-of-christianity-in-the-middle-east.html?_r=0.

22. Pierre Tristam, "Christians of the Middle East: Country-by-Country Facts: A Presence Dating Back Two Millennia," *Thought Co.*, accessed January 18, 2016, http://middleeast.about.com/od/middleeast101/a/christians-middleeast.htm.

23. Avi Asher-Schapiro, "Who Are the Yazidis, the Ancient, Persecuted Religious Minority Struggling to Survive in Iraq?" *National Geographic*, August 11, 2014, http://news.nationalgeographic.com/news/2014/08/140809-iraq-yazidis-minority-isil-religion-history.

Chapter 2. The Ancient Middle East

1. William L. Cleveland and Martin Brunton, *A History of the Modern Middle East*, 6th ed. (Boulder, CO: Westview Press, 2016), 1.

2. "The Behistan Inscription," in *The Behistan Inscription of King Darius*, trans. Herbert Cushing Tolman (Nashville, TN: Vanderbilt University Press, 1908), published online in 1998, accessed January 29, 2016, http://mcadams.posc.mu.edu/txt/ah/Persia/ Behistun_txt.html.

3. Gareth C. Sampson, *The Defeat of Rome: Crassus, Carrhae, and the Invasion of the East* (Barnsley, UK: Pen and Sword Books, 2008), 169–81.

Chapter 3. The Prophet Muhammad and the Emergence of Islam

1. Quotations from the Qur'an appearing in this book are from "The Meaning of the Glorious Quran: Text, Translation, & Commentary by Abdullah Yusuf Ali," *The Glorious Quran*, IslamicBulletin.org, accessed October 20, 2017, http://www. islamicbulletin.org/free_downloads/quran/quran_yusuf_ali2.pdf. To facilitate the reader's understanding, the authors have replaced some original (vintage) English words with their modern equivalents. For example, "thee" has been replaced with "you."

2. John Alden Williams, ed., *The World of Islam* (Austin: University of Texas Press, 1994), 37–40.

3. Scott Horton, "Tacitus on the Costs of War," *Harper's Magazine*, November 26, 2007, https://harpers.org/blog/2007/11/tacitus-on-the-costs-of-war/.

4. "The Last Sermon of the Prophet Muhammad," *Hadith of the Day*, September 8, 2012, http://hadithoftheday.com/the-last-sermon/.

5. Because the *shahada* is foundational to Islam, you can appreciate the outrage throughout the Muslim world when Syrian security forces loyal to President

Bashar al-Asad forced captured protesters to shout, "There is no god but Bashar!" The images were captured on cell phone, posted on social media, and shown on antiregime television channels. This blasphemous act helped transform many Syrian demonstrators into armed insurgents and fueled the recruitment of foreign fighters to engage in battle against the al-Asad government.

Chapter 4. The High Caliphate

1. This hadith, "The Hadith of Ghadir [the Oasis] of Khumm," is not included in the al-Bukhari volumes of hadith but can be found in the Ibn Hanbal volumes (16:152, 4:281, 368, 372–73) and the volumes of al-Tirmidhi (16:165). Two scholarly studies in English on this particular hadith are *Shi'ism: Doctrines, Thought, and Spirituality*, edited by Seyyed Hossein Nasr, Hamid Dabashi, and Seyyed Vali Reza Nasr (Albany: State University of New York Press, 1988), and *Charismatic Community: The Shi'ite Identity in Early Islam* by Maria Massi Dakake (Albany: State University of New York Press, 2008).
2. This hadith can found in the volumes of Ibn Maja (2:1303) and the volumes of Abu Dawud (bk. 35, no. 4240). Both are referred to as *Kitab al-Fitan* (Book of Dissention).
3. For a time, the 'Abbasids governed from al-Raqqa, in present-day Syria. Fast-forwarding nearly thirteen hundred years, al-Raqqa served as the seat of government for ISIS, but comparisons between the Islamic State and the 'Abbasids end with that historical coincidence.

Chapter 5. Islamic Law and Medieval Muslim Civilization

1. Thomas W. Lippman, *Understanding Islam: An Introduction to the Muslim World*, rev. ed. (New York: Penguin Books, 1990), 70.
2. This hadith, also quoted in response to Question 17, can be found in the volumes of Ibn Maja (2:1303) and the volumes of Abu Dawud (bk. 35, no. 4240). Both are referred to as *Kitab al-Fitan* (*Book of Dissention*).

Chapter 6. Invaders, Conquerors, and Warriors

1. The Nur al-Din Zangi Mosque in Mosul was deliberately destroyed by ISIS when they withdrew from the city in 2017. The mosque, built in 1174, was an important symbol of Iraqi and Islamic heritage.
2. When the French army occupied Damascus in 1920, General Henri Gouraud (1867–1946) reportedly mocked the tomb of Salah al-Din by declaring, "We are back!" Whether true or not, the account illustrates the impact of the Crusades on popular imagination.
3. Akh. Minhaji, *Islamic Law and Local Tradition: A Socio-Historical Approach* (Yogyakarta, Indonesia: Kurnia Kalam Semestra Press, 2008), 93.
4. At the site of the Battle of Marj Dabiq, ISIS declared the ultimate battle between the forces of Islam and Christianity—a precursor to end times. Interestingly, the English-language magazine published by ISIS (2014–16) was titled *Dabiq*.

Chapter 7. The Rise of the Ottoman and Safavid Dynasties

1. Bogomilism, named for the priest Bogomil, originated in Bulgaria in the tenth century. It was a Christian Gnostic movement that rejected the physical church and all its trappings; instead, it regarded the human body as the sacred temple. Its adherents engaged in various forms of ritual cleansing and purging of the body. Bogomils also believed in a dualistic world, one divided between God and Satan.

Believing that institutions were creations of Satan, Bogomils refused to pay taxes and resisted the feudal social order. Bogomilism threatened the peace and stability of the Balkans.

2. Marshall G. S. Hodgson, *The Gunpowder Empires and Modern Times*, vol. 3, *The Venture of Islam: Conscience and History in a World Civilization* (Chicago: University of Chicago Press, 1974), 1, 26.

Chapter 8. The Rise of Western Influence in the Middle East

1. 'Abd al-Rahman al-Jabarti, *Napoleon in Egypt: Al-Jabarti's Chronicle of the French Occupation, 1798*, intro by Shmuel Moreh, trans. Robert L. Tignor (Princeton, NJ: Markus Weiner, 1993), 24, 26.
2. Jabarti, 106.
3. Mehmet 'Ali's ascent to power in Egypt was the first time in Egyptian history that the voice of local leaders was considered in the selection of their governor. In this case, the Ottoman sultan acceded to the wishes of prominent Egyptians, namely, 'Umar Makram (d. 1822), who had been a leading anti-French dissident. Once in power, Mehmet 'Ali discarded Makram and governed Egypt as an absolute ruler, thus perpetuating foreign domination over the country until the Egyptian Revolution of 1952. A mosque and statue adjacent to Cairo's Tahrir Square honor 'Umar Makram.
4. The Turkish term "pasha" loosely equates to the title "lord." The term is also used in Arabic although it is literally transliterated as "basha" because there is no equivalent of the letter *p* in the Arabic alphabet. The Turkish term "bey" is equivalent to "sir."

Chapter 9. The Emergence of Nationalism in the Middle East

1. Arthur Goldschmidt and Aomar Boum, *A Concise History of the Middle East*, 11th ed. (Boulder, CO: Westview Press, 2016), 164.
2. Sultan Murat V, a nephew of 'Abdulaziz, ruled from 30 May to 31 August 1876. A committed liberal, Murat was deposed on the grounds of mental instability and replaced by his brother 'Abdulhamid II. Murat died in 1904.
3. The argument that a caliph must be an Arab persists among militant Islamists today. It was a criticism hurled by militants at the so-called Commander of the Faithful, Mullah Muhammad 'Umar (d. 2013), leader of the Afghan Taliban. Mullah 'Umar, a Pashtun, was born near Kandahar, Afghanistan.
4. Walter Laqueur and Barry Rubin, eds., *The Israeli–Arab Reader: A Documentary History of the Middle East Conflict*, 7th ed. (New York: Penguin Books, 2008), 10.
5. Laqueur and Rubin, 16.

Chapter 10. The Middle East between the World Wars

1. During Operation Iraqi Freedom (2003–11), American combat forces battled an Iraqi insurgent group named the 1920 Brigades.
2. Robert Lacey, *The Kingdom: Arabia and the House of Sa'ud* (New York: Avon Books, 1981), 526–29.

Chapter 11. Egyptian Independence, the Zionist Movement, and the Creation of Israel

1. Egypt has since memorialized the event as Police Day, but on 25 January 2011 antigovernment demonstrators used that holiday to initiate their nationwide protests, illustrating just how low the public's esteem for the police had fallen.

2. Other founders of the Non-Aligned Movement were Josip Broz Tito (1892–1980) of Yugoslavia, Sukarno (1901–70) of Indonesia, Jawaharlal Nehru (1889–1964) of India, and Kwame Nkrumah (1909–72) of Ghana.

3. In 1906 Alfred Dreyfus was exonerated, restored to the army, and promoted to major. The actual spy in the pay of Germany was Major Ferdinand Esterhazy (1847–1923), who fled to Great Britain, where he lived out the rest of his life.

4. Laqueur and Rubin, *Israeli-Arab Reader*, 28.

5. Laqueur and Rubin, 45.

6. Deborah Dayan, *Pioneer*, trans. Michael Plashkes (Tel Aviv: Massada Press, 1968), 83.

7. In 1950 Ralph Bunche became the first African American to win the Noble Prize for Peace, and in 1963 President John F. Kennedy awarded him the Presidential Medal of Freedom.

Chapter 12. Turkey after Atatürk, Iran under Mohammed Reza Shah, and the Arab World after World War II

1. Peacock Throne is a metonym referring to the Persian monarchy since the time of Nadir Shah. The original Peacock Throne was constructed by the Mughal emperor Shah Jahan (r. 1628–58), who also built the splendid Taj Mahal in Delhi, India. Nadir looted the throne from the Mughals, but it was lost after his assassination. Later Persian sovereigns sat on a replica throne. The Qajar shah Fath-'Ali (r. 1797–1834) ordered construction of the exquisite Naderi (Sun) Throne, which is erroneously referred to as the Peacock Throne. The Pahlavi shahs used the Naderi Throne in their coronations.

2. According to documents declassified in June 2017, CIA headquarters had attempted to abort the coup against Mosaddiq, but Roosevelt ignored the cable and pressed on. The documents also show that Ayatollah Abol-Ghasem Kashani (1882–1962), believing that Mosaddiq was too weak to contain the growing strength of the communist Tudeh Party, collaborated with the Americans to oust the prime minister. Bethany Allen-Ebrahimian, "64 Years Later, CIA Finally Releases Details of Iranian Coup," *Foreign Policy*, June 20, 2017, http://foreignpolicy.com/2017/06/20/64-years-later-cia-finally-releases-details-of-iranian-coup-iran-tehran-oil/.

3. Michel 'Aflaq, "In Memory of the Arab Prophet," April 5, 1943, trans. Ziad el Jishi, Al Baath Online, accessed June 11, 2017, http://albaath.online.fr/English/Aflaq-00-In-Memory-of-the-Arab-Prophet.htm.

4. With the onset of civil war, the al-Asad regime replaced absolute Arabism with absolute Syrianism in the singular quest to remain in power.

5. Nasser's close friend Field Marshal 'Abd al-Hakim 'Amer (1919–67), the Egyptian minister of defense and army chief of staff, proved incompetent in managing the union with Syria. Nasser was blind to 'Amer's mismanagement of important governmental matters, which would culminate in the debacle of the Six-Day War of June 1967. 'Amer, who panicked during Israel's lightning fast drive toward the Suez Canal, had no plan to evacuate his troops from the Sinai. In the aftermath of the defeat, the two friends had a tragic falling out that led to 'Amer's suicide.

6. The term "fatah" means conquest. It is also a reverse Arabic acronym standing for the Palestinian National Liberation Movement.

Chapter 13. The Arab-Israeli Conflict, 1967–73

1. General Riad (1919–69) is considered one of the Egyptian military's most innovative thinkers. He was unmarried, apolitical, and dedicated to Egyptian arms. He later

served as armed forces chief of staff. He died when an Israeli artillery shell hit his foxhole while he was inspecting defense works along the Suez Canal in 1969.

2. "The Six-Day War: Resources, Documents, Photos and Video: The Khartoum Resolutions, September 1, 1967," Committee for Accuracy in Middle East Reporting in America (CAMERA), accessed November 8, 2017, http://www.sixdaywar.org/content/docs.asp#khartoum.

3. Some Muslim clerics, such as Egypt's Shaykh 'Abd al-Hamid Kishk (1933–96), argued that the main reason for the Israeli victory in 1967 was the Jewish people's commitment to their faith and that the only remedy for this humiliating defeat was a return to Islam.

4. Laqueur and Rubin, *Israeli-Arab Reader*, 116.

5. Laqueur and Rubin, 152.

6. The state of peace between Egypt and Israel is described by many observers as cold. It remains to be seen if radical Islam can serve as a catalyst to move both sides toward full reconciliation. Of note, every Egyptian leader from al-Sadat's successor Hosni Mubarak to the current president, Abdel Fatah al-Sisi, and even the Muslim Brotherhood's Mohammed Morsi, has expressed his commitment to upholding the 1979 peace treaty.

7. British Overseas Airways Corporation (BOAC; now British Airways), Swiss Air, and Trans World Airlines airliners were flown to Jordan. A Pan American airliner was flown to Cairo.

8. "Black September Plea to Israel," BBC News World Edition, January 1, 2001, http://news.bbc.co.uk/2/hi/middle_east/1095221.stm.

9. "Jordan Asked Nixon to Attack Syria, Declassified Papers Show," CNN, November 28, 2007, http://edition.cnn.com/2007/POLITICS/11/28/nixon.papers/.

10. "The War of Attrition: The Rogers Plan (December 9, 1969)," Jewish Virtual Library, accessed June 24, 2017, http://www.jewishvirtuallibrary.org/the-rogers-plan-december-1969.

11. Abraham Rabinovich, "Moshe Dayan's Yom Kippur War," *Jerusalem Post*, October 6, 2013, http://www.jpost.com/Opinion/Op-Ed-Contributors/Moshe-Dayans-Yom-Kippur-War-328029.

12. The United States increased its Defense Readiness Condition (DEFCON) posture from level 4 to 3, with 1 being all-out war, to deter the Soviets from intervening in Egypt. CIA documents declassified in 2016 reveal the decision was driven by intelligence that Moscow had prepared the deployment of nuclear weapons to Egypt. Tim Naftali, "CIA Reveals Its Secret Briefings to Presidents Nixon and Ford," CNN, August 26, 2016, www.cnn.com/2016/08/26/opinions/secret-briefings-to-presidents-from-cia-naftali.

13. The October 1973 Arab-Israeli War included some of the largest tank battles in military history. Thousands of Soviet-supplied tanks were deployed by Egyptian and Syrian forces against American-supplied Israeli armor.

Chapter 14. Revolutionary Iran

1. Jimmy Carter, "Tehran, Iran, Toasts of the President and the Shah at a State Dinner, December 31, 1977," *American Presidency Project*, ed. Gerhard Peters and John T. Woolley, accessed July 3, 2017, http://www.presidency.ucsb.edu/ws/?pid=7080.

2. For a brief documentary review of Mohammed Reza Shah's departure from Iran and the return of Ayatollah Khomeini, see "7 Million People Fill the Streets—the Imam Has Returned!" YouTube, 14:59, episode 5 of Al-Manar's documentary *Ruhollah*,

posted by Middle East Observer, February 1, 2013, https://www.youtube.com/watch?v=2iCzeO1OksA.

3. "Iran (Islamic Republic of)'s Constitution of 1979 with Amendments through 1989," Constitute, last modified June 6, 2017, accessed July 4, 2017, https://www.constituteproject.org/constitution/Iran_1989.pdf?lang=en.

4. Ayatollah Khomeini charged Hassan Habibi (1937–2013), a French-educated sociologist, lawyer, and Iranian political figure, with drafting the constitution of the Islamic Republic. The document was influenced by the constitution of the French Fifth Republic and contained ideas from modern Islamist political thought. See Siavush Randjbar-Daemi, "Building the Islamic State: The Draft Constitution of 1979 Reconsidered," *Journal of Iranian Studies* 46, no. 4 (2013): 641–63, https://doi.org/10.1080/00210862.2013.784519.

5. A prominent Iranian officer who was influenced by the brutality of the Iran-Iraq War is General Qassem Suleimani (b. 1957), commander of the IRGC's Quds Force. Since the late 1990s, he has played a leading role in Iran's clandestine activities in Iraq, Syria, and Afghanistan; he is a formidable adversary of the United States. Dexter Filkins, "The Shadow Commander," *New Yorker*, September 30, 2013, www.newyorker.com/magazine/2013/09/30/the-shadow-commander.

Chapter 15. Developments in Egypt since 1973

1. Laqueur and Rubin, *Israeli-Arab Reader*, 206.

2. It is important to remember that the Muslim Brotherhood is generally considered an Islamist political organization, meaning it wishes to impose its interpretation of Islam on Muslims and non-Muslims alike through electoral or other nonviolent means. Over the past nine decades, however, it has demonstrated periods of extreme violence.

3. While attending Egyptian universities, several Sudanese, Palestinian, Syrian, and Yemeni students were exposed to the teachings of the Muslim Brotherhood, and after they had returned home, they established local branches of the Brotherhood. Nasser's repression of the Brotherhood forced thousands of its members to seek asylum in Saudi Arabia and other gulf states. Many of them filled teaching positions in schools and universities, where they introduced a new generation of Arabs to their brand of Islamist political activism. Among these teachers was Usama Bin Ladin, who became a critic of Islamist political activism and embraced the theories of Sayyid Qutb, who argued that violence was an effective means of establishing an Islamist social order.

4. Mohamed Heikal, *Autumn of Fury: The Assassination of Sadat* (New York: Random House, 1983), 255.

5. Gilles Kepel, *Muslim Extremism in Egypt: The Prophet and Pharaoh* (Berkeley: University of California Press, 1986), 192.

6. The judges found electoral irregularities that favored organized parties, namely, the Islamist parties. For example, there were several instances of candidates running as independents in the first round of voting and then running as members of a political party for the same office in the second electoral round.

Chapter 16. National Tragedies in Lebanon and Syria

1. Thomas Hobbes, "Hobbes: *The Leviathan*," in *The Western Tradition*, vol. 2, *From the Renaissance to the Present*, 4th ed., ed. Eugen Weber (Lexington, MA: D. C. Heath, 1990), 442.

Chapter 17. Iraq from the Rise of Saddam to the Fragile Beginnings of Democracy

1. In 2003 Saddam was hidden by the same Tikriti clan that protected him after his participation in the failed attempt to assassinate General 'Abd al-Karim Qasim in 1959.
2. Saddam Hussein's declarations in July 1990 were not the first time an Iraqi leader threatened to invade Kuwait. In 1961 'Abd al-Karim Qasim blustered that he would restore the small shaykhdom to the Iraqi state. He backed down when he was confronted by demonstrations of British military power in the Persian Gulf.
3. George H. W. Bush, "Public Papers: Remarks and an Exchange with Reporters on the Iraqi Invasion of Kuwait," August 5, 1990, George H. W. Bush Presidential Library and Museum, College Station, TX, https://bush41library.tamu.edu/archives/public-papers/2138.
4. Among the Arab forces participating in Operation Desert Storm were 50,000 Syrian troops, deployed by President Hafiz al-Asad, Saddam's longtime Ba'thist rival.
5. Patrick Cockburn, *Muqtada al-Sadr and the Shia Insurgency in Iraq* (London: Faber and Faber, 2008), 116.
6. United Nations Security Council, Resolution 677, S/RES/677 (Nov. 28, 1990), http://www.un.org/en/ga/search/view_doc.asp?symbol=S/RES/677(1990).
7. Saddam Hussein's invasion of Kuwait and Operation Desert Storm directly affected the lives of this work's two authors. While a graduate student in the United States, Youssef Aboul-Enein was paralyzed with worry over his parents and brothers then living in Riyadh, which came under attack from Iraqi Scuds. Months earlier he had almost not made it back to the United States because he was visiting his family for the summer holiday when Saddam attacked Kuwait. He managed to board one of the last flights out of Riyadh for New York. This experience instilled in him a desire to join the U.S. military, which he did in 1994, after he had completed two master's degrees. Four years later, he deployed on board the USS *Guam* (LPH 9) and with the 24th Marine Expeditionary Unit in support of Operation Southern Watch, finally getting a chance to check the actions of Saddam. In 1992 Joseph Stanik served as the Tomahawk Land Attack Missile (TLAM) strike planner on the staff of the Commander U.S. Naval Forces Central Command (now the U.S. Fifth Fleet), embarked in the flagship USS *La Salle* (AGF-3), in the Persian Gulf. He served successively under Rear Admiral Raynor A. K. Taylor and Vice Admiral Douglas J. Katz. At a time when Saddam repeatedly hindered the efforts of the UN's weapons of mass destruction inspection teams, he was preoccupied with ensuring the Navy's arsenal of Tomahawk cruise missiles in-theater was mission ready.
8. Colin Freeman, "Saddam Hussein's Palaces, *Telegraph*, July 16, 2009, www.telegraph.co.uk/news/worldnews/middleeast/iraq/Saddam-Hussein-palaces.html.
9. In September 2017, the autonomous Kurdistan Regional Government held a referendum on independence for Iraqi Kurdistan. The measure passed with 94 percent of the votes cast, a cause of concern for the governments of Iraq, Turkey, Iran, and the United States, which had long supported a unified Iraqi state.
10. Saddam developed an extensive smuggling network to ship petroleum through Syria and Turkey thereby eluding the watchful eyes of coalition monitors. When ISIS took control of parts of Iraq and Syria, they used these routes to trade oil to finance their "caliphate."
11. Nomyr El-Hadi, "Ayat Seestani Opposes Any Foreign Dominion," Jafariyanews.com, April 26, 2003, http://www.jafariyanews.com/2k3_news/apr/26_seestani.htm.

Chapter 18. The Israeli-Palestinian Conflict and Peace Process since the Late 1980s

1. "2000: 'Provocative' Mosque Visit Sparks Riots," *BBC Home: On This Day, 1950–2005: 28 September*, updated 2008, accessed August 25, 2017, http://news.bbc.co.uk/onthisday/hi/dates/stories/september/28/newsid_3687000/3687762.stm.

2. U.S. Department of State, "Israel and the Occupied Territories," *2004 Country Reports on Human Rights Practices*, February 28, 2005, https://www.state.gov/j/drl/rls/hrrpt/2004/41723.htm.

3. After Netanyahu reclaimed the prime minister's office in 2009, he ordered two armed incursions into Gaza: Operation Pillar of Defense in 2012 and Operation Protective Edge in 2014.

Chapter 19. Understanding Islamist Extremism in the Twenty-First Century

1. "Interview Osama Bin Laden (May 1998)," *Frontline: Hunting Bin Laden*, accessed September 30, 2017, http://www.pbs.org/wgbh/pages/frontline/shows/binladen/who/interview.html.

2. Abu Bakr al-Baghdadi also claims that he is a descendant of the Prophet Muhammad, but this assertion is most probably contrived. The claim is likely the invention of al-Baghdadi's acolyte, the Bahraini-born Turki Mubarak 'Abdullah Ahmed al-Binali (1984–2017), who served as spiritual leader of ISIS until he was eliminated in a U.S. air strike.

Chapter 20. Combatting Islamist Extremism in the Twenty-First Century

1. In the early 2000s, followers of Turkish Islamist Fethullah Gülen supported Recep Tayyip Erdoğan's rise to national power, but at the time of this writing, they are viewed by Turkish authorities as a cabal bent on overthrowing Erdoğan's government. Gülen, who lives in exile in Pennsylvania, is a convenient scapegoat for the Turkish leader's political difficulties.

2. In the first round of voting for the Egyptian assembly, several candidates ran as individuals. Then, in the second round, they stood for election as part of a political bloc. The Egyptian high court ruled that, in effect, they had run as different candidates in the two rounds of voting—a practice that favored an organized political group, such as the Muslim Brotherhood.

3. In 1994 Ayman al-Zawahiri published *The Bitter Harvest*, in which he attacks the Muslim Brotherhood as a failed experiment in Islamist politics. His strategy for achieving a desired political outcome is direct violent action.

4. Dana Ford, Salma Abdelaziz, and Ian Lee, "Egypt's President Calls for a 'Religious Revolution,'" CNN World, January 6, 2015, http://www.cnn.com/2015/01/06/africa/egypt-president-speech/index.html.

5. Fareed Zakaria, "The Road to Reformation; Al Qaeda Had Hoped to Rally the Entire Muslim World against the West, but Now It Is in the Middle of a Dirty Sectarian War within Islam," *Newsweek*, February 12, 2007.

6. "Muslim Reform Movement," Muslim Reform Movement: A Global Coalition of Muslim Reformers, December 4, 2015, https://muslimreformmovement.org/wp-content/uploads/2017/08/Declaration-1.pdf.

Selected Bibliography

General Readings and Viewings

Armajani, Yahya, and Thomas M. Ricks. *Middle East: Past and Present.* 2nd ed. Englewood Cliffs, NJ: Prentice Hall, 1986.

Ash, David, and Dai Richards, dirs. *The 50 Years War: Israel and the Arabs,* 1999. Arlington, VA: PBS Home Video, 2000. DVD.

Bacevich, Andrew J. *America's War for the Greater Middle East: A Military History.* New York: Random House, 2017.

Bickerton, Ian J., and Carla L. Klausner. *A History of the Arab-Israeli Conflict.* New York: Routledge, 2018.

Bolger, Daniel P. *Americans at War, 1975–1986: An Era of Violent Peace.* Novato, CA: Presidio Press, 1988.

———. *Savage Peace: Americans at War in the 1990s.* Novato, CA: Presidio Press, 1995.

Brockelmann, Carl, and Moshe Perlmann. *History of the Islamic Peoples.* Translated by Joel Carmichael and Moshe Perlmann. New York: G. P. Putnam's Sons, 1947.

Cleveland, William L., and Martin Brunton. *A History of the Modern Middle East.* 6th ed. Boulder, CO: Westview Press, 2016.

Egger, Vernon O. *A History of the Muslim World since 1260: The Making of a Global Community.* 2nd ed. New York: Routledge, 2018.

———. *A History of the Muslim World to 1405: The Making of a Civilization.* 2nd ed. New York: Routledge, 2017.

Gardner, Robert H., dir. *Islam: Empire of Faith.* 2002; Arlington, VA: PBS Home Video, 2005. DVD.

Gasiorowski, Mark, and Sean L. Yom, eds. *The Government and Politics of the Middle East and North Africa.* 8th ed. Boulder, CO: Westview Press, 2017.

Gelvin, James L. *The Israel-Palestine Conflict: One Hundred Years of War.* 3rd ed. New York: Cambridge University Press, 2014.

———. *The Modern Middle East: A History.* 4th ed. New York: Oxford University Press, 2016.

Gettleman, Marvin E., and Stuart Schaar, eds. *The Middle East and Islamic World Reader.* Rev. ed. New York: Grove Press, 2005.

Gilbert, Martin. *The Routledge Atlas of the Arab-Israeli Conflict.* 10th ed. New York: Routledge, 2012.

Goldschmidt, Arthur, and Aomar Boum. *A Concise History of the Middle East.* 11th ed. Boulder, CO: Westview Press, 2016.

Held, Colbert C., and John Thomas Cummings. *Middle East Patterns: Places, Peoples, and Politics.* 6th ed. New York: Routledge, 2018.

Herzog, Chaim, and Shlomo Gazit. *The Arab-Israeli Wars: War and Peace in the Middle East.* Rev. ed. New York: Vintage Books, 2005.

Hodson, Marshall G. S. *The Venture of Islam: Conscience and History in a World Civilization.* 3 vols. Chicago: University of Chicago Press, 1977.

Hudson, Michael C. *Arab Politics: The Search for Legitimacy.* New Haven, CT: Yale University Press, 1977.

Kerr, Gordon. *A Short History of the Middle East: From Ancient Empires to Islamic State.* Harpenden, UK: Pocket Essentials, 2016.

Lapidus, Ira M. *A History of Islamic Societies.* 3rd ed. New York: Cambridge University Press, 2014.

Laqueur, Walter, and Barry Rubin, eds. *The Arab-Israeli Reader: A Documentary History of the Middle East Conflict.* 7th ed. New York: Penguin Books, 2008.

Lee, Robert D. *Religion and Politics in the Middle East: Identity, Ideology, Institutions, and Attitudes.* Boulder, CO: Westview Press, 2013.

Lenczowski, George. *The Middle East in World Affairs.* 4th ed. Ithaca, NY: Cornell University Press, 1980.

Lewis, Bernard. *The Middle East: A Brief History of the Last 2,000 Years.* New York: Touchstone, 1997.

Lust, Ellen, ed. *The Middle East.* 14th ed. Washington, DC: CQ Press, 2016.

Mansfield, Peter. *A History of the Middle East.* 4th ed. New York: Penguin Books, 2013.

Martin, David C., and John Walcott. *Best Laid Plans: The Inside Story of America's War against Terrorism.* New York: Harper and Row, 1988.

Ochsenwald, William, and Sidney Nettleton Fisher. *The Middle East: A History.* 7th ed. Boston: McGraw Hill, 2010.

Rogan, Eugene. *The Arabs: A History.* New York: Basic Books, 2017.

Smith, Charles D. *Palestine and the Arab-Israeli Conflict: A History with Documents.* 9th ed. Boston: Bedford/St. Martin's, 2017.

Smith, Dan. *The Penguin State of the Middle East Atlas.* 3rd ed. New York: Penguin Books, 2016.

Tessler, Mark. *A History of the Israeli-Palestinian Conflict.* Bloomington: Indiana University Press, 2009.

Tucker, Ernest. *The Middle East in Modern World History.* Boston: Pearson, 2013.

Tyler, Patrick. *A World of Trouble: The White House and the Middle East—From the Cold War to the War on Terror.* New York: Farrar, Straus and Giroux, 2009.

Recommended Readings and Viewings
Chapter 1: The Physical and Human Geography of the Middle East

Barr, James. *A Line in the Sand: The Anglo-French Struggle for the Middle East.* New York: W. W. Norton, 2012.

Beaumont, Peter, Gerald H. Blake, and J. Malcolm Wagstaff. *The Middle East: A Geographical Study.* 2nd ed. London: David Fulton, 1988.

Coon, Carleton S. *Caravan: The Story of the Middle East.* Rev. ed. New York: Holt, Rinehart and Winston, 1958.

Glubb, John. *A Short History of the Arab Peoples.* New York: Barnes & Noble, 1995.

Hammond Atlas of the Middle East and Northern Africa. Union, NJ: Hammond World Atlas, 2006.

Hitti, Philip K., and Walid Khalidi. *History of the Arabs.* Rev. 10th ed. New York: Palgrave Macmillan, 2002.

Hourani, Albert. *A History of the Arab Peoples*. Cambridge, MA: Belknap Press of Harvard University Press, 1991.

Johnson, Paul. *A History of the Jews*. New York: Harper Perennial, 1987.

Jones, Toby Craig. *Desert Kingdom: How Oil and Water Forged Modern Saudi Arabia*. Cambridge, MA: Harvard University Press, 2010.

Kertzer, Morris N. *What Is a Jew? A Guide to the Beliefs, Traditions, and Practices of Judaism That Answers Questions for Both Jew and Non-Jew*. Rev. ed. Revised by Lawrence A. Hoffman. New York: Touchstone, 1996.

Khalaf, Samir, and Roseanne Saad Khalaf, eds. *Arab Youth: Social Mobilization in Times of Risk*. London: Saqi Books, 2012.

Koppes, Clayton R. "Captain Mahan, General Gordon, and the Origin of the Term 'Middle East.'" *Middle East Studies* 12, no. 1 (1976): 95–98.

Lewis, Bernard. *The Arabs in History*. 6th ed. Oxford: Oxford University Press, 2002.

Mansfield, Peter. *The Arabs*. 3rd ed. New York: Penguin Books, 1992.

Masani, Rustom. *Zoroastrianism: The Religion of the Good Life*. New York: Macmillan, 1971.

National Geographic Atlas of the Middle East: The Most Concise and Current Source on the World's Most Complex Region. 2nd ed. Washington, DC: National Geographic, 2008.

Nydell, Margaret K. *Understanding Arabs: A Contemporary Guide to Arab Society*. 5th ed. Boston: Intercultural Press, 2012.

Peters, James. *The Arab World Handbook: The Essential Guide for Business Travelers, Expatriates and Tourists*. Arabian Peninsula and Iraq ed. London: Stacey International, 2010.

Rogan, Eugene. *The Arabs: A History*. New York: Basic Books, 2017.

Sharkawi, Muhammad Al-. *History and Development of the Arabic Language: From Pre-Islamic Times to the Age of Conquests*. New York: Routledge, 2017.

Yergin, Daniel. *The Prize: The Epic Quest for Oil, Money, and Power*. New York: Simon & Schuster, 1991.

Chapter 2: The Ancient Middle East

Dzeilska, Maria. *Hypatia of Alexandria*. Translated by F. Lyra. Cambridge, MA: Harvard University Press, 1995. (See also the film based on the book: *Agora*. Directed by Alejandro Amenábar. 2009; Santa Monica, CA: Lionsgate Home Entertainment, 2010. DVD.)

Farrokh, Kaveh. *Iran at War: 1500–1988*. Oxford: Osprey, 2011.

Goldberg, Andrew, and Ray Suarez. *Jerusalem: Center of the World*. Produced and directed by Andrew Goldberg. 2009; Arlington, VA: PBS Home Video, 2009. DVD.

Grant, Michael. *The Ancient Mediterranean*. New York: History Book Club, 2002.

———. *Constantine the Great: The Man and His Times*. New York: Barnes & Noble, 1998.

———. *The History of Ancient Israel*. New York: History Book Club, 2002.

Hoyland, Robert G. *Arabia and the Arabs: From the Bronze Age to the Coming of Islam*. New York: Routledge, 2001.

Jenkins, Philip. *Jesus Wars: How Four Patriarchs, Three Queens, and Two Emperors Decided What Christians Would Believe for the Next 1,500 Years*. New York: Harper One, 2010.

Kriwaczek, Paul. *Babylon: Mesopotamia and the Birth of Civilization*. New York: Thomas Dunne Books, 2010.

Snell, Daniel C. *Life in the Ancient Middle East, 3100–332 B.C.E.* New Haven, CT: Yale University Press, 1997.

Starr, Chester G. *A History of the Ancient World*. 4th ed. New York: Oxford University Press, 1991.

Wilkinson, Toby. *Rise and Fall of Ancient Egypt*. New York: Random House, 2013.

Chapter 3: The Prophet Muhammad and the Emergence of Islam

Ali, Abdullah Yusuf, trans. *The Holy Qur'an*. Hertfordshire, UK: Wordsworth Editions, 2000.

Allen, Roger, and Shawkat M. Toorawa, eds. *Islam: A Short Guide to the Faith*. Grand Rapids, MI: Wm. B. Eerdmans, 2011.

Armstrong, Karen. *Muhammad: A Prophet for Our Time*. New York: HarperCollins, 2006.

Barker, Greg, dir. *Koran by Heart*. 2011; New York: HBO Home Entertainment, 2011. DVD.

Bonney, Richard. *From Qu'ran to Bin Laden*. New York: Palgrave Macmillan, 2004.

Donner, Fred M. *Muhammad and the Believers: At the Origins of Islam*. Cambridge, MA: Harvard University Press, 2012.

Esposito, John L. *Islam: The Straight Path*. 5th ed. New York: Oxford University Press, 2016.

———. *What Everyone Needs to Know about Islam: Answers to Frequently Asked Questions, from One of America's Leading Experts*. 2nd ed. New York: Oxford University Press, 2011.

Flaster, Alex. *Decoding the Past: Secrets of the Koran*. 2006; New York: History Channel, 2006. DVD.

Gibb, H. A. R. *Mohammedanism: An Historical Survey*. 2nd ed. London: Oxford University Press, 1982.

Guillaume, Alfred. *Islam*. New York: Penguin Books, 1981.

Hazleton, Lesley. *The First Muslim: The Story of Muhammad*. New York: Riverhead Books, 2013.

Lings, Martin. *Muhammad: His Life Based on the Earliest Sources*. Rev. ed. Rochester, VT: Inner Traditions, 2006.

Lippman, Thomas W. *Understanding Islam: An Introduction to the Muslim World*. Rev. ed. New York: Penguin Books, 1990.

Mehdi, Anisa, and John Bredar. *Inside Mecca*. Directed by Anisa Mehdi. 2003; Washington, DC: National Geographic Society, 2009. DVD.

Omaar, Rageh. *The Life of Muhammad*. Produced and directed by Faris Kermani. 2011; Arlington, VA: PBS Home Video, 2013. DVD.

Qattan, Omar al-, dir. *Muhammad: Legacy of a Prophet*. 2002. Potomac Falls, VA: Unity Productions Foundation, 2011. DVD.

Quinn, Anthony. *The Message*. Directed by Moustapha Akkad. 1976; Beverly Hills, CA: Anchor Bay Entertainment, 2005. DVD.

Sells, Michael. *Approaching the Qur'an*. Ashland, OR: White Cloud Press, 2007.

West, Douglas Brooks. *Inside Islam: A Sweeping Story of One of the World's Great Faiths*. Directed by Mark Hufnail. 2002; New York: History Channel, 2002. DVD.

Williams, John Alden, ed. *Islam: The Traditions and Contemporary Orientation of Islam: A Religiously Integrated Way of Life Revealed in the Writings of Its Scriptures and Prophets, Its Legalists, Theologians, and Mystics*. New York: George Braziller, 1962.

Williams, John Alden. *The Word of Islam*. Austin: University of Texas Press, 1994.

Chapter 4: The High Caliphate

Bobrick, Benson. *The Caliph's Splendor: Islam and the West in the Golden Age of Baghdad*. New York: Simon & Schuster, 2012.

Gabriel, Richard. *Muhammad: Islam's First Great General.* Norman: University of Oklahoma Press, 2007.

Glubb, John Bagot. *The Great Arab Conquests.* New York: Barnes & Noble, 1995.

Halm, Heinz. *Shi'ism.* Translated by Janet Watson and Marian Hill. 2nd ed. New York: Columbia University Press, 2004.

———. *The Shi'ites: A Short History.* Translated by Allison Brown. Princeton, NJ: Markus Weiner, 2007.

Hawting, G. R. *The First Dynasty of Islam: The Umayyad Caliphate, AD 661–750.* 2nd ed. New York: Routledge, 2000.

Hazleton, Leslie. *After the Prophet: The Epic Story of the Shia-Sunni Split in Islam.* New York: Anchor Books, 2010.

Hoyland, Robert G. *In God's Path: The Arab Conquests and the Creation of an Islamic Empire.* Oxford: Oxford University Press, 2017.

Kennedy, Hugh. *The Armies of the Caliphs: Military and Society in the Early Islamic State.* New York: Routledge, 2001.

———. *The Great Arab Conquests: How the Spread of Islam Changed the World We Live In.* Philadelphia: Da Capo Press, 2008.

———. *The Prophet and the Caliphates: The Islamic Near East from the Sixth to the Eleventh Century.* 3rd ed. New York: Routledge, 2016.

———. *When Baghdad Ruled the Muslim World: The Rise and Fall of Islam's Greatest Dynasty.* Cambridge, MA: Da Capo Press, 2005.

Madelung, Wilfred, and Paul Walker, eds. and trans. *The Advent of the Fatimids: A Contemporary Shi'i Witness.* New York: I. B. Tauris, 2000.

Momen, Moojan. *An Introduction to Shi'i Islam: The History and Doctrines of Twelver Shi'ism.* New Haven, CT: Yale University Press, 1985.

Nasr, Vali. *The Shia Revival: How Conflicts within Islam will Shape the Future.* Updated ed. New York: W. W. Norton, 2016.

O'Shea, Stephen. *Sea of Faith: Islam and Christianity in the Medieval Mediterranean World.* New York: Walker, 2006.

Peacock, A. C. S. *Early Seljuq History: A New Interpretation.* New York: Routledge, 2010.

Rodinson, Maxime. *Mohammed.* Translated by Anne Carter. New York: Vintage Books, 1974.

Sachedina, Abdulaziz Abdulhussein. *Islamic Messianism: The Idea of the Mahdi in Twelver Shi'ism.* Albany: State University of New York Press, 1981.

Spuler, Bertold, and Jane Hathaway. *The Age of the Caliphs: History of the Muslim World.* Translated by F. R. C. Bagley. Princeton, NJ: Markus Wiener, 1995.

Tucker, Ernest S. *Nadir Shah's Quest for Legitimacy in Post-Safavid Iran.* Gainesville: University of Florida Press, 2006.

Von Grunebaum, G. E. *Classical Islam: A History, 600–1258.* Translated by Katherine Watson. New York: Barnes & Noble, 1996.

Chapter 5: Islamic Law and Medieval Muslim Civilization

Ahmed, Akbar S., and David M. Hart, eds. *Islam in Tribal Societies: From the Atlas to the Indus.* New York: Routledge, 2010.

Ali, Shaheen Sadar. *Modern Challenges to Islamic Law.* Cambridge: Cambridge University Press, 2016.

Black, Antony. *The History of Islamic Political Thought: From the Prophet to the Present.* 2nd ed. Edinburgh, UK: Edinburgh University Press, 2011.

Brend, Barbara. *Islamic Art.* Cambridge, MA: Harvard University Press, 1991.

Crone, Patricia. *God's Rule—Government and Islam: Six Centuries of Medieval Islamic Political Thought.* New York: Columbia University Press, 2004.

Gardner, Carrie. *Cities of Light: The Rise and Fall of Islamic Spain.* Produced and directed by Robert Gardner. 2007; Arlington, VA: PBS Home Video, 2007. DVD.

Goodwin, Jan. *Price of Honor: Muslim Women Lift the Veil of Silence on the Islamic World.* New York: Plume, 1995.

Hallaq, Wael B. *An Introduction to Islamic Law.* Cambridge: Cambridge University Press, 2009.

———. *The Origins and Evolution of Islamic Law.* Cambridge: Cambridge University Press, 2004.

Hassani, Salim T. S., Al-. *1001 Inventions: The Enduring Legacy of Muslim Civilization.* 3rd ed. Washington, DC: National Geographic, 2012.

Hitti, Philip K. *Islam and the West: A Historical Cultural Survey.* Malabar, FL: Krieger, 1979.

Ibn Khaldun. *The Muqaddimah: An Introduction to History.* Edited by N. J. Dawood. Translated by Franz Rosenthal. Princeton, NJ: Princeton University Press, 1969.

Morgan, Michael Hamilton. *Lost History: The Enduring Legacy of Muslim Scientists, Thinkers, and Artists.* Washington DC: National Geographic Press, 2007.

Sait, Siraj, and Hilary Lim. *Land, Law and Islam: Property and Human Rights in the Muslim World.* London: Zed Books, 2006.

Turner, Howard R. *Science in Medieval Islam: An Illustrated Introduction.* Austin: University of Texas Press, 1999.

Von Grunebaum, Gustave E. *Medieval Islam: A Study in Cultural Orientation.* 2nd ed. Chicago: University of Chicago Press, 1953.

Watt, William Montgomery. *Islamic Political Thought.* Edinburgh, UK: Edinburgh University Press, 1987.

Chapter 6: Invaders, Conquerors, and Warriors

Asbridge, Thomas. *The First Crusade: A New History.* Oxford: Oxford University Press, 2005.

Bedser, Richard. *Richard the Lionheart and Saladin: Holy Warriors.* 2005; Arlington, VA: PBS Home Video, 2005. DVD.

Hillenbrand, Carole. *The Crusades: Islamic Perspectives.* New York: Routledge, 2000.

Holt, P. M. *The Age of the Crusades: The Near East from the Eleventh Century to 1517.* New York: Longman, 1992.

Ibn-Munqidh, Usamah. *An Arab-Syrian Gentleman and Warrior in the Period of the Crusades.* Translated by Philip K. Hitti. New York: Columbia University Press, 2000.

Jones, Terry. *Crusades.* Produced and directed by Alan Ereira and David Wallace. 1995; New York: History Channel, 2001. DVD.

Kronemer, Alex. *The Sultan and the Saint.* 2016; Potomac Falls, VA: Unity Productions Foundation, 2017. DVD.

Lewis, Mark, dir. *The Crusades: Crescent and the Cross.* 2005; New York: History Channel, 2005. DVD.

Maalouf, Amin. *The Crusades through Arab Eyes.* Translated by Jon Rothschild. New York: Schocken Books, 1984.

Man, John. *Genghis Khan: Life, Death and Resurrection.* London: Bantam, 2005.

Marozzi, Justin. *Tamerlane: Sword of Islam, Conqueror of the World.* Cambridge, MA: Da Capo Press, 2006.

Morgan, David. *The Mongols.* 2nd ed. Malden, MA: Blackwell, 2007.

Museum with No Frontiers. *Mamluk Art: The Splendor and Magic of the Sultans.* Madrid, Spain: Museum with No Frontiers, 2001.

Reston, James, Jr. *Warriors of God: Richard the Lionheart and Saladin in the Third Crusade.* New York: Anchor Books, 2001.

Rogerson, Barnaby. *The Last Crusaders: The Hundred-Year Battle for the Center of the World.* New York: Overlook Press, 2009.

Spuler, Bertold. *History of the Mongols.* Translated by Helga and Stuart Drummond. New York: Barnes & Noble, 1996.

Spuler, Bertold, and Arthur N. Waldron. *The Mongol Period: History of the Muslim World.* Princeton, NJ: Markus Wiener, 1994.

Streusand, Douglas E. *Islamic Gunpowder Empires: Ottomans, Safavids, and Mughals.* Boulder, CO: Westview Press, 2011.

Sverdrup, Carl Fredrik. *The Mongol Conquests: The Military Operations of Genghis Khan and Sube'etei.* Solihull, UK: Helion, 2016.

Waterson, James. *The Knights of Islam: The Wars of the Mamluks.* London: Greenhill Books, 2007.

Chapter 7: The Rise of the Ottoman and Safavid Dynasties

Axworthy, Michael. *A History of Iran: Empire of the Mind.* Rev. ed. New York: Basic Books, 2016.

———. *The Sword of Persia: Nader Shah, from Tribal Warrior to Conquering Tyrant.* London: I. B. Tauris, 2009.

Blow, David. *Shah Abbas: The Ruthless King Who Became an Iranian Legend.* London: I. B. Tauris, 2009.

Capponi, Niccolò. *Victory of the West: The Great Christian-Muslim Clash at the Battle of Lepanto.* Cambridge, MA: Da Capo Press, 2006.

Clot, André. *Suleiman the Magnificent.* London: Saqi Books, 2012.

Crowley, Roger. *Empires of the Sea: The Siege of Malta, the Battle of Lepanto, and the Conquest for the Center of the World.* New York: Random House, 2008.

———. *1453: The Holy War for Constantinople and the Clash of Islam and the West.* New York: Hyperion, 2005.

Farrokh, Kaveh. *Iran at War, 1500–1988.* Oxford: Osprey, 2011.

Finkel, Caroline. *Osman's Dream: The History of the Ottoman Empire, 1300–1923.* New York: Basic Books, 2007.

Goodwin, Godfrey. *The Janissaries.* London: Saqi Books, 1997.

Hopkins, T. C. F. *Confrontation at Lepanto: Christendom vs. Islam.* New York: Tom Doherty Associates, 2006.

Itzkhowitz, Norman. *Ottoman Empire and Islamic Tradition.* Chicago: University of Chicago Press, 1980.

Lewis, Bernard. *The Emergence of Modern Turkey.* 2nd ed. London: Oxford University Press, 1968.

———. *Istanbul and the Civilization of the Ottoman Empire.* Norman: University of Oklahoma Press, 1987.

Lord Kinross. *Ottoman Centuries: The Rise and Fall of the Turkish Empire.* New York: Morrow Quill Paperbacks, 1979.

Morgan, David. *Medieval Persia, 1040–1797.* New York: Longman, 1990.

Newman, Andrew J. *Safavid Iran: Rebirth of a Persian Empire.* London: I. B. Tauris, 2009.

Reston, James, Jr. *Defenders of the Faith: Christianity and Islam Battle for the Soul of Europe, 1520–1536.* New York: Penguin Books, 2010.

Smith, Mike. *The Ottomans: Europe's Muslim Emperors.* London: British Broadcasting Corporation, 2013.

Wheatcroft, Andrew. *The Enemy at the Gate: Habsburgs, Ottomans, and the Battle for Europe.* New York: Basic Books, 2008.

Chapter 8: The Rise of Western Influence in the Middle East

Barber, Noel. *The Sultans.* New York: Simon & Schuster, 1973.

Cole, Juan. *Napoleon's Egypt: Invading the Middle East.* New York: St. Martin's-Griffin, 2008.

Fahmy, Khaled. *All the Pasha's Men: Mehmed Ali, His Army, and the Making of Modern Egypt.* New York: Cambridge University Press, 1997.

Jabarti, 'Abd al-Rahman al-. *Napoleon in Egypt: Al-Jabarti's Chronicle of the French Occupation, 1798.* Introduction by Shmuel Moreh. Translated by Robert L. Tignor. Princeton, NJ: Markus Weiner, 1993.

Lewis, Bernard. *The Middle East and the West.* New York: Harper Torchbooks, 1966.

———. *What Went Wrong? The Clash Between Islam and Modernity in the Middle East.* New York: Oxford University Press, 2002.

McMeekin, Sean. *The Berlin-Baghdad Express: The Ottoman Empire and Germany's Bid for World Power.* New York: Belknap Press, 2012.

Tahtawi, Rifa'a Rifi' Al-. *An Imam in Paris: Account of a Stay in Paris by an Egyptian Cleric (1826–1831).* Translated and introduced by Daniel L. Newman. London: Saqi Books, 2011.

Taylor, A. J. P. *The Struggle for the Mastery in Europe, 1848–1918.* New York: Oxford University Press, 1954.

Ufford, Letitia W. *The Pasha: How Mehmet Ali Defied the West, 1839–1841.* Jefferson, NC: MacFarland, 2007.

Yapp, M. E. *The Making of the Modern Middle East, 1792–1923.* New York: Longman, 1993.

Zorlu, Tuncay. *Innovation and Empire in Turkey: Sultan Selim III and the Modernization of the Ottoman Navy.* Rev. ed. London: I. B. Tauris, 2011.

Chapter 9: The Emergence of Nationalism in the Middle East

Antonius, George. *The Arab Awakening: The Story of the Arab National Movement.* Beirut: Librairie du Liban, 1969.

Arslan, Shakib. *Our Decline: Its Causes and Remedy.* Kuala Lumpur, Malaysia: Islamic Book Trust, 2004.

Barr, James. *A Line in the Sand: The Anglo-French Struggle for the Middle East.* New York: W. W. Norton, 2012.

———. *Setting the Desert on Fire: T. E. Lawrence and Britain's Secret War in Arabia, 1916–1918.* New York: W. W. Norton, 2008.

Churchill, Winston S. *The River War: An Account of the Reconquest of the Sudan.* New York: Award Books, 1964.

Farwell, Byron. *Prisoners of the Mahdi: The Story of the Mahdist Revolt Which Frustrated Queen Victoria's Designs on the Sudan, Humbled Egypt, and Led to the Fall of Khartoum, the Death of Gordon, and Kitchener's Victory at Omdurman Fourteen Years Later.* New York: W. W. Norton, 1989.

Ford, Roger. *Eden to Armageddon: World War I in the Middle East.* New York: Pegasus Books, 2010.

Golkap, Ziya. *The Principles of Turkism.* Translated by Robert Devereaux. Leiden, Netherlands: E. J. Brill, 1968.

Graves, Robert. *Lawrence and the Arabs.* New York: Paragon House, 1991.

Hart, B. H. Liddell. *Lawrence of Arabia.* New York: Da Capo Press, 1989.

Haslip, Joan. *The Sultan: The Life of Abdul Hamid II.* New York: Holt, Rinehart and Winston, 1973.

Hawes, James. *Lawrence of Arabia: The Battle for the Arab World.* 2003; Arlington, VA: PBS Home Video, 2003. DVD.

Jabarti, 'Abd al-Rahman al-. *Napoleon in Egypt: Al-Jabarti's Chronicle of the French Occupation, 1798.* Introduction by Shmuel Moreh. Translated by Robert L. Tignor. Princeton, NJ: Markus Wiener, 1993.

Kaplan, Robert D. *The Arabists: The Romance of an American Elite.* New York: Free Press, 1995.

Khalidi, Rashid, Lisa Anderson, Muhammad Muslih, and Reeva S. Simon. *The Origins of Arab Nationalism.* New York: Columbia University Press, 1991.

Lawrence, T. E. *Seven Pillars of Wisdom: A Triumph.* New York: Anchor Books, 1991.

Lean, David. *Lawrence of Arabia.* Produced by Sam Spiegel and David Lean. 1962; Culver City, CA: Sony Pictures Home Entertainment, 2001. DVD.

Lord Kinross. *Between Two Seas: The Creation of the Suez Canal.* New York: William Morrow, 1969.

Mansfield, Peter. *The Ottoman Empire and Its Successors.* New York: St. Martin's Press, 1973.

McMeekin, Sean. *The Ottoman Endgame: War, Revolution, and the Making of the Modern Middle East, 1908–1923.* New York: Penguin Books, 2016.

Moorehead, Alan. *Gallipoli.* Baltimore: Nautical and Aviation Publishing, 1985.

Mostyn, Trevor. *Egypt's Belle Epoque: Cairo and the Age of the Hedonists.* London: Tauris Parke Paperbacks, 2007.

Murphy, David. *The Arab Revolt, 1916–18: Lawrence Sets Arabia Ablaze.* Oxford: Osprey, 2008.

Oren, Michael B. *Power, Faith, and Fantasy: America in the Middle East, 1776 to the Present.* New York: W. W. Norton, 2008.

Price, Tim Rose. "A Dangerous Man: Lawrence after Arabia." *Great Performances.* Directed by Christopher Menaul. May 8, 1992; Richmond Hill, ON: BFS Entertainment, 2004. DVD.

Rogan, Eugene. *The Fall of the Ottomans: The Great War in the Middle East.* New York: Basic Books, 2015.

Ruthven, Malise. "The Map ISIS Hates." *New York Review of Books,* June 25, 2014. Accessed November 1, 2017. http://www.nybooks.com/daily/2014/map-isis-hates/.

Sayyid Marsot, Afaf Lutfi Al-. *A Short History of Modern Egypt.* Cambridge: Cambridge University Press, 1998.

Schneer, Jonathan. *The Balfour Declaration: The Origins of the Arab-Israeli Conflict.* New York: Random House, 2012.

Sharabi, Hisham B. *Nationalism and Revolution in the Arab World.* Princeton, NJ: D. Van Nostrand, 1966.

Spilsbury, Julian. *The Thin Red Line: An Eyewitness History of the Crimean War.* London: Weidenfeld & Nicholson, 2005.

Thompson, Jack H., and Robert D. Reischauer, eds. *Modernization of the Arab World.* Princeton, NJ: D. Van Nostrand, 1966.

Tibi, Bassam. *Arab Nationalism: Between Islam and the Nation-State.* New York: St. Martin's Press, 1997.

VanDeMark, Brian. *American Sheikhs: Two Families, Four Generations, and the Story of America's Influence in the Middle East.* Amherst, NY: Prometheus Books, 2012.

Vatikiotis, P. J. *The History of Modern Egypt: From Muhammad Ali to Mubarak.* Baltimore: Johns Hopkins University Press, 1991.

Wilson, Jeremy. *Lawrence of Arabia: The Authorized Biography of T. E. Lawrence.* New York: Atheneum, 1989.

Chapter 10: The Middle East between the World Wars

Aboul-Enein, Youssef H., and Basil Aboul-Enein. *The Secret War for the Middle East: The Influence of Axis and Allied Operations during World War II.* Annapolis, MD: Naval Institute Press, 2013.

Abrahamian, Ervand. *A History of Modern Iran.* Revised and updated. Cambridge: Cambridge University Press, 2018.

Axworthy, Michael. *A History of Iran: Empire of the Mind.* Rev. ed. New York: Basic Books, 2016.

Barr, James. *A Line in the Sand: The Anglo-French Struggle for the Middle East.* New York: W. W. Norton, 2012.

Feroz, Ahmed. *The Making of Modern Turkey.* New York: Routledge, 2000.

Fromkin, David. *A Peace to End All Peace: The Fall of the Ottoman Empire and the Creation of the Modern Middle East.* New York: Holt Paperbacks, 2009.

Hanioglu, M. Sukuru. *Atatürk: An Intellectual Biography.* Princeton, NJ: Princeton University Press, 2011.

Haykel, Bernard, Thomas Hegghammer, and Stephane Lacroix, eds. *Saudi Arabia in Transition: Insights on Social, Political, Economic and Religious Change.* New York: Cambridge University Press, 2015.

Lacey, Robert. *The Kingdom: Arabia and the House of Sa'ud.* New York: Avon Books, 1981.

Lippman, Thomas W. *Inside the Mirage: America's Fragile Partnership with Saudi Arabia.* Boulder, CO: Westview Press, 2004.

Lord Kinross. *Ataturk: A Biography of Mustafa Kemal, Father of Modern Turkey.* New York: William Morrow, 1965.

Mackey, Sandra. *The Saudis: Inside the Desert Kingdom.* New York: Signet, 1990.

Mango, Andrew. *Ataturk: The Biography of the Founder of Modern Turkey.* New York: Overlook Press, 2012.

Marr, Phebe, and Ibrahim al-Marashi. *The Modern History of Iraq.* 4th ed. Boulder, CO: Westview Press, 2017.

Ozoglu, Hakan. *From Caliphate to Secular State: Power Struggle in the Early Turkish Republic.* Santa Barbara, CA: Praeger, 2011.

Shenk, Robert. *America's Black Sea Fleet: The U.S. Navy Amidst War and Revolution, 1919–1923.* Annapolis, MD: Naval Institute Press, 2012.

Tahri, Jihan al-, and Martin Smith. *Frontline.* "House of Saud." Directed by Jihan al-Tahri. Aired February 8, 2005. Arlington, VA: PBS Home Video, 2005. DVD.

Winkler, David F. *Amirs, Admirals and Desert Sailors: Bahrain, the U.S. Navy, and the Arabian Gulf.* Annapolis, MD: Naval Institute Press, 2007.

Yapp, M. E. *The Near East since the First World War.* New York: Longman, 1992.

Yergen, Daniel. *The Prize: The Epic Quest for Oil, Money and Power.* New York: Free Press, 2008.

Chapter 11: Egyptian Independence, the Zionist Movement, and the Creation of Israel

Botman, Selma. *Egypt from Independence to Revolution, 1919–1952.* Syracuse, NY: Syracuse University Press, 1991.

Gilbert, Martin. *Israel: Birth of a Nation.* Produced and directed by Herbert Krosney. Written by Martin Gilbert and Herbert Krosney. 1997; New York: History Channel, 2006. DVD.

Heikal, Mohamed H. *Cutting the Lion's Tail: Suez through Egyptian Eyes.* London: Andre Deutsch, 1986.

Laqueur, Walter. *A History of Zionism: From the French Revolution to the Establishment of the State of Israel.* New York: MJF Books, 1972.

Lloyd, Selwyn. *Suez 1956: A Personal Account.* London: Jonathan Cape, 1978.

Loeterman, Ben. *1913: Seeds of Conflict: Early Encounters between Jewish and Arab Nationalism.* July 10, 2014; Arlington, VA: PBS Home Video, 2014. DVD.

Marshall, S. L. A. *Sinai Victory: Command Decisions in History's Shortest War, Israel's Hundred-Hour Conquest of Egypt East of Suez, Autumn 1956.* New York: William Morrow, 1958.

Morris, Benny. *1948: A History of the First Arab-Israeli War.* New Haven, CT: Yale University Press, 2008.

Nasser, Gamal Abdel. *Egypt's Liberation: The Philosophy of the Revolution.* Washington, DC: Public Affairs Press, 1956.

Neguib, Mohammed. *Egypt's Destiny.* London: Victor Gollancz, 1955.

Nichols, David. *Eisenhower 1956: The President's Year of Crisis: Suez and the Brink of War.* New York: Simon & Schuster, 2012.

Pargeter, Alison. *The Muslim Brotherhood: From Opposition to Power.* New ed. London: Saqi Books, 2013.

Sadat, Anwar El-. *Revolt on the Nile.* New York: John Day, 1957.

Schama, Simon. *The Story of the Jews.* Written by Simon Schama. 2014; Arlington, VA: PBS Home Video, 2014. DVD.

Shafir, Gershon, and Yoav Peled. *Being Israeli: The Dynamics of Multiple Citizenship.* Cambridge: Cambridge University Press, 2002.

Shipler, David K. *Arab and Jew: Wounded Spirits in a Promised Land.* Rev. ed. New York: Penguin Books, 2002.

Van Creveld, Martin. *The Sword and the Olive: A Critical History of the Israeli Defense Force.* New York: Public Affairs, 2002.

Wickam, Carrie Rosefsky. *The Muslim Brotherhood: Evolution of an Islamist Movement.* Princeton, NJ: Princeton University Press, 2013.

Chapter 12: Turkey after Atatürk, Iran under Mohammed Reza Shah, and the Arab World after World War II

Aburish, Said K. *Arafat: From Defender to Dictator.* New York: Bloomsbury, 1999.

———. *Nasser: The Last Arab.* New York: Thomas Dunne Books, 2004.

———. *Saddam Hussein: The Politics of Revenge.* New York: Bloomsbury, 2000.

Bill, James A. *The Eagle and the Lion: The Tragedy of American-Iranian Relations.* New Haven, CT: Yale University Press, 1988.

Bourges, Herve. "Algeria: Test of Power" (two episodes). *Al-Jazeera.* October 2013. Accessed November 8, 2017. https://archive.org/details/AlgeriaTestOfPower.

Doulah, Suhaib Abu. "Syria: The Reckoning" (two episodes). *Al-Jazeera.* March 2016. Accessed November 8, 2017. https://topdocumentaryfilms.com/syria-reckoning/.

Heikal, Mohamed. *The Cairo Documents: The Inside Story of Nasser and His Relationship with World Leaders, Rebels, and Statesmen.* Garden City, NY: Doubleday, 1973.

———. *The Sphinx and the Commissar: The Rise and Fall of Soviet Influence in the Middle East.* New York: Harper and Row, 1978.

Kelly, J. B. *Arabia, the Gulf and the West: A Critical View of the Arabs and Their Oil Policy.* New York: Basic Books, 1980.

Kerr, Malcolm. *The Arab Cold War, 1958–1964: A Study of Ideology in Politics.* London: Oxford University Press, 1965.

Kinzer, Stephen. *All the Shah's Men: An American Coup and the Roots of Middle East Terror.* 2nd ed. Hoboken, NJ: Wiley, 2008.

Lacouture, Jean. *Nasser: A Biography.* New York: Alfred A. Knopf, 1973.

Mackey, Sandra. *The Iranians: Persia, Islam and the Soul of a Nation.* New York: Plume, 1998.

Mansfield, Peter. *Nasser's Egypt.* Middlesex, UK: Penguin Books, 1965.

Nutting, Anthony. *Nasser.* New York: E. P. Dutton, 1972.

Pope, Nicole, and Hugh Pope. *Turkey Unveiled: A History of Modern Turkey.* Woodstock, NY: Overlook Press, 2011.

Seale, Patrick. *The Struggle for Syria: A Study of Post-War Arab Politics, 1945–1958.* New Haven, CT: Yale University Press, 1986.

Stephens, Robert. *Nasser: A Political Biography.* New York: Simon & Schuster, 1971.

Chapter 13: The Arab-Israeli Conflict, 1967–73

Aboul-Enein, Youssef H. *Reconstructing a Shattered Egyptian Army: War Minister Gen. Mohamed Fawzi's Memoirs, 1967–1971.* Annapolis, MD: Naval Institute Press, 2014.

Ajami, Fouad. *The Arab Predicament: Arab Political Thought and Practice since 1967.* Updated ed. New York: Cambridge University Press, 1992.

Ennes, James M. *Assault on the Liberty: The True Story of the Israeli Attack on an American Intelligence Ship.* New York: Random House, 1979.

Heikal, Mohamed. *The Road to Ramadan.* London: William Collins Sons, 1975.

Herzog, Chaim. *The War of Atonement: The Inside Story of the Yom Kippur War.* Philadelphia, PA: Casemate, 2010.

Kipnis, Yigal. *1973: The Road to War.* Translated by Barbara Doron. Charlottesville, VA: Just World Books, 2013.

McDonald, Kevin, dir. *One Day in September.* 2000; New York: Sony Pictures Classics, 2005. DVD.

Oren, Michael B. *Six Days of War: June 1967 and the Making of the Modern Middle East.* New York: Presidio Press, 2003.

Phizicky, Stephen. *Six Days in June: The War That Redefined the Middle East.* Directed by Ilan Ziv. 2007; Boston: WGBH Educational Video, 2007. DVD.

Pollock, Kenneth. *Arabs at War: Military Effectiveness, 1948–1991.* Lincoln: University of Nebraska Press, 2002.

Quandt, William B. *Decade of Decisions: American Policy toward the Arab-Israeli Conflict, 1967–1976.* Berkeley: University of California Press, 1977.

———. *Peace Process: American Diplomacy and the Arab-Israeli Conflict since 1967.* 3rd ed. Washington, DC: Brookings Institution, 2005.

Rabinovich, Abraham. *The Yom Kippur War: The Epic Encounter That Transformed the Middle East.* New York: Schocken Books, 2004.

Reeve, Simon. *One Day in September: The Full Story of the 1972 Munich Olympics Massacre and Israeli Revenge.* New York: Arcade, 2000.

Seale, Patrick. *Abu Nidal: A Gun for Hire: The Secret Life of the World's Most Notorious Arab Terrorist.* New York: Random House, 1992.

Segev, Tom. *1967: Israel, the War, and the Year That Transformed the Middle East.* Translated by Jessica Cohen. New York: Metropolitan Books, 2007.

Shazly, Saad El-. *The Crossing of the Suez.* Rev. ed. San Francisco, CA: American Mideast Research, 2003.

Snow, Peter, and Dan Snow. *20th Century Battlefields.* Episode 6, "1973 Middle East." Produced by Danielle Peck. Directed by Paul McGuigan. Aired July 9, 2007, on BBC.

Wallach, Janet, and John Wallach. *Arafat: In the Eyes of the Beholder.* New York: Lyle Stuart, 1990.

Chapter 14: Revolutionary Iran

Aboul-Enein, Youssef H. *Militant Islamist Ideology: Understanding the Global Threat.* Annapolis, MD: Naval Institute Press, 2013.

Axworthy, Michael. *Revolutionary Iran: A History of the Islamic Republic.* Oxford: Oxford University Press, 2016.

Bowden, Mark. *Guests of the Ayatollah: The First Battle in America's War with Militant Islam.* New York: Atlantic Monthly Press, 2006.

Buchan, James. *Days of God: The Revolution in Iran and Its Consequences.* New York: Simon & Schuster, 2013.

Hiro, Dilip. *The Longest War: The Iran-Iraq Military Conflict.* New York: Routledge, 1991.

Lewis, Bernard. *What Went Wrong? Western Impact and Middle Eastern Response.* Oxford: Oxford University Press, 2002.

Martin, Vanessa. *Creating an Islamic State: Khomeini and the Making of a New Iran.* London: I. B. Tauris, 2007.

Mottahedeh, Roy. *The Mantle of the Prophet: Religion and Politics in Iran.* 2nd ed. Oxford: Oneworld Publications, 2000.

Murray, Williamson, and Kevin M. Woods. *The Iran-Iraq War: A Military and Strategic History.* Cambridge: Cambridge University Press, 2014.

Osman, Tarek. *Islamism: What It Means for the Middle East and the World.* New Haven, CT: Yale University Press, 2016.

Pollack, Kenneth M. *The Persian Puzzle: The Conflict between Iran and America.* New York: Random House, 2004.

Wright, Robin. *In the Name of God: The Khomeini Decade.* New York: Simon & Schuster, 1989.

———. *Sacred Rage: The Wrath of Militant Islam.* Updated ed. New York: Touchstone, 2001.

Zatarain, Lee Allen. *America's First Clash with Iran: The Tanker War, 1987–88.* Philadelphia, PA: Casemate, 2010.

Chapter 15: Developments in Egypt since 1973

Achcar, Gilbert. *Morbid Symptoms: Relapse in the Arab Uprising.* Stanford, CA: Stanford University Press, 2016.

Al Aswany, Alaa. *On the State of Egypt: What Made the Revolution Inevitable.* New York: Vintage Books, 2011.

Calvert, John. *Sayyid Qutb and the Origins of Radical Islamism.* New York: Columbia University Press, 2010.

Cook, Steven A. *The Struggle for Egypt: From Nasser to Tahrir Square.* Oxford: Oxford University Press, 2013.

Cooley, John K. *Libyan Sandstorm: The Complete Account of Qaddafi's Revolution.* New York: Holt, Rinehart and Winston, 1982.

Gerges, Fawaz A. *Making the Arab World: Nasser, Qutb, and the Clash That Shaped the Middle East.* Princeton, NJ: Princeton University Press, 2018.

Haas, Mark L., and David W. Lesch, eds. *The Arab Spring: The Hope and Reality of the Uprisings.* 2nd ed. Boulder, CO: Westview Press, 2017.

Heikal, Mohamed. *Autumn of Fury: The Assassination of Sadat.* New York: Random House, 1983.

Kandil, Hazem. *Soldiers, Spies and Statesmen: Egypt's Road to Revolt.* London: Verso, 2012.

Kirk, Michael. *Frontline.* "Revolution in Cairo." Aired February 22, 2011. Arlington, VA: PBS Home Video, 2011. DVD.

Maher, Shiraz. *Salafi-Jihadism: The History of an Idea.* Oxford: Oxford University Press, 2016.

Noujaim, Jehane. *The Square: The People Demand the Downfall of the Regime.* 2013; New York: City Drive Films, 2015. DVD.

Pargeter, Alison. *The Muslim Brotherhood: From Opposition to Power.* London: Saqi Books, 2013.

———. *Return to the Shadows: The Muslim Brotherhood and An-Nahda since the Arab Spring.* London: Saqi Books, 2016.

Sadat, Anwar El-. *In Search of Identity: An Autobiography.* New York: Harper Colophon Books, 1979.

Stanik, Joseph T. *El Dorado Canyon: Reagan's Undeclared War with Qaddafi.* Annapolis, MD: Naval Institute Press, 2016.

Stein, Kenneth W. *Heroic Diplomacy: Sadat, Kissinger, Carter, Begin, and the Quest for Arab-Israeli Peace.* New York: 1999.

Venkus, Robert E. *Raid on Qaddafi: The Untold Story of History's Longest Fighter Mission by the Pilot Who Directed It.* New York: St. Martin's, 1993.

Wickham, Carrie Rosefsky. *The Muslim Brotherhood: Evolution of an Islamist Movement.* Princeton, NJ: Princeton University Press, 2015.

Yaqub, Salim. *Imperfect Strangers: Americans, Arabs, and U.S.-Middle East Relations in the 1970s.* Ithaca, NY: Cornell University Press, 2016.

Chapter 16: National Tragedies in Lebanon and Syria

Doulah, Suhaib Abu. "Syria: The Reckoning" (two episodes). *Al-Jazeera.* March 2016. Accessed November 8, 2017. https://topdocumentaryfilms.com/syria-reckoning/.

El Khazen, Farid. *The Breakdown of the State in Lebanon, 1967–1976.* Cambridge, MA: Harvard University Press, 2000.

Frank, Benis M. *U.S. Marines in Lebanon, 1982–1984.* Washington, DC: History and Museums Division Headquarters, U.S. Marine Corps, 1987.

Friedman, Thomas L. *From Beirut to Jerusalem.* New York: Farrar, Straus, Giroux, 2000.

Hammel, Eric. *The Root: The Marines in Beirut August 1982–February 1984.* St. Paul, MN: Zenith Press, 2005.

Hiro, Dilip. *Lebanon Fire and Embers: A History of the Lebanese Civil War.* New York: St. Martin's Press, 1993.

Lesch, David W. *The New Lion of Damascus: Bashar al-Asad and Modern Syria.* New Haven, CT: Yale University Press, 2005.

———. *Syria: The Fall of the House of Assad.* Updated ed. New Haven, CT: Yale University Press, 2013.

Saad-Ghorayeb, Amal. *Hizbu'llah: Politics and Religion.* London: Pluto Press, 2002.

Seale, Patrick. *Asad: The Struggle for the Middle East.* Berkeley: University of California Press, 1992.

Van Dam, Nikolaos. *Destroying a Nation: The Civil War in Syria.* London: I. B. Tauris, 2017.

———. *The Struggle for Power in Syria: Politics and Society under Asad and the Ba'th Party.* 4th ed. London: I. B. Tauris, 2011.

Chapter 17: Iraq from the Rise of Saddam to the Fragile Beginnings of Democracy

Atkinson, Rick. *Crusade: The Untold Story of the Persian Gulf War.* Boston: Houghton Mifflin, 1993.

———. *In the Company of Soldiers: A Chronicle of Combat.* New York: Henry Holt, 2004.

Clancy, Tom, and Fred Franks. *Into the Storm: A Study in Command.* New York: G. P. Putnam's Sons, 1997.

Coughlin, Con. *Saddam: His Rise and Fall.* New York: Harper Perennial, 2005.

Fick, Nathaniel. *One Bullet Away: The Making of a Marine Officer.* Boston: Houghton Mifflin, 2005.

Gordon, Michael R., and Bernard E. Trainor. *Cobra II: The Inside Story of the Invasion and Occupation of Iraq.* New York: Vintage Books, 2007.

———. *The Endgame: The Inside Story of the Struggle for Iraq from George W. Bush to Barack Obama.* New York: Vintage Books, 2013.

———. *The Generals' War: The Inside Story of the Conflict in the Gulf.* New York: Little, Brown, 1995.

Hiro, Dilip. *Desert Shield to Desert Storm: The Second Gulf War.* New York: Routledge, 1992.

Hirsch, Linda, Martin Smith, and David Fanning. "Bitter Rivals: Iran and Saudi Arabia." February 20, 2018; Arlington, VA: PBS Home Video, 2018. DVD.

Kirk, Michael. *Frontline.* "Bush's War." 2008; Arlington, VA: PBS Home Video, 2008. DVD.

———. *Frontline.* "The Lost Year in Iraq." Aired October 17, 2006. Arlington, VA: PBS Home Video, 2006. DVD.

Makiya, Kanan. *Republic of Fear: The Politics of Modern Iraq.* Updated ed. Berkeley: University of California Press, 1998,

Ricks, Thomas. *Fiasco: The American Military Adventure in Iraq, 2003 to 2005.* New York: Penguin Press, 2006.

———. *The Gamble: General David Petraeus and the American Military Adventure in Iraq, 2006–2008.* New York: Penguin Press, 2010.

Sassoon, Joseph. *Saddam Hussein's Ba'th Party: Inside an Authoritarian Regime.* Cambridge: Cambridge University Press, 2012.

Smith, Martin. *Frontline.* "Obama at War." 2015; Arlington, VA: PBS Home Video, 2015. DVD.

Tripp, Charles. *A History of Iraq.* 3rd ed. Cambridge: Cambridge University Press, 2007.

West, Bing. *No True Glory: A Frontline Account of the Battle for Fallujah.* New York: Bantam Books, 2005.

Woodward, Bob. *Bush at War.* Updated ed. New York: Simon & Schuster, 2003.

———. *Obama's Wars.* New York: Simon & Schuster, 2010.

———. *Plan of Attack: The Definitive Account of the Decision to Invade Iraq.* New York: Simon & Schuster, 2004.

———. *State of Denial: Bush at War, Part III.* New York: Simon & Schuster, 2006.

———. *The War Within: A Secret White House History, 2006–2008.* New York: Simon & Schuster, 2009.

Chapter 18: The Israeli-Palestinian Conflict and Peace Process since the Late 1980s

Anderson, Mark. *Elusive Peace: Israel and the Arabs.* 2005; Arlington, VA: PBS Home Video. 2005. DVD.

Bennis, Phyllis. *Understanding the Palestinian-Israeli Conflict: A Primer*. 6th rev. ed. Northampton, MA: Olive Branch Press, 2015.

Dowty, Alan. *Israel/Palestine*. 3rd ed. Oxford: Polity Press, 2012.

Gilbert, Martin. *Israel: A History*. New York: Harper Perennial, 2008.

Goodman, Hirsch. *Frontline*. "Shattered Dreams of Peace: The Road from Oslo." Directed by Tor Ben-Mayor and Dan Setton. 2002; Arlington, VA: PBS Home Video, 2002. VHS.

Kurtzer, Daniel C., Scott B. Lasensky, William B. Quandt, Steven L. Spiegel, and Shibley Z. Telhami. *The Peace Puzzle: America's Quest for Arab-Israeli Peace, 1989–2011*. Ithaca, NY: Cornell University Press, 2013.

Milton-Edwards, Beverly, and Stephen Farrell. *Hamas: The Islamic Resistance Movement*. Cambridge: Polity Press, 2010.

Primakov, Yevgeny. *Russia and the Arabs: Behind the Scenes in the Middle East from the Cold War to the Present*. New York: Basic Books, 2009.

Ross, Dennis. *The Missing Peace: The Inside Story of the Fight for Middle East Peace*. New York: Farrar, Straus and Giroux, 2005.

Tyler, Patrick. *A World of Trouble: The White House and the Middle East—From the Cold War to the War on Terror*. New York: Farrar, Straus and Giroux, 2010.

Chapter 19: Understanding Islamist Extremism in the Twenty-First Century

Bergen, Peter L. *Holy War, Inc.: Inside the Secret World of Osama Bin Laden*. New York: Touchstone, 2002.

———. *Manhunt: The Ten-Year Search for Bin Laden from 9/11 to Abbottabad*. New York: Broadway, 2012.

———. *The Osama Bin Ladin I Know: An Oral History of al-Qaeda's Leader*. New York: Free Press, 2006.

Bonney, Richard. *Jihad: From Qur'an to Bin Laden*. New York: Palgrave Macmillan, 2004.

Brisard, Jean-Charles, and Damien Martinez. *Zarqawi: The New Face of al-Qaeda*. Cambridge, MA: Polity Press, 2005.

Coll, Steve. *Directorate S: The CIA and America's Secret Wars in Afghanistan and Pakistan*. New York: Penguin Press, 2018.

———. *Ghost Wars: The Secret History of the CIA, Afghanistan, and Bin Laden, from the Soviet Invasion to September 10, 2001*. New York: Penguin Books, 2005.

Cran, William. *America at a Crossroads*. "Jihad: The Men and Ideas Behind al Qaeda." Aired April 15, 2007. Arlington, VA: PBS Home Video, 2007. DVD.

Esposito, John L. *The Islamic Threat: Myth or Reality?* New York: Oxford University Press, 1999.

Evolution of Evil. Season 1, episode 8, "Bin Laden: A Terrorist Mastermind." Aired September 13, 2015. Elizabeth, NJ: American Heroes Channel, 2015.

Fanning, David. *Frontline*. "The Al Qaeda Files." 2000–2005; Arlington, VA: PBS Home Video, 2006. DVD.

Fishman, Brian H. *The Master Plan: ISIS, al-Qaeda, and the Jihadi Strategy for Final Victory*. New Haven, CT: Yale University Press, 2016.

Gelvin, James L. *The New Middle East: What Everyone Needs to Know*. New York: Oxford University Press, 2018.

Gerges, Fawaz A. *ISIS: A History*. Princeton, NJ: Princeton University Press, 2016.

Hashim, Ahmed S. *The Caliphate at War: Operational Realities and Innovations of the Islamic State*. New York: Oxford University Press, 2018.

Kepel, Gilles. *Jihad: The Trail of Political Islam.* Translated by Anthony F. Roberts. London: I. B. Taurus, 2006.

Kepel, Gilles, and Antoine Jardin. *Terror in France: The Rise of Jihad in the West.* Princeton, NJ: Princeton University Press, 2017.

Lia, Brynjar. *Architect of Global Jihad: The Life of al-Qaida Strategist Abu Mus'ab al-Suri.* New York: Columbia University Press, 2008.

National Commission on Terrorist Attacks upon the United States (The 9-11 Commission). *The 9/11 Commission Report: Final Report of the National Commission on Terrorist Attacks upon the United States (Authorized Edition).* New York: W. W. Norton, 2004.

Scott-Clark, Catherine, and Adrian Levy. *The Exile: The Stunning Inside Story of Osama Bin Laden and Al Qaeda in Flight.* New York: Bloomsbury, 2018.

Smith, Martin. *Frontline.* "The Brothers." Aired February 22, 2011. Arlington, VA: PBS Home Video, 2011. DVD.

Warrick, Joby. *Black Flags: The Rise of ISIS.* New York: Anchor Books, 2016.

Weiss, Michael, and Hassan Hassan. *ISIS: Inside the Army of Terror.* New York: Regan Arts, 2015.

Wright, Lawrence. *The Looming Tower: Al-Qaeda and the Road to 9/11.* New York: Vintage Books, 2007.

Wright, Robin. *Rock the Casbah: Rage and Rebellion across the Islamic World.* Updated ed. New York: Simon & Schuster, 2012.

Chapter 20: Combatting Islamist Extremism in the Twenty-First Century

Bassiouni, M. Cherif. *Chronicles of the Egyptian Revolution and Its Aftermath, 2011–2016.* Cambridge: Cambridge University Press, 2017.

Cagaptay, Soner. *The New Sultan: Erdogan and the Crisis of Modern Turkey.* London: I. B. Tauris, 2017.

Hamid, Shadi. *Islamic Exceptionalism: How the Struggle over Islam Is Reshaping the World.* New York: St. Martin's Press, 2016.

Harris, Sam, and Maajid Nawaz. *Islam and the Future of Tolerance: A Dialogue.* Cambridge, MA: Harvard University Press, 2015.

Jones, Seth G. *Waging Insurgent Warfare: Lessons from the Vietcong to the Islamic State.* New York: Oxford University Press, 2017.

Lynch, Marc. *The New Arab Wars: Uprisings and Anarchy in the Middle East.* New York: Public Affairs, 2017.

Maher, Shiraz. *Salafi-Jihadism: The History of an Idea.* New York: Oxford University Press, 2016.

Manji, Irshad. *Allah, Liberty and Love: The Courage to Reconcile Faith and Freedom.* New York: Atria, 2016.

———. *The Trouble of Islam Today: A Muslim's Call for Reform in Her Faith.* New York: St. Martin's Griffin, 2005.

Masri, Safwan M. *Tunisia: An Arab Anomaly.* New York: Columbia University Press, 2017.

McLeod, Ian, dir. *America at a Crossroads.* "Faith without Fear." Aired April 19, 2007. Arlington, VA: PBS Home Video, 2007. DVD.

Nance, Malcolm, and Chris Sampson. *Hacking ISIS: How to Destroy the Cyber Jihad.* New York: Skyhorse, 2017.

Nawaz, Maajid. *Radical: My Journey Out of Islamist Extremism.* Guilford, CT: Lyons Press, 2013.

Index

'Abbasid caliphate, 54, 63–67, 68, 70, 71, 72, 75, 85, 94, 95, 98, 105, 109, 117, 137, 381n3 (chap. 4)

'Abdullah, King, 171, 178, 179, 182, 195, 217, 238, 239

'Abdulmejid I, 143, 146–47, 148

Afghani, Jamal al-Din al-, 370–72

Afghanistan: geography of, 9; Middle East region inclusion of, 4, 5; Persia invasion by, 125; refugees from Soviet-Afghan War, 353–54; resources for U.S. war in, 331; Soviet invasion of, 270, 353; U.S. invasion of, 355; U.S. military presence in, 2; U.S. support for government of, 2

agriculture, 2, 8–9, 20, 25, 72–73

'Alawis, 14, 302–3, 314

Alexandria, 7, 29, 87, 294

Algeria, 14, 136, 140, 205, 239, 242

'Ali Ibn Abu Talib: conversion of, 32; death of, 17; as first Imam, 67; governing as caliph, 58, 60–61; relationship to Muhammad, 14, 17; selection as caliph, 14, 17, 55–56, 60; Shi'a as Partisans of 'Ali, 14, 17–18; spiritual authority of Shi'a, 14, 67

Allah, 20, 25, 28, 39

almsgiving (*zakat*), 43, 44, 58, 109

Anglo-Egyptian Treaty of Alliance, 201, 202

Anglo-Persian Oil Company (Anglo-Iranian Oil Company), 164–65, 192, 229–30

Ansar (helpers/Medinan converts), 34, 55–56, 59, 60, 61–62, 63, 65

Arab League, 239, 291, 316

Arab Legion, 182

Arab Revolt, 173–74, 195–96

Arab Spring protests, 8, 137, 350, 363

Arab world, 5–6, 11, 238–46

Arabian Peninsula, 4, 5, 9, 28–29, 171–72, 173–74

Arab-Israeli conflicts: Arab victory in 1973, 265, 266–67; Arab-Israeli War (1948–49), 202, 204, 215–18, 238–39, 244;

Arab-Israeli War (1956), 217; Arab-Israeli War (1967, Six-Day War), 207, 217, 237, 247–53, 269–70, 383n5 (chap. 12); Arab-Israeli War (1973), 217, 254, 258–63, 346, 384nn12–13; Arab-Israeli War (1982), 217; Israeli victory in 1967, 249–51, 252, 384n3; War of Attrition, 259–60

Arab-Israeli peace negotiations and agreements: Annapolis Peace Conference, 349; Camp David Accords/Camp David Frameworks for Peace (1978), 254, 266, 285, 287–88; Camp David II, 345, 347; Israel-Egypt Peace Treaty (1979), 254, 384n6; Israel-Jordan Peace Treaty (1994), 254; Israel-Palestine negotiations, 341–46; Jewish settlements in occupied territories as barrier to peace agreement, 252; negotiations after 1967 war, 252; negotiations after 1973 war, 263–65; Oslo I Accords (1993), 254, 342–43; Oslo II Accords (1995), 254, 342, 343; prospects for peace, 346–51; Quartet for the Middle East, 345–46; Rogers cease-fire plan, 259; Sinai and Golan Interim Agreements, 254; Sinai I agreement, 264–65; Sinai II agreement, 265; two-state solution, 339–40; UN role in peace settlement, 251, 252, 253–54; Wye Mills Accords, 344–45

Arabs: ancient artifacts as symbols of nationalism, 22; background, culture, and language of, 11–12, 165–66; Bedouin as representatives of Arab culture and virtues, 10, 165; clans, tribes, and tribal federations organization of, 26; definition of, 6, 165–68; nationalism and definition of, 6; nationalist movement, 174–76, 178–79, 183; pre-Islamic Arab society, 26–29; "pure" and Arabized Arabs, 26; traditional values and tribal concerns, decline in interest in, 27–28; 'Uruba

About the Authors

Youssef Aboul-Enein is a U.S. Navy Medical Service Corps commander who since 9/11 has advised on counterterrorism and Middle East affairs at the highest levels of the Defense Department and intelligence community. He has trained thousands of deploying U.S. military personnel in his more-than-twenty-year military career and has taught graduate-level courses on Islam and the Middle East at both the National Intelligence University and National Defense University. He is the author of *Militant Islamist Ideology: Understanding the Global Threat* (2010), *Iraq in Turmoil: Historical Perspectives of Dr. Ali al-Wardi, from the Ottoman Empire to King Feisal* (2012), *Secret War for the Middle East: The Influence of Axis and Allied Intelligence Operations during World War II* (with Basil Aboul-Enein, 2013), and *Reconstructing a Shattered Egyptian Army: War Minister Gen. Mohamed Fawzi's Memoirs, 1967–1971* (editor, 2014).

Joseph T. Stanik, a retired U.S. Navy officer, is the author of *"Swift and Effective Retribution": The U.S. Sixth Fleet and the Confrontation with Qaddafi* (1996) and *El Dorado Canyon: Reagan's Undeclared War with Qaddafi* (2016). A 1978 graduate of the U.S. Naval Academy, he is a long-term teacher of history at the secondary and collegiate levels.